The Bootle Boy

Les Hinton
The Bootle Boy

an untidy life in news

SCRIBE

Melbourne · London

Scribe Publications
18–20 Edward St, Brunswick, Victoria 3056, Australia
2 John St, Clerkenwell, London, WC1N 2ES, United Kingdom

Published by Scribe in Australia, New Zealand, the UK,
and North America 2018

Typeset in Garamond Premier Pro by the publishers.

Printed and bound in the UK by CPI Group (UK) Ltd,
Croydon CR0 4YY

Scribe Publications is committed to the sustainable use of natural
resources and the use of paper products made responsibly from
those resources.

9781925322828 (Australian edition)
9781911617013 (UK edition)
9781925548730 (e-book)

CiP records for this title are available from the British Library
and the National Library of Australia.

scribepublications.com.au
scribepublications.co.uk

For my Kath,
thank you, thank you

CHAPTERS

CHAPTER 1

Uncle Bill's wedding ring

A life builds on itself, but its architecture follows no rules. It can appear at the beginning to have a strong foundation and then be swept away in the first storm, mystifying those who failed to see the flaws in its design. It can seem ramshackle, yet rebuild itself to withstand whirlwinds. My own life has surprised itself again and again. In my first 15 years, we moved so many times I didn't understand what people meant when they talked about the comfort of being 'home'. I still don't get it, but eventually, when I was older, I worked out my own personal definition. We lived in Egypt, Eritrea, Libya, Singapore, and the British occupied zone in West Germany — all places where, for one imperial reason or another, the British had some kind of control. They were the dying days of the Empire, and everywhere we went the sun was setting on it.

Between these postings — most of them lasting a couple of years — we existed in a limbo the Army called 'transit', which meant spending weeks or months any place the military could make a deal to accommodate us. We stayed at seaside boarding-houses in the seedy charm of Blackpool by the promenade and near the pier in

1

Southend-on-Sea. We lived in a green, corrugated-iron hut, insulated with asbestos, in a Liverpool suburb; and spent six months in a worn-out village hotel in the Scottish Highlands.

The rest of my life might be explained by the ingrained restlessness this childhood wandering created in me. I went to so many schools I cannot be sure of the count — in some, I was only there a couple of weeks — but they number somewhere around 13 in 10 years. I didn't keep any childhood friends until the age of 15, when Dad left the Army and we went to live in Australia. The only name I remember is Brenda Laidler in Singapore, but she hardly even noticed me.

These foreign places evaporated behind us. Everyone was a nomad, so the families we left melted away as we did, off to their own new postings and own new worlds.

The only constant place for me was Bootle, a once-prosperous Lancashire hamlet, jammed hard against the docks of Liverpool, and shattered by war. If ever I had roots, they were here, and if a life's foundation begins with the ground from which it emerges then tough and blighted Bootle, and the people there who loved me, must go some way to understanding mine. First, I found safety and happiness there; then, in a complicated way, it was terrifying; and then, almost when I wasn't looking, the heart of my childhood was lost forever, its people gone and all its physical evidence erased.

Malcolm Street, where I was born, was a narrow, grey honeycomb of cobblestones, a dead-end flanked by small, bay-fronted Victorian terraces with no bathrooms, hot water, or indoor plumbing, except for a tap at each scullery sink. At the bottom of each hard-paved backyard was a brick outhouse.

At one end of the street, beyond a high red-brick wall, panting steam trains billowed coal smoke that clung to windows and washing. At the other end, St John's Road ran parallel to the mighty Liverpool docks half a mile west, near the point where the grey waters of the

River Mersey flowed into Liverpool Bay. Auntie Gladys' house was here, and just before dawn on Saturday 19 February 1944, I was born in her front parlour and placed on the floor in a laundry basket prepared with white cotton and lace. It was 110 days before D-Day, so there was a lot of grief to counterbalance this happy family moment.

A few doors down, on the corner of Malcolm Street, at 149 St John's Road, was the home of my uncrushable grandmother, Edith Emily Bruce, the widowed mother of 10. Her house was the chaotic and crowded gathering place for the extended Bruce family. Our house was three doors away from Auntie Gladys, who was my mother's identical twin; their sister, Emily, lived a hundred yards away; brothers and cousins were a walk.

The four-page edition of the *Liverpool Echo* announcing my birth carried more significant news: 'STUTTGART Attacked In GREAT STRENGTH By Our HEAVIES' ... 'Battering For Great Nazi Rail Centre' ... 'NAZIS FALL BACK' ... 'DEAD GERMANS IN HEAPS'. By the time I was born, the Luftwaffe had already devastated our dockside neighbourhood. After London, Merseyside got the worst of the Blitz; newspapers said bombs destroyed or damaged up to 90 per cent of the homes in Bootle.

Merseyside was the key western port in the Battle of the Atlantic, and destroying its docks and railway system was central to the Nazi effort to starve and subjugate the country. Britain was isolated from occupied Europe, and ships carrying food and arms from the United States and Canada had to reach here past a blockade of enemy U-boats.

Living in the middle of this was my family of cleaning ladies, cooks, seamstresses, boilermakers, dockworkers, and tailors. Their terraced homes were in the bull's-eye, sandwiched between railway lines and docks. They had nowhere to go except the uncertain safety of their Anderson shelters, the build-it-yourself refuges that came with a spanner, nuts and bolts, and a page of instructions. An Anderson was less than 6-foot high, not much longer, and intended to accommodate six people. Each day, they carried gas masks to their jobs in the factories and wharves nearby, past the ruins and wrecked ships. Above them, tethered by long cables, were the floating hulks of barrage balloons, there to thwart low flying attacks. At night, they lived behind blackout curtains.

The worst time was the May blitz of 1941, Merseyside's deadliest air raid. In seven days, 680 German bombers dropped 960 tons of bombs and 112,000 firebombs. The May blitz killed more than 1700 people on Merseyside, including Uncle Bill, my mother's brother. He was the quiet son in a raucous family, a tailor, tall and thin with horn-rimmed spectacles. He went to work as an air raid warden on 4 May and was never seen again. In the ruin of a warehouse, they found a left hand and knew it was Uncle Bill's by the wedding ring engraved with the name of Rose, his wife. He was 34.

The scale of events overwhelmed such family tragedies. Mr and Mrs Richard Cruise, of Kirkdale, lost their three sons — Harry, William, and Peter — in action within eight months, and that only rated a short single column in the *Echo*.

I was born 18 months before the war ended, but in Europe the obliteration of German cities had already begun. When I was two days old, *The Times* of London reported that 2000 Allied aircraft had mounted 'the greatest daylight air assault of the war'. The night before, 1000 RAF bombers dropped 2300 tons on Leipzig alone.

Liverpool did what it could to live a normal life. A front-page advert in the *Echo* announced that Vera Lynn, the wartime singer famed as the British Forces' Sweetheart, was appearing at the Empire Theatre, two performances at 5.20pm and 7.45pm. *Gentleman Jim*, starring Errol Flynn, was showing at the Commodore, our local cinema.

The *Echo*'s conscientious editors found space to correct a mistake — a judge at Liverpool Assizes had not described the plaintiffs in a case as 'abominable' but 'admirable'.

An anxious Mr Edmund Percy wrote to the Editor:

> Whilst one hails with delight the advent of a few oranges in this country, one views with dismay and disgust the amount of orange peel carelessly thrown upon our streets and sidewalks. Quite apart from untidyness [sic] this is a very dangerous practice and is likely to lead to very serious, if not fatal, accidents, especially in the blackout.

The peril of Mr Percy's killer orange peel is overshadowed on the page opposite, beneath dense columns of type headlined 'Local Casualties — News Of Our Men in The Forces'. The bleak listing of Merseyside's latest dead, missing, and captured is broken with tiny headshots of the smiling, tragic faces of young men in uniform. The headlines three pages later provide the context for Liverpool's grief — 'NAZIS' GREAT Anzio LOSSES' ... 'AIR, SEA ONSLAUGHT' ... 'Furious Gun Duels' ... 'CASUALTIES "ENORMOUS"'.

My big sister Marilyn was three years old when war began. She remembers the noise and how buildings shook as the bombs fell, and being forbidden from using the top bunks because sleeping there meant being the first to die. During raids, the family shelter filled with the howls of Annie Laurie, the family's Scottish Terrier, who Mum said was 'shell-shocked' and driven crazy by the blitz.

In the panic of Bootle's first air raid, Marilyn — we always called her Mal — slipped from the satin-covered eiderdown in which our mother had wrapped her, and bounced down the stairs. Next morning, as the family gathered in the back room at 149, my grandmother was less annoyed by the bombs than her daughter's carelessness. 'Well,' she said, picking up her bruised and swollen granddaughter, 'if Hitler doesn't get her, you certainly will.'

Along with the entire nation, my family was placed on a strict wartime diet to ration supplies of sugar, butter, margarine, cheese, jam, bacon, ham, and poultry. Ration books were buff-coloured for most people, but when my mother was expecting me she received a special green version, which meant extra eggs and milk, and the pick of what fruit there was. Blue books were for children between five and 15, guaranteeing more meat, fruit, and milk.

Ministry of Food advertising lauded the versatility of rationed food, even offering recipes. 'No limit to the tempting dishes you can make with dried eggs,' it promised.

Other advertising offered help in coping with the stresses of the time, promoting numerous and improbable cures for wartime nerves. Beecham's Powders showed a woman's anguished face with the line, 'I can't go on'. Beecham's, it promised, was 'a quick and certain remedy' for 'nerve pains' — 'thousands upon thousands resort to it with gladness the moment the attack commences', adding, 'Also recommended for toothaches, colds, and chills.'

For suffering children evacuated away from their families and the bombing, help was at hand — 'How Lucozade mothers home-sick kiddies.' Three or four glasses a day was the recommended dose.

Even chocolate was a necessity — 'Education officers all over the country have ordered supplies of Fry's chocolate as emergency rations for children. Because chocolate is a most valuable, highly-concentrated and energy-giving food, it is just the thing to keep children going in the event of temporary food-dislocation by air raids.'

Families were scattered by the war. In 1941, my father, Frank Arthur Hinton, was already enlisted when Mum joined the women's branch of the Army, the ATS — Auxiliary Territorial Service. She signed on while angry after a row with my dad, the cause of which she since forgot. It was an impulsive thing to do, especially since she had a five-year-old daughter. The recruitment office was unsympathetic when she returned next day, and declined to cancel her application.

Marilyn was sent to live with my father's parents, Frank and Magdalene Hinton, at their flat in Huyton, eight miles east. Huyton was not a Luftwaffe target. When the air raid siren sounded, instead of running to the public shelter, the family sat it out in the windowless hall of the flat. Grandad Hinton wore a big, black surgical boot on his left foot and was too slow to get to the shelter. He was a chef and had worn the boot since contracting blood poisoning after cleaning a contaminated rabbit.

My father's parents had a three-bedroom flat, with an indoor bathroom, and a kitchen with hot and cold running water. In the living room was a small electric fire; Marilyn had never seen one. Trees grew along the street, and wartime rationing somehow had less impact in the home of a chef. Visitors were offered tea, sandwiches, and cake, which sailed into the living room aboard a glistening chrome trolley. At Sunday lunch, strawberries and cream was served for 'afters'. Grandad Hinton was not so fearsome as first indicated by his wintry face and alarming limp. In the evenings, he would sit in his chair crafting butterflies and spiders out of silver wrapping paper, allowing himself a little smile as he presented them to Mal. Together, they planted apple seeds in a window box because Marilyn imagined they would quickly become trees.

When I was born, the war in Europe had 15 months to run, but the last air raid had been two years before. The closest I came to wartime action was when I was two and my mother rushed with me into the street when an explosion rattled our windows. She said people were running and crying, and a column of smoke was rising from a fighter plane that had crashed in St John's Road. It was a Fleet Air Arm Fairey Firefly fighter. The pilot bailed out, but his plane killed a neighbour's child.

The last family casualty was Uncle Joe, who was an infantryman in the South Lancashire Regiment and went to fight the Japanese in Burma. Uncle Joe came home with terrifying tales of hacking his way through the jungle in steaming heat, and of his perilous crossing of the Irrawaddy River under machine-gun fire as his regiment advanced against the Japanese. When a soldier yards ahead of him was shot dead in the back of the neck, Uncle Joe said he ran to his side to see the fatal bullet stuck between his friend's teeth like a cigarette.

Disease was another lethal foe in Burma and that is what killed Uncle Joe. Dysentery, dengue fever, and malaria were common enemies in his war. He came home with tropical sprue, a digestive disease that basically destroys the body's ability to absorb nutrients. After the war there was no sure treatment, and Uncle Joe was almost always sick, constantly thin and pale. He spent much of his post-war life in and out of the Liverpool School of Tropical Medicine. He suffered the fatal wound of his war far longer than he was in action. Uncle Joe died in 1954, aged 41, nine years after the war ended. Sprue was responsible for many Allied deaths — an Indian research team estimated in 2006 that the disease accounted for one-sixth of casualties in India and Southeast Asia.

Air raids killed about four thousand on Merseyside, but few knew the scale of the carnage at the time. The morning following attacks, after hours spent in the cramped darkness of their Anderson shelters, my family would turn on BBC radio news, reacting with bleak amusement as the announcer played down, or even ignored, what they had just been through.

For years after, lost buildings left great gaps in the streets. In many there were no buildings at all, only stretches of rubble, dusty pyramids of bricks, and high, lonely walls. The sight of young men in wheelchairs, or with missing arms and legs, was normal to me.

Mum said she never imagined that Germany would win the

war, which was a testament both to her powers of self-delusion and a brilliant wartime propaganda machine. I wonder now how the country's spirit would have stood up in the era of 24-hour news, with Hitler's blitzkrieg coming live into their living rooms, his mighty Panzer divisions spearheading the greatest war machine in history as it swept across Europe.

While Bootle was a wasteland when I was born, my Auntie Gladys' parlour was meticulous. Families lived in cramped homes but reserved their front parlours for occasions. This is where people gathered around newborns and coffins. I would sit alone in my grandmother's parlour as a little boy. The room was cold and stale with a frayed effort at gentility. Antimacassars rested on the backs of chairs of carved wood and satin. They were laced and bright white, and no heads ever touched them. A yellowing music book was opened on the rack of an untuned upright piano. A grandfather clock stood still at 5.26. Photographs of long-dead relatives made it a shrine. Beautiful Auntie May, who died aged 20 in 1922, regarded visitors with an unwelcoming gaze. The parlour was dense with unlovely aspidistra plants. Aspidistras thrive in heat, cold, drought, bad light, and poor soil. Such an unconquerable survivor, so well adapted for hardship, must have been easy to identify with.

This may have been a tough and sooty dockland, but its streets bore incongruous names bestowed by high-minded Victorian burghers. They evoked Oxbridge colleges — Pembroke, Balliol, Exeter, and Hertford — and Shakespearean characters — Othello, Romeo, Juliet, and Viola. 'William Shakespeare' was the name of a local pub, and the art deco facade of the Commodore cinema stood between Portia and Falstaff streets. Malcolm Street was named after the good guy in Macbeth. My younger brother was given the name of the next street, Duncan. My name was more up to date. I was named after Leslie Howard, who was a matinee-idol when the Luftwaffe shot down his plane 8 months before I was born.

Once a village seaside resort, Bootle had long ago been swallowed by Liverpool; its gentility sacrificed for the industrial prosperity that made Merseyside one of the great trading posts of the British Empire, and a place of riches and proud architecture. By the end of the nineteenth century, Bootle was itself thriving. New railways crisscrossed the town, and its riverside houses and pubs had yielded to bustling docklands.

Bootle's promise made it a mecca for hopeful young men, including James Downie Bruce, a Scot from Kilwinning, Ayrshire. James was an apprentice boilermaker, and would become my maternal grandfather. On 15 September 1897, aged 21, he married a local girl, Edith Emily Brooks, who was 19. They had 10 children. My mother, Lilian Amy, was the eighth but only just; her twin sister Gladys arrived 10 minutes later.

My grandmother's marriage was unhappy. No one said a fond word about James Downie. The Bruce daughters repeated stories about their father: he had been a violent drunk whose arrival home, swaying and swearing, filled the house with fear.

One night, Grandma mistakenly put her hatpin into her husband's flat cap on the hallway hat stand. The hatpin was still there when James Downie put on his hat and walked to the pub. When he came home, my grandfather beat his wife for the mockery he had suffered from his drinking pals.

My grandmother attempted several times to leave her brutal husband, but he tracked her to every rooming house. When he died in 1916 after an accident at work, he left his wife seven gold sovereigns. My mother told stories of her unloving father as if she had been an eyewitness, but she was only two when he died.

If my grandfather was a brute, Grandma was forgiving to the point of saintliness. She always kept her dead husband's picture on the wall in the back room above the fireplace. It was a huge photograph of a solemnly handsome man who always seemed about to speak. His apprehensive gaze may have represented some quality of his personality, but was possibly nothing more than shock at the strange, new-fangled camera equipment that would have confronted him. He wore a fine moustache that was beginning to curl at each end, and a stiff Edwardian collar. A watch chain looped neatly across his waistcoat. To his left, in an elaborate pot, was an aspidistra.

All her life, my mother told stories of my grandmother's difficult life with her father. But the deepest sadness of the Bruce family was for my grandmother's lost children. Even allowing for the working-class mortality rates of the time, this was an unlucky house. Edith, her first-born, died as baby; John Douglas was 15 months; Auntie May was 20; Bill was killed in the blitz at 34. In 1916, a few weeks after the death of her 40-year-old husband, Grandma's tenth and last child, Jean, died aged three months.

Growing up with tales of James Downie seems to have rendered Bruce women suspicious of men. It was clear to me even when I was small, listening to my mother and her twin sister. They didn't often talk warmly of men. With the exception, that is, of Gregory Peck. My mum liked him, and always told me we looked exactly alike.

She also loved her older brothers, and her cousin Don, who had been brought up as a brother after his mother died. I think they were the big laughing men who threw me high in the air until I touched Grandma's ceiling. Mum made them sound wild and admirable.

Dad was short and, when Mum brought her fiancé home to meet the family, her tall brothers walked around on their knees. She said her brothers were always in trouble, but smiled when telling stories about them. Uncle Jim, she said, had fired an air gun through the front door letterbox at a passing policeman's helmet and knocked it off.

I only remember Cousin Don and Uncle Dave. Dave was once

a musician, and on the piano in the parlour he appeared in a framed photo, wearing a tuxedo, with a trumpet on his lap. He had a neat Clark Gable moustache and dark hair pasted back from his forehead. As a young man, he had played with big orchestras, but took a job in insurance after catching tuberculosis. Cousin Don had gone to night school, qualified as a ship's engineer, and gone on to a successful career in the maritime industry. All my childhood, he was held up to me as an example. Uncle Dave gave me a few piano lessons, and I wish I had kept them up.

Grandma Bruce — Edith Emily Bruce — was monumental to me. Born in 1878, when Disraeli was prime minister, she was a widow at 38, and worked two shifts a day as a cleaner while caring for her family. She had little money and no prospect of improving her circumstances, but was proud never to have ignored the landlord's knock. Her children were educated away from home by a charity for the poor.

Somehow she managed to save, and after her death in 1960 my mother bought me my first typewriter with the little she inherited. It was a portable Olivetti Lettera 22, a sleek and beautiful machine that travelled the world with me and now sits nearby, a battered veteran in happy retirement, as I type this on a MacBook Air.

Grandma Bruce was held in awe by her daughter as a woman of indestructible will who kept everything together in the face of engulfing challenges. When her son's wife committed suicide, she had taken in their two children, a baby and a toddler, and raised them as her own. When another son had a daughter, and abandoned the mother, she had paid for the baby's upkeep — seven shillings and sixpence each month until she was 15. Nothing made her break.

It would be too tidy and romantic to say she coped with it all and managed to bring up a healthy and happy family. I'm not sure she did, but it must be some success in such a hardscrabble life that none of them ended up in prison.

Unable to support a big family, she had sent Mum and her twin sister Gladys to a children's home 55 miles away in Lancaster. They were eight years old. It was called the Ripley Hospital, but Mum always told us it was the 'Ripley School for the Children of Poor but Respectable Families'. The school had been built with the legacy of Thomas Ripley, a Lancaster publican's son who made his fortune as a merchant prince of Liverpool. It was a home for orphans and fatherless children in Lancaster and Liverpool, and there was an idiosyncratic condition for entry that qualified my mother and her twin; they lived within seven miles of Liverpool's Anglican cathedral.

Ripley offered strange lessons to its poor pupils, teaching little girls how to curtsy when presented in court, or how to behave in front of their servants. They were taught how to talk and how to walk. Mum liked demonstrating how she was made to walk balancing a book on her head, while making sure her toes touched the ground first with each step. I was confused, never having seen anyone walk in this fashion, before or since.

This kind of finishing-school learning was not much use when my mother left at the age of 14 for a job operating the lift in a dry-cleaning factory. It was a tough life in Bootle for a girl, her Scouse accent sanitised by elocution lessons, who had been given the sense of entitlement that goes with preparations for the moment she would curtsy before the King.

Ripley teachers were strict. Talkative pupils were made to sit cross-legged facing the corner with large cotton reels thrust into their mouths. Ripley helped poor families for years after my mother left, but it became a regular school after the war when the support of the welfare state allowed one-parent families to stay together.

The Bruce clan, my mother's side of the family, had more difficult lives than the Hintons. Dad's family was a success compared with hers. The Hintons had migrated to Australia and thrived in farming, real estate, and the food business. A distant cousin was a veteran of Gallipoli and Passchendaele who won the Military Cross, was twice Mentioned in despatches, and became a brigadier. Dad's father had worked at Boodle's, an exclusive gentlemen's club in St James's, London. His name appeared in a 1922 edition of *The Times* in a story headlined 'The Cook's Art' registering his attendance at the opening of the 26th Universal Cookery and Food Exhibition.

For a long time, the Hintons earned their living from food. My dad, Frank, was a chef. His dad, also Frank, was a chef. His grandfather, another Frank, was a baker. Isaac Langley Hinton, my great-great-grandfather owned his own bakery in Great Chapel Street, Soho, in the mid-nineteenth century.

My father was born in London. He grew up in leafy suburbs in the southwest, near Wimbledon Common. His main mischief was squeezing through the fence to watch tennis at the All England Tennis and Croquet Club. He augmented his pocket money foraging for lost balls and selling them to departing players.

Seen from the tough streets of Merseyside, the Hintons were lucky people. My mother told stories of lost wealth and hardship. Her mother's parents had a thriving leather processing business. They had lived in a big house with their own housekeeper, and travelled the prosperous streets of nineteenth century Liverpool in their own horse and carriage.

All this was lost when Grandma's father died, and his grief-stricken widow turned to drink and ended up penniless. Grandma Bruce, still a small girl, had been raised by her own grandparents.

Frank met Lilian in Liverpool when she was 19 and he was 23. She became engaged to him when she was 20, but Grandma wouldn't let her marry until she was 21. Her birthday was 27 May 1935, and she married on 8 June. They posed on the steps of St John's Anglican Church in the next street. The wind had caught my mother's long white dress, sweeping it to one side. In her left arm, Lilian carried a huge bouquet of namesake white lilies. With her right, she seemed to hold my father tightly. He was wearing a large white carnation and a dark suit with gigantic lapels, the sort that have gone in and out of fashion ever since. Mum was beaming brightly, a picture of happy sweetness that was to fade with the years. My father was taking the day more seriously, only a slight smile breaking round his mouth. He was never a big smiler.

It was a happy start to an unsteady relationship. For my mother, marrying Frank Hinton was to be a way out of Bootle. Before the war they moved frequently around Britain, travelling with Marilyn, who was born 11 months after their wedding. My father changed jobs often. One of the quirks of this otherwise quiet man was his quick temper. Kitchen conflicts led again and again to him storming out of a job, or being fired. My mother said she dreaded the days he brought home the black canvas bag that held his work knives — they only came home with him after he'd lost another job.

Dad volunteered as an army chef in February 1940, six months after Britain declared war. Dad liked telling us that Napoleon had said an army marched on its stomach, and that helping them march was his job. He spent the war in Britain. He wanted to go abroad, and once got as far as the dock before his departure was cancelled. Dad remained a soldier for 19 years: Army no S/173319.

My mother was one of millions of women who volunteered for non-combatant jobs. There was the Women's Land Army, whose members stood in for farm workers conscripted to fight, and 'Canary Girls', who worked in munitions factories, earning their name because exposure to toxic TNT turned their skin yellow. For ATS volunteers like my mother, duties stretched from driving and repairing vehicles to acting as kitchen maids. My mother could never drive, or even ride a bicycle. She did her share of humdrum work, but most remembers waking to sirens, and running through dark woods to anti-aircraft guns. She would provide the ammunition while men did the firing.

The war brought the first of my parents' many separations. Dad's peripatetic military life caused most of these separations — but not all of them. They tested their marriage without ever quite breaking it.

The war years gave women left at home a new sense of independence. Between 1939 and 1945 divorce petitions increased fivefold. In a reversal of pre-war trends, two out of three were filed by men against their wives, many on the grounds of adultery, brought by soldiers returning from the front.

When the war was over, and soldiers returned looking for jobs, most women went back to being housewives, many reluctantly. By the late 1940s fewer than 20 per cent of married women worked. Mum returned to being a housewife, and my sister Mal, who was nine, had to get to know her parents all over again. Her grandparents hated parting with her.

Fifty-nine years after the war, when I was running Rupert Murdoch's British newspapers, Baroness Boothroyd visited my office in London. Betty Boothroyd, a former Labour MP, had been a colourful and popular Speaker of the House of Commons. She strode forcefully into my office, immaculate in red, her shining white hair perfectly in place, and said immediately: 'I need you to give me some money.'

The baroness was raising funds for a monument to the women of the Second World War. She visited me on 27 May 2004, and could not have chosen a better moment. It was Mum's ninetieth birthday.

My company offered a generous donation, and I was told Lilian Amy Hinton's name would be placed in a time capsule beneath the monument, along with many thousands of others who had joined the war effort.

On 9 July of the following year, I watched Queen Elizabeth unveil this monument to my mother — a 22-foot tall bronze monolith set in the middle of Whitehall, north of the Cenotaph. London was in the grip of a new wartime tension; two days earlier, Islamic extremist suicide bombers had killed 52 Londoners and injured more than 700. It was a difficult and moving day.

It was also 10 months after my mother had died. I think that day would have pleased her.

CHAPTER 2

149 St John's Road

Bootle is an unprepossessing place even today, and back then it was especially battered and bleak. But I loved Bootle because I could count on it. I probably loved it more than those people who had no choice but to live there all the time. Bootle was always there when not much else was. Even Dad vanished for a while when I was very young — it was years before I found out about the army butcher Mum met in Egypt.

Our life abroad was luxury compared with life in Bootle. Dad was only a staff sergeant, but we had maids and houseboys who cooked and cleaned. We ate bananas, tangerines, prickly pears, coconuts, pineapples, and pomegranates. In Britain, all I remember were pears and apples.

It wasn't easy leaving the heat and bright skies, but nothing could beat a foggy Bootle homecoming — seeing the weary flicker of old gas street-lamps on the wet pavement, breathing in the familiar coal-filled air. Even the cold wind cutting through my hot-weather clothes felt like a welcome. We always spent time there during our periods of 'transit'. We stayed at my grandmother's terrace at 149 St John's Road.

My grandmother's house was as predictable and comforting as a favourite story. The same two wooden pickets would be missing from the green fence around the weedy patch beneath the front window. Below the pickets were the rusty stumps left when the original iron railings had been taken away to provide metal for the war effort. Inside, across the brass doorstep and beyond the unvisited parlour, was the back room where everything happened. The big black kettle would sit above the fire in the tall hearth. On the ledge next to it was the long fork for making toast. Fire-toasted bread was crisped on one side only and covered with Tate & Lyle Golden Syrup or a thick layer of bittersweet lemon curd.

A plastic red-checked tablecloth with the same two burn rings covered the table beneath the window overlooking the backyard. You couldn't actually look at the backyard because Grandma kept the curtain drawn so visitors couldn't see the weeds fighting through the dull white distemper peeling off the brick walls.

In the lightless hallway, on a small table next to the hat stand, was a heavy black Bakelite telephone. I was allowed to answer it, always with the words 'Bootle 3048'. Lifting the receiver required both hands, and you placed a call by giving the operator a number.

The only lavatory was at the bottom of the yard. The seat was cold and there was no toilet paper, only torn squares of the *Daily Mirror* on a hook. This might be how printer's ink got into my blood. Or maybe it was because of Uncle Joe, the Burma veteran who worked for a while as a watchman and cleaner in the offices of the *Daily Post* and the *Liverpool Echo*, and brought home large and exciting black-and-white photos he picked out of the waste bins.

Grandma kept a mad Border Collie named Bobby in the backyard, where he had nowhere to run and nothing to chase. Whenever Bobby was let into the outside world, he went wild with excitement, which Grandma said was bad for him.

Bath time was Saturday morning, when a small zinc tub was placed in front of the hearth and filled with hot water from the black kettle. When I was older everyone had to sit among the aspidistras in the cold front parlour before I took off my clothes.

The only heat in the house came from the back room fire, which was fed with real coal. The pyrotechnics of real coal was lost long ago to the tame glow of smokeless coke, which is healthier but not so much fun. Real coal was fierce, and unpredictable. It crackled and sizzled, and its flames changed colour — blue, orange, white, yellow. Sometimes it spat out tiny red missiles, filling the back room with the singe of the hearthrug.

Upstairs, we slept in beds with noisy springs. The mattresses were old and sunk in the middle; it was like cradling in a big nest. Beneath each bed was a metal bed pot to avoid a trip outdoors. When Grandma's scary sister, my great aunt Grace, stayed, I would get into bed with Mum and put the hook on the door, while she wandered the house crying about creatures she couldn't identify that were crawling on the walls.

The bread man's horse clattered along the street in low-headed resignation, its giant hooves sliding on the cobbles. I would lift my hand with carrot ends and stale bread — 'Keep your fingers straight, lad, or he'll bite them off' — and feel his soft wet lips.

The coal men's smiles were white and pink in their blackened faces. They aimed the entire contents of the heavy sacks on their backs exactly down our coalhole. I would help lift the round heavy metal cover on the pavement outside our front door then run downstairs and shovel the stacking lumps so they could all fit into the cellar. It was brilliant and messy fun, but made me cough.

The chimneysweep covered the hearth with newspaper and made his brush handle longer and longer, and I ran into the street to see its black bristles peep out of the chimney top. The rag-and-bone man would ride past with his pony and cart, crying out and ringing a bell. My grandmother never had anything to sell him. Twice a day, lamplighters carried along their narrow ladders to light or extinguish each gas lamp. Mum said they earned extra in the morning banging on doors to wake people so they weren't late for work.

The back room was my Wild West prairie. Bobby the Border Collie was Lassie, but never did what he was told. My horse was the right arm of the torn brown sofa. I was a hard rider and the sofa arm eventually fell off.

In the mid-fifties, Grandma rented a 12-inch Baby Bush television and sat it high in a corner of the back room on a small shelf above the table. Until then, the only television I saw was through a crack in the lace curtains of the front window two doors down from Auntie Gladys' in Malcolm Street. I watched the test pattern, waiting for Bill and Ben the Flower Pot Men, who lived in two flower pots at the bottom of a garden and spoke their own dialect. My mother said she couldn't understand them, but I could, and thought it must be a language for children only.

Much later, I enjoyed watching a blonde singer named Jill Day, who wore clinging dresses, and, at the end of a song, would turn her back on the camera and wink at me over her shoulder.

When television advertising arrived, there was one for Gibbs SR toothpaste, which meant our toothpaste was famous. There were other things advertised that I had never heard of. Horlicks was a drink you needed for a good, sound sleep, and Lucozade made sick people better. My mum said these advertisements were not true and, even if they were, we couldn't afford Horlicks or Lucozade.

People on television and radio had strange voices. Grandma called them 'posh'. They also used different words. Dad was from London, and said, 'Cor, blimey' or 'Cor, lumme,' when he was surprised. Posh people on the television and radio said, 'I say!'

I'm not sure what my first memory was; I was told so many stories about being a baby that I'm sure I've created mental films about them. But I'm certain of one early memory because no one was there who could have told me about it. I saw a blazing light changing places with the face of a black woman. It terrified me. I remember crying and struggling against a hand planted firmly on my chest. I remember a voice saying softly, 'Stop, stop.' A stinking white square was placed on my face, and then there was nothing. The material was cotton wool, the smell chloroform, and the hand was pinning my struggling body beneath the beam of a surgery light. My mother had decided I should be circumcised. I do not know the reason, but it was not religious and, since I was three years old, she left it late.

It was at Grandma's that my mother discovered I was a better reader than she thought. I was five, with a copy of the *News of the World*, when I asked her what 'sexually molested' meant. It was a while before I got my hands on another copy of the *News of the World*. Years later, when I was an adult, the *News of the World* would get me into far worse trouble.

School was Bedford Road Primary, which was an epic trek from St John's Road. When I measured the distance years later, it turned out to be half a mile. This daily journey began with the morning malt ordeal. Each day, a dessert-spoon overflowing with malt and cod-liver oil was forced into my mouth. There was so much of it that I couldn't breathe properly until it began to melt. Malt was medicine to ward off all ills, I was told, and it was unsafe to leave home without taking it.

Suitably immunised, I would set off, past the terraces along St John's Road. Some of these terraces were boarded-up and derelict. At the old bomb site on the corner stood two prefabs — the quick-build homes for families left homeless by the blitz. I would turn right, passing through the echoing cobbled subway under the train lines where, in February 1952, a stranger told my dad and me, 'The King is dead' and that Princess Elizabeth, aged 25, was now the queen.

On the left, upon emerging, was Auntie Elsie Silk's corner shop, where customers' feet had worn a deep curve into the wooden step at her door. I called her 'Auntie' but she was only Grandma's best friend. On my way home, I would pop in to say hello and sometimes she gave me a stick of liquorice, or a Barratt's Sherbet Fountain, but not often.

Across Stanley Road, and then Miranda Road, was my school, a red-brick Victorian building with small and narrow windows. There was a concrete playground with no grass.

When Princess Elizabeth visited Bootle before becoming queen, we had a day off to stand in the street with flags. Everything the princess wore was bright red — her coat, hat, gloves, handbag, and shoes. She made Bootle seem black-and-white.

Life was not idyllic for the extended Bruce family. There were fights — constant fights — followed by long silences: sometimes one sister against another, sometimes with the family split into factions. I cannot remember the cause of a single argument, but no one seems to have suffered a serious injury — at least, not when I was alive. Before my birth, one of my aunts — as well as Grandma — was married to a man who beat her.

I think all the Bruces were working-class Tories. If Labour's 1945 election victory created a post-war sense of working-class liberation and opportunity, word of it didn't arrive at 149 St John's Road. Each election day, Grandma accepted a ride to the polling station from the Labour Party and voted Conservative.

My mother regarded the upper classes with admiration rather than resentment. She said Tory gents, high born and pinstriped, were better to rule us than uncouth workers, with their coarse ways and raw regional accents — people like us. Mum had a forceful way of expressing herself, and it took me a while to shake off this idea.

My family was Protestant and never spoke well of Roman Catholics. My mother did not like the Sacrament of Confession; she said we should admit our sins directly to God and not via another human being. When the Orange Day Parade happened everyone stayed home. This was a big day for Protestants but my grandmother said we should stay home because Catholics and Protestants would get into fights.

In 1968, Mum wasn't happy when I married a Catholic. She would have been in despair knowing I married another in 2009, but it was almost five years after she died. At least my second wife was from Liverpool.

Edith Emily Bruce, my grandmother, was 66 when I was born. By the time I was conscious of her, she was sallow and old, but still tall, unbent, and never slow. Even then, compared with other women, she wore clothes from another age. Her simple dark-coloured dresses always ended a little above her ankles, and her black shoes had low thick heels and were held on with buttoned straps. Every evening, she draped around her shoulders the same navy-blue loose-knit shawl. Her hair was long, tied in a bun during the day, but brushed out every night in front of the fire. It was white and shining, and stretched to below her waist. She would throw loose hair into the fire where I watched it curl and disappear.

She always polished the brass top of the front doorstep and scrubbed the step below it. 'It shows you have respect,' she said. Each Saturday morning, with her Brasso and a scrubbing brush, Grandma got on her hands and knees at the doorstep to pay homage to her respectability. Her steps were the shiniest and cleanest in the street.

I last saw my grandmother standing on her gleaming doorstep in 1959, the day before we left for Australia. My mother was giving her a long, last embrace. She died the following year.

Grandma was not a jolly woman. I don't remember her smiling

much, or ever laughing. But she was always gentle with me, with the same soft smell. When she was babysitting we had a secret pact: I could stay up 30 minutes after bedtime — until half past eight.

I have Grandma to thank for my Bootle liberation. My mother never wanted me to play in the streets at home. I could wander the Egyptian desert by the Suez Canal, watching camel trains wind through the dunes; ride a white horse in the Eritrean highlands at the age of eight; trek alone through the back streets of Tripoli; clamber the bomb sites of Germany; play soldier in the jungly tropics of Singapore, where snakes could kill with a single bite. I could even walk to school, but I could never go out to play. Rough Bootle boys were bad company for little Les.

I presume my mother was trying to protect me from the toughness and difficulty Bootle represented to her. But when Mum was out, Grandma would set me free to roam. When Mum complained, Grandma wouldn't retreat. 'It's not healthy to keep him cooped up in here all day,' she would say. Eventually Mum surrendered, and Bootle was at my feet. I could walk to Auntie Elsie's shop to buy my comics — *Beano, Dandy,* and *Eagle* — kick a ball in the streets, dash through the narrow back alleys, and play hide-and-seek in the bomb sites. The only rule was no sitting on the wall at the end of Malcolm Street watching the trains, not since a boy down the street fell off and a goods train missed him by inches.

On Saturday morning, I would visit Mum's sister, Emily, who lived three doors away in St John's Road. Auntie Emily was big and always wore the same wraparound pinafore with a print of tiny flowers. When we played draughts, she allowed me to take lots of her pieces, but never let me win. The centrepiece of the mahogany sideboard in her back room was a wireless, domed like a church, made of brown Bakelite with a large dial and big tuning knob.

We listened to serials like *Dick Barton — Special Agent* and

Journey Into Space. Dick Barton began with a roll of drums and pounding music. Arch-villains threatened the world with weapons of indescribable power. There were flaming buildings to escape, and high-speed car chases. In moments of great danger, Dick would say things like 'Great Scott!' and 'Blast!' and advise his sidekicks, Snowy White and Jock, to flee by saying: 'We better buzz off.' *Journey into Space* was set far into the future — in 1965. Captain Jet Morgan flew a rocket ship to the dark side of the moon with his crew — Lemmy, Doc, and Mitch — where they were kidnapped by UFOs and taken thousands of years into the future.

I would lean against the sideboard to listen, head on my arms, right next to the radio, which was so loud you could see the brown fabric cover of the speaker throbbing with the drama taking place inside. I would be so impatient to listen to these programmes that I played with the radio dial, thinking I could find them at any time. Auntie Emily told me that was useless and I had to wait until a certain time — I think it was 11am. I never quite understood why. More than half a century later, technology caught up with my complaint, and we could watch and hear anything any time.

Auntie Emily was a widow with no children. Her husband Bert dropped dead in a cinema queue. As they stood in line, a woman went by wearing a large hat, and Auntie Emily laughed when Uncle Bert said, 'The wind is going to take her and her hat in a minute.' They were his last words; when Auntie Emily looked round, her husband was lying dead on the pavement. Mum said Uncle Bert would hit Auntie Emily regularly until my uncles took him into the back alley one night, knocked him down, and banged his head on the cobblestones.

On Saturday afternoon, I would go with my big sister Marilyn and our cousin Judith to the matinee at the Commodore Cinema, which was across a blackened railway footpath leading to Stanley

Road. Marilyn and Judith never much liked having me around. When they were babysitting, they put the clock forward an hour to fool me into going to bed early. Taking me to the cinema with them was the price they paid for their tickets. Before the main film, there was a short pre-war American serial, ending with an impossible cliffhanger that hooked me every time. We had to wait all week to see what happened next.

We bought fish and chips on the way back, wrapped in newspaper, but at home Grandma made us put our food on plates and sit at the table with knives and forks. The crockery was old and battered, and we were not allowed to drink from the chipped side of teacups.

We had our own delicacies: chip butties — chips, covered with HP Sauce, between two slices of Sunblest bread; bread and dripping — beef cooking fat, laced with tasty brown bits, smeared thickly over bread with lots of salt; sugar sandwiches — bread and margarine sprinkled with Tate & Lyle white sugar. I never kicked the habit of chip butties.

Our cousin, Neil Brooks, was manager of the Liverpool Empire in Lime Street, the city's biggest theatre. This made him a family success. Later, he gained legendary status by becoming manager of the famous London Palladium. Cousin Neil would get us free front-row tickets at the Empire, which we could never have afforded. We saw performers such as Guy Mitchell, Lita Roza, Cab Calloway, Alma Cogan, and Winifred Atwell. I had never heard of any of them, but the audience was excited, so I knew they must be famous.

We were the first to leave Bootle, and Britain. Working-class people did not leave the country much in those days, and everyone back home thought our lives lucky and adventurous. When we went back, everyone looked pallid against our deep tans.

My widowed Auntie Gladys, Mum's twin, married a bank clerk called Harvey Gibbs. Her first husband was the Burma veteran who died from a tropical disease. Uncle Harvey was posher than us, and my aunt moved away to a pebbledash semi-detached at 33 Willow Avenue in Huyton with a garden in the front and back, three bedrooms, a separate dining room, and a garage for their black Ford Popular.

Streets had the names of trees: Laburnum, Cypress, Sycamore, Lilac. Auntie Gladys and Uncle Harvey ate with serviettes on their laps and we had to do the same when we visited. Between meals, they kept their serviettes rolled up in silver rings carved with their initials. When Uncle Harvey was a child, his parents would not let him talk at the table. After meals, he had to go to his room and couldn't sit with his parents in the living room. We called our evening meal tea, but Auntie Gladys started calling it dinner.

The Willow Avenue house overlooked a big field and woods, but in the 1970s the new M62 motorway cut right across it. The tentacles of the new motorway system were spreading across the country, and when my aunt and uncle found out their bit of country was to be sacrificed, they bought a bungalow in an even nicer place, near a nature reserve by the sea, in Formby.

We would visit Auntie Gladys and Uncle Harvey on Sundays. Uncle Harvey loved routine and precise timing. Afternoon tea was always 4pm. He would drive us home at night at exactly the same time, and through the window of the corner house we passed, the television always seemed to be showing the finale of *Sunday Night at the London Palladium*, when all the performers waved from the revolving stage.

No one was more important to my mother than her twin sister Gladys. Gladys and Lilian had epic fights, yet talked of their closeness as if it were something mystical. Once, when they lived more than 10,000 miles apart in Adelaide and Liverpool, they went into hospital on the same day with heart trouble. Old stories of people struggling to tell them apart were repeated more and more as they aged; their delight in telling them made it impossible to be bored.

My mother missed Gladys deeply when they were separated, which was for most of their adult lives. She talked of her constantly. They never spoke by telephone; we didn't have a telephone in the house until Australia. There was a constant back and forth of letters and photographs. Important news of birth, illness, and death arrived by telegram.

I never lived in Bootle again after we went to Australia. I became afraid of going back. I drove there many times without getting out of the car. The poor, cold, dark streets and houses had once been the only familiar place I knew on earth.

But in Australia, in her warm and safe Adelaide suburb, Mum talked about our leaving Bootle as if we had made a lucky escape, as if going back would have doomed us all; that nothing her children made of themselves would have been possible. Many people, when they improve their lives, talk fondly about the rough streets where they began. Not Mum. She made Bootle sound like hell, and I think, in her own mind, that's what it was — full of the memory of grinding unhappiness, of poverty and hardship and grief.

Even going back to Liverpool for a long time made me feel as if I were tempting fate, walking among dangerous spirits, heading into a trap that would never let me go. The prospect of every visit depressed me. This feeling made no sense, and I shook it off years ago. Kath, my second wife is a south Liverpool girl, and I go back often, even to the few remaining Bootle pubs.

Forty years after settling in Australia, as Mum's old mind began to wander, she talked about going home. Every time I visited, she said the same thing. Take me back home with you, she would say, I don't like it here any more, I want to go home. She must have meant Bootle, there was nowhere else, but it was too late to remind her how desperate she had been to leave. Her mind was full of dreams by then — reborn memories of lost people, of imaginary visitors to her care-home room. Maybe moments of Bootle happiness surfaced through the confusion.

There was nothing left in any event. She was the last of her generation, and every house in our stretch of St John's Road had been razed. The last time I visited Bootle, I spent that day alone, wandering the streets — past the derelict Commodore Cinema, the boarded-up shops, and the new but already run-down estates. I had a pint and a microwaved pie in an empty pub, and chatted to the barmaid who, incongruously, came from Los Angeles. She missed the sun, she said.

It had started to rain, the same soft, soaking rain of my childhood that drifts suddenly in from the Irish Sea. I stood under the old railway bridge over which the goods trains used to rattle, belching soot at us.

Kath was shopping with her mother and had promised to pick me up there at four. As usual, she was late, but I didn't care. I stood and remembered a thousand things about my family and my life here. My mother's Bootle, the place she had yearned so unexpectedly for in her final months, had melted away, and so had mine.

When finally Kath pulled up in the hire car, her mother, Angela, waving merrily at me, I climbed into the back and stared out the window. We passed our lost neighbourhood. Grandma's place was gone: the aspidistra parlour that was a shrine to her lost children; the backyard, with its weed-sprouting walls, where Bobby the Border Collie spent his life in confinement; the crackling real-coal fire in the back room, where we toasted bread on one side only. Auntie Emily's had vanished, too, where I listened to those Saturday morning adventures on her giant Bakelite radio set and never once won a game of draughts. The back alleys and the cobblestoned dead-end streets where I ran — Malcolm Street, my birthplace, and Duncan Street — were entombed beneath concrete car parks and a vast grey warehouse. It had become the site of an industrial packaging company called Weir & Carmichael. Near the spot I was born, the company's proud sign said: 'Packaging Your World'. It felt like a taunt.

CHAPTER 3

There's a minefield at the bottom of our yard

I was five when it started, when I first left the familiar comfort of Bootle and the tall, loud uncles who tossed me into the air, and cheered me up with glove puppets when I lay sick on the back room sofa.

I remember the journey; the world turning from grey to green, from tight and closed, to bright and open. I remember a glistening field on a frosty morning; the evening sun through the sinewy branches of a gigantic tree; and strong country smells. I remember squealing on the back of Mal's bike as we sprayed through the stream that crossed a lane near us; the shrill of a dive-bombing bird when I found its nest; learning the name of my first flower — bluebells, clustered along the banks of the stream; and discovering that tadpoles turned into frogs. We had a black-and-white mongrel called Patch who could find me wherever I hid.

It was the first alien place I visited, even though we were only 130 miles away from Bootle, in Yorkshire. Catterick Camp was our first Army 'posting' and we were living in a vast military garrison.

There were khaki uniforms everywhere, and big, shiny black boots thumping along the pavement. And guns, lots of guns. My brother, Duncan, was born there, and Marilyn fell out of a tree and broke her nose, which remained beautifully bent until she had it straightened 30 years later. German prisoners-of-war were still at the camp, although by now they walked pretty freely. They did odd jobs around the barracks. One painted the outside of our house and drank cups of tea in the kitchen.

Catterick was only the first stop on the expeditionary life that lay ahead of us. For the next 10 years, we were swept along, wandering extras in a world-changing game, as the sun set on the British Empire.

Once the jubilation of victory had faded, post-war Britain was a shaky place. Its economy was a wreck, and large parts of many cities were shattered wastelands. As the 1940s ended, the United Kingdom was still bitter and confused that an exhausting victory had delivered no premium in peace.

In its gilded age, the Empire had embraced twenty per cent of the world's population. Now the word 'empire' itself had been displaced by another — 'superpower' — and it applied only to the United States and the Soviet Union. Across the world, Britain's colonies, possessions, and 'protectorates' were beginning to rattle their chains. India, the most prized possession, was to become a constitutional republic in 1950. The country's leaders struggled on in the belief that sustaining the Empire was the path to recovering power and prosperity. Awakening from this delusion took a while; until 1966, a senior politician had the title 'secretary of state for the colonies', which by then sounded like a character from a Gilbert and Sullivan comic opera.

Everything was changing, and not only Britain's place in the world. The country itself would change beyond recognition in the coming decades. The tiny island that called itself Mother Nation to millions of Africans, Indians, and Asians, was itself almost pure white. Property rental ads still advised: 'No coloureds or Irish need apply.' Only 100,000 people were of ethnic origin, many of them clustered in port cities like Liverpool and Cardiff. Fifty years later that number would exceed 4 million. In 1950, it would be another quarter of a century before it became illegal to sack a woman who became pregnant. Abortion would be outlawed for another 17 years, until 1967, the year in which homosexuality would also cease being a crime. There were only 100,000 household TV sets, and each year 1.4 billion cinema tickets were sold to see mainly black-and-white films; 60 years later that number had dwindled to 170 million. There was no portable music; even the transistor radio boom was in the future. Heavy, stationary radios played a limited variety of music from the BBC Light Programme; that was it, unless, through crackling static, you could pick up Radio Luxembourg nearly five-hundred miles away, as it broadcast popular tunes and commercials — and, by the mid-1950s, rock and roll.

This was the Britain I marched away from with my soldier dad to spend years in alien places in new climates, among different peoples speaking peculiar languages and eating strange food. It made a catastrophe of my formal education, but I learned a lot.

We travelled by sea in battered troop ships; old relics that would be war heroes if ships won campaign medals. They braved the early retreat from Europe, the Battle of the Atlantic, the North Africa campaign, the invasion of Italy, and later Korea, Cyprus, Kenya, and Malaya. *Georgic* had been salvaged after German bombers sunk it near the Suez Canal in 1941. *Dilwara* attended the Allied evacuation of Greece 1940, the Sicilian campaign of 1943, and the liberation of Burma. *Empire Medway* was at the Yalta conference when the United States, the Soviet Union, and Britain re-shaped post-war Europe; American and British delegates had slept in our cramped cabins. *Asturias,* an armed merchant cruiser declared scrap after a torpedo strike, was reborn to carry troops, and migrants to Australia. We went to Singapore on her final voyage. It was also the last journey of the whisky-breathed ship's captain; he was buried at sea soon after presenting me with first prize in a fancy-dress competition. I dressed as a robot in cardboard boxes.

On board these ships, locked gates separated two worlds. We were from the 'non commissioned' ranks; Dad was not an officer but a sergeant. A sign warned us to keep our place — 'Officers and Families Only Beyond This Point.' We would peer through the grille of the gates from the crowded stern and see well-dressed strollers wandering the empty deck, and a few others in deck chairs, reading books.

On our crowded side of the fence, bare-chested squaddies would scuffle and banter and increase my vocabulary with words not found in any dictionary of the day. They had tattoos — the old-fashioned sort with rampant eagles, skulls, bloodstained bayonets, and big red hearts, pierced by arrows, declaring love for 'Mum' or 'Doris'. These young soldiers were almost all doing their National Service, the universal two-year military call-up that lasted until 1960.

As ever, when my father encountered an officer he snapped his hand to his forehead in a stiff salute. In return, the passing officer might give a token tap of his cap with a swagger stick. These officers were often smooth-faced men far younger than my father. Dad said an officer would only salute a sergeant if the sergeant had won the Victoria Cross.

I would often share with boys my age a six-bunk cabin deep below, near the throbbing engines. Sometimes the cabin had a porthole, but usually not. Baths and showers were salt water. The crew were strange and interesting men. A steward started waiting for me each night after dinner, with fruit as a gift. I was 11, he must have been 30. My unworldly parents thought he was being nice, but I soon decided to refuse his fruit. The old cockney steward with shiny Brylcreemed hair and a thin black moustache, who cleaned my cabin every day, told me he had not set foot on land for six years.

'You don't even get off at home in Southampton?'

'No. This is where I live. I have seen everywhere there is to see.'

Other stewards were nautical hermits like him.

There was no real school in troop ships, only a couple of hours of makeshift classes if one of the army wives happened to be a teacher. The closest to a geography lesson was playing the daily contest of guessing how far the ship had travelled by sticking a pin in a large map.

Ashore in Durban, on the east coast of South Africa, when I headed to the top deck of a local double-decker bus, two firm hands lifted me into the air as the conductor returned me to the lower deck. Upstairs was for 'non whites' only. A new kind of segregation.

My mother was a smuggler. She never failed to sneak through British Customs with more cigarettes than the law allowed. She always had a victorious smile after getting through with her contraband. Breaking the rules excited her. When we arrived in Southampton once, and Mum was attempting to avoid paying duty, I told the Customs officer she was wearing a new gold watch. Mum wasn't pleased. I could never explain why I did it, but I was only eight. I don't think my mother had a criminal mind, although in the sergeants' mess once, when her fountain pen disappeared from the table where she had been sitting, she promptly stole a different one. 'Someone stole mine,' she said, 'so I'm stealing someone else's.' Mum seemed happy with this logic, although even as a boy it seemed dubious to me.

We went to Egypt when I was six, and lived on the edge of an army camp. There were four single-floor houses and nothing much to see but sand and ships sailing across the desert half a mile away — we could see the ships from our house, but not the Suez Canal. When the wind blew, the sand was whipped into a stinging brown fog.

When Dad and I walked in the dark one night towards the garrison gate, a soldier raised a rifle to his shoulder and shouted, 'Halt! Who goes there,' and started counting loudly: 'One. Two. Three ...'

'Stay here,' said Dad, and he marched forward and showed some paper to the gunman who was threatening us. The sentry smiled down at me as we passed and stroked the top of my head. Dad said the soldier was there to keep us safe and counting to ten gave Dad time to prove he was not an enemy. 'But what happens after he counts to ten?' Dad didn't answer me.

When we approached our house at night, a searchlight beaming from a tower would follow us to our front door like a giant cinema usher guiding us to our seats. When I went to school each day, on a hard bench in the back of a three-ton Army lorry, two soldiers travelled with us carrying Lee–Enfield .303 rifles.

We had a 'houseboy' named Hassan, who wore a bright-white robe, made perfect strawberry-jam tarts, and scoured the kitchen pans with sand outside the back door instead of the Brillo pads Mum bought at the camp store, the NAAFI, which was short for the Navy, Army, and Air Force Institutes. Returning from school one day, I saw him standing near the garrison gate, a soldier holding him by the arm. When I shouted and waved, Hassan only looked at me sadly. Mum said the Army wouldn't allow Hassan to work for us any more.

'Why?'

'They say it's not safe to have him here.'

We lived in the Suez Canal Zone near Ismailia in a place called Gebell Maryam. At the time, Britain controlled this zone under an agreement reached with Egypt before the Second World War. It was a shaky deal whose days were numbered, and the reason we were all in Egypt.

When we visited Ismailia, it looked very poor. Egyptians lived in huts made of pieces of tin and palm fronds. People tried to sell us things, and beggars followed us along the street. Every time we went to Ismailia, I saw a man with no legs who sat on a piece of wood with wheels and pushed himself along with his clenched fists.

It was in Egypt I taught myself to swim. We went to a small lake off the canal, where I would stand on a diving board, throw a rubber ring into the water, and then jump. I would sink into the dreamy underwater silence, look up to the light, locate the ring, and float up to it. My parents never worried — Dad couldn't have helped because he didn't swim either. Eventually, I jumped without the ring. My little brother said his first words there. Some of them confused my mother until she was told they were Arabic.

My own personal sandpit covered acres. There were birds and chameleons and many insects, but ants outnumbered them all. They built cities outside our front door, thousands and thousands of ants in orderly lines, carrying objects many times their size. It amazed me how organised they were without anyone telling them what to do. I once found some candle-like sticks in the sand near the barbed wire around the barracks. Years later, when I told Dad, we agreed it was most likely dynamite. 'There was a lot of trouble going on there,' he said. Camel trains would pass outside the barbed-wire perimeter of our garrison. When they rested, the camels would drop to their knees and sink into the sand with their legs folded, and I would fit myself through the barbed wire to get close to them. They were huge, haughty-eyed, and odorous. The Arab camel handlers would let me pat them and lift me onto their backs. I never smelled anything so bad as a desert dromedary.

At the bottom of our sandy backyard, a skull and crossbones sign was attached to a barbed wire fence. Mum said that if we ever, ever climbed over that fence we would be blown to pieces and die. We lived next to an uncleared minefield laid by the British. During the war,

Rommel's army invaded Egypt and intended seizing control of the Canal. In 1942, seven years before we arrived, Montgomery's Eighth Army defeated Rommel at El-Alamein, which was 240 miles from our house. It was an important early victory for the Allies, prompting Churchill's famous remark: 'This is not the end. It is not even the beginning of the end. But it is perhaps the end of the beginning.'

Outside our back door, to the left, beyond our next-door neighbour, was a stream where we had our own rowboat, which was blue and leaky. My friends and I would row along the stream and fish. Once, the boat began to sink, and we shouted for help. Without pause, Mum leapt the fence with the skull and crossbones sign and ran across the ground we had been warned we could never tread without dying. The barbed wire had torn her dress and streaks of blood were running down her legs. I kept shouting, 'Mum, jump in the water,' and when she finally did the water was waist deep. My fearless mother walked to our rescue and towed us home in our sinking rowboat. This was when I knew my mum loved me, but also was brave and perhaps a little crazy.

We bought a dog to take the place of Patch, who had been given to friends in Catterick. It was a German Shepherd puppy, and my sister called him Pepper. Pepper had a short and unlucky life. He never stood a chance; he was a martyr to the English class system. The camp adjutant, a captain, lived next door, and Pepper didn't like him. Each day, he greeted the captain home with barks and growls. The captain might have been frightened of dogs, but I could not understand why Pepper's conduct deserved the death penalty. Nor did I work out why my father took me to the execution. Pepper was tied to a barbed wire fence and a young soldier with a revolver, who did not have a good aim, started firing at him from a distance. After several shots, with Pepper howling in pain, my father took the revolver from the soldier, walked close to Pepper, and fired one shot.

My dad didn't speak afterwards, but there were tears on his cheeks. I don't know whether I cried, but I have always believed that Pepper died because my father was out-ranked by the man next door.

Dog lovers who hear this story are inclined to become emotional, sure that it must have been a deep childhood trauma for me. If it was, it's stayed well buried. But I never again formed a close attachment to a pet. The shooting of Pepper was my first experience of death, and irretrievable loss.

I don't think we ever ventured beyond the Suez Canal Zone and I never made a single Egyptian friend. The British Army was isolated and unwelcome. That's why our desert neighbourhood was hedged with barbed wire and guarded by searchlights and shouting sentries. The Sphinx and the Great Pyramid of Giza were only 80 miles away, but we never saw them.

Soon after the Army moved us to our next posting, rioters killed British civilians in Cairo, and in Ismailia, a few miles from where we lived, British soldiers with tanks fought Egyptian police and armed militia — Fedayeen — killing dozens.

We were there during the final years of British control of the Suez. It ended in 1952 when the military overthrew the monarchy, declared a republic, and forced the British to leave. Soon after, I saw Egypt again from a troop ship passing through the Suez Canal. Everyone was instructed to stay below decks, but from a porthole, I saw crowds of angry people shouting from the banks and throwing things at our ship.

In 1956, Gamal Abdel Nasser, the country's new president, nationalised the Canal, and the armies of Britain, France, and Israel tried to seize it back. The invasion provoked international outrage, led by the United States and Soviet Union, and a rapid withdrawal of the invading armies. The Suez Crisis was the swansong of the British Empire.

It was 1965 before I finally saw the Sphinx and the pyramids. I was on my way back to Britain from Australia, seeking my fortune in Fleet Street, and the ship had docked for a day or two in Egypt. A couple of us hired a taxi to take us there, and our driver was cheerful and talkative and spoke good English.

'Where you from?'

'Australia.'

'Ah, beautiful. I drive many Australians. Nice people.'

'I'm originally English. I lived in Egypt as a child.'

'English? Why were you here?'

I caught his eye in the rear vision mirror and could see the cheerfulness leaving his face.

'My father was a British soldier. We lived in the Canal Zone.'

For the next five hours we did not exchange a word.

———

The British garrison in Asmara, the capital of Eritrea, became so small that the Army closed our school. The military didn't care much about leaving children stranded and uneducated in faraway places, and naturally I didn't complain. For six months, instead of lessons, I went riding on a white horse with a shorn mane called Karushan. I renamed him Silver. I went alone to the stable every day, galloping round the paddock for hours, the Lone Ranger chasing the bad guys.

Asmara was perched on a plateau more than seven thousand feet above sea level in the Horn of Africa. We went there after Egypt, catching a train at the Red Sea port of Massawa, and travelling through mountains, along the edges of high cliffs, in an open carriage pulled by a slow and ancient steam engine. Dad's friend Sergeant Chalkie White told me to watch out for the baboons clambering on the side of the train. They were big and unafraid of humans, with huge fangs, frizzy manes, and weird, close-set eyes 'They kidnap babies,' he said. When I told him I couldn't see any babies on the train, he said that was because the baboons had kidnapped them all. Sergeant Chalkie had a big scar on his stomach after being shot by a German with a Luger pistol. The German had been standing at the top of the stairs when Chalkie kicked in the door of a house. He said being shot felt the same as being punched very hard.

This time, we weren't living in an army camp, and there were no guards, or searchlights and barbed wire. We lived in a house on a hillside with lots of neighbours. Our housekeeper came to work in traditional dress of colourful robes, like a sari, with her hair plaited in tight, narrow rows that ran back along her head. The housekeeper once plaited my mother's hair in the same way. It took a long time. She brought her own food to work, and it was shocking at first when she ate everything with her fingers, wrapping food from a bowl in pieces of flatbread. The food looked like the stew from Liverpool — we called it Scouse — but with a different smell. Mum said we should eat our own food — she always said that, whichever country we lived in, except for Germany. It didn't seem unusual until later, but we virtually never mixed with local people, only with other army families.

Dad was no longer a cook. He had caught typhoid in Egypt and, because typhoid is so infectious, was no longer allowed to handle food. He now worked as an army store manager. This was the time I noticed a lot of things in the house — like blankets, sheets, and toilet paper — had WD printed on them, with an arrow between the letters. This meant they were the property of the War Department. I think we were supposed to buy our own blankets and sheets, but these were the perks of Dad's new job. When he was a chef, he came home with large cuts of meat.

We arrived in Eritrea in early 1952 and were among the last remnants of Britain's presence. Italy had occupied Eritrea since the

1880s, until Britain drove the Italian army out in 1941. Britain had governed it as a protectorate ever since, but in 1952 gave up control when the country was to be united with neighbouring Ethiopia. There was a ceremony in Asmara, and crowds watched British soldiers marching through the streets beating drums and blowing bugles before the Union Flag was lowered.

Leaving Asmara was the next scariest thing in my life, after watching my mother run through the minefield in Egypt. We were among the final families to leave, and had to travel in an armed convoy back to Massawa to board a troop ship. My dad told me we had to travel in a convoy through the mountains instead of catching the train because of gangs of bandits called Shiftas. These bandits had ambushed trains and vehicles, burnt villages and crops, stolen cattle, and killed many people. They also hated the British. Dad had been chosen to remain behind as part of the last, tiny military presence, but went with us to Massawa. Dad was at the end of our lorry, holding a submachine gun with a long curved magazine, which he said held more than 30 bullets. The backs of the lorries were covered by khaki canvas, and families had to sit well inside and out of view. A soldier stood behind a heavy machine gun that was mounted on the back of a Jeep that followed us. When we stopped in a village for a break, we had to stay inside the trucks while Dad and the other soldiers searched the buildings.

The Shiftas didn't attack us, and we boarded our troop ship safely to sail to our next home, through the hostile crowds on the banks of the Suez Canal, and on to Tripoli, the capital of Libya, on the north coast of Africa. As our ship pulled out of Massawa, heading up the Red Sea, I could see Dad on the dock, standing with the one other soldier from the convoy who also stayed behind. He was smiling and waving, and I kept looking until he was just a dot, worried about leaving him alone in such a dangerous place.

Considering its history in the decades to follow, Tripoli was far more tranquil than Egypt or Eritrea. Libya was a monarchy and the king, Idris, had been raised to power by the Allies after he rallied locals to help drive out the Germans and Italians during the Second World War. The country had an agreement allowing British and US military bases. American supersonic fighter jets would fly above us, so low that the palm trees would shudder in the blast of their engines. You didn't hear the sound these fighters made until they had passed.

Our home was in a block of flats on a road called the Lungomare, the Italian word for 'seafront'. It was lined with palm trees, and curved around Tripoli harbour towards an ancient fort near the white-stoned buildings of the old city. In the early 1800s, US warships attacked the fort and bombarded the city when President Thomas Jefferson declared war on the Barbary Coast pirates terrorising merchant ships. This campaign is immortalised in the opening lines of the hymn of the US Marines:

> From the Halls of Montezuma,
> To the shores of Tripoli;
> We fight our country's battles
> In the air, on land, and sea.

We saw much more of Libya than we had of Egypt. In Tripoli, I don't remember seeing a single British sentry. Our flat was on the second floor, and our neighbours were Libyan and Italian. The first time I heard the Muslim call to prayer, it came from the high minaret of a mosque in the old city; it was a lilting, beautiful song with no words I understood. The old city was a maze of narrow streets with stalls selling jewellery, gold, carpets, and strong-smelling spices. We could go home in a horse-carriage called a *gharry*, which were usually brightly decorated. The horses wore shining black harnesses and golden buckles with feathers rising high above their heads.

An Arab chased me and some friends one day after one of us threw stones at him. It was a stupid, pointless thing to do, and he was furious. His billowing white robe made it look as if he was running in slow motion. I fell off a wall, splitting open my chin, and the Arab caught up with me, lying bleeding and crying on the ground. He said a few angry words then walked with me back to our flat. I had to go to hospital for stitches. I still have the scar.

Outside Tripoli, we saw troglodyte communities, living in caves carved out of mountains by their distant ancestors. They were dug vertically around circular courtyards, several levels below ground, like inverted blocks of flats. They were basic homes, but these people were not primitive. Some caves had wooden front doors with furniture, pottery, and carpets. They had existed for hundreds of years because they provided insulation from savage daytime sun and cold desert nights. Some were used as shelters during the 2011 Libyan Civil War. Dad bought a small blue-painted bowl from them, but dropped and broke it on the way home.

I went to school in Tripoli, but it was never as informative as those days wandering the old city and discovering troglodyte caves. I don't remember the lessons, but never forgot the teacher who demanded I stop writing with my left hand. Whenever I used my left hand this teacher hit it with a ruler. Not the flat side of the ruler, which only stung, but the hard edge. Mum went to the school demanding an explanation, and later told me: 'She said you must use your right hand otherwise it makes the class look untidy. I told her she was talking bloody nonsense, so from now on ignore her.'

Torn between Mum's instructions and the hard edge of a ruler, I struggled on with my right hand. This ordeal triggered a contest between the hemispheres of my brain. Today I write with my right hand; bat right, but throw left at cricket and softball; golf right; play tennis and kick left. This must explain why my hand-eye coordination renders me useless at all ball games.

My biggest discovery in Tripoli was America; it was where I first saw Americans in the flesh. While I waited each morning for a noisy three-ton army lorry to take me to school, they sailed by in gigantic, silent cars with exotic names such as Pontiac, Packard, Studebaker, and Cadillac. These cars were all glittering chrome with big fins and white-wall tyres. I read that America had a lot of cars — 50 million of them — that were enough to stretch around the world at the equator seven times. Dad said he didn't like American cars because they used too much petrol. But we didn't own a car at all. No one in our family did, and besides, Dad couldn't drive.

I never actually met an American in Libya; I only saw them in their cars and at the cinema. They talked louder than us, which annoyed Dad, and walked differently. The men had crew-cuts, checked shirts, and Levi jeans. They leaned against the wall outside the cinema with thumbs sticking in their pockets, chewing gum much more obviously than we did. They lived in bigger homes farther along the Lungomare, and had their own special store, called the PX, which sold things you couldn't buy anywhere else.

This was around the time my cousin Jean started sending me packages of American comics. Cousin Jean had married an American GI in Liverpool after the war and now lived in the Gulf Coast town of Pascagoula, Mississippi, which sounded exotic. The comics she sent were filled with stories of superheroes — Superman, Batman, Captain Marvel, the Flash — and cowboys with two gun holsters — Tex Ritter, Gene Autry, Lash LaRue, Hopalong Cassidy, Roy Rogers. The cowboys were great aims and also humane — they only ever shot guns out of the hands of the bad guys.

The comic stories were fine, but the advertising was really exciting. American children could buy Daisy air guns that looked like Winchester rifles used by the US Cavalry, and Bazooka bubble gum that was, according to the advertising, capable of inflating into gigantic pink bubbles. A man called Charles Atlas, who had sand kicked in his face when he was skinny, had built himself into a muscle man no one could push around, and was offering to do the same for all skinny American boys. The Schwinn Phantom, bright coloured and silvery, was the 'swellest' bicycle. One ad said it was the most popular kids' bike in the world, but I had never seen one.

I decided in Tripoli that one day I would live in America and drive one of their big shiny cars; it took me a while.

CHAPTER 4

Don't mention Hitler

Münster was inside the post-war British Zone of Occupation, and the British Army of the Rhine had a large garrison there. By the time we arrived the 'occupation' had ended and we were part of NATO forces protecting Western Europe against the Soviet Union.

I was 10 years old when we moved to West Germany and I met Joachim. It was an officially arranged friendship; Joachim was German, it was nine years after the war had ended, and the British Army and the city authorities of Münster were clearly thinking ahead.

Joachim and I were paired, along with dozens of other children, in a scheme to further Anglo–German reconciliation. A teacher, explaining it to me, talked gravely about the importance of healing the wounds of war and, before my first meeting with Joachim, recommended: 'It's best not to talk about the war or to mention Hitler.'

Avoiding the subject wasn't difficult — Joachim couldn't speak English and the only German I knew were a few phrases needed to go shopping for Mum: *'Zehn pfund kartoffeln bitte'* ('Ten pounds of potatoes, please'); *'sechs eier'* ('six eggs'); and *'ein kleines brot'* ('one small bread'). My German reached its peak when I managed to tell our housekeeper the complete story of *Little Red Riding Hood*.

Joachim was a quiet and fastidious boy with his own bedroom, which was always in impeccable order, with impossibly tidy bookshelves, and walls with maps and, for some reason, lots of photographs of snow-capped mountains. He did not appear to possess a single toy, but spent hours drawing elaborate pictures with crayons, or leafing through his stamp collection. He gave me a number of stamps bearing Hitler's head; I gave him a set commemorating the Queen's coronation. We visited each other on Sunday afternoons until I went to boarding school 30 miles away. By that time, we had learned to communicate in a fractured dialect mixing English and German. He would write letters in beautiful calligraphy on paper like parchment, with complicated drawings around each page. Mine were written in plain fountain pen on small blue Basildon Bond pages. I still have the Hitler stamps he gave me.

I didn't know much about Hitler before arriving in West Germany. I knew he had bombed our town and killed many people, including my Uncle Bill, the tailor. I had no idea why the war was fought, only that Dad had told me Hitler was an evil man and crazy. It was easy to understand why an evil and crazy man would drop bombs on people's houses, but it was a shock to discover we had done the same thing. Münster looked a lot like Bootle; Allied air raids had destroyed two-thirds of the city.

A few years later, in my teens, I picked up a book by George Orwell, *The Lion and the Unicorn*, published in 1941. I'm not sure I ever finished it, but his first sentence reminded me of that mystifying, childish discovery of what two countries had done to each other: 'As I write, highly civilized human beings are flying overhead, trying to kill me.'

Our home was in Hüfferstraße, overlooking woods and a moat with green water surrounding a castle. It was easily the most spacious place we ever had. The kitchen was nothing like my gran's scullery. It was so big and the floor so smooth that I learned to roller skate there.

Germany was like Bootle in many ways, in addition to the ruins of war. The weather and the smells were familiar, and the people looked more like us than Egyptians and Eritreans, although men clicked their heels and bowed at the neck when they were introduced, and married women wore wedding rings on their right hands. There was no television but we listened to radio on the British Forces Network. *Educating Archie* starred a dummy and its ventriloquist, Peter Brough. It didn't occur to me then how odd it was that a ventriloquist could be a radio star. I watched television only once in all the time we were in Germany. We crowded into the sergeant's mess at Dad's barracks in front of a small black-and-white set to watch Grace Kelly, an American actress, marry Rainier, the prince of Monaco, a pocket-sized principality on the Mediterranean coast. It was the first wedding I remember, on or off television, and I was surprised at how excited the mothers were about Grace Kelly's dress.

Münster was where we owned our first car, and I became interested in newspapers. When my father said we were buying a car, I remembered the long red-and-white Studebaker that had been my favourite American model in Tripoli. But we bought a second-hand German Opel Olympia, coloured beige. It was a 1951 model, but looked very old-fashioned, with the spare wheel attached to the outside of the boot. Dad said the Opel Olympia hadn't changed shape since before the war. He learned to drive in it at the age of 44.

At primary school in Münster, my class was assigned to write an essay in the form of an autobiography. Having just read that some species of butterfly have a lifespan of only days, I wrote 'My Life as a Butterfly' about a beautiful creature doomed to counting out its life in hours as humans did in years. My butterfly was depressed about this, which made the story implausible since he lived as long as every member of his species and would have known no better. A few days after submitting this story, the door to our classroom swung open, and in marched the headmaster.

'Which of you is Hinton?' he called, in an irritated voice.

'Me, sir.'

He waved a piece of paper above his head. 'Did you write this story about a butterfly?'

'Yes, sir,' I said.

He frowned. 'You wrote it all by yourself?'

'Yes, sir, I did.'

He looked at me for another moment in silence. 'Really?' he said, and left the room.

I did not hear another word about my essay and never got a grade, but it was the first inkling in my life that I might be good at something.

Music lessons at Münster always meant singing American songs such as 'The Black Hills of Dakota'; 'Anything You Can Do I Can Do Better'; 'There's No Business Like Show Business'; and 'The Deadwood Stage'. They were all songs from the musicals *Annie Get Your Gun* and *Calamity Jane,* which I had seen at the Commodore in Bootle. Our pretty, young teacher said they were her favourite films, and we sang these songs again and again while she played happily at the piano, singing in what she must have thought were approximations of Doris Day and Betty Hutton. The music teacher wore her shiny black hair back in a bun; she was slightly overweight and had a large, soft, white chest.

I never felt popular at school. I was once caned, to the acclaim of my classmates. Our teacher was reprimanding us for skating on the school balconies, and warning that the punishment for doing so was a caning. As he spoke, a girl interrupted, 'But, sir, Hinton did it first and we thought it was allowed.' For some reason, this accusation led to a chorus from the rest of the class alleging other misdemeanours. Unfortunately, I was guilty of all of them. Mr Bryant, a short, small-framed man who always wore a brown Harris Tweed jacket, shook his head sadly. 'Well, I think the jury has spoken,' he said, and picked up the long cane resting in the corner behind his desk. The pain of betrayal lasted longer than the sting of his two quick strokes, one for each palm.

At the age of 11, I was separated from my family for the first time. Dad had often been absent, travelling ahead to new postings — he was gone for longer when Mum fell for the army butcher. But I had never been without my mother and big sister, or my brother since he was born when I was five. Münster did not have an Army secondary school, and I was sent away to a boarding school. I was not happy. My life was a constant migration, but I could depend on those four familiar people: the sister who bullied me but hugged me, too; the brother who shadowed my every step; the fiercely caring mother; my remote but always loving father.

I sat gloomily in the front of our old car, driving south to the Windsor School in Hamm. To me, the journey dragged on, but we arrived after only 30 miles to the place where I was to be abandoned. It was a monotony of identical and featureless buildings, each of red-brick and five floors, lined up next to a cricket field. Previously living quarters for German soldiers, they were now school dormitories. These former barracks were divided into school houses, and named by the conquering British after homeland castles: Caernarvon, Edinburgh, Marlborough, Hillsborough, and my house, Balmoral.

Each dormitory had empty cream walls, a single ceiling light with a white conical shade, and six iron-framed beds with a small locker beside each. There were showers and sinks for everyone at the end of the corridor, and trouble from matron if we failed to leap from our beds and head straight for them at the sound of the morning bell. We learned to make our own beds and clean our dorms, which meant dusting and polishing the brown linoleum floor. Boys from the tidiest dorm got to stay up an hour after lights out on Sunday and listen to the radio.

At night, a duty master prowled the corridors with a large white plimsoll gym shoe. If one boy in a dorm was caught talking, the duty master would line up all six for a swipe of his shoe across our pyjama-clad backsides. One master hit us much, much harder than the others. Perhaps it gave him some secret pleasure, but we made sure we kept quiet when he was on duty.

We wore school uniforms of crimson jackets and grey flannel trousers. On the jacket breast-pocket was the school badge, bearing the motto 'Concordia,' which was at odds with the accompanying motif of castle turrets and crossed swords.

I still have the claret-coloured plastic writing compendium my parents gave me with their instructions to write each Sunday. Even now, the smell of it brings back the misery and abandonment I had felt; the desperate knowledge that no matter how much I wanted, I could not see or speak to my family. My life was in the hands of people I didn't know or like. I had to live with boys I had never met and didn't choose. Everywhere were hundreds of strange people I couldn't escape. I felt crowded and lonely at the same time.

With no choice but to assimilate into this unwelcoming world, the torment slowly eased. I ended up tougher, more confident, and able to stand up to occasional bullies. I also learned to satisfy prowling night masters by exaggerating the suffering inflicted by the great white plimsoll. I developed a lifelong antipathy to body contact sports after 45 seconds on a rugby field, a crushing tackle, and the distant voice of the sports master: 'Hinton, Hinton, answer me. What day is it? What date is your birthday?' I became the only boy in the St Boniface chapel choir, sang the descant, didn't care about the mockery of rugby-playing schoolmates, and fainted once while carrying the cross into church. At an ecumenical service, the Protestant soprano sang 'Ave Maria' with the Catholic contralto and it was easily the most beautiful thing I had ever heard. 'Ave Maria' also taught me how repetition can ruin great music.

At the age of 11 in the 1950s, British children were divided into two groups by the Eleven-Plus exam. Those who passed were identified as bright children who would receive a more academic 'grammar school' education. This meant studying other languages, English literature, and more advanced science and mathematics, in order to prepare for university and the professions. The rest were classified as better suited to more practical pursuits and attended 'secondary modern' classes. While grammar kids studied Latin and the classics, the others spent more time learning to, as it was described, 'work with their hands' at woodwork, metalwork, and digging the ground to grow vegetables in 'rural science'.

Before arriving at Hamm, I took my Eleven-Plus exam. I never heard the result, but must have done all right because I was placed into a grammar school class. We started learning French, and were told we would study *Great Expectations* by Charles Dickens.

All new arrivals were interviewed, and my interview happened two weeks after I arrived. I sat beside the teacher, whose desk was facing a window overlooking the cricket pitch. He didn't look up from his desk, where there was a book for his notes and a sheet of paper from which he read questions. There was one question and answer I never forgot:

'What do you want to do when you finish your education?'

'I haven't decided yet, sir, but I want to be either an actor or a car mechanic.'

The actor part of the answer was true — I appeared in school plays and amateur dramatics until I was 20. But a car mechanic? I never understood why I said that; the words came from nowhere. I had an illustrated book at home with a chapter about the internal combustion engine and had been fascinated that millions of sparks made car wheels go round, but I had never wanted to be a mechanic.

I knew at once I had given an unwelcome answer. The master shook his head slightly and wrote a note. 'We don't really teach acting, but we can certainly help you understand how cars work,' he told me. And that was that. I became a 'secondary modern' boy, never to take another French class or study *Great Expectations*.

In Britain, grammar and secondary modern educations were segregated into different schools. At Windsor, we were integrated in dorms but went to separate classes. I was looking through the locked troop ship gate at those first-class passengers all over again.

I learned to operate a lathe, bend hot metal over an anvil, make a dovetail joint, and build a trellis to grow peas. I hated it. These were decent and important things to learn, if you wanted to, and if you were good at them, but I didn't want to and was no good at them anyway. Never again have I sown a seed or planed a piece of wood. To be fair, there was a little literature, too. I was once made to learn William Blake's 'The Tyger' by heart — as a punishment for talking in class.

For years, the testament to my education was not a framed certificate, but the white-painted wrought-iron lamp on my parents' television. It was still there in my thirties, rocking on its misshapen base.

We left for Dad's next posting, Singapore, in November 1956. Before leaving West Germany — on 5 May 1955 — the country gained full sovereignty and was allowed to establish a military force and manufacture weapons. It would be 35 years before the fall of the Iron Curtain and the reunification of West and East Germany.

The Cold War was still intense: just before we left, the Soviet Army, killing thousands of people, crushed an uprising in Hungary. Hungary was a long way from Hamm — about six hundred miles east on the other side of Austria — but the Hungarian Revolution was hugely important to us. Hamm was a British Forces school, and we had already been told that the Soviet Union was now our enemy and determined to rule all Europe. A teacher told us about the North Atlantic Treaty Organisation and that our fathers were part of a military alliance pledged to defend Western Europe against 'aggression.' It was the first time I heard the word aggression. Dad told me not to worry about Hungary, that it was the Russians claiming back their own territory, and that they would never invade West Germany.

Singapore was on the tip of the Malay Peninsula, 85 miles north of the equator, where the climate had no clear seasons except for wet and wetter, and the temperature hovered between the mid-seventies and mid-eighties. It was a rainforest world, luxuriantly green compared with the sands of North Africa. Huge open drains along the streets were torrents during downpours. Tropical surprises became routine: a long emerald snake coiled round a palm tree; the brown-eyed gaze of a long-tailed macaque monkey; a lizard darting across our living room wall; a raucous cloud of colourful birds. There was no air conditioning and our windows were always open, each covered with wrought-iron lattices. I learned a new word: acclimatise. We were instructed how to cope with the weather and avoid exertion for at least three weeks while our bodies adjusted.

The people looked strange and small, and smelt different. They walked differently, too, the women with quick, short, sliding steps. They would sit without chairs outside shops and front doors, their bottoms resting on their heels in total comfort, eating from bowls held to their lips, scooping rice with chopsticks. In a miracle of balance and strength, tiny women transported towering bundles balanced on their heads.

Our first Singapore home was in the Serangoon Gardens Estate, which had been built after the war for British families. It was a Surrey suburb with an Asian twist. The streets were called Brighton Avenue, Medway Drive, and Chislehurst Grove. We lived in a spacious bungalow with a garden and room for a live-in maid. Our home was opulent, especially compared with Bootle, and far above the local living standards.

We bought our first record player, but only ever had four long-playing records. There was *Salad Days*, a musical about upper-class university life and a magical piano that made people dance, written by Julian Slade, an Old Etonian; the Chopin nocturnes played by a little-known Dutch pianist, Cor de Groot; Oscar Hammerstein's *Carmen Jones*; and *Deep in My Heart,* the soundtrack of a 1954 film about the composer Sigmund Romberg, featuring Rosemary Clooney, Gene Kelly, Jane Powell, and Howard Keel. I played them for hours, and knew every note and every word.

I went to day school in Singapore — to Alexandra Secondary Modern. James Dean had died in his speeding Porsche the year before and a lot of boys were copying his look — acting tough and sulky, with the collars of their white school shirts turned up, and their hair greased back at the sides and styled high at the front. Almost all the boys seemed to carry flick knives — they were easy to find in Singapore — and would occasionally threaten each other with them, although I never saw an actual knife fight. I quickly copied them, but I never told Mum about the knife.

Just as in other schools, we were given daily milk, only in Singapore it came in cartons rather than bottles, which meant milk bombing was common. Cartons were thrown from an upper balcony into the playground; the heat guaranteed every milk-soaked target would be rancid by the time the home bell sounded. Milk bombing was a serious offence but I was never caught.

During this time, British and Commonwealth troops were involved in a conflict known as the Malayan Emergency, a Communist insurgency in Malaya, which was only 14 miles from Singapore across the Straits of Johor. Dad was never sent there, but we travelled back to Britain on the same ship as members of the King's Own Scottish Borderers and one soldier had a missing arm. The Malayan Emergency lasted 12 years, until 1960. More than 500 British and Commonwealth soldiers were killed.

My sister fell in love in Singapore. She was working as a secretary with the Australian Army and brought home a boy from Adelaide. Don Duberal was a blond, curly-haired corporal with a cocky Australian style, an unfamiliar accent, and a strange dialect. I learned phrases like 'Dinkum', which meant true or honest; 'I'm feeling crook', which usually meant a hangover; and, to be used in moments of celebration, such as when Don won on the horses, 'You beauty'.

Don was posted to Singapore after spending time in Malaya. He liked horse racing and beer, and giving my mother cheek. This immediately endeared him to Dad, but definitely not Mum, whose relationship with her future son-in-law never recovered from the night he arrived at our place after celebrating another good bet. Under his arm was a struggling chicken, purchased with his winnings and presented to my mother for family dinner. Helpfully, but not soberly, Don volunteered for the task of killing the bird. He held it down on a cutting board, took unsteady aim, and severed its head with a kitchen knife. Carelessly, he did so while holding only the chicken's head, and the decapitated body immediately took off in my house-proud mother's immaculate kitchen. It bounced crazily around us to the sound of Mum's screams and the crash of crockery and glassware, blood spraying from its neck over the white walls and kitchen cabinets. Finally, it landed on top of the cooker, dead at last. Our kitchen looked like a scene from a Quentin Tarantino film.

Don's rapid retreat prevented an actual homicide. Don and Mum were never best friends, but I think Mum was privately proud years later when he retired from the army as a lieutenant colonel.

Singapore was my father's final posting before he would return to 'civvy street'. Singapore was still a colony and the British had a vast military base on the island. As well as thousands of army and navy personnel and their families, the base employed ten per cent of the local population. A young Cambridge-educated lawyer, Lee Kuan Yew, who would become the founding father of the nation, led demands for independence. When elections were held in Singapore, our school would close and British families had to stay at home. Singapore ceased to be a colony in 1963 after 144 years of British rule. It became a republic two years later when it left the Federation of Malaysia.

Mal and Don married in Singapore in 1958. We had the reception at our newly built quarters on an army housing estate, and Dad did the catering. They sailed away to live in Adelaide, and for Mum it was like a death in the family. She hardly spoke for weeks and ate almost nothing. She was so thin I thought she might die, but Dad didn't seem to know what to do; I don't think it occurred to either of them that she needed medical attention.

We returned to England soon after, and when Dad left the Army we had to decide where to live. I think Mum had made her mind up already to take us all to Adelaide, but Dad looked at other options. Bootle was ruled out quickly. We considered Canada, but decided it was too cold after all those hot weather years. New Zealand looked attractive, but at nearly 50 Dad was too old to be accepted there as a migrant.

In May 1959, after my final months of school at Maghull Secondary Modern near Liverpool, where I was awarded a C-minus in metalwork for that wrought-iron lamp, we left Southampton for

Adelaide on the P&O liner *SS Orion*. Our passage was subsidised by the Australian government, at that time engaged in a mass immigration programme to populate the country. The four-week voyage cost migrants £12 for each adult, but children went free.

I had already written to the *The Advertiser*, Adelaide's morning newspaper, looking for a job. I knew it was useless to stay at school; my education had been too haphazard. I had been dropped, at random times of the school year, into one Army school after another, and left to catch up with the class. Each time I arrived, they seemed to be teaching what I had learned in a previous school. Apart from woodwork and metalwork, I had heard the same lessons over and over: Britain in the Iron and Bronze Ages; the Roman conquest; medieval crop rotation. I sat through at least three introductions to Pythagoras's Theorem. I also wasn't much of a student — even in secondary modern, my grades were modest with the exception of English 'composition'.

I had seen a lot of the world, but felt apart from it most of the time. In each new place we remained on the edge, in our own parallel 'colonial' world. Maybe it was a culture of detachment borne out of years of 'occupying', and a sense we were better than the people we lived among — wealthier, smarter, and cleaner. We never mixed with the natives, or ate their food. In Singapore, food carts would pass the house, their luscious smell coming through the windows, while we ate chops and chips. Today, much of what I experienced is familiar to everyone through television and cheap travel, but then it was utterly new.

It didn't help me pass an exam, but I gathered a lot of informal knowledge and experience of the world. For instance, I became a worldwide authority on different methods of corporal punishment. Teachers like Mr Bryant in Münster kept a cane in the classroom corner, visible and menacing. The night masters at Hamm stalked the corridors with the great white plimsoll. In the Scottish Highlands, where we were in transit for six months at the Highland Hotel in Strathpeffer, each teacher kept a thick leather strap in their desks, designed for the purpose of pain. These straps were a foot or so long, three inches wide, and cut in narrow strips at the end where it struck the hand — my hands had blisters for weeks before the skin hardened. In Maghull on Merseyside, teachers used the cane but also improvised. At lunch, it was common for a talkative pupil to receive a hard slap across the back of the head; my face landed once in a plate of semolina. In Singapore, there was more ceremony; the headmaster handed out all canings and an appointment would be made for the following day, adding to the punishment by giving the pupil a long night to live in dread. I know of no ongoing cases of historic school assault; teachers must have been given a blanket pardon.

Without the help or support of a school, I had discovered newspapers and narrowed my career choices to two: I wanted to be a journalist or an actor. The acting ambition faded fast in Adelaide, which was not a theatrical mecca. I did a lot of amateur performances and wrote to the Royal Academy of Dramatic Art in London and Lee Strasberg at the Actors Studio in New York. Their replies were not encouraging.

I was 11 when I began to think about working in newspapers. I didn't grow up on the posh side of newspapers; the literature in my life was in the columns of the *Daily Mirror* and the *Daily Mail*. The English papers arrived each day, one day late, at our Münster flat. The *Mail* was an unwieldy broadsheet and the *Mirror* had huge headlines and more photos. I liked the *Mirror* better. While we lived in Germany, the *Mirror* launched *Junior Mirror* for children, and I collected all but one edition before it ceased publishing. It was the first time I was associated with the closing of a publication, but not the last.

The first big newspaper story I remember was about Ruth Ellis, a nightclub hostess who was hanged for murder at Holloway Prison in London on 13 July 1955. The story was on the front page of the *Daily Mirror* and started with these words: 'It's a fine day for haymaking. A fine day for fishing. A fine day for lolling in the sunshine. And if you feel that way — and I mourn to say millions of you do — it's a fine day for a hanging.'

This story continued with a chronology of what had happened to Ruth Ellis the morning she was executed for shooting her lover, David Blakely outside the Magdala public house in South Hill Park, Hampstead, London. 'If you read this before nine o'clock this morning, the last dreadful and obscene preparations for hanging Ruth Ellis will be moving up to their fierce and sickening climax ... If you read this at nine o'clock, then — short of a miracle — you and I and every man and woman in the land with a head to think and a heart to feel will, in full responsibility, blot this woman out.'

After reading the *Daily Mirror* that morning, I never wanted to be responsible for anyone's execution, and also thought it would be good to work for newspapers. The author of that Ruth Ellis piece was Cassandra, the pen name of William Connor. The Cassandra column was a daily event and I always read it. The *Mirror* sold more than 4 million copies then, and its readers were working-class people like us. Connor wasn't a fancy writer using big words and complicated sentences, but he was funny and angry and weaved wonderful images with simple language. Two years after Ruth Ellis was hanged, Connor witnessed a British hydrogen bomb test on Christmas Island in the Pacific and summed it up in a stark sentence: 'It was a dress rehearsal for the death of the world.'

I kept that Ruth Ellis newspaper for years. In 2005, 45 years after writing my first newspaper story, the Magdala became my local pub. The *Mirror* story was hanging in a frame, and on the tiled wall outside there was still the bullet hole from the errant first shot Ellis aimed at her lover.

I also saw when I was young how newspapers not only covered a big story, but could shape attitudes about it among millions of readers, especially at the time of a big sporting event, when the British come closest — apart from during a war — to expressing genuine nationalist fervour.

My first lesson in this Fleet Street technique — and the globe girding magic of communication — came in May 1955 when the boxer Don Cockell, a former blacksmith from south London, challenged the American world heavyweight champion, Rocky Marciano. In those days, heavyweight title fights were huge events and British newspapers were running excited stories about the coming combat. These reports were partial in every way towards the brave boy from Balham who had crossed the Atlantic to take on Marciano — 'The Rock' — who had knocked out Joe Louis himself, although Louis had been 37 by the time this happened.

Even Dad became a boxing fan. He didn't care about sport, except when he was checking his football pools coupon, but got us out of bed in Münster to listen on our Telefunken radio to the live broadcast as Cockell fought Marciano in San Francisco. It was a famous massacre; Cockell was far outclassed, and took a mighty beating for nine rounds before the referee ended the match. It was a brutal fight, and Marciano was a roughhouse boxer, but the British newspapers for the following few days provided an unforgettable example of how Fleet Street could create a sporting hero from the ashes of total defeat.

Cockell had gone into the ring an underdog and taken the beating most people expected. But Fleet Street whipped itself into a glorious fury over Rocky Marciano, and made my dad and millions of others furious, too.

The verdict was the same in every newspaper I read, and Dad brought them all home after the Cockell fight: Marciano was a merciless, savage, cheating brute. In the *Daily Mirror*, Peter Wilson, a writer in the same league as Cassandra, said Marciano was 'like a gorilla, except a gorilla does not eat meat, and Marciano is the most carnivorous fighter I have ever seen ... We still conduct boxing as a stylised sport under a formal set of rules. Here it is legalised cobblestone brawling.' The *Mirror* always described Wilson as 'The Man They Can't Gag', which made him seem intrepid even though he looked like a suburban banker in his by-line photo. But he was a powerful writer who would deploy wonderful hyperbole to touch the millions of people reading the *Mirror*. Cockell's courage, Wilson said, had given rise to a 'kind of primeval mass sympathy and acclamation', which made it sound as if he were writing about the Crucifixion.

Don Cockell, brave as he had been in the ring, never had a prayer of beating Marciano, but Fleet Street had the power and imagination to transform a painfully one-sided fistfight into an epic injustice. Cockell arrived home bruised and battered but heroic, a lion-hearted loser.

This Fleet Street power to excite the nation endured well into the twenty-first century but it was far stronger in the 1950s; at the time of the Cockell–Marciano fight only one in three households had television, with choice limited to two channels. It was more than 10 years before early satellite allowed live international broadcasting. All that most people saw of this fight was a few moments on the cinema newsreel. But 21 million national newspapers were sold each day in a country with 14 million homes. Newspapers were still the dominant messengers, and descriptive writers like Wilson and Cassandra became household names because they could bring great events alive. Writing for newspapers was the most exciting job I could imagine — unless, of course, I could become a film star.

CHAPTER 5

Guglielmo's happy voice

My excitement about a new life in Australia lost its edge when I thought I might go blind. In the ship taking us to Adelaide, a veil of brown had suddenly clouded my vision. Since I was a small child, I had been virtually blind in my right eye, and now this blurring curtain had descended over my left.

The young eye-surgeon's face was pressed so close to mine I could feel his breath. My left eye ached from the white light shining into it through a large magnifying glass. When Dr Peter Stobie had finished his examination, I was too blinded to see him deliver the news.

'You have a detached retina.'

I had no idea what these words meant, but the doctor's voice was grave.

'We must operate right away.'

I learned quickly that the retina layers the back of the eye, and without it you cannot see. It is a medical emergency when a retina detaches, and within two hours I was a patient at the Royal Adelaide Hospital. For the next five weeks I would be blindfolded, confined to bed, and required to keep my head in the same position at all times

65

— elevated and leaning slightly to the left.

Through an opening he would cut through the bottom of my eye, Dr Stobie would attempt to re-attach my errant retina by performing a diathermy, a process involving heat and electricity that was a common remedy at the time, but abandoned long ago.

My eyes had always been trouble. After catching measles at the age of three months, I developed a disorder known as strabismus — crossed eyes. Years of operations and eye patches failed to cure this condition, and by the age of 10 I was essentially what doctors describe as monocular; my right eye was almost useless. With my good eye alone to lead me through life, its unemployed partner had drifted lazily off to the right. While one eye took perfect aim at a person's face, the other gazed sightlessly over their left shoulder. People I spoke to would look back thinking I was addressing someone else.

Being unable to make eye contact with people is a handicap one has to suffer in order to understand. Through the years, it was a source of pain, and other people's amusement. I would be called 'Cyclops' and the 'man with one eye on the world'. 'Here's not looking at you, kid' was common. Even my loving mother was entertained: 'You've got one eye and a ball of fat.'

It was a handicap with many drawbacks. At parties, my friends could catch the eye of a girl they liked. When I tried, it would be the girl's neighbour, the one less interesting to me, who reacted. When reading on trains, women sitting opposite would fiercely tug down their skirts, certain I was sneaking an uninvited look. On the other hand, when I was admiring their legs, they never knew. Approaching strangers as a young reporter, I would sometimes resort to closing my blind eye. This must have looked odd, but at least guaranteed I could make immediate contact without having first to explain my deformity.

I considered wearing a black eye-patch, which, as well as having a practical benefit, was certain to supply mystery and allure. I imagined enjoying the fascination of beautiful women as they learned the story of my lost eye. I could tell them how I defended my family against a maddened attacker in the dangerous backstreets of Tripoli; or fought off a gang armed with flick-knives surrounding me and my girl in Singapore's seedy Bugis Street, as the famous transvestites parading there cheered on my bravery. I had a long list of other colourful story ideas, but decided there was a high risk that no one would believe a word of them. I forgot the eye patch and settled for the dull truth. My story of catching measles as a baby never once brought a glitter to a pretty girl's eye.

But my eye problems were never more alarming than when I was 15, lying in an echoing ward in the Royal Adelaide Hospital, where I had been blinded in order to see.

It was an unexpected lesson in life, becoming a refugee from the sighted world, learning what it was to have no eyes. It amplifies the senses that remain, but leaves the main canvas blank. I knew I was in a ward with 15 other patients because I had been told as much. But I could not see them, or the colours of the ward, or the owner of the soft woman's voice that described it to me. I began to wonder how people existed in this new world, what it must be like to live with smells, tastes, and sounds, yet unable to attach them to an image. I had been able to see, so I had memories, and the ability to guess at and shape pictures in my head. But was it better for a blind man to have once been sighted, or more merciful to be blind from birth? What is beauty if you have never been able to behold a face, or a cathedral, or a bird on a branch? Was it better never to have seen these things than to have them snatched away?

When I put my thoughts about blindness to Bob, whose bed was across the ward, I could tell he was hearing nothing original. Bob had been blind all his life. 'Everything is clear enough to me,' he said.

I was an unhappy visitor to Bob's world. I knew the surgery had come without guarantees, that my five prostrate weeks were key to the cure. But why was Bob teaching me Braille? 'One dot equals A, two vertical dots B, two horizontal dots C,' he would tell me. Had the hospital asked him to prepare me? Was I recovering, or rehearsing to be blind forever?

I started thinking about what Bob had meant when he said everything was clear to him. I decided that the unseen hospital space could become whatever I wanted it to be; the faceless people could look however I wanted them to. The world would be at my command, and having invisible friends would provide infinite flexibility. Eyes, hair, height, shape, skin — each doctor, nurse, patient, hospital orderly could be designed in my mind to the last detail. They could be tall or short, thin or fat, redheads or blondes, pretty or ugly, and wear whatever I chose. It would be like dressing dolls.

I engineered a vision for each voice. Bob sounded tall and big shouldered, with lank blond hair slightly matted across his forehead and bony cheeks, and skin like parchment. Guglielmo, the young Italian in the next bed who was to become my best friend in the ward, was short and wiry, with cropped black hair, blue eyes, and crooked teeth. The nurse who held my hand and told me I looked much more than 15 was petite and blue-eyed, and her hair a lovely crowd of chestnut curls. The booming senior sister whose arrival always hushed the ward was definitely short and stout, with white hair.

I could change my mind about people who displeased me. A beautiful person could be condemned to ugliness. One nurse became Marilyn Monroe the moment we first talked. She had a low and throaty voice, so the image fit perfectly. I had a crush on her, which she didn't reciprocate. When I tried to chat she never had time for me. My revenge was to make her plain — narrow-faced, small-mouthed, hook-nosed, and skinny.

The best of my imagined designs never changed, but seemed more perfect as the weeks passed. It was dedicated to Sophie, whose soft voice had described the ward to me. This voice came to my bed sometimes and read me stories, and I fell in love with it. It belonged, I decided, to a woman with shining raven hair descending to the bottom of her long neck without reaching her shoulders. Her skin was smooth and clear and the colour of cream; her smile wide and white; her lips full, red, and mobile; her breasts just large enough to see as they began to cleave apart at the top of her uniform; her legs tapering at the bottom towards slim ankles.

For five weeks, I lived with these conjured images, but there was one I did not need to manufacture, and I never forgot. Every third day, my eyes had to be uncovered and cleaned, and when this happened the same vision interrupted the darkness.

I will never forget the first time. Rolled slowly on to my back, I had to look straight at the ceiling, to fix on a single spot, and on no account turn my eyes. As I lay there, two warm hands touched my face and peeled away the dressing. Reflexively, I shut my eyes against the strange, sharp light, squinting tightly until they could bear the brightness. My freed eyes finally fixed their open stare on the ceiling. And then they arrived, hovering above me: two beautiful saucers of blue. Big and deep and dazzling. Perfect kaleidoscopes of sapphire, flecked with sky blue; disembodied, flying objects suspended between a nurse's starched cap and a surgical mask. The most magnificent eyes the world had ever seen now leaned very close, less than a foot away, searching deeply into mine. As a 15-year-old, it is a dream come true being looked at like that with eyes like those.

Touch and smell matter a lot when you are a teenage boy trapped in bed at the mercy of invisible nurses who are as beautiful as you choose them to be.

A bed-bath must normally be a humiliating experience; naked, rolled from side to side, swabbed head to toe by an unsmiling nurse, seeing from the scowl on her face that the task was high on the list of things she most hated. But Sophie of the raven hair and red lips administered my bed baths. Each day, she took a tender journey down my body, a warm flannel touching my face and neck and shoulders, progressing softly to the very tip of my toes. Sophie never took long enough at the task before drying me with a towel and combing my hair. But then, finally, she would lean across me, stroking and straightening my cover of sheets and blankets, so close I could smell her freshness and feel the brief breeze of her breath.

My neighbour and new friend, Guglielmo was 25 years old and had arrived soon after me, temporarily blinded by using an oxy-acetylene torch without eye protection. He had immigrated to Australia from Italy, leaving his family behind. Guglielmo was loud, laughing, and funny, the bright heart of our ward of sufferers. He was a dreamer who talked non-stop and at high speed. His fractured English demanded total concentration.

'Jeez, mate, slow down will you,' Bob would say, 'You sound like a chicken being bloody strangled.'

But Guglielmo was never deterred, and his answer was always the same. 'All right, tell me, how good you speak Italian?'

He was engaged to be married, and each night his 17-year-old fiancée would sit beside his bed. This was the only time Guglielmo did not speak English. None of us understood what they said to each other, and they talked in whispers.

Guglielmo and I would dream together about what we would do with our lives in Australia, and what would become of us.

'Les, this is a beautiful country. It is good we both came here. In Italy my people are poor, but here I will be rich. I will have my own company and I will build houses. Many people will come here, like we have. They will need houses and I will get rich building them.'

But first he would marry. 'I will save money and marry Anna. You should see her, Les, she is beautiful, very beautiful. Then I will take her home to meet all my family in Italy. We will not go by ship but by jet plane. For my honeymoon, I will fly in a jet plane all the way back to Italy with my wife, Anna. I will work and save to do it. And Anna will have children and we will live in a big house.'

And I would tell him what would happen to me, how I would become a newspaper reporter and travel the world, visiting every continent, meeting famous people — film stars and prime ministers — and that my name would be seen by millions of readers.

When he left hospital, Guglielmo stood beside my bed. 'Les, don't forget me when you are a big important newspaper reporter and we are both rich. One day, when you are old enough, I will teach you to drink. We will go to the pub and I will buy you a schooner. You must drink it slowly. Maybe you will bring along one of these pretty nurses. They like you — really, they do. Oh, if only I was not engaged.'

He took my hand and kissed it, then patted my chest. 'Good luck, Les, good luck.'

Guglielmo's voice faded as he walked away, down the ward, joking with the other patients he was leaving behind, and teasing the giggling nurses in his flirty, broken English. Everyone shouted goodbye to Guglielmo, and when he was gone the ward was very quiet.

As the day approached when my blindfold would come off, I became afraid. My only vision for weeks had been those brilliant blue flying saucers, the dazzling eyes of the nurse. Now the real world out there was waiting to shatter my imagination.

The nurses were enjoying it. 'You don't have a clue what anyone looks like, do you?' said beautiful Sophie of the breezy breath.

'You don't know what I look like either,' said Bob, my braille teacher. 'But I don't suppose even I know what I look like.'

I was convinced being blindfolded had changed my personality.

Freed of the lifelong burden of being Les with the lazy eye, I had shed my shyness. It had been a liberation never having to see strangers discover I couldn't look straight — those looks of blank confusion, that searching glance over the left shoulder. I was now an extrovert. I could talk with easy charm and sparkling humour. Older women — some as old as 20 — found my company irresistible, and would sit at my bedside laughing at my jokes. I had become bolder with a blindfold.

Actually, this entire feeling turned out to be a drug-induced illusion. A few years later I could recapture that sense of invincible charm by drinking a couple of glasses of wine. I had clearly been under the influence of mind-altering medication designed to get me through those weeks of bedridden stillness.

I hadn't yet worked that out on the day Dr Peter Stobie, my eye surgeon, arrived to remove the blindfold. After hating the darkness, I was dreading the light.

The first face I saw was no surprise. The last person I had seen before the general anaesthetic took me away was Dr Stobie. Here he was again — balding, pallid and serious. Immediately after removing the blindfold he replaced it with a pair of strange spectacles; the lenses were covered but for two tiny circles of light at the centre of each frame. So I re-entered the seeing world through these two tiny portals; they were intended to stop my eye moving too much while it continued to heal.

The ward was vast, like a great hall, with a soaring ceiling, yellow walls, tall windows, and a floor of polished brown linoleum. The beds were spaced far apart, their frames made of black iron, and nurses paced along the wide middle passageway dressed in light-blue uniforms under starched-white aprons.

As I squinted at it all, I could see in a blur one blue-and-white nurse waving far across the ward as she walked in my direction. She stood beside my bed, smiling. She was short, a little over five foot, with an ample figure, very ample. Her cheeks were full, very full, and her short hair frizzy and unkempt, as if she did not take much trouble with it. But her smile was a warm and caring smile, and her bright hazel eyes were smiling, too. 'Hello, Les,' she said, taking hold of my arm. 'I'm Sophie.'

This was the real Sophie, the raven-haired beauty of my imagination, with the long neck, red lips, and perfect ankles. Nothing I imagined about her was true. Yet the warm and gentle voice was still there, and the kindness. And I could never have imagined her beautiful smile.

One by one, reality replaced my imagination. The stern, stout senior sister was statuesque, slender, and beautiful; Bob, my braille teacher, was very short with a big round stomach, and almost entirely bald; the petite, handholding nurse was not petite, and her chestnut hair was black and quite straight. I got only one right. Marilyn Monroe really was blonde and shapely. She also remained uninterested in chatting to me. As a 15-year-old, the gift of those five weeks was that it gave me no choice but to get to know people from the inside first.

After five weeks in bed, the body grows accustomed to being out of use. My ignored muscles had atrophied. My legs were useless. I could not walk, or even stand. I took my first shower sitting in a chair because my legs would not bear the weight of my body.

The operation had saved my sight and stemmed the damage, but the shadow across the top right of my vision had not gone, and distortions also remained, and colours were less sharp. I was also unable to recognise a face at 50 paces, but presumed after the operation that this was a handicap I must learn to live with. For some reason, no one thought it might be a good idea to test me for spectacles — not until I was learning to drive and my brother-in-law

Don refused to continue with his lessons until I had my eyes tested.

In 1960, the requirements for a driving licence in Adelaide were undemanding — probably no stricter than those needed to drive a horse-and-carriage 100 years before. You did not need to take a driving test at all, and could be given a licence without ever sitting behind the wheel of a car. I was asked about 20 questions on the rudiments of the road. It was not a challenging examination — red lights mean stop, don't accelerate driving past a school, don't rev your engine to hurry old ladies crossing the street, when it's dark turn on headlights.

Also, reasonably enough, you were not allowed to drive if you were blind. For me, this was the tricky part. In a doctor's eyesight test I might have nailed the big letter at the top, but it would be pure guesswork after that. Luckily, this test was not so sophisticated.

The examiner just took me into the street, and pointed. 'See that street?'

I could tell from the direction he was pointing where the street must be — beyond the large garden in front of us.

'Yes.'

'OK, tell me what model car that is.'

Since I could hear engines but see only blurring movement, I had to think quickly. At that time, by far the most popular car in Australia was a local product called a Holden. So I replied: 'It's a Holden, sir.'

'That one?'

'Another Holden.'

'That?'

'Holden.'

After the same question had been followed 10 times by the identical answer, the examiner wrote something on his clipboard.

'Seven out of ten — that'll do,' he said.

And I was let loose on the roads of Adelaide.

What alarmed my brother-in-law was not so much my inability ever to take a corner without mounting the pavement as my failure to notice any approaching stop sign until I was within 20 feet and travelling at 35 miles per hour. My first pair of spectacles changed everything, and I have driven accident free, more or less, ever since.

Although safe to drive, I still didn't see all that well, and imperfect vision has many drawbacks. Sports, for instance. Seeing through a single eye does not aid hand-eye coordination, or help in judging the direction of a fast-moving ball. Cricket did not come naturally to me. Facing a fast bowler, my only defence was quiet prayer, since I had no chance of seeing the approaching missile.

People who didn't like me exploited this weakness. I was sometimes played at a position called silly mid-on, which requires the fielder to stand suicidally close to the batsman. I only ever stopped one ball while playing in this position, and that was when it scored a direct hit a little below my throat while travelling at least 100 miles per hour. The only sound I heard as I lay near death at the batsman's feet was my captain's cackle and his words: 'Well stopped, Les.' That was 50 years ago; I finally forgave the captain five years ago — when he died.

Watching sport was not easy, either. Even with spectacles, it was difficult to identify players. In Adelaide, I earned an additional £3 10s a week writing about soccer. These were the days when soccer was a minor sport in Australia — so minor no one else wanted the job. But being the soccer writer for *The News* made me a big-shot in a small world. I joined a panel to judge the man of the match at every game. I enjoyed the prestige of this position until the day I forgot to bring my binoculars. There was an awkward silence when I handed in my choice for best player: 'Err, Les — he wasn't playing today.'

———

I was old enough to drink when I heard the news. It was 7 July 1962, and I was an 18-year-old cadet reporter arriving for a Saturday shift on *The News*' sister paper, the *Sunday Mail*. Before I could find a desk, the *Sunday Mail*'s chief reporter, Bill Reshcke, hurried towards me. 'There's been plane crash. An Alitalia jet flying out of Sydney has crashed in India, and it looks like there are no survivors. We need to check if any locals were on board.'

Alitalia Flight 771, bound from Sydney to Rome, via Bangkok, Bombay, and Tehran, had 94 people on board, and had been approaching Bombay through a blinding summer monsoon when it crashed into a jungle hilltop 50 miles northeast of the airport. Search parties trekked through miles of rough terrain to reach the wreckage. Two days later, only half the bodies had been recovered, but it was clear everyone on board had died.

Four victims had begun their journey in Adelaide: a six-year-old girl, Dagmar von Brasch, had been flying to Frankfurt to visit an aunt, and Luigi Monti, 70, was going home to Forli, Italy, after a three-month visit to see his daughter and two grandsons. They were two tragic stories, but by now I was learning the necessary detachment; too much terrible misfortune filled the columns of a newspaper. At times, however, bad news breaks through your defences, and that is what happened when I learned the names of the other two victims. They were Mr and Mrs Guglielmo Proietti of Frederick Street, Stepney, newlyweds who were flying to Rome on their honeymoon.

Guglielmo, my hospital friend, had worked and saved, and gone home in a jet plane, not a ship, to introduce his new bride to his Italian family. It was just as he had promised himself as we lay in our hospital beds plotting our lives. He had talked to me of becoming wealthy building homes, but Guglielmo had started his own trucking business. He would have been so pleased with himself climbing aboard that plane, off to see the poor relatives he talked about, to arrive with his beautiful bride and tell them of his new life in a lucky country.

The grainy photo we published had been taken two weeks before, on their wedding day. A tiny tiara pinned to the beaming bride's dark hair held in place a long white veil. She was beautiful, just as Guglielmo had said. The groom to her right was neatly combed, with a big knot in his dark tie, a slight smile, and delighted eyes.

But it was the face of a stranger. I would always remember my vibrant unseen friend as short and wiry, with close-cropped black hair, blue eyes, and teeth askew. And his happy, hopeful voice.

CHAPTER 6

'Yes, Mr Murdoch'

The Australian immigration officer in Liverpool wasn't encouraging when I told him I was going to be a newspaper reporter. 'It's a tough business to get into, son,' he said. 'You should stay in school and improve your education.' My parents weren't hopeful, either — Mum thought it was a fantasy I would soon work out of my system.

The immigration man gave me one address. *The Advertiser*, he said, was by far the better daily newspaper in Adelaide. It was a morning broadsheet and the city's leading daily. The other newspaper, he said, was 'a tabloid'.

I did not have high hopes after my interview at *The Advertiser*'s offices on King William Street, the city's central boulevard. It was a warm day, but Mum said I must look my best, which was why I arrived beneath a heavy, brown Harris Tweed jacket, and wearing thick grey flannel trousers. Dad provided his regimental tie from the Royal Army Service Corps to perfect the outfit. Even before the interview, I could feel the perspiration travelling down the middle of my back.

Whatever appeared on *The Advertiser*'s list of required qualities for an aspiring journalist, the man who interviewed me gave no indication that I possessed a single one. I had, however, stepped inside my first newsroom; walked into the glamorous blue haze and down the ranks of cigarette-burned desks, heard the hammer and ring of massed typewriters, smelt the musty blend of newsprint and ink, and discovered how a newspaper building trembles to the rhythm of its great basement presses. It seemed like a fine place to be.

Five days later, the letter from *The Advertiser* delivered an unexpected problem. No, there was no vacancy in the editorial department — no surprise there — but there was a position in the accounts department to which it was felt I would be ideally suited.

I knew what Mum would say before she looked up from the letter. She had sat down on her squeaking bed in the grimly utilitarian immigration hostel where we were lodged, leaning one hand on its rough grey blanket and holding my letter in the other.

'Great, love, you've got a job.'

'But I don't want to work in an accounts department. I hate maths. I'm useless with numbers. I want to be a reporter.'

These were the moments when my mother adopted her famous look of furrowed, dark-eyed threat. But not yet of anger — the anger was held in reserve, to be unleashed if resistance continued. It was a familiar sight, my mother coiled for battle, but it no longer scared me.

She spoke slowly, each word uttered with thumping menace. 'You must go back to see them and take the job. You need a job.'

'No. I'm not going to do it. Don't keep telling me because I won't.'

I understood this was her survival instinct. The rule for her was simple: take what you can get when you can get it. It had been a tough childhood — born into a large, struggling dockland family, her widowed mother's daily double-shifts cleaning, her education at a home for the poor, operating the lift at a dry-cleaning factory at the age of 14. Why would I knock back the offer of a job, any job? But I had made my stand and waited for the counter-attack. What happened next was unheard of in the history of Hinton family skirmishes. Mum let out a long, surrendering sigh. 'Well, okay, but you've got to find a job somewhere. What are you going to do?'

The News was Adelaide's evening newspaper, the one the immigration officer disdained as a 'tabloid'. Its offices were on North Terrace, one of four streets that were the boundary of this neat square mile of a city, each named by its literal-minded founders after the four points of the compass. It was a plain building, painted desert-brown, and much less majestic than *The Advertiser*'s sleek new tower on King William Street.

I climbed one flight of stairs, as the letter had instructed, and arrived in a corridor of tall, white partitions. Sounds spilled over these walls: shouts and laughter, clattering typewriters, and the clamour of unanswered telephones. I pressed a bell beside the unmanned reception desk. A boy a little older than I arrived to lead me through a wide, blue door 20 feet along the corridor, where a woman about my mother's age looked at me seriously. Her grey cotton dress had a tight white collar and her hands were poised above the keys of a huge Remington typewriter, its oily innards visible inside a black steel frame. 'Mr Rivett will be here in a minute. Sit down there.'

I sat on a hard chair with a high back of wooden slats, and waited outside the office of Rohan Deakin Rivett, the editor-in-chief of *The News*. A framed cartoon on the wood-panelled wall showed an angry man beside a closed door marked 'Editor'. The man was wielding a long bullwhip and looming over a terrified secretary. The cartoon caption said: 'I want to see him NOW!'

I have no idea why Rohan Rivett gave me a job. I'm not sure whether he did it out of pity, or because he had mixed me up with someone else, but I left that meeting and ran through the bright sun of North Terrace with the title of 'copy boy', a promised salary of

£5 10s a week, and an instruction to be in the office the following morning at eight.

The cheerless hostel where we were staying was only a five-minute walk away, set improbably in beautiful riverside parkland at the city's heart. I was there delivering my breathless news within two minutes.

The meeting had lasted half an hour. Rivett's low-lit office was sealed against the noise outside. On his desk were four telephones. Along the front of a large wooden intercom to his left were two rows of switches, one red and all the others black. Newspapers sat in neat piles on shelves against the wall, held together by pink ribbon. He studied my letter in the light of a green-shaded desk lamp. It was an honest letter, so I knew it offered no qualifications likely to impress him. He put the letter aside and asked me to tell him about my life so far. So I talked about Bootle, the British Army, and our wandering life, and how we had come here because my sister had met and married an Adelaide soldier in Singapore. 'I lived in Singapore,' he said.

When he asked me why I wanted to be a journalist, I delivered my prepared answer, which I knew contained nothing original. I wanted to meet people, go places, tell stories, and I liked to write. I had read every page of *The News* for the previous few days, and talked about what I admired: the feature articles of John Miles; Doug Easom's quirky 'Odd Spot' column; Norm Mitchell's cartoons; Douglas Brass' dispatches from London.

Rohan Rivett pressed down on one of the black intercom switches.

'Murray, can you come down please?'

Murray Willoughby James was the newspaper's chief of staff, and when he arrived Rivett rose to stand beside him. They were two silhouettes against the sunlight through the window.

'Mr Hinton will be joining us as a copy boy tomorrow morning.'

I had a job.

Even though Rohan Rivett's next words sounded reproachful. — 'He's *fifteen years* and *three months old*,' — he said them while looking at me with a faint smile and I knew that, somehow, I had made the right impression.

I was too young, without any useful education, had no testimonials, no family connection, and knew nothing about Australia except that Don Bradman had been a good batsman, which is the same as knowing nothing about the United States except that Babe Ruth could hit baseballs. And yet I walked straight off the boat to be given a job on a whim by Rohan Deakin Rivett, the patrician son of one of Australia's leading scientists, and the grandson of its second prime minister, Alfred Deakin. I think Murray James was as surprised as me.

Newspapers are high-functioning dictatorships. One all-powerful mind is in control. In a world of instant decisions, in the late-night heat of an oncoming deadline with a silent pressroom waiting, there is only so much time for debate. At *The News,* I witnessed for the first time the power and frailty of an editor's life. Even in the saluting subservience of the British Army, I had never known such deference to one person's beliefs and requirements. Journalists, junior editors, and sub-editors fretted constantly. 'I'm not sure about this? Does Rohan know?'; 'Who wrote that head? He'll hit the roof'; 'I know it's long, but he says we've been underplaying the story.' Day-to-day, page-by-page, an editor's decision must be final and unassailable.

But editors are not invulnerable. Their power is great, but it is also frail. Regime change will follow if readers fall away, or if one of those split-second decisions proves to be wrong once too often. An impatient proprietor will quickly overthrow an editor who loses their grip. Cassandra of London's *Daily Mirror* wrote about the shadow that hovers over editors: 'Editors! I seen 'em come. And I seen 'em go. But way up on the mountain overshadowing Fleet Street the Abominable Snowman goes on for ever.'

Rivett's fatal moment came a year after I arrived. He was the first editor Rupert Murdoch ever fired.

Rivett died in 1977 of a heart attack, aged 60, an early death almost certainly brought on by the biggest story of his life. When I began at *The News,* John Tulloh, a tall, bony-faced cadet came to me with firm advice: 'You must read Rivett's book, *Behind Bamboo.* Everybody who comes here has to read it.' When I did, a brief, half-forgotten sentence Rivett had uttered at my job interview was explained. 'I lived in Singapore,' he had said.

Behind Bamboo was the story of Rivett's war, an epic of death, courage, cruelty, plague, starvation, and, for him at least, ultimate survival. When Japan entered the war in December 1941, Rivett, a cadet reporter aged 23 from Melbourne, had volunteered to go to Singapore to work for the Malaya Broadcasting Corporation. *Behind Bamboo* begins as Rivett performs the chilling duty of broadcasting stunning news to the world on 9 February 1942: 'I took a deep breath and as the red light flashed on behind the microphone ... I went on to read out the announcement which told the world that Britain's Eastern fortress had been violated and that the Japanese had landed on Singapore Island.'

Behind Bamboo is about the three years Rivett endured as a prisoner-of-war, written secretly and hidden 'in the roof of attap huts, in the bottoms of tins and bamboo containers, under the ground, in the framework of my bed and inside bandages strapped around my thighs and waist'.

He recorded life inside the broiling hold of a 'Jap hellship' carrying prisoners-of-war to slavery along the infamous Burma–Thailand railway. He wrote of summary executions in prison camps, prisoners beaten to death for violating minor rules, and of sick and dying men reduced to 'cadaverous wrecks' by their Japanese guards. 'They cared nothing and did nothing as these men rotted to death before their eyes,' he wrote. Rivett scorned them in defeat; their 'cringing servility' was 'only equalled by their arrogance and brutality while they had been on top'.

More than sixty thousand Allied prisoners-of-war were forced into slave labour in Japan's drive to carve a 250-mile path through Burma's unyielding terrain of hills and dense jungle. For Japan, the railway was crucial to accelerating its advance across Asia, but it lives in history as the scene of one of the Second World War's great atrocities. More than 12,000 prisoners-of-war were driven to their deaths.

Nothing about Rivett betrayed the three-year nightmare he had been through. I couldn't imagine what he had witnessed, what demons haunted him, or even if he had any demons. He was tall, more than six feet, with academically rounded shoulders — a reader's stoop — and he favoured double-breasted suits. His hair was fair and thinning, and his face was intense even when he was telling you what sandwich he wanted for lunch.

He was one of many war veterans working at *The News*. Among them, the 'Japs' were almost universally loathed, and none had better cause to hate than Rohan Rivett. But he stood apart from his wartime comrades and became a vocal advocate of reconciliation with Japan. I remember the impact of a memo he circulated after returning from a goodwill visit to Japan. The memo announced a change to the newspaper's style book. Henceforth, the name of Japan's capital city would no longer be spelt 'Tokio' but 'Tokyo'. The old spelling, said the memo, offended the Japanese. To many of us, it was a small change, but a huge gesture; the bitter old war veterans in the office were not amused.

I performed many tasks for Rivett. Some were nerve-wracking, like making cash deposits into his bank account. As well as being forgiving, he was trusting. He once handed me £300 — a huge amount in 1959 — to deliver to his King William Street bank.

I had never seen so much money. Another duty was updating the newspaper files in his office. He required all local, Melbourne, and Sydney newspapers to be maintained in orderly piles. This involved threading pink ribbon through a giant darning needle and lacing it through the newspapers so they stayed in tidy packs without being tied so tightly that the Editor could not turn the pages. It was not a demanding task, and I was daydreaming the day Rivett strode into the office and shook me with a booming and excited voice: 'I must tell you that this is a day you will remember all your life. It is the day that Rupert Murdoch stepped beyond Adelaide to begin growing a great Australian newspaper company.'

I turned towards him with a puzzled look.

'News Limited is now the owner of the Sydney *Daily Mirror*. It is one of many more newspapers this company will own,' he said.

I don't think Rivett — or even Rupert Murdoch — could have guessed at the scale of his understatement, and that the little 'News' of Adelaide was the genesis of the mighty News Corp. For the next half century, the word News existed in almost every subsidiary company name — News Limited (Australia), News International (London), World News in America, then News America Publishing. For years, the intro to every 20th Century Fox film, with its trumpet fanfare and searchlight beams, declared across the bottom of the screen 'A News Corporation Company'. But that was before Fox became the big brother of the Murdoch corporations.

That was in May 1960. It was a heady day for Rivett, but two months later he was out of a job. The letter from Rupert was handed to him by his tearful secretary. It said: 'I have never loathed writing a letter more.'

The office reeled with shock, and regret. Departing editors leave dread and uncertainty in their wake. I have, once or twice, seen these departures bring glee, but most often a newspaper suddenly without an editor is bereft. People who knew him said Rivett was deeply distressed. He had been a Murdoch family friend; in the early 1950s, when Rivett was a London-based correspondent, young Rupert, then an Oxford student, had been his regular houseguest.

Years later, Rupert described his fallen editor as 'headstrong' and told an interviewer: 'I felt I just could not leave him in charge in Adelaide because he had become so emotional in his editorial writing. It was a very sad day for me.'

I knew Rohan Rivett for a short time, and not well at all, but he was the stranger — charismatic, and maybe headstrong — who gave me my first big chance. He never again set foot in the office, but a few times after he was sacked I saw him driving slowly by the office in his grey Humber, seeming to search for a familiar face. Upon seeing me he would wind down his window, wave, and drive on.

———

Not much made sense on my first day at work. It was a whirl of speed and noise and curses. My orders were to follow around an experienced copy boy and learn from him. His name was Trevor Bitmead, and he slicked back his red hair in a Tony Curtis style.

It was early morning and 20 reporters at three rows of desks were typing on pieces of paper large enough to contain only about 50 words. When a reporter cried, 'Copy!' Trevor seized a completed page, hurried it next door to the sub-editors' room, and placed it in a metal tray. For about 90 minutes, Trevor and a dozen other boys carried these small pages to the same basket.

In the subs' room, a large man with blue braces and a loose tie was in charge. He handed the pages to other men with instructions such as: 'Ten inches of copy across eight ems. Two decks of seventy-two point Century Bold caps across four. Make the intro twelve point bold across fourteen.' The sub-editors knew what he was talking about.

When a sub-editor finished writing on these pages he also called, 'Copy!' and a boy would fold the pages into a metal cylinder, and push the cylinder into a thick pipe that made a loud sucking noise. This pipe would carry the cylinder, rattling at great speed, across the ceiling and out of sight.

'Trevor, where does that pipe go?' I asked.

Trevor led me out of the newsroom to a place that was even noisier and also very hot. Men sat at a dozen gigantic black machines typing on keyboards with dozens more keys than a typewriter. As they worked, they studied the pieces of paper that had been typed by reporters and marked by sub-editors. Wells containing molten lead were attached to these linotype machines, and the reporters' words and the sub-editors' headlines were turned into lines of hot type.

This type was then carried to another room where yet another group of men put the lines of lead type into a frame on a heavy metal table. At the same time, they referred to large pieces of paper that were sketches of page designs that the sub-editors had also provided. When this was done, the men tapped gently over the entire metal page with a wooden hammer before wheeling it to the foundry, where other men used more molten metal to turn these pages into curved plates to be fitted to the rotary press.

The pressroom was the loudest place of all. It was also dangerous. When the press was running, it was impossible to talk. Some men working there wore hearing aids and had missing fingers.

I went home that night overwhelmed, exhausted, and fearful. Would I ever fathom the mysterious precision of the place, the chaotic choreography that somehow produced a newspaper? I didn't know how I would manage the pace or the intensity. Everyone had seemed angry or anxious or both. Maybe the accounts department was the place for me after all. But, after a week or so, I began to get the hang of, and would soon fall in love forever with, the rowdy glamour of the newspaper world.

Copy boys were lined up each morning on a bench at the back of the reporters' room. We were there to do whatever we were told: run copy, deliver new editions around the office, buy sandwiches or cigarettes, feed parking meters.

Hanging on the wall facing us was a big, black, square panel, which was perilous to ignore. When a buzzer sounded, the board displayed the name of an editor, beckoning from somewhere in the building, and the boy at the top of the bench would hurry to receive his orders. Any boy slow off the mark faced the anger of the Head Copy Boy. Despite the title, it was a tradition to give this job to a retiree. Roy Hussey was a short and growling man whose deeply lined face sank into hollows beneath the bulging cheekbones that supported his oversized black spectacles.

Mr Hussey was our boot-camp sergeant, there to knock us into shape. He went about this task with dour enthusiasm, sitting at his corner desk imperially surveying his boys as we sat in silent discomfort on the hard wooden bench, waiting for the call to action.

Each of us adhered to the strict Hussey dress code — suit and tie at all times. No slip-up was too minor to provoke his anger: not a moment's lateness arriving for work or coming back from lunch; not a split second of delay when the dreaded buzzer sounded, or an impatient reporter's cry of 'Copy!' went too long unheeded. Mistakes, or misconduct, could bring instant dismissal. Sometimes Mr Hussey was within his rights. He escorted out of the building the copy boy who took an elastic band and fired a large metal paper clip into a moving press, shredding the fast-moving newsprint and bringing the machine to a messy halt.

I had a near miss myself one night when Rupert Murdoch arrived unexpectedly at his office on the ground floor. The only television in the building was in this room. On Saturday nights, when it was slow, copy boys sometimes sat on the floor behind his leather sofa watching Westerns. I was alone when he arrived and I lay quietly panicking behind the sofa for an eternity — or maybe 90 seconds — the television still playing, before he turned it off and left. Rupert laughed when I told him this story years later, but didn't disagree that he would have fired me on the spot.

I never felt closer to serious trouble than the day I lost the midday news bulletin minutes before it was to be broadcast on Adelaide's most popular radio station. My job was to deliver the bulletin to 5DN, another News business, a mile or so away.

In the days before fax and email, this task was performed with a delivery mechanism relied upon for more than a century: a bicycle. I set off on the uphill trek with the noon bulletin tucked into my back pocket. This was not wise. When I arrived 15 minutes before midday, my back pocket was empty.

In all the experiences of my career — on the receiving end of a prime minister's anger, sitting in the White House to be attacked over a television show I oversaw, the rain of shattered glass caused by a Belfast bomb, the Turkish rocket that exploded at my Cyprus hotel — none was worse than the grip of helpless terror I felt at that moment.

I ran into the studio to see the presenter, sitting alone at his microphone. He gave me a smile and a friendly wave through the glass soundproofing. I couldn't bring myself to admit what I had done. I leapt back on the bicycle, retracing my journey, but felt doomed for sure. It was a windy day and the loose pages had been held together by a single paper clip. I felt no hope and saw no future.

And then there was a scatter of white paper blowing across the road on a downhill slope. Cars were running through it, single sheets were airborne. But there it was — my lost midday news — and I raced around the road, heedless of swerving traffic, reassembling every tire-marked page.

I sped back to the studio and delivered my errant bulletin moments before the strike of noon. The presenter looked up at me quizzically as he read, turning the smudged and crumpled pages, but the newscast went smoothly, and afterwards I went into the soundproof booth and confessed.

'Why didn't you tell me, mate,' he said. 'I'd have re-read the news from 10am and saved you the trouble.'

Some experiences never fade, and that is one. Here's another. Early one morning, a plump-cheeked man with a cigarette turned away from the newspaper file at the bottom of the reporters' room.

'Can you buy me a ham sandwich, please?' he said, handing me a 10s note.

'Yes, sir,' I said.

This was my first exchange with Rupert Murdoch. For 15 years we discussed nothing more elevated.

CHAPTER 7

'Christ, Hinton,
don't you know . . .'

I was learning about newspapers, and I was also learning about a new country. This time, there was no plan to move on after a couple of years. My parents had bought their first house: a new three-bedroom L-shaped bungalow at 23 Minchinbury Terrace, Marion. We lived next to a vineyard growing grapes for 'Minchinbury Champagne', before the French seized back control of the word and made them call it sparkling wine.

Across from our narrow street was the railway station, and the regular din of diesel engines and brakes from commuter trains heading to and from the Adelaide city centre seven miles northeast. On hot evenings, with the windows open, the sound of our television — the first we owned — was overwhelmed by this noise. After years of wandering, my father, who was now 49, and my mother, 45, were here to stay.

The garden was an expanse of empty earth when we arrived, but everything grows fast and big in Australia. When he was not working in a kitchen, Dad spent much of his life weeding, planting, and mowing in his garden. On Saturdays, he kept his tiny transistor radio with him, listening to the races. He planted trees — an orange tree, a lemon tree, an apple tree, and gum trees. He grew dozens of flowers: from tulips and roses, to rambling bougainvillea. A vegetable patch flourished behind the garage that contained our new two-tone Hillman Minx with whitewall tyres.

Adelaide was a wonderful place: the weather, the air, the open spaces, and the ease of life in a small city. As for Australians, it took a while to understand them. For a young country built by immigrants, they didn't seem to like newcomers much.

The British, who came in the largest numbers, were 'Poms'. No one was sure why we were Poms. One theory held that it was an acronym of 'Prisoners of Mother England', harking back to the eighteenth and nineteenth centuries when British offenders were transported to penal colonies in Australia. Another theory claimed that it came from Australian rhyming slang, and that pomegranate was the word for immigrant. Non-British immigrants were distinguished from us as 'New Australians', a description often uttered with disdain. New Australians were virtually all Europeans, largely from Italy and Greece. When we arrived Australia had a 'White Australia' policy, which resisted immigration from neighbouring Asian nations. It was already being dismantled when we arrived and had disappeared by the 1970s.

But I knew from Rohan Rivett that Australians were willing to give people a chance. Now I had to make the most of it.

I had a lot to learn. While Mum and Dad discovered the joys of endless television, I locked myself away in my bedroom — the first of my own — and ploughed randomly through books of biography, history, and fiction. I read everything I could: Steinbeck, Faulkner, Dickens, Waugh, Greene, Defoe, Swift, Dumas, Melville, Ian

Fleming, Agatha Christie. Many of them were books that kids my age were still at school reading. I checked every word I didn't know in the *Concise Oxford English Dictionary* Dad bought me. There were a lot of them. I still have the remains of that dictionary, dismembered long ago by overuse. I read Churchill's *The Second World War* — all six volumes — years before understanding that it might not be entirely objective, and his *A History of the English-Speaking Peoples*. I browsed *Fowler's Modern English Usage*. I read *Time* magazine every week, every page. I could see how it slanted things, and used words that didn't exist, but I loved the exciting places it wrote about.

Every week, I went to the newsstand at the Adelaide railway station and bought a yellow-bound copy of one week's editions of the London *Daily Mirror*. When I became a cadet sub-editor, I drove compositors crazy trying to copy *Mirror* layouts, insisting on wild column measures, complicated rules, and weird photo crops, which they had great difficulty creating.

I read about the history of newspapers, and how the 'heavies' were born at a time when printing technology was as miraculous as the internet would seem centuries later. I read the history of *The Times* of London, founded in 1785 by John Walter, and what Abraham Lincoln had told its fabled war correspondent, William Howard Russell: 'The London *Times* is one of the greatest powers in the world — in fact, I don't know anything which has much more power — except perhaps the Mississippi.'

I read about the eccentric founding fathers of Fleet Street's popular newspapers: Lord Northcliffe, who created the *Daily Mail* and the *Mirror*, and the Canadian Lord Beaverbrook, whose *Daily Express* was both a huge success and his personal bully pulpit. I read about the yellow press war in New York between Joseph Pulitzer and William Randolph Hearst, and how they were accused of using their newspapers to provoke the Spanish–American War of 1898.

Above all, I read books by journalists. The first was *Teach Yourself Journalism* by E. Frank Candlin. It was a tiny volume in a yellow-and-black dust jacket, and I practically memorised it. I learned that if you were a success and managed to get a job in Fleet Street, which was unlikely given the talent required and the intense competition, you could earn as much as £1000 a year. That was when I started saving for a ship's ticket to London.

But my favourite books were about the adventures of foreign correspondents. James Cameron tracking down Albert Schweitzer in the African jungle; Russell of *The Times* covering the Charge of the Light Brigade. 'Surely that handful of men are not going to charge an army in position? Alas! It was but too true — their desperate valour knew no bounds,' he wrote. René MacColl of the *Daily Express* wrote in his *Deadline and Dateline*: 'Humanity can be divided roughly into the statics and the transients.' If you were a static by disposition, his advice was to forget about being a foreign correspondent. My wandering life, I decided, was definitive proof I was perfectly qualified.

Certain books by the great editors of Fleet Street became well known even outside the obsessive and self-regarding world of journalism. Hugh Cudlipp's *Publish and Be Damned*, about the *Daily Mirror* in its heyday, was like that. The *Mirror*, Britain's first 'red top', was a brilliant, buccaneering paper for the workers. Cudlipp and crew exulted in the risk of pushing against the boundaries of contemporary taste. He wrote of the *Mirror*: 'Millions swear by [it], regard it as their daily Bible; others loathe it, curse it, reject its news and views as the modern works of Satan. It has been threatened with suppression by Parliament, attacked by other newspapers, denounced by prelates ... Some politicians who have flayed it in public have enjoyed, or sought in private, its approbation.' I heard the echo of these words years later when I was executive chairman of News International and *The Sun* had deposed the *Mirror* as the newspaper to love or hate.

Arthur Christiansen was editor of the *Daily Express* for 24 years. In his autobiography, *Headlines All My Life*, he wrote of the importance of mixing entertainment with serious news: 'The reader requires cakes and ale as well as bread and butter.' Every day, before lunch, Christiansen wrote a review of that day's edition. I remember these most:

Here is a three-fold rule of conduct for our paper:

1. Never set the police on anybody.
2. Never cry down the pleasures of the people.
3. Remember our own habits and frailties when disposed to be critical of others.

Are we not in danger of becoming a nagging paper, simply because it is much easier to criticise than to praise?
There are too many stories about things and not enough about people ...
News, news, news — that is what we want. You can describe things with the pen of Shakespeare himself but you cannot beat news in a newspaper.

Cudlipp called Christiansen 'the patron saint of urgency'.

An editor's job didn't seem so much fun to me as the lives of Cameron and MacColl. Christiansen wrote despairingly about being the victim of a harrying proprietor who was forever on the telephone: 'The telephone constantly rang. Wherever Beaverbrook went, the telephone followed.'

When he cracked under the pressure, a Harley Street doctor

injected Christiansen for 12 days with a preparation of strychnine, iron, and arsenic. He said this treatment restored his shattered confidence, but the remedy seemed drastic to me. He also died when he was 59. I decided as a teenager that I never wanted to work at close quarters with an overbearing proprietor. Not everything works out in life.

Christiansen was a popular newspaper genius — circulation of the *Daily Express* reached 4 million under him — but coverage of his death exposed the everlasting rift between posh and popular newspaper cultures. His 1963 obituary in *The Times* was sniffy: 'By one yardstick at least he was a successful editor; how good an editor he was is another matter.' He defined for decades much of the style of popular newspapers — the sharpness of their writing, the style of their layouts and photo selection — but in those days, as now, some 'heavy' newspaper editors regarded themselves as the officer class, and their popular counterparts as members of the other ranks.

All this reading I was doing mattered, but back at the office the objective was to be selected from among the copy boys to become a trainee reporter — a 'cadet'.

Running copy and buying coffee, cigarettes, and sandwiches was how you earned your pay. But no matter how good you were at that, it was not going to get you a cadetship. They were hard to get — 8 out of 10 copy boys would give up and look for other work. You had to find stories and get them into the newspaper. To get stories, you needed contacts. This was tricky for a new boy in town who knew no one. But the first lesson I taught myself was that everyone was a potential contact. My first was my dad.

Dad had become the chef at the immigration hostel where we first lived, and came home one night complaining how hard he would be working the next few weeks cooking for hundreds of new immigrants heading for Adelaide aboard the *SS Strathaird*. It was the biggest single intake of migrants ever to arrive at the hostel.

That was my first story — my first words in print. It was a 17-line single column brief, and it appeared on 7 September 1959. The headline said: '265 migrants due Friday'.

Nothing compares to the first time you see in print words you have thought up yourself, knowing they will appear in tens of thousands of newspapers delivered to every corner of your small town. Thousands of people would read my words — in the pub, on the train going home, over their evening meals. This was powerful stuff. I was 15 years and 7 months old.

Once you realise everyone has a story fit to print, especially if they live in a small town, it gets easy. A couple that had arrived from Britain on the same ship as us opened their own barbershop, and, unheard of in Adelaide in the 1950s, the wife was cutting men's hair. My first picture story — 'Mrs Gwen Urch adds a feminine touch to her very masculine trade'.

What are those men doing on the big vacant lot at the end of our street? They turn out to be surveyors, happy to answer my casual questions. My first page-three top: 'A new shopping centre, the biggest of its type in South Australia'.

The surest story source was council meetings. The hard part was spending evenings with the droning burghers of Marion Council. But it yielded results: 'Dogs kill 84 sheep'; 'Kindergarten for Oaklands estate'; 'Talks sought on level crossing'; 'Fire sprinklers needed in schools'.

I kept up a routine of books before bedtime, and tried for a minimum of two stories a week in the paper. I learned shorthand. In those days, the smallest tape recorder weighed 20 pounds and cost a fortune. You couldn't complete your cadetship without a 120-word shorthand note, and I wanted to get an early start. I learned the version created in the nineteenth century by Sir Isaac Pitman.

Even today, when I'm writing rapid notes, it creeps in. My sister Mal taught me to touch type on an Olympia portable she still had 50 years later.

In November 1960, three men with uniformly grey hair sat side-by-side in the editor's office of *The News*. Ron Boland, the new-ish editor, Jim Wilson, his deputy, and Murray James, the chief of staff, had to make a decision. Their grave-eyed gazes were fixed on me.

Every year, they awarded cadetships to one of the 25 copy boys, and I was among the five candidates to be interviewed. I had joined the newspaper 17 months before, and was flattered, but not hopeful.

Reporters who had been through this ordeal told me what to expect. The editors would need to be convinced I followed events and read the whole newspaper; they'd ask questions about the front-page lead on, say, Monday of last week. They'd want to know what the second editorial was yesterday, and the names and jobs of cabinet ministers. They'd spring odd foreign questions, too: who is the American secretary of state; who was the British prime minister before this one. And, inevitably, they'd ask me why I wanted to be a journalist, and what I wanted to be doing 10 years from now.

That's about how it went. I answered the questions and left the room. The conclave began. The next morning brought judgement. The panel had decided, unusually, to create two additional cadetships. I'm sure my best friend Rex Jory, who started at *The News* within a few days of me, was frontrunner, and I was a close second. We were both 16 years old.

I learned of this decision from Murray James, and it was one of the most bizarre encounters I ever had with a boss. James beckoned me through a big blue swinging door into his glass-walled corner office. He was a short, square, hurrying man, who was forever on his way somewhere else. His hair was wavy and grey, swept back from his forehead, and kept so firmly in place it looked like curves of cement.

'Les. You've done well. Really well. The editor wants to make you a cadet.'

It was a total and wonderful surprise. I could feel my heart pounding and my face flushing as I gathered myself to speak. But James had not finished. He was now looking down, studying the scribbles that covered the green blotting-pad on his desktop. 'However, there is an issue,' he said. 'It's your eye, son. You can't be going out representing *The News* with that eye.'

I stood there in dazed silence, wondering what plan he was about to announce for my intolerable eye.

'To be a cadet, you need to get it fixed,' he said. 'Go to a doctor. Get it straightened. We'll pay whatever it costs, and then everything will be good. Will you do that?'

In the years since, I have retold this story many times, mainly to young colleagues and human resources directors, enjoying their outrage, listening to them outline the terrible consequence for any modern employer who would make such a demand. But life was different in 1960, especially for a 16-year-old who had left secondary modern school only 18 months before. I couldn't believe my luck.

James was still looking down at his blotting-pad, so I addressed the hard top of his head: 'Yes, Mr James, I will go to the doctor and I will ask him to straighten my eye — and thank you very much for this opportunity.'

I became a cadet journalist, but the operation to straighten my eye was a failure. For decades to come, my wilful wandering eye would stare blindly out at nothing. Still, we managed to cope with life together, until 2003 when a persuasive Manhattan doctor convinced me modern straightening procedures were almost certain to succeed — as they did.

As for Murray James, he never mentioned the matter again, and I avoided at all times making eye contact with him.

I was made editor of 'Possum's Pages' in *The Sunday Mail,* the daily *News*'s sister. Possum's Pages was a two-page spread for children, and I was now 'Possum'. I was inundated each week with mail from hundreds of young readers. They sent letters, drawings, jokes, and puzzles, and I chose some to publish. It was a child's section edited by a child.

I shared space behind partition walls with two people. Helen Caterer was a permanently excited feature writer who seemed about to break into a sprint whenever she walked. Cecil de Boehme, the features editor, was my boss. He had one arm that did not work properly, and a stern manner. Everyone else called him Cec, but he was Mr de Boehme to me.

As Possum, I had to do everything in the production of my pages. I had to write copy and headlines, choose and edit stories, draw layouts, and make everything fit on the page. I had learned to write brief stories, but knew nothing about anything else. Cecil de Boehme was my teacher, and I learned from him the rudiments of newspaper production: selecting type sizes, counting out headlines, scaling pictures, shaping a page on a layout sheet.

I also learned the dialect of newspapers: that ems, ens, and picas were printer's measures; routed blocks were photographs with the background removed; that nonpareil was tiny type; and that serif meant fonts with curves, and sans serif those without.

I had to edit the weekly horoscope, which arrived by mail each week. The week it failed to turn up, I wrote it myself.

This was my baptism into journalism, a 12-month hazing. I made terrible mistakes and suffered Mr de Boehme's terrible anger.

After Possum, I moved to the reporters' room of the daily newspaper, which looked like a classroom but was permanently shrouded in a blue fog of cigarette smoke. Small wooden desks were arranged in three rows with hard, numbing chairs. The typewriters were cast-iron monsters, some dating back to before the First World War, indestructible Royals, Remingtons, Underwoods, Coronas, and Olympias. Unlike their fragile electronic successors, no technicians were needed to keep these beasts running. Manual typewriters are more romantic to remember than they ever were to use — the jamming keys, the inky-fingered task of changing ribbons, and the pain of retyping whole pages to correct or re-write. That was all fine when we didn't know any better. They were hard on the fingers, too. The last time I played with my Lettera 22 — now nearly 60 years old — it was like driving a car without power steering.

Newspapers in Australia inexplicably used military vocabulary to describe levels of seniority: trainee journalists were cadets, from first year to fourth; trained journalists were given ranks — from D grade through to A, with Super A for the most highly rated; the news — or city — editor was grandly titled chief of staff. In keeping with this military structure, desks were occupied according to rank. At the head, just outside the swinging door of the chief of staff's office, was Ken May, political editor, who would go on to run Murdoch's Australian company and become Sir Kenneth. Behind him, sat the chief reporter, Frank Shaw, and behind him, the best writer in the room, Brian Gill, known as Beagle. He was furious when the subs deleted his funny pay-off lines, especially on the occasion he wrote about a poodle breeder's failed attempts at artificial insemination: 'It all goes to show that the poodle prefers a doodle.'

I occupied the middle-row desk at the back of the room. Each morning, having read at home every page of our rival, *The Advertiser*, I waited to be summoned by the chief of staff. A copy boy sitting in the corner of his office summoned us in order of seniority.

Mine were beginner's jobs: hunting for stories among passengers arriving on the Melbourne Express; covering the wool auctions; sitting for hours in courtrooms, hoping for a headline; shadowing the chief crime reporter — specialist reporters were called roundsmen — and learning which violent deaths matter to newspapers; there was almost no interest in suicides.

Stories spilled onto the platform when the Melbourne Express arrived each day at 9am. In 1960, this was how people came to town. The local airport was tiny and passenger jets so new that people were excited when they flew low and loud over the city. Deafening potential customers was a marketing tactic.

The Melbourne Express came from the outside world bringing fame, glamour, and drama. Public relations were primitive then. To find out which actors, singers, and politicians were on board, you spoke to the guards. For human interest, you stood and watched, and had to be willing to interrupt emotional reunions. These reunions were often routine, but not always. Sometimes people arrived dressed differently, speaking a foreign language, and were held in long, weeping embraces. When that happened it was likely to be your story for the day. Even 25 years after the war, 'New Australian' immigrants struggled to bring together families it had divided. It was in 1960 that Dad's deputy chef finally rescued his wife from behind the Iron Curtain in Ukraine. It was a great story for me when she arrived on the Melbourne Express.

———

I was working among a great cavalcade of characters, unlike any I had known — editors and reporters a world apart from my Bootle uncles and my dad's army mates. There were few women in those days, and the most senior was 'editress' of the social pages.

You cannot typecast a newsman. Never trust any effort to do so. They can be loud, as well as timid; mighty drinkers, or tee-totallers; lyrical writers, or great reporters with limited vocabularies;

scrupulously principled, or shady chancers. Editors can be calm and measured, or rampaging bullies. It would be good to say the calm version got better results, but there is no pattern; brutal genius can provoke great work.

Murray Hedgcock was a tee-totaller and a cricket obsessive, a Methodist who never swore or even raised his voice. His sense of humour was dry and sharp, but his response to the most uproarious moment was limited to a mild smile. Hedgcock was features editor, and all that agitated him was sloppy copy. He was the office grammar despot; a tyrant in the face of redundant words, passive sentences, split infinitives, wayward apostrophes, and the overuse of adverbs and adjectives. Hedgcock taught me to take care with my copy, especially when I knew he would be editing. Even now, with him long retired and in his eighties, I still read and re-read emails to him before hitting 'send'.

Jeff Medwell was the editor of 5DN radio news, and taught me to write the spoken word. This is a special skill, which basically inverts the sequence of facts. In a newspaper, a story would begin: 'Six people died in a head-on collision on North Terrace today.' For radio you would write: 'Two cars collided head-on in North Terrace today, killing six people.' In radio, you delay the main information, first using the fact of the crash to gain the listener's attention.

Medwell was not a tee-totaller. His great feat was to return from drinking copious lunchtime pints and still produce flawless copy. I learned a lot from Jeff Medwell, but never matched his performance when drunk in charge of a typewriter.

Ted Smith was a gentle feature writer with a round, owlish face and a wry laugh. He was the same age as my parents, but a wonderful drinking companion, full of wit and tales. Off duty, he produced a stream of short stories and pacy novels with titles like *A Lively Form of Death*, *Northward the Coast*, and *The Killers of Karawala*. He used a different name to write his fiction — Edward Lindall — that was derived from the names of his children. When I started writing features, I would show them to Ted Smith. I was amazed how quickly he saw the holes in them. He had brisk advice about writing: 'Just sit at your typewriter and never retreat.'

Each Wednesday, Blake Brownrigg would gather cadets for our weekly 'cadet lecture', although the word 'lecture' gives an inflated idea of these events. Most of the time, we listened to the more elderly and less occupied staff members telling stories about the old days. Brownrigg was a semi-retired columnist whose job was to oversee our training. When he failed to dragoon someone to spend an hour talking to us, which was often, we would have to listen to him reminisce. Most often he repeated stories of his spell in public relations, when Maureen O'Hara and Peter Lawford made a film in South Australia called *Kangaroo*. It had been a flop, he told us, mainly because the film misunderstood Australia. His principal contribution had been persuading the director to remove a scene in which a mob of marauding kangaroos attacked and destroyed a country town.

These people were the informal faculty that shaped my further education. Over the next six years, everything I learned came from people such as them — and the books in my bedroom. They weren't teachers in the school and university sense, forcing their knowledge on me. They answered my questions helpfully enough, but most of the time I watched them in action and learned painful lessons when my frequent mistakes irritated them. The subs were the most easily irritated and the sub-editors' room the toughest classroom at *The News*. I was landed there, in a mist of cigarette and pipe smoke and beery breath, when I was 18. The subs were older, more experienced, and crustier than the rest of the staff. Terrorising new boys put a shine in the eyes of every sub. Arch Bell, the chief sub-editor, was towering and quick-tempered, with a mysterious growth on the back of his neck that would redden when a deadline was approaching. Bell once handed me sheets of copy with instructions attached. I followed his instructions closely, or I thought I had. Twenty minutes later the door into the subs' room flew open, to his storming arrival. He loomed over me, and growled: 'Jesus Christ, Hinton, don't you know what stet means?'

The room went into a hush. The sub-editors lined up around the desk kept their heads down, but I knew they relished my predicament. I was the only person in the room who did not know what 'stet' meant, and my ignorance had left a big hole in the paper and delayed the entire edition. Stet is a word with Latin roots that means that edited cuts should be ignored. It was common in the age of hand-written editing.

I wish I'd had the wit to question why 100 words of copy would be topped by two decks of inch-deep type across three columns. Or why I had been handed so many pages of copy that had been firmly crossed out. And, of course, why, on each of those pages there appeared clearly, in capitals, the word 'STET'.

Everyone grumbled about sub-editors, but they were the editorial assembly line, the craftsmen who made the paper happen. They made everything fit, shaped every page, placed and trimmed every story, selected and sized every photograph, filtered out mistakes and bad language.

They seemed so awesome and fierce when I was a teenager. Arch Bell was a passionate man, but generous beneath the bluster, and lived for his work. Indeed, within months of retiring he was dead. Marty Ryan gave me the first lesson in writing a picture caption: 'Son, it's no use simply saying what's in the picture — we can see that. Say something more.' Ryan lost an eye in the war flying bombers over Europe. He wore an eye patch, not a black and glamorous one, but a white dressing to treat the unhealed wound. Jack Fahey taught me about headlines: 'There better be a bloody good reason if you ever again give me a headline that doesn't contain a verb.' Fahey was a big, vulnerable man who would announce to the office the joys of sobriety each time he went on the wagon, which was never for long. Norm Sewell, his white hair always groomed, had a huge midriff around which he was able — just — to fasten the suit jacket he always wore. Sewell hated florid prose. He once disapproved of a re-write of mine: 'This makes my skin crawl, lad. Keep it simple, always keep it simple.' Sewell left the office early one day, grey and unwell, and died that afternoon.

These heroes are almost all gone now; ghosts from a lost world, but their shadows have stayed, along with the lessons they passed on to a boy standing at ground zero in his career.

CHAPTER 8

Frank and Lilian

It was quiet at home on Thursday 13 May 1965, the day I left Adelaide for London. Quiet, except for Mum's loud sobbing. Dad was at the bottom of his garden, crouched in the cool morning sun on his weeding stool beneath the orange tree he had planted when we moved in. His transistor was tuned in to horse-racing news, and a few magpies pecked in the grass. Dad's weeding stool was one of his sanctuaries when Mum was upset or angry; other times, he sat in the car with a beer, reading westerns. Mum was never easily consoled, and Dad was no good at it anyway.

Dad got the worst of it when Mum was in a bad mood. He usually sat wordlessly, waiting for her mood to pass. The only time I saw him lose his temper was when Mal had left home, and we thought Mum would starve to death. She was so hard on him one day that he gave a sudden cry of rage, shoved his plate of food across the table, scattering peas and chips, and stormed upstairs. Mum was so shocked she apologised to him later, which was very out of character.

While Dad hid in his weeds, Duncan was on his bed looking solemn, and I was alone with Mum in my room, where she was making a ritual of stripping my bed, acting out her pain by eliminating all evidence of me from the home I was abandoning.

She removed everything — sheets, blankets, the single pillow — until there was only a naked mattress and an empty wardrobe and the bare blue walls I had painted myself. She did it slowly, folding and refolding into a perfectly neat pile, now and then sitting to sob some more. She was not a teary woman and never wept for effect, so it was shocking when she cried. Her body would shake and rock, her mouth would freeze into a wet gape, and her crying was like a scream.

The emotion of that day had been building for weeks. A couple of nights before, when I came home late after seeing a girl, she hammered on my chest with her fists and wept. 'You've been out all night with that tart,' she said. This was not entirely true; the night had not been so eventful as Mum appeared to think, and it was harsh describing my sweet friend Josephine as a tart. I stood there until she exhausted herself. Mum may have been a distant wife, but she was an intense mother.

My departure was no surprise to my parents. For four years, each Friday, I had collected my weekly pay from the cashier's counter and made a deposit into a savings account at a bank branch across the street from the office. When I had enough, I was going to flee the bucolic comfort zone of Adelaide with my pal Rex Jory and head for London. I even took Mum's advice on the return fare: 'Make sure you have enough to get back if things go wrong.'

But in my mother's dreams, I was going to marry, and stay in Adelaide. She had high hopes when I was seeing a lovely blonde with a double-barrelled name whose grandfather was a knight; but I liked her more than she liked me. But still Mum had hoped each date with a girl would anchor me. By the time I said goodbye to Josephine, Mum was in despair.

Adelaide was the first permanence of my parents' adult life: a red-brick bungalow with white-framed windows, our own car in its own garage, the tidy concrete driveway Dad had laid himself, the garden he proudly created in the rich soil that had nurtured orchards and vineyards before houses like ours consumed it.

For me, a restless 21-year-old, it was bland suburbia, far from where I wanted to be. For them, it was a destination. Our home looked like a department store showroom with its Danish-style furniture and shiny blue Formica kitchen tops. It was impeccable, dustless, even soulless unless you accepted the deep but unclear importance that keeping it that clean represented to my mother. She was house-proud even when she wasn't at home: years later, when we took her on holiday, she made the hotel beds before we checked out.

After so many rootless years, they needed the unthreatened rhythm of Adelaide. But it was their fault I was leaving. I had spent my childhood travelling the world with them. They had had enough of it, but I wasn't ready to stop. London was 10,000 miles from Adelaide, but in 1965 it felt to me like the heart of life.

Australia, even in its own mind, was a far-flung British province. Some resented the old country, others felt deeply attached to its monarch and traditions. Australians could never read enough about Britain. Newspapers were full of the news and excitement of London. It was the height of Swinging London and Carnaby Street, and the dawn of what would be known as the 'Permissive Society', which, looking back on it, seems quaint. London, I had also decided, published the world's best newspapers.

Adelaide, by comparison, was a Victorian freeze-frame, where the pubs closed at 6pm, and housewives dressed up to go shopping in the city, wearing hats and long white gloves. Everything exciting was happening somewhere else.

On our way to the ship, everyone was silent as Dad reversed down the drive in his Hillman Minx. I scraped that car when it was new and took it to a garage for a secret paint job. Dad spotted it right away doing the Sunday wash and got his revenge soon after when he found a nylon stocking on the back seat and showed it to Mum. I told her the truth — the girl took if off to walk on the beach — but she wasn't convinced.

The beaming white liner that was taking us away, *SS Orcades*, was at Port Adelaide. Everyone came aboard with Rex and me to see our windowless two-bunk cabin. There was no anti-terrorist security then, and the ship was full of people saying goodbye.

In the 1960s, before flying was routine, there was no quick way to Britain, except for the wealthy, and therefore no mercifully swift farewell in the airport terminal. A ship's departure was ceremonial. And very long.

Orcades crept away from the dockside in slow motion, with a soulful, shuddering blast of its horn. The air was thick and bright with thousands of coloured streamers connecting passengers on deck with people they were leaving. Farewell streamers were a tradition in the days of big ocean liners, and every departure had an atmosphere of festive sadness.

As the ship edged away, the streamers tightened and then broke. Their happy colours became streaks of litter in the harbour's water. Shouts from the disappearing docks slowly died in the throbbing of the ship's engines. I feel bad now remembering how delighted I was to be leaving, and how I wished the ship would hurry up.

My family stood together in a tight group. Mum clutched the broken streamers and cried. Her hair, not yet grey, was permed in place for the occasion. Mal had her arm in Mum's. Dad, hands in his pocket, looked dazed. Duncan, who was 16, looked abandoned. He told me later that Mum wouldn't leave until the ship had vanished over the horizon. I don't know how Dad felt. I didn't know how he felt about most things. Mum's big emotions crowded out his.

From that day, we were a long-distance family. They visited me in London and the United States, and I went home again, but never for long. I felt guilty about this, and tried to make up for it by visiting them more as they grew older.

My quiet father was an onlooker in my upbringing. I don't remember a moment of advice from him, or much reproof. I remember, once or twice, when he put me to bed, feeling the brush of his moustache when he kissed me goodnight. He only hit me once, lightly across the back of the head with a rolled newspaper when we were crossing a street on the way to the cinema. I can't remember why, but it was a shocking moment. When we entered the cinema, a song was playing with the lyric, 'Oh, my papa, to me he was so wonderful'. He was, in his muted way. He didn't often use words to show his feelings. He made things for people he loved. When I was interested in amateur dramatics, he built me a beautiful box for my stage make-up with my name carved on the lid. When Mum wouldn't let me have a sheath knife, he carved a full-size Bowie knife from a log. Mal and Duncan both have furniture he made. There was never any ceremony. He would make something and quietly present it.

For years, he did the football pools. We would study his face for any signal of success as he listened to the results on his radio. These were given gravity by the solemn lilt of the presenter's voice and the glorious names of competing teams: Tranmere Rovers, Heart of Midlothian, Partick Thistle, Wolverhampton Wanderers, Hamilton Academical, Stenhousemuir. The biggest Littlewoods prize was £75,000. We were overjoyed the day Dad won £11.

Dad was short, about five foot five, with an oversized, beaky nose. On parade, he marched in the back row so he could skip to catch up without breaking everyone's stride. He stroked his moustache perpetually while reading his Zane Grey westerns. He read every inch of the newspapers. Long after I became a journalist, he would catch me out spotting stories I had missed. On payday, when he came home happier than usual, he would throw banknotes into the air.

Lilian, my mum, was extremely sharp, but not particularly knowledgeable, or curious about the world. She did not read much, but loved crosswords, was unbeatable at Scrabble, and could quote long passages from the Bible and snatches of poetry learned long ago. With her energy, fury, and inarticulate ambition, she was not easy to live with. She had a hard edge, which showed in her dark and frightening eyes when she was angry. When upset, she sometimes shouted, and her vocabulary could be educational for a boy; other times, she would sink into sulks that lasted for days. It wasn't always clear what she was angry about. Sometimes she was wound up so tightly any small thing made her snap.

Mum was on the front line of every battle: difficult neighbours, inept schools, and whenever Army high-ups messed up our accommodation or travel arrangements. When she argued with our neighbour in Germany about a shared garden, she dug up the entire lawn and planted vegetables. It was a land grab. Mum might have been a little mad, but people didn't mess with her.

In our house, she made the rules. She hit me often, but never with real intent. She mostly used one of her shoes, and, whenever she raised it in anger, I fled. When she caught me, cowering in the corner of a room, she would be satisfied with one swipe so long as I followed it with a cooperative cry of pain.

No one got sick in our house. Missing school or work was not an option. No cold, however severe, kept me at home. A morning vomit after something you ate? 'You'll be fine.' Flu symptoms? 'Here's a glass of water — off you go.' And off I would go, with an extra handkerchief and my nose stuffed with a lump of Vicks VapoRub.

For years, our home was a pocket of Prohibition. I had never seen

Mum drink, but she did often tell a story of being sick once after too much crème de menthe. Whenever Dad arrived home with whisky on his breath, the atmosphere was combustible. I was a teenager when I found out most families had alcohol with Christmas dinner; we had water with our goose, followed by a cup of tea.

In Adelaide, however, the temperance was overwhelmed by our new Australian life. At first, my mother would react with alarm when guests, in the local tradition, arrived bearing bottles of chilled beer and flagons of wine. Meanwhile, her elder son was learning the ways of Australian newspapers, a world not known for abstinence.

I began arriving home dizzy after a couple of schooners in the Strathmore Hotel, next to the office. When Mum didn't complain about my beers, Dad seized the moment and started lacing his coffee with whisky. Mum sat silent and scowling in front of the television.

I think my drinking gave Dad cover. He felt safer when we had a beer together. Dad was a master at retrieving a bottle of West End Bitter from the freezer just as it was beginning to crystallise. We would share one in the garden on a hot Sunday afternoon. Even Mum relented and was known to have an occasional shandy — one-quarter beer, three-quarters lemonade — but only ever one.

Mum didn't drink, but was a helplessly hooked chain-smoker. The house was filled with tobacco accoutrements: cigarette holders, fancy table-lighters, ashtray souvenirs collected on our travels, and a wooden cigarette-box into which I would place neat rows of filter-tipped du Mauriers when guests were expected. Mum liked fancy cigarette brands; in Bootle, she had rolled her own or bought Woodbines. When she went out, I filled a brown leather-covered cigarette case for her handbag and topped up the fuel in her silver Ronson lighter. The fingers of her right hand were stained dark-brown and the insides of her teeth were black. The haze and smell in our house meant nothing to me. I never smoked, but on a train it made no difference to me whether I travelled in a smoking carriage or not.

After a heart attack at the age of 47, Mum quit, but a stroke 18 years later left her with slurred speech and a severe limp for the rest of her life.

She loved her children intensely, but the love didn't overflow. I would wrap my arms around her while she washed the dishes, pressing my head against her back, and say, 'Do you love me, Mum?'

Every time, her answer was the same: 'Give me one good reason why I should.'

But I knew that's what she would say, and I knew she was saying 'yes'.

She was ambitious for her children, but she didn't have big dreams for us. To her, success meant a secure job — any job — and a house in a nice neighbourhood, and a steady, safe, respectable, law-abiding life. That was far better than the wandering, out-of-control existence of an Army sergeant's wife. Or living in Bootle.

She drove us hard at school. It was agony when I was eight and struggling to master the times-tables. She made me recite them over and over every night until I got them right, which I never quite did.

Duncan went to university, earned degrees, and became a teacher. I pressed on more haphazardly, but I knew I had pleased her the day she could show the neighbours a story in *The News* with my by-line. When Marilyn married a soldier, her heart must have sunk, but in the end the sergeant's wife was happy to have a lieutenant colonel as a son-in-law.

She never wanted us to step out of line. 'Don't get into arguments at work — your father did that again and again,' she would say. She was horrified when my first wife Mary and I provided accommodation for a friend fresh out of prison after serving six months for embezzlement. 'You will disgrace the family,' she said. 'What if people find out?'

Her children meant more to her than her husband, and she was haunted, as we grew older, by the knowledge we would abandon her. She could never hide her distress when we found other people; no girlfriend or spouse was good enough.

Mary and I went to Adelaide for nearly a year in 1970. It was by far our longest visit, and Mum was desperate for us to stay, although she knew we never would. When we told her one evening that Mary was pregnant with our first child, she didn't even smile or look up from her crossword. 'I suppose you'll be going back to England to have it,' she said.

My parents' marriage could not correctly be called fiery, with the fire only coming from one side. I remember a story — I think it was a TV comedy sketch — in which a man with a complaining wife had the ability to make himself go deaf. It was about my dad.

Lilian dominated her husband, but at the same time was powerless in the life he had chosen. Whenever and wherever the Army told my father to go, we followed. She had no choice but to take a back seat to his unglamorous, unpredictable job as a non-commissioned officer.

Most of the time, Mum appeared to disapprove of Dad, but it was impossible to know why. Maybe it was his gentle satisfaction with life, his low threshold of contentment, his quietness, and his pleasure in solitude; his hobbies — westerns, horse racing, gardening, and the exotic birds he bred for a few years in a big cage in the back garden. It wasn't an ideal marriage. As a boy, I must have thought it was normal for loving grown-ups always to be in a temper with each other and to sleep in twin beds. That was before I learned their painful history.

In 1950, when I was six, and Mum was 36, she met a married Army butcher called Freddie. He had been posted to Egypt without his family, and Mum met him at a party in the sergeants' mess.

Their affair must have been intense because, when Freddie went back to England, my mother followed him. She walked out on her husband of 15 years, and took her three children with her. It must have been an act born out of great and unexpected love, or desperate unhappiness. She can't have had much money, so presumably had no doubt that she and Freddie were going to spend the rest of their lives together.

Mal was 14 and remembers Mum telling her what had happened and that she would have to decide whether to stay with Dad, or leave with her.

We lived for a year at Grandma's in Bootle without seeing Dad once. I remember his absence, and I remember Mum being out at night so often and so late that I became terrified she might never return. I couldn't sleep until I heard her laughing outside and saying good night to people.

I don't know whether Mum changed her mind, or Freddie decided to stay with his wife, but at the end of that year, my parents reconciled.

Grandma must have known what was happening, but no one was going to tell a small boy, so the rift did not shatter me. I knew nothing about the reasons for Dad's absence, or our year back in Bootle, for 60 years, until I questioned Mal for this book. By then, Mum and Dad had been dead many years. The news would have horrified me when I was younger, but by then I understood more of the foibles of life and marriage, and knew it was mostly impossible to judge the relationships of others. It didn't cause me to question my parents' love for me — I never questioned that — but it helped explain my mother's torment and, possibly, Dad's acquiescent approach to his marriage. I'll never know now why she left, or if Dad's conduct contributed to hers. There was never anything evidently romantic in their relationship that I could see, but it didn't seem odd when I was a child, having grown up with it. Still, even though the Bruces and Hintons were never families to hang out their emotions and problems, it's amazing I was never told. I'm not angry with anyone and, whatever went wrong then, they were together in the end for 60 years.

Mum calmed down a little and, in their later years, I finally saw my parents show affection. It was an easy fondness; they smiled at each other a lot and even touched, but I never saw them actually kiss or embrace. Dad was tenderly protective of Mum after her stroke, and when he died — seven years before Mum — she was bereft.

In their old age, they left Adelaide for Canberra, where Mal and Duncan lived with their families. In 2004, Mum died there, aged 90, in a nursing home, remembering Dad, her children, her sister Gladys, and her mother, but not much else. Afterwards, I found every letter I had sent her from London, those blue weight-saving 'aerogrammes', neatly preserved in a shoebox. She was buried, as she had wanted, in the same grave as Dad.

I last saw Dad in 1996, when he didn't have long to live. He was sitting low in his high-backed chair, his tired old head resting on a white lace-trimmed antimacassar, chest heaving, and an ugly cylinder of oxygen at his side next to a tabletop of pill bottles. Every few moments, he took deep breaths from a mask. His old hands, scarred long ago by years with his kitchen knives, were now covered with marks left from skin cancer surgery. Through the French windows of the living room, he could see his plants and trees blooming beneath the Canberra sun, and the flower beds he would never touch again.

Of course, neither of us acknowledged we were together for the last time. He looked at me with his pale blue eyes, but it was only a glimpse; Dad's looks never lingered.

I kissed him on the forehead, 'See you, old man.'

'Safe trip,' he said.

Two months later, in a hospital bed, gasping but still lucid, he took hold of Duncan's shirtfront. 'I can't take this any more,' he said. Duncan spoke to his doctors and signed some papers. Dad died the next day. He was 86.

Back in Australia for his funeral, I found among his things a card addressed to me, dated 19 February 1945, my first birthday and four years before Duncan was born.

In it, he had written: *To my one and only son, wishing him all the wishes I've wished myself. Dad.*

I had never seen it until then.

CHAPTER 9

Warm beer, cold rain

The passage to 'the old country' was a rite for young Australians in the 1960s. Britain was an inviting place; its borders were open to Australians, and they could work and vote the moment they came ashore.

The voyage took a month. It was half happy recklessness, half a grim introduction to life beyond a lucky country's safe shores. To reach the cultural comfort of Britain, we had to pass through less familiar places; north through the Indian Ocean to Colombo and Bombay, into the Red Sea towards Egypt and the Suez Canal, and on to the Mediterranean.

We saw the Pyramids of Giza on the banks of the Nile when tourism was so undeveloped the only sign of it was a tiny Coca-Cola stand alongside the Sphinx, which was so unprotected we climbed it and put crumbling pieces in our pockets. But the streets of Colombo and Bombay were desperate. Great Victorian buildings, remnants of British rule, were juxtaposed against seething poverty. In Colombo, crowds of begging children were whipped away by police under orders to make life easier for cash-carrying tourists. But they were so desperate they kept returning until we paid them to go away.

In Bombay, there was the hot, sour smell of street sleepers, hundreds of them packing the pavements, and prostitutes crouched behind small windows, like ragged mannequins, trapped by their pimps. In Egypt, not much had changed in the 15 years since I had lived there. Beggars with missing limbs still cried for help, and crouching women held out pleading hands, as they cradled undernourished babies, black flies crawling on their faces.

It was far from the orderly, sanitised world we had left behind, and not new to me. But the girls wept and the boys stood in silent shock. They might have seen brief black-and-white images of scenes like these on their small-screen televisions, but this was living, reeking real life.

In the days before instant, all-seeing video, when the world was more isolated from itself, Australia was especially alone. Television newsreels arrived by air from America and Europe long after the event. When John Kennedy was murdered in 1963, television stations made a special effort and were proud to broadcast footage from Dallas a day or so after the event. Newspaper photos from overseas were 'radio photos' — so raw in detail that artists were employed to paint it in.

We would return from these trips ashore to the cocoon of *Orcades*, where our own reality ruled. *Orcades* was like every ship making this voyage in the 1960s — a teeming party boat, quiet every hung over morning, and jumping by early evening. Drink was cheap, the bars closed late, and the music was loud.

It would not be long before giant jet planes were carrying more than 300 passengers to London in less than a day, forcing passenger liners to rethink their business models. Sea travel would become luxury, slow-going excursions to nowhere, catering to mature passengers looking for tranquillity — the same generation who were in *Orcades* in 1965, dancing wildly to Tom Jones and 'What's New Pussycat?', and closely and hopefully to The Beatles' 'If I Fell In Love With You'.

I didn't dance much. It was rutting season in these ships, the sole social interaction involved girls and boys hooking up, and I never quite worked out the rules. Making casual conversation with strange women was impossible for me, at least when I was sober. At home, I would walk around the streets for an hour searching for the courage to phone and ask someone for a date.

In *Orcades*, I watched confident — and sober — men strike up casual conversations with pretty women, and by midnight be arm-in-arm, laughing and drinking. It looked miraculous to me — I wondered how they did it.

When I found the courage, it wasn't real courage at all; and too much brandy and ginger ale makes you bad at picking the right moment. When The Righteous Brothers were singing 'You've Lost that Lovin' Feelin'', I thought it was the perfect time to ask a woman, crying in a corner, if she wanted to dance. 'Oh, please, fuck off,' she said.

Rex attracted women without even trying. Sometimes they even asked him to dance. He was lucky with women — even after the car accident that nearly killed him and completely changed his face.

We were driving too fast along a dirt road in his mother's sky blue VW Beetle when we were both 17. Rex was at the wheel, and when the car went into a skid he braked, which is never a good idea. 'We're going to roll,' he shouted, and sure enough his mum's bright new VW made one complete flip before landing on its side in a roadside ditch. I stayed inside but Rex was thrown out. I found him squirming in the dirt 20 yards from where the car had landed. He was delirious — cheering on a football game — and blood was seeping from his head in several places. We were way out in the country, and the only visible structure was a farmhouse about a quarter-mile away. The farmer's wife gave me a flannel to wipe my face while she called an ambulance.

I was unhurt, apart from a lot of aches next day, but pretty well every bone in Rex's face was shattered. He was in hospital for weeks. Even when he came out, his head was locked in a metal cage to keep it in place. His face was so altered that old school friends didn't recognise him.

That was the bad news.

The good news was that Rex's new face looked pretty handsome, and he was chosen to read the news on NWS 9, Adelaide's first television station, which Rupert launched in 1959. Three or four times each night, for 60 seconds, he would read the *Minute News* — right through prime time on the station almost everyone in the state of South Australia was watching.

Rex became famous, which meant that going to parties with him was complete misery. It also made him very confident with girls. In the ship, only South Australians recognised him, but he had started behaving like a television personality by then, and it was useless to compete.

At sea with Rex, there were gratifying moments when even the best of the women-catching men knew they were beaten. The ship's officers changed the game whenever they marched into a room, braid shimmering on the epaulettes of their starched-white uniforms. When the ship's surgeon showed up, shoulders bright with gold and crimson, everyone backed away as if a twelve-point stag had arrived in the glen. Even Rex was in awe; whenever the surgeon walked into the dining room — tall, blond, and glamorous — Rex would stand to attention, salute, and shout, 'I honour you', and the surgeon would look mystified.

Four weeks is a long time to be sealed off in a cruising village. It leaves a lot of time for romance to bloom and then go wrong. There were break-ups and jealousies and mild scuffling. But everything had a limited sense of consequence simply because we all knew it could not last. The days cooled, Tilbury was getting closer, and when we arrived our perishable world would vanish like a midnight coach.

The sky was the colour of concrete at the Tilbury dock, and the cold wind forced a thick drizzle into our faces. The puddles on the uneven dockside soaked through my white canvas shoes. England felt wintry, even in June, after sailing through the baking Red Sea.

We could see Mike Quirk, our Adelaide friend, among the welcoming crowd, jumping and waving. He was wearing a black polo-neck sweater underneath a brown corduroy jacket, and boots with long, pointed toes. We admired his London modishness.

Our first stop was a pub, the first English pub I ever set foot in. It was a heart-sinking moment.

'A lager, please.'

'A what?'

'A lager. Really cold.'

'We've got bitter. You can have a pint or a half. But it's not very cold, mate.'

These were the first two unpleasant surprises awaiting all Australians: rain and warm beer. In the 1960s, cold beer was overwhelmingly the favoured drink in Australia. It represented three-quarters of the country's alcohol consumption. In British pubs, the only beer on tap was room temperature. In bottles, the most popular was something called Watney's Pale Ale. It had a medicinal taste, but Brits seemed to love it. The closest to home for a beer-loving Aussie was a Carlsberg, a Danish invasion that was kept on a 'cold shelf' that managed to chill slightly the bottom quarter of the bottle.

But London was a dream of familiar sights, most of which I had never seen. The wandering old River Thames, St Paul's Cathedral, Westminster Abbey, Horatio Nelson glowering from his mighty granite column; the grey importance of Whitehall sweeping towards the Gothic Revival limestone of Big Ben and the Palace of Westminster; the Mall, wide, red, and flag-lined, heading long and straight to Buckingham Palace; the diesel grumble of black cabs; the high, narrow red buses. I was in a film set.

Much of central London was a sprawling memorial to its triumphs and pride. A country had to have felt good about itself once to celebrate its success in such a glorious, permanent way.

But in 1965 the people living amid these everlasting monuments were going through a historic update. A new generation, conceived in the relief of peace, was through adolescence and into adulthood and the world was tilting towards them. They liked different music and clothes, but above all they were gripped by a dawning sense of possibility and iconoclasm that reached deep into the country's working-class.

The sclerotic class system I had seen as an Army sergeant's son was not looking so invincible. The Prime Minister, Harold Wilson, had a rich Yorkshire accent, even if he did amplify it in public; bright new playwrights such as Arnold Wesker and Harold Pinter, were East End boys; film stars and high-profile photographers like Albert Finney, Michael Caine, and David Bailey were the sons of bookies, porters, and tailors. Jean Shrimpton, a former typist, was the world's most famous model, and Sandie Shaw had quit her job in the Ford factory at Dagenham to reach number one in the hit parade. A new kind of self-esteem was rising, it was said, to replace the lost grandeur of empire.

It was more than their music that made The Beatles a triumph. They were class liberators, too. As a Liverpool boy in Adelaide, I watched these rough-tongued Scouse lads on television acting cheeky and confident with the Royal Family. No one had done it until them, and they talked just like me.

Time magazine, in the days when it had a serious influence, would soon make Londoners even more pleased with themselves by coining a description that would stick for years — Swinging London. 'In a once sedate world of faded splendor, everything new, uninhibited and kinky is blooming,' it said. 'London is switched on. Ancient elegance and new opulence are all tangled up in a dazzling blur ...' The Rolling Stones, it ruled, were 'a new breed of royalty'.

It turned out that this era was not so much bringing down elitism as redefining it. We re-distributed our wealth upwards to rising musicians, shilling by shilling, and forgave them when they left their tenements and pebbledash semis and disappeared into Surrey mansions in the back seats of psychedelic Rolls-Royces, raising their own dynasties and sending their children to private schools where they grew up without provincial accents and led pro-hunting protests. We forgave them because, while our money made them rich, their music made us happy. It was a trade we understood, just as we accept the wealth of modern footballers — we can see what we have paid for with our satellite subscription and season ticket.

Socialism was on the march in the 1960s, and capitalism was on the defensive, but few complained about the wealth of our new working-class heroes. For us, the sinners were complicated corporations and banks, and tycoons whose abstract fortunes we couldn't understand.

Although our heroes may have joined the upper crust we had loved to see them mock, because of them it never seemed so inaccessible again.

You could see in the streets, in the fashions, how old traditions were crumbling — miniskirts and bright colours confronting staid bowler hats and striped pants. There has been a clear victor: 50 years later, skirts are still short, and the bowler hat extinct.

I had seen a little of London as a child. We had passed through after disembarking from troop ships at Southampton, but we always headed straight to Euston station for the connecting train to

Liverpool. We might have waited hours to catch the Liverpool train, but Mum thought we were safer waiting on the hard seats at Euston, and that is always what we did.

Australians in London carved out their own ghettos and dominated certain pubs. Before high commissions and embassies became fortresses against terrorism, the vast ground-floor of Australia House in Aldwych was open to anyone, and was a hangout for young visitors. Scores of newspapers from home were kept on file. The streets outside were a marketplace where young Australians back from a European tour would park their camper vans with 'For Sale' signs in the window, ready for new arrivals to make the trip — sleeping bags and Primus stoves included. Parking rules were more relaxed then.

The Surrey, a pub down the hill towards the river, was an Australian-occupied zone. So was Earl's Court, then a cheap and rowdy world of shabby bedsits with perhaps London's highest ratio of gas rings per head of population. So many Australians arrived there in the 1960s it was nicknamed 'Kangaroo Valley'. There were no livelier pubs or noisier neighbours. Rising property prices would later civilise Earl's Court, and make it duller, as the Australians scattered.

Rex and I stayed with Mike Quirk and a group of other Australians and Canadians. The tough street in Willesden where they lived was badly lit, and the flat itself had only a one-bar electric fire in the tiny living room. There was a sofa and a chair. We slept on the sloping floor. The tiny kitchen's tabletop was an old door resting on a bathtub. There was no running hot water.

But here I was in the big city, excited and broke apart from the sacrosanct return fare in the bank back in Adelaide, and £50 cash. I needed a job.

I first set foot in Fleet Street when Rex and I went job hunting without appointments. We were getting desperate for work, and thought it was a bold, Australian thing to do — I wasn't really Australian, but my British passport certified me as an 'Australian Resident'. We walked up the dusty stairway circling the brass cage of an elevator shaft in 10 Bouverie Street, just off Fleet Street, across from the *News of the World*, the newspaper Mum caught me reading when I was five years old.

All along one side of the street, tightly parked lorries were piled with huge reels of newsprint. The reels were being slung with thick rope and lifted by cranes off the lorries and into a building. People walked nonchalantly along the pavement beneath their crushing weight.

No one was expecting us at the office of British United Press. It was the British wing of United Press International, the US news agency that had employed famous journalists such as Walter Cronkite, Harrison Salisbury, and Martha Gellhorn. On the third floor, we stood at a high wooden counter, and banged on a rusty desk bell. Rex and I wore suits and ties; our jackets buttoned very high, our ties very thin, according to the fashion of the day. Behind the counter were a horseshoe of desks and a battery of black teleprinters. It was a small room and the teleprinters filled it with their rattling and ringing. No one sitting at the desks heard us until we began shouting.

A tall man in a white shirt with pencils in the breast pocket came towards us. He was slim apart from the belly pressing against his belt. His hair was combed close to his head on each side of a dead straight parting. It was shiny and pure black, but he was not young.

'We are journalists from Adelaide in South Australia looking for work,' Rex said.

Frank H. Fisher, the editor of British United Press, looked at us in fierce silence. I felt an urge to flee, but Rex was closer to the exit and in my way. He was also less timid.

'Even a few shifts would be good,' he said.

'Where are your CVs?'

Fisher took them and read quickly, for less than a minute.

'Come back at ten tomorrow morning and we can talk,' he said.

We left feeling exhilarated and brave, and went across the street to The Tipperary pub to settle our nerves and drink alongside actual Fleet Street journalists.

Next day, Frank Fisher gave us each a handful of cables from UPI correspondents. 'Choose two stories from them and edit them for transmission,' he said. 'No more than five hundred words a story. You've got an hour.'

This is when I discovered 'cable-ese' — a long-dead prose form dating to the days when distant correspondents filed stories by telegram. Every word in a cable cost money, and cable-ese is a compressed, money-saving dialect. Instead of writing 'does not know', a cable would say 'unknows'. If something was not wanted, it was 'unwanted'. If a correspondent was heading to Saigon, he was 'Saigonwards'. If there were no news on American casualties in a particular conflict, but the correspondent would send a story as soon as possible, his cable would say — 'unnews khe sanh casualties will file soonest'.

This lost language created memorable lines. A UPI correspondent, quitting in frustration, wired his office: 'upstick job asswards'. Evelyn Waugh, when he was a journalist, was cabled in Ethiopia about a nurse said to have died in an Italian air raid: 'require earliest name life story photograph american nurse upblown'. Discovering the story wasn't true, Waugh replied, 'nurse unupblown'. One journalist was fond of signing off memos sardonically, 'ellenkay' — love and kisses.

These cables were sometimes riddles. Acronyms saved words, and politicians would often be referred to by job title only.

Fisher had told us not to refer to the clippings library for information — this was to be a test of how we wrote and how much we knew. The first cable I looked at said: 'exlagos stop pm nairobiwards prooau talks president'. I had to make a coherent intro from these words. My throat dried.

exlagos — Fine, the capital of Nigeria. That's the dateline.

PM — Prime minister, obviously.

nairobiwards — He's heading to the capital of Kenya.

prooau talks — He was going for talks about the OAU. That, I was pretty sure, was the Organisation of African Unity.

president — Kenya's president was Jomo Kenyatta.

All good, except who was the prime minister of Nigeria? I had no idea, so I skipped to another story. I passed my test, and in June 1965 became a desk editor at British United Press. I also discovered, and never forgot, the lyrical name of the Nigerian prime minister at the time: Sir Abubakar Tafawa Balewa.

Within a few weeks, I learned other new and exotic names: Kenneth Kaunda, Julius Nyerere, Mobutu Sese Seko, Jean-Bédel Bokassa, Moïse Tshombe, Souvanna Phouma, Hastings Banda. I discovered countries and tyrannies I had never heard of — places boiling with revolution, civil war, martial law, insurgencies, or riven with apartheid. The main thing I learned was how little I knew.

The important break for me was that British United Press was tiny and strapped for cash. Within two months, at the age of 21, having just discovered a country called Upper Volta, I was in total charge for 10 hours a day of the BUP news feed to national and provincial newspapers all over the country. I'm not sure paying customers were well served by my good fortune, but it was great for me.

I worked from 10pm to 8am four days a week, including weekends. While I was wrestling with a long read on the Mekong

Delta, my happy Aussie friends would phone me with drunken accounts of their Earl's Court parties. But midnight in London was late afternoon in California, and the day was just beginning across Asia. In Vietnam, where American escalation had begun after the 1964 Gulf of Tonkin Resolution, terrible events were unfolding. While the rest of Britain slept or caroused, I was happily lost down a black hole of lonely nights and no social life, learning about the world, buried in a mountain of foreign cables, and guided by the big atlas I kept hidden in a drawer until I was alone.

Working in a small office is the best thing a young journalist can do; it forces you to learn at the deep end. This did not mean I was unsupervised. The ever-looming Fisher marked my overnight work — literally. His first daily task was to sit with the overnight file and read it, page-by-page, armed with a thick pencil and a constant frown. Fisher was looking for factual mistakes and clumsy sentences, but his fetish was the purging of all American terms before copy went on the British wire. This was a challenge, since all but a few correspondents were Americans writing for their home audience. Fisher was bad company when he was displeased, and nothing angered him more than Americanisms. No one seems sure who first said that the Americans and British were two peoples divided by a common language, but it could easily have been Fisher.

He gave a loud grunt at every mistake, pressing a heavy black circle around it with his pencil. Sometimes he would type a stern note, put a copy on every desk, and pin the original to the notice board.

Some translations were easy. 'Fanny' refers to the human backside in America, but definitely does not in Britain. We knew that *labor* needed a *u* and that *center* should be *centre*, and *defense defence*. But others were subtler, and a small misunderstanding could lead to a big mistake. When American negotiators want to *table* an issue, they mean put it aside. When the British say it, they mean they want to discuss it, often urgently.

There were dozens of other traps: it was *lorry* in Britain — not *truck*; *tin* — not *can*; *pram* — not *baby carriage*; *hotel porter* — not *bellhop*; *burgled* — not *burglarized*; *cheque* — not *check*; *lift* — not *elevator*; *rubbish* — not *garbage* or *trash*; *spring onion* — not *scallion*; *launderette* — not *laundromat*; *maths* — not *math*; *city centre* — not *downtown*; *anti-clockwise* — not *counterclockwise*.

This crash course in language and world affairs proved a great education, but did not pay well. Fisher was a good teacher, but he was also cheap, with a tight budget to manage. His first pay offer before I joined didn't even cover my share of the rent for the bedsit in Swiss Cottage that Rex and I had found. When he told me to take it or leave it, I told him I couldn't afford to work for him, that I was a member of the National Union of Journalists, and his offer was lower than the union minimum. I accepted his increased offer, although it was still beneath the NUJ minimum. Fisher told me the minimum only applied to national newspaper journalists who had reached the grand old age of 24.

After a while, when I was more confident and learning fewer new things, the BUP job began to feel like solitary confinement. I was reading and writing about the world's turmoil, while sealed away from it in my ticker-tape tomb, released each morning to head home to bed, against the rush-hour tide.

The excitements of London were taking place in my absence. After almost a year of lonely learning, I began writing to national newspapers. I wrote to dailies and Sundays, tabloids and broadsheets, and papered the wall next to my bed with their curt rejections. At first, I pinned them up in defiance, but took them down when there were so many they became discouraging.

I got a couple of interviews. John Grant, the brusque Home

Editor of *The Times*, spent 30 minutes with me, and Jack Crawley at the *Daily Mail*, who liked to conduct his job interviews over drinks, took me upstairs at The Harrow in Whitefriars Street. I was told it was traditional for the interviewee to buy Crawley his drinks. Both told me I was too young and inexperienced, and needed to learn the ropes at a local paper somewhere in Britain before attempting the London big time. They refused to count *The News* in Adelaide.

I wrote my final letter to the runt of Fleet Street, a broadsheet with dwindling sales and a doubtful future. It was called *The Sun*. The paper was bottom of my list, and I lied in my application letter and said I was 24 instead of 22. This was a great age, I decided, and quite old enough for a job in Fleet Street. It would also qualify me for the NUJ minimum wage.

Within a week Barrie Harding, news editor of *The Sun*, had invited me to an interview.

CHAPTER 10

Hired. Fired. Hired

The Sun had its offices in Covent Garden long before it became fashionably famous for its restaurants and boutique stores. For 300 years it had been London's wholesale garden market. Covent Garden smelt country fresh early in the day, but later, on a hot afternoon, it was pungent with rotting fruit and vegetables littering its lanes.

Covent Garden overlapped with London's theatre district. The Royal Opera House was at its heart, and Drury Lane along its edge. It was a nocturnal world, an all-night intersection of bohemian theatre people, flat-capped garden porters, and lingering newspaper workers. This odd mix crowded into the all-night cafes, and pubs opened at 5am when most of the garden workers finished their shifts.

When I arrived one mid-morning in July 1966 for my meeting with Barrie Harding, the working day was winding down. The fruit and vegetable stalls were mostly empty. Lorries had driven off with their purchases to distribute them among shops and supermarkets, and the flower ladies were making their late daily visits in search of bargains to take back to their street stands.

Barrie Harding was blond and softly plump, and he laughed in explosive and disconcerting bursts. I told him about my work at *The News* in Adelaide.

'Ha,' he laughed. 'I don't know much about Australian newspapers.'

I told him of my experience at BUP.

'Ha. Working at an agency is very different to newspapers.'

I could tell my interview was not progressing well, but then he surprised me.

'We have a vacancy for a holiday relief reporter. It will last for six months or so. I can't guarantee anything full time, but you will have to leave your BUP job.'

'That will be absolutely no problem,' I said calmly. On the street outside, I jumped in the air, and the fruit and veg men looked at me oddly. I had a job on Fleet Street.

The Sun then was an unglamorous poor cousin of the mighty *Daily Mirror*. It struggled with a sale below 1 million while the *Mirror*, with sales above 5 million, was the country's biggest daily. *The Sun* was an experiment by the *Mirror*'s owners, the International Publishing Corporation, to produce a modern newspaper for Britain's growing middle-class. It was born out of the *Daily Herald*, a paper with its roots in the trade union movement. In the 1930s it became the country's biggest daily, but its circulation was eaten away by the intense post-war competition. The plan was to make *The Sun* subtly upscale, and it was given a dry-witted, whimsical style. This approach succeeded in setting *The Sun* apart from other newspapers; the trouble was it also set it apart from readers.

The Sun was the most intense place I had worked. Everyone was so sure of themselves, so competitive and combative, and so impatient, that I longed for the quiet, sealed loneliness of BUP. Most of the editorial staff worked in the so-called Big Room. At one end, the sub-editors sat bowed and silent, wielding their pens. At our end, it was raucous. Reporters sat in rows of dark metal desks. The old hands were expansive and noisy, and relaxed in an exaggerated way, putting their feet up on the desks, flicking cigarette ash from their shirts. They debated loudly who had come back from lunch the drunkest, and told one another crude stories and jokes. They went quiet only when cursing the bosses who sat across the room.

Few of the heavy black telephones had dials, and there weren't enough typewriters for everyone, or even desks. We were hot-desking before anyone had thought of the term. This created a pecking order. If Sid Williams, the chief reporter, needed the typewriter I was using, he would snatch it mid-sentence from my desk. 'Sorry, old boy, I have work to do.'

Reporters congregated in two places during working hours: in the newsroom, or across the street in the Cross Keys. It was debatable where we spent more time. The Keys was a tiny pub, whose narrow front was a thicket of flowers and shrubbery with granite columns beneath two winged and naked cherubs holding huge, crossed keys. This was a version of the papal seal displaying the keys of heaven; certainly arrivals looked happy as they walked through its gates.

Every day, from 1pm until closing time at 3pm — or a bit longer if Ann, the landlady, was in a good mood — we crowded into the Cross Keys. We might have received our assignments before lunch, but unless they required us to leave the neighbourhood, everyone walked over to the Keys. At 3.30pm we would be back at our desks to make a few more phone calls. When the pub reopened at 5.30pm there was time for a quick pint, then back to the office to file by 7pm or so.

There were a lot of drunks among us, and a few geniuses. Sometimes both qualities were present in one person. The film critic Ann Pacey, wild and profane in the pub, would return to the office after lunch to write flawless pieces on the morning screening she had seen. Jon Akass was my hard-living hero, a debauched Ben Franklin, with long, shaggy hair receding at the front. I wanted to be him right down to the drinker's paunch.

Akass travelled the world, drinking and smoking, and producing colourfully descriptive copy from US presidential elections, African wars, and Iron Curtain countries. Akass was candid when drunk; his career faltered, but recovered, when he called the editor a 'swivel-headed cunt'. He found writing a torture; on bad days, he would fill a room with cigarette smoke and empty a half-bottle of Scotch. This didn't make him unique. Harry Arnold was short and slight, and baffled everyone with his capacity for accommodating beer.

Akass and Arnold were at the two ends of the spectrum of newspaper writers. Akass was a 'creative', and studied in his shambly untidiness. Arnold was a straight newsman, presenting powerful stories in brisk, unadorned prose. Regular reporters were required to wear suits and ties, and Arnold bought his suits from Savile Row. He was fastidious about his appearance, and it was a bad day for him when he arrived at work with his usual shining shoes — one, however, being black, and the other brown. He dealt well with his embarrassment, announcing: 'I have another pair at home exactly the same.'

Arnold was peerless at writing hard news and fiction. The fiction was confined to his dazzling expense claims, which possibly explained his Savile Row suits. Expenses were a grey area then. The first stern words I received at *The Sun* were in a lecture from the newsdesk on the importance of claiming expenses every week: 'At least ten quid, more if you actually spend anything.' This was a tax-free tenner on top of my weekly salary of £26 10s, making me rich.

The Sun was struggling, and its offices were shabby, but there was no sign of austerity when it came to the number of staff. Each reporter would get one, maybe two, stories a day. There were teams of industrial reporters, diplomatic reporters, theatre critics, science writers, correspondents dotted round the world, and feature writers happy to get a piece in every month. The full-time motoring editor didn't get much in the paper, but took us for a spin round the pubs whenever a new Rolls-Royce or Austin Princess came on the market.

A regiment of assistant editors wandered the Big Room with no clear duties. One was Ted Castle, husband of the cabinet minister Barbara Castle, who struck some of us as commissar at a union newspaper still loyal to its roots. Joe Haines, one of our political correspondents, whose grand by-line was 'J. T. W. Haines', would go on to work for Harold Wilson in Downing Street.

A large staff meant competition for good stories was intense, and I started at the bottom. My jobs were modest, and when a big story broke I was usually on the sidelines. In October 1966, 116 children and 28 adults were killed when a slagheap, loosened by rain, buried a school in the Welsh mining village of Aberfan. It was a massive tragedy, but my contribution to the next day's newspaper was a three-paragraph weather piece.

I was often landed with the lonely night shift, manning the newsdesk in case of a big breaking story. I spent much of the time answering crank calls. One man called twice a week to tell me he was Elvis Presley, and sang 'Love Me Tender' to prove it. His voice was quite good, but the Newcastle accent raised suspicions.

My stories appeared far from the front page: a too-noisy toy drill taken off the market; Lord Snowdon, the Queen's brother-in-law, gets a 'slight electric shock' using welding equipment on a factory visit; 'girl' flight attendants warned: Don't drink the leftovers.

My first by-line, with my name credited in print, was on a story about a new issue of postage stamps celebrating technology. Images included a hovercraft, a nuclear power station, and an E-Type Jaguar. It was a dull story, but that 'by Leslie Hinton' pleased me. It always had to be Leslie: 'It must be your full name — always beware the diminutive,' editors told me.

The news agency prose I had used at BUP, which might have worked in a heavy broadsheet, was too cold and clunky for a popular. 'Give it a bit of zip, mate, this isn't *The Daily Telegraph*,' I was told.

I knew I was not an instant hit in a place crowded with talent, and I remembered Barrie Harding's warning: no guarantee of a permanent job.

There must have been a shortage of staff the day I was sent to report on an address Prince Philip was making to 500 British exporters. I was sent late, and when I arrived the prince was already speaking.

Fleet Street reporters operated under a code of guarded cooperation. The competition was cutthroat, but there were circumstances in which they helped each other. If a rival reporter arrived late, it was common for his friend from another paper to tell him what he had missed. I was not aware of this custom, nor did I know anyone at the event. My tame story revealed the prince's desire to eliminate Britain's trade gap and appeared beneath a bland headline, 'The Merchant Prince'.

It's bad enough when a single newspaper scoops the rest of Fleet Street on a story that is your responsibility, but at least you share the pain. It is a lonely terror when you miss a story every other newspaper plays big.

What I'd missed was the prince delivering a fierce attack on his audience. He had protested about late deliveries, poor after-sales service, and constant strikes. 'I am sick and tired of making excuses for this country,' he said. 'We are all in this unpleasant soup together.'

It was huge in all our rivals. The *Daily Mirror*'s headline was, 'The Angry Duke Lashes Out'; the *Daily Express*, 'I'm Sick And Tired Of Making Excuses For Britain'. *The Times* reported angry political reaction on its front page, and ran the entire speech inside.

The prince had placed his royal boots squarely on the forbidden parade ground of politics. It was explosive stuff, and my story had contained none of it.

It was an unhappy trip to the office that Friday morning. As soon as I arrived, I was ordered to the office of Tony Boram. I had never met Boram, a senior editor of more power and importance than Barrie Harding.

A bright lamp lit up the surface of Boram's desk. His spectacles were thick and he peered at me with an apologetic expression. 'I have to tell you, we will not be able to offer you a full-time job,' he said. 'We will keep you on for the time being, but you should begin looking elsewhere.'

I found a desk outside and sat in silence. No one spoke to me. I was sure they knew what had happened. I had capped five months of average work with a serious mistake. Had I done a decent job before my Prince Philip moment, I might have survived, but I had brought disaster on myself by being too tentative. I had felt unsure, out of my depth, and it left me paralysed.

But getting sacked was like shock therapy for me. The moment I knew nothing worse could happen to me at *The Sun* newspaper, my head cleared. I became brave. Over the next few, carefree weeks, I produced four front-page stories. One was the front-page lead. I started to get better assignments, all while waiting for the promised axe to descend. Seven months later, I was still collecting a salary and claiming each week my minimum £10 expenses. By then, I decided they had forgotten to fire me.

I wrote a story about an ingenious food company boss, Freddie Fox, from St Albans, who sold 200 cases of English spaghetti to an Italian supermarket chain. His back-to-front trade of the national dish stirred indignation in the Italian media. It was a short piece, fun to write, and the newsdesk people laughed out loud when reading it. It appeared as a single column on the front page.

This happened at exactly the right time. It was August, the main holiday month. I was one of the few people in the office and the heavyweight reporters were away. Bill MacLelland, the deputy news editor, had laughed loudest at my spaghetti story. He came over and sat in the chair next to mine with a smile still on his face. His eyes were red and half-closed. MacLelland was always mildly drunk.

'We need to send someone to the Scilly Isles for a week,' he told me. 'You can leave in the morning.'

I had never been on an out-of-towner before. I had never been valued highly enough for a newspaper to actually pay to fly me anywhere, or put me up in a hotel. But now I was heading for the Isles of Scilly, an archipelago reaching into the Atlantic Ocean off the southwest tip of the English mainland. It was a quiet place, and its economy depended on a gentle climate that appealed to tourists, and early spring flowers it sold to chillier parts of the country.

That summer, the Queen and her family were arriving on the Royal Yacht Britannia. It was the first visit by a monarch since the turn of the twentieth century. At the same time, Harold Wilson, the determinedly understated prime minister, was spending his summer holidays in a modest local bungalow he owned. On top of this, wreckage had been discovered of a British fleet that had run aground in 1797, killing almost two thousand people. Dozens of treasure hunters were on the scene.

August is always a month for light news. Parliament isn't sitting, courts are out of session, and big business on holiday, so less serious news fills the vacuum. In Fleet Street, August is known as the Silly Season, and there I was in the Isles of Scilly with my own private harvest of stories. I wrote of treasure hunters staring coldly at each other over the bounty of an ancient wreck; manhole covers painted green to match the grass on a new housing estate the Queen would visit — the joke is the Queen thinks the whole world smells of fresh paint — and of the Royal Family's arrival after sailing through rough waters. I filed stories about Prince Andrew being too seasick to come ashore, and how pale the Queen looked. I wrote about the prime minister draping his bungalow with a giant flag of the Union, and the Queen meeting his dog, Paddy, while royal security officers ordered pleasure boats to stay ashore, and local boatmen planned a loss-of-profit claim against Buckingham Palace.

The newsdesk loved me.

The day I arrived back, I was summoned again to the office of Tony Boram. This time a bright smile came with the poor-sighted peer: 'That was a good trip. We want to give you a full-time job.'

That was how Prince Philip got me fired, the Queen got me hired, and I discovered the fickle ways of Fleet Street.

———

In a dark downstairs bar off London's Park Lane, a small group of journalists listened to a young man singing a love song he had written himself. His name was Steven Georgiou, he was 18 years old, and it was the silliest love song I ever heard.

Georgiou stood in the light of a tiny stage swaying to his own melody as he sang, 'I love my dog as much as I love you/But you may fade, my dog will always come through.' The singer had recently changed his name to Cat Stevens, and his appearance that night was the beginning of his effort to become a star. I did not hold out much hope for him.

'Why did you call yourself Cat and decide to sing about a dog?' I asked.

He looked wounded.

'I called myself Cat because a girl I know said I looked like one,' he said.

I thought it was a terrible song and a stupid gimmick, so I drank the free champagne and didn't write a word.

The debut of Cat Stevens was the first event I covered as *The Sun's* new show business reporter.

Frank Fisher had been right, when trying to talk me out of leaving BUP, to warn me that the job of a national newspaper reporter was not all serious work. *The Sun* might have been staid compared to the redtop tabloid it would soon become, but it nevertheless demanded entertaining news, just as Arthur Christiansen of the *Express* had said: 'The reader requires cakes and ale as well as bread and butter.'

As the newest staff reporter, I spent a lot of time providing the cake and ale. Were UFOs visiting the West Country, or was it just Venus 'cruising' through the sky thanks to the optical illusion of fast-moving clouds? Was that a puma stalking the Surrey countryside, or an overweight tabby cat? When hippy squatters clashed with Covent Garden locals, my story was about the flower people versus the fruit and veg men.

My personal favourite was the story of the Reverend Hunter A. Tomlinson, an American who had arrived from New York saying he was king of the world. This might have been a false claim, but Tomlinson had once run for the US presidency, pledging to establish a cabinet post of secretary of righteousness; he deserved some attention. After failing to win the presidency, Tomlinson was now travelling the world with an aluminium throne. This throne was apparently a temporary one; later in the month, he was going to set his permanent throne on Mount Zion, shortly after his planned visit to West Germany. 'I am going to will away the Berlin Wall,' he told me.

There was also the quiet afternoon I was sent to a protest outside the British Board of Film Censors in Soho Square. John Trevelyan, secretary of the board, was the son of a parson, a man in his sixties with gentle manners and shocking black eyebrows. Trevelyan was wrestling with rapid changes in public taste and new levels of acceptability, and was gaining respect for his efforts. But Trevelyan had limits, and the protesters at his door had reached them.

Fewer than a dozen people were walking in a circle under the gaze of a single glum policeman as Trevelyan stood at his office window looking down on them, and shaking his head.

'It's a film showing nothing but close-ups of bottoms, human backsides in the act of walking on a treadmill,' he told me. 'The real problem is that every now and then, between the moving legs, there is a clear glimpse of male genitalia. I cannot possibly allow it to be released.'

There was a bunch of daffodils on Trevelyan's desk. 'They were sent up to me by the young lady who organised the protest. She's Japanese.'

The protest leader was short, with long black hair and a serious face. She was offering a daffodil to a smartly dressed passer-by when I introduced myself. The man was studying a large sign covered with photographs of bottoms and the question: 'What is wrong with these pictures?' He adjusted his bowler hat and walked on frowning, a daffodil in one hand, and his umbrella in the other.

The protest leader was Yoko Ono. She told me she was 25 years old and a 'performance artist'. I had never heard of a performance artist, so my story called her an actress. It turned out she was really 34 and had met John Lennon at an art exhibition the year before. Her husband at the time, a New York film producer called Anthony Cox, accompanied her at the protest, and seemed unaware of his wife's new friendship.

'The bottom is beautiful. It has great expression,' Yoko Ono said, in a helium-tone voice. 'It should not be less exposed than any other part of the body.'

Her art would become famous everywhere in the near future, and my story might have been the first written about it. I kept the clipping of this story, and its headline expresses perfectly the difference between the two *Suns*. The tabloid that became a runaway hit would have run something like: 'What A Cheek! Censor Smacks Bare Bum Protesters'. But its sedate predecessor ran the following, two decks over five columns: 'An Indignant Protest, So Fragrantly Expressed'.

I don't know why the newsdesk appointed me to the job of full-time show business reporter. I went to the films once or twice a year, watched almost no television, and neither knew nor cared much about music, except for an interest in The Beatles because they were from Liverpool. But I took the job — it was worth £3 more a week — and found myself at the centre of a cultural earthquake, on the edge of the Swinging Sixties, watching 'counterculture' turn mainstream.

Show business reporters floated along on an ocean of entertainment provided by a new breed of power broker: the Public Relations Man. Within days, I had a call from Les Perrin, the most famous PR of the day, the pontiff of showbiz flacks, whose biggest clients were the Rolling Stones. 'Come to lunch. I'll book a table at the Cafe Royal,' he said.

The Cafe Royal was a mythical place, the height of old London. It would soon fade away with the changing times, but then the Cafe Royal was still one of Europe's most glamorous spots. It was a world of silver carving-trolleys, crimson velvet, naked carvings, and mirrored walls that bounced around its rooms the refracting light of huge chandeliers. Oscar Wilde, H. G. Wells, and D. H. Lawrence had once eaten here. Elizabeth Taylor, Richard Burton, Brigitte Bardot, and Laurence Olivier were now clients. It was a seductive place to take someone whose most frequent dining-out experience was the cafe at Euston Station.

Les Perrin and his rivals jostled for the attention of newspapers.

They needed to reach readers because print was still the medium of the masses. Each time a struggling artist such as Cat Stevens came along, we were lured to clubs in Mayfair, with the promise of free alcohol and food. These events — and many others concocted to showcase musicians, actors, films, and plays — went on all day and every day, beginning at 11am. It was the closest I came to living in the 1960s without remembering them. I saw a lot of 'future superstars' who never reached the peaks their managers predicted.

Newspapers were important because television and radio were overwhelmingly state-funded and still waking up to the new world. There was no commercial radio, and the BBC had yet to hand a microphone to an actual 'disc jockey'. That didn't happen until September 1967. Until then, most pop music came from illegal pirate-radio stations on ships in the North Sea.

Public Relations Men had another job. While they were promoting newcomers, they were also protecting established stars. They gave us champagne, but they also lied and deceived when they wanted to prevent awkward news from leaking. The tricks of PR people became an occupational hazard, but they were new to me then.

To most superstars, we were beneath them. No one was more charmless than Frank Sinatra. He arrived once to rehearse at the Royal Albert Hall, and a reporter friend tried hard for a quote, 'You're my hero, I have bought all your records, and seen you live three times. Will you answer a few questions?' he begged.

Sinatra glanced over his shoulder at his admirer, without adjusting his stride. 'Fuck off,' he said.

When The Beatles formed their own company and called it Apple Corps, I spent hours standing outside their headquarters at 3 Savile Row being ignored.

I went to Paul McCartney's house in St John's Wood in March 1969 because he was expected to marry Linda Eastman, a photographer from New York. McCartney wouldn't tell me anything. He bounded towards me from his front door and aimed a mighty swing at my stomach. I braced for the pain and imagined the excellent story that would result from being attacked by a Beatle. But he pulled the punch and patted me on the belly. 'Evening. Got nothing to say.' He and Eastman married the next day.

John Lennon could be unkind to reporters. Judith Simons of the *Daily Express* was allegedly one of his favourites, but he could be cruel to people he liked. Judith was a heavy smoker, and when she walked into a press conference he greeted her with: 'Here comes Judy Simons — she doesn't menstruate, she just drops ash.'

At the Isle of Wight pop festival, I walked down the street with Bob Dylan and George Harrison, asking them questions and getting no answers. I sat in a bar next to a gloomy Charlie Watts, and he wouldn't speak to me either, except to say 'No, thanks' when I offered to buy him a drink. A group of musicians calling themselves Fat Mattress were happy to talk; they needed publicity, but it didn't help. They split up soon after.

Performers at the Isle of Wight included Dylan, The Who, Joe Cocker, the Bonzo Dog Doo-Dah Band, The Moody Blues, Tom Paxton, and Richie Havens. In the audience were John Lennon, Eric Clapton, Ringo Starr, Keith Richards, and, I discovered later, a young musician called Elton John no one had yet heard of. Other stars of the day came to watch, including Liz Taylor and Richard Burton, Roger Vadim, and Françoise Hardy.

It was a special 'counterculture' event because Dylan had been a recluse since a motorbike accident three years before and this was his scheduled resurrection. The mood of homage had faded by the time he arrived on stage three hours late.

No one knew at the time that the Isle of Wight festival would make history. This and Woodstock both happened in the same month, and both turned out to be primitive dress rehearsals for the sophisticated, hyper-produced outdoor festivals that followed.

It was civilised, more or less, and good-natured. I was present for the most unexpected event, a moment that earned more column inches than Dylan's music, and resulted in the unlikeliest interview I ever conducted.

A young couple, embracing the free spirit of the age, had sex in front of a large audience, including me. They did this in a sea of foam provided by the concert organisers as an added attraction. The foam did not provide much camouflage. I have never since stood up to my waist in foam questioning a naked woman about the rights and wrongs of sex in public. Her answers to my questions were not entirely coherent, but revealed no regret. Her name was Vivian, she was 19 and came from 'nowhere'.

I witnessed big show business events from a distance in the 1960s only to put together the pieces years later. In the summer of 1967, I stood on the doorstep of a Georgian house in Belgravia as the body of The Beatles manager Brian Epstein was taken away in a coffin. Epstein was 32. He died of an overdose of sleeping pills at the peak of his most famous clients' fame. It was a tragic story. Years later I told the singer Cilla Black that I had been standing outside Epstein's home that day. I knew John Lennon had persuaded Epstein to become Cilla's agent.

'I was on the other side of that front door the very moment his coffin was taken away,' she said.

The grief, she told me, had been terrible.

'It was so awful. Everyone was crying and crying and crying.'

A few days after Epstein's death, The Beatles held a secret meeting in Ringo Starr's basement flat in Marylebone. Peter Brown, who worked closely with The Beatles and Epstein at the height of Beatlemania, told me about it over a drink — but not until 2010.

Paul McCartney had insisted the group get down to business quickly to plan the future without their manager. It was a difficult meeting; Peter was standing by a window, stunned by the loss of one of his closest friends, when two arms embraced him from behind and a head rested on his back. 'You all right, mate?' asked John Lennon.

I found out about that meeting the same year I sat with Mick Jagger at a dinner party in Manhattan, and he gave me a wonderful quote that was decades too late. We talked about the media and how they treated celebrities. He was remarkably uncomplaining, considering the stories written about him. I told Jagger I'd been amazed at how unconcerned he looked in 1967 when he was sentenced to three months in prison for possessing four unprescribed amphetamine pills. It was a crazy sentence, and Jagger was quickly released, but his treatment became a landmark confrontation between the new age and traditionalists.

At the time, Jagger had found an unexpected ally in *The Times*, whose editor William Rees-Mogg wrote a fierce editorial in his defence: 'Who breaks a butterfly on a wheel?'

Jagger was not so relaxed as he looked, he told me over dinner. 'It was terrible,' he said. 'But that editorial changed everything for me. It saved my career.'

By 1968, it was clear that *The Sun* in its existing form was doomed. Even if I wanted to spend my life trailing fruitlessly after superstars and ruining my liver, *The Sun* was reaching the end of its days.

Not long after deciding the time had come for another change, I was sitting in the newsroom and the foreign editor, John Graham, a big-voiced Ulsterman, looked up from a piece of agency copy and addressed the room.

'Anyone here ever heard of Rupert Murdoch?'

CHAPTER 11

The Dirty Digger storms Fleet Street

Until 1968, the name Rupert was associated by much of Britain with a talking bear in a *Daily Express* comic strip. As a child, I hated comics featuring anthropomorphic characters, and Rupert to me became a weird and unlikeable name. Rupert Bear was a mild, eager-to-please fellow, nothing like the real-life version who was about to descend on Britain. But the bear's friends did appear to foretell some details of the life ahead for his namesake — there was Tigerlily, the mischievous Chinese girl, and the Fox boys, who were always causing trouble.

Rupert Murdoch was a stranger to Fleet Street. When word spread that I knew him, senior editors started paying attention to me. I played up my acquaintance to keep their interest, but he had only addressed me by name once or twice.

When Rupert's father, Sir Keith, died in 1952, a long and admiring obituary in *The Times* — headlined 'Northcliffe of Australia' — merely mentioned that among those surviving him was a son. Sir Keith had built a large Australian newspaper group, but in the complicated unwinding of his interests, Rupert was left to manage only a remnant of it.

It was not until May 1960 that Britain got a sniff of Rupert's ambitions. A seven-line brief in *The Times* — 'Sydney Newspapers Change Hands' — reported that 'Mr K. R. [Rupert] Murdoch ... has entered the daily newspaper field in Sydney by buying a controlling interest' in the city's *Daily Mirror* and *Sunday Mirror*. Newspaper accounts of Rupert would become less benign over the years.

Perhaps the first recorded British insult thrown at him was in January 1969 after he outwitted Robert Maxwell, the millionaire Labour MP, in a bitter battle to gain control of the *News of the World*. 'Mr Maxwell called me a moth-eaten kangaroo,' Rupert said at the time, with the wide, gap-toothed grin we all knew when he was young, before the cosmetic dentistry.

The *News of the World* was Rupert's first foothold in Britain. The Carr family had controlled it since 1891, but the chairman in the 1960s, Sir William Carr, did not have a reputation as an attentive manager. The family owned a third of the shares and lived well off the proceeds of a flourishing newspaper.

For a while, Carr was an admirer of Rupert. He saw him as the white knight to keep Robert Maxwell at bay. Maxwell's dodgy business practices were attracting attention even then, 22 years before he pillaged the pension fund of the Mirror Group and toppled mysteriously off his yacht into the Atlantic Ocean.

In persuading *News of the World* shareholders to support Rupert's bid, Carr talked warmly of his new Australian friend: 'You'll not only like him, but he'll prove to you he has much to offer us.' When the deal was done, Carr remained chairman of the company, and Rupert became managing director. He immediately swept through the company, driving for change. Within six months, Carr had resigned and Rupert was in the chair. He was 38.

Rupert moved into his London headquarters at the *News of the World* offices in Bouverie Street. With a printing plant in the heart of London that operated only one day a week, he was now sitting on a valuable, under-used asset. He started looking for another newspaper. A mile away in Covent Garden, a daily was dying.

The experiment to position *The Sun* as a broadsheet for the up-and-coming 'middle-class' had failed. It was selling around 800,000 and sinking fast. Its owners, the International Publishing Corporation, had decided they were fighting a lost cause. The company chairman was the legendary tabloid editor, Hugh Cudlipp, whose books I had read and re-read as a boy. He agreed to sell *The Sun* to Rupert.

Before the deal was closed, Robert Maxwell emerged again to fight Rupert. He tried wooing journalists from the paper by inviting us for drinks and snacks to hear what a great owner he would be. He didn't make a good impression — we had no control in the matter anyway — and Rupert prevailed once more.

After the sale was complete in November 1969 — Rupert paid £800,000 — Cudlipp was dismissive: 'I wish him well in his bold venture. If he succeeds, as well he may, I will be the first to applaud.' There is no record of Cudlipp's applause nine years later when *The Sun* became Britain's number one newspaper. His beloved *Daily Mirror* was selling around 5 million at the time of the sale, and Cudlipp had thought it invincible.

Rupert adapted quickly to the role of a Fleet Street mogul, cruising London in a chauffeur-driven Rolls-Royce. But he never slipped into some of his competitors' easy-going ways. Not many proprietors could be spotted stalking the streets, rearranging newsstands to give their newspapers the best display.

Murdoch's new edition of *The Sun* copied the *Mirror* unashamedly, right down to adopting the paper's old front-page battle cry to the workers — 'Forward with the People' — and spoofing the great *Mirror* columnist Cassandra by running a daily column that was displayed in exactly the same style and called 'Son of Cassandra'. Its author was Robert Connor, son of the real Cassandra, William Connor.

But no British newspaper had been so graphic, in words or pictures, on the subject of sex. *The Times* gave the new arrival a frowning review in an editorial on 18 November, the day after the tabloid's debut: 'The formula is a simple one ... sex, sport and sensation,' it said.

> This is an old way to create a new newspaper. Sex and sensation ... were a normal plot for Daniel Defoe, the first begetter of almost every striking invention in British journalism. Sport as an aid to circulation came in with the Victorians.
>
> It will be interesting to see whether the new *Sun* is a commercial success. It very well could be. Mr Murdoch has not invented sex but he does show a remarkable enthusiasm for its benefits to circulation, such as a tired old Fleet Street has not seen in recent years.

———

While Rupert was plotting to buy *The Sun* in 1969, I was getting to understand British tabloids. I worked five days a week for the broadsheet version of *The Sun,* but earned extra working Saturday shifts on Sunday newspapers.

My induction into the raw culture of the Fleet Street popular press came on the night of Saturday 9 August 1969, while working a shift on the *News of the World. The News of the World* was a broadsheet then, but had the style of today's redtop tabloids.

Charlie Markus was the squat, bullet-headed news editor. He bellowed a lot, and no one argued with him except, occasionally, his deputy, Robert Warren, whose courtly, soft-spoken manner seemed misplaced in the hectic newsroom.

That night, a two-line news agency snap dropped on Markus' corner desk in the room he shared with his reporters. Sharon Tate, the beautiful 26-year-old wife of the film director Roman Polanski, had been found murdered in her Bel Air home. It was a good story for the newspaper, given added spice by the fact Polanski was famous for dark horror films such as *Rosemary's Baby*.

But as more details emerged, a fever gripped the *News of the World*. Four others had also been killed: two bodies were on the lawn outside; one was in a car; and another in the house. A white nylon rope was tied around Tate's neck, looped over a ceiling beam, and attached to another victim with a hood over his head. Tate had been eight months pregnant. She was wearing a bra and knickers. Her front door was daubed with blood. An American flag was mysteriously draped over a couch in the living room.

Markus was in such a state of excitement I thought he might levitate. For him, this story had it all. Beauty, riches, stardom, Hollywood, and an abundance of hideous detail. All this, before it became known the killers were members of Charles Manson's helter-skelter cult.

If an IBM mainframe computer of the day had been asked to assemble the entire history of homicide and conjure up the ultimate late-breaking story for the *News of the World,* this would have been it. Long-distance calls were made to Los Angeles, appointing every available freelancer to the job. Every known acquaintance of Roman Polanski and his murdered wife — colleagues, neighbours, rivals, old lovers — were sought for comment. Library clippings were scoured for similarities with Polanski's grisly films. I was instructed to prepare a list of the twentieth century's foulest mass murders.

As well as urgency that night, there was a mood of muted appreciation. The *News of the World* wasn't enjoying what had happened; there was no ghoulish delight. With the exception of Markus' near delirium, there was mostly a cold and practical understanding of the task. For their readers, it was a shocking story, and irresistible reading; this was the kind of event they expected their Sunday newspaper to cover in every detail. For journalists doing their jobs, serving their customers, this reduced an awful crime to a commodity, to be packaged and delivered as perfectly as possible.

Saturday shifts on other newspapers gave me first-hand lessons in the differing personalities of Fleet Street, but nothing compared with the atmosphere at the *News of the World* when it was rising to the occasion of a celebrity mass-murder. I did regular work at *The Sunday Telegraph*. No newspaper was less like the *News of the World*, but its reporters were not sombre; they would take me to a pub in Ludgate Circus, where we peered over our pints at women dancing topless.

Editors at the *Telegraph* liked copy to be straight, just as I had written it at British United Press. Stories ran longer, but we were encouraged to keep adjectives to a minimum. We were permitted to write long first paragraphs, with multiple commas, even occasional semicolons — intros that would have guaranteed a blast from Charlie Markus.

Broadsheet sub-editors believed it was their duty only to trim and tidy a reporter's work while inspecting it for errors. Most of the time, original work appeared on the page with few changes. The subs' desks of popular newspapers were mincing machines, and teams of editors would routinely re-write a reporter's copy beyond recognition. It was infuriating how much better it often was when they'd finished.

When Rupert took over *The Sun,* I did not stay. I wanted to take Mary, my new wife, to Australia to meet my family and friends, and to show her the country. I was offered a job or a payoff, and the redundancy was enough for a down payment on a house. I was 24 and Mary 23, and we decided to quit our jobs and wander. I took the money, put it in the bank, and we sailed away.

I met Mary in September 1966, one Saturday night at the flat of an Australian dentist in Earl's Court. I didn't know the dentist and hadn't been invited to the party. A few of us heard about it in a local pub and turned up at the door armed with Party Fours, which were usually enough to gain entry to a regular Australian Earl's Court party. These were four-pint cans of beer that were ubiquitous in the 1960s, but inexplicably went out of fashion sometime in the 1980s.

We went to the party after being thrown out of the pub. I had emptied a pint of beer over the head of an annoying friend, which distressed the landlady.

Mary was standing across from me in a room full of jostling people. I think The Kinks were playing on the stereo. She was with a redhead who was also beautiful. But Mary had a perfect face, with a square Celtic jaw, and gentle eyes. She was wearing a knitted hat.

She said later that the first thing I ever said to her was: 'Your thin and faintly curling lips look most attractive.' I do not actually remember saying this because it had been a long and tiring evening, but it was a good description. I do remember that, in spite of my untidy condition, Mary tolerated my company and before she left agreed to give me her telephone number. I have never forgotten it — 953-6564.

I called her the next day and we agreed to meet at seven o'clock that evening at the Earl's Court tube station. Mary arrived very late — she was never a good timekeeper.

We married on 30 March 1968, a rainy Saturday, in a red-brick Catholic church in Elstree, Hertfordshire, not far from the council house where Mary lived with her mother, Sally, a cleaner, and her younger brother, Danny. Her father, Martin, a merchant seaman, had died of cancer eight years earlier at the age of 52.

There was a patriotic campaign sweeping Britain at the time, intended to raise the country's morale during an economic downturn. People were wearing Union Flag 'I'm Backing Britain' badges, and the *Daily Express* was running the strapline every day on its front page. We found the mood disagreeable — an earlier symptom of the jingoism and lurking xenophobia that contributed to the 2016 Brexit vote — so we staged our own mild protest by spending more than we could afford hiring two Mercedes as our wedding cars.

As a non-Catholic, I was required for several weeks before the ceremony to attend religious instruction meetings with the gaunt and ancient parish priest, Father Murray. We sat in our overcoats in front of an inadequate electric fire while he explained the superiority of the Roman Catholic faith over the Anglican version into which I had been baptised. We failed to agree most of the time, and for our last few evenings together we talked about photography, which was his hobby. He tried to sell me a second-hand camera.

Mum travelled by ship from Adelaide for the wedding. As a Liverpool Protestant, she had not reacted well to the news I was marrying a Catholic of Irish descent. It took a while, but Mary won her over and they became close.

Mary and I sailed to Australia in the autumn of 1969. For the one-way trip to Adelaide I got a job as a 'press liaison officer' on the P&O-Orient liner *SS Oriana*. We received free passage and two first-class cabins, in return for which I had to find interesting stories to offer reporters greeting the ship at every port. It was not hard. I found a flood of human-interest stories by running a competition in the ship's newsletter. Passengers were given free drinks in exchange for stories about their lives and their reasons for going to Australia.

When we arrived in Fremantle in Western Australia, one local television channel ran the first 10 minutes of its nightly news with stories from the ship.

Mary liked Australia, but not its attitude to women. The personnel manager who gave her a job behind the information desk of David Jones department store did so only after she promised not to become pregnant. Mary immediately broke this promise, and enjoyed the angry glares of the personnel manager at the growing evidence of her disobedience.

They welcomed me back when I asked for a job on *The News*. Ron Boland, the editor-in-chief, wanted me on the subs' desk, but I resisted and became a feature writer. The office had been rebuilt. Instead of separate rooms for reporters, subs, sports, and features, we were all in one huge desegregated newsroom.

Five years in Fleet Street had taught me a lot. *The News* was a first-rate local newspaper, better than most of its British counterparts. But for me the place that had been so frantic and intimidating years before now seemed leisurely. Nothing improves a newspaper more than the stress of competition, and in Adelaide there was almost none.

After 10 months living with Mum and Dad in their bungalow, we sailed back to England. We had never intended to stay, and Mary, who was five months pregnant, wanted our baby to be born in Britain. We might not have made the best decision. It was a six-week journey, and by the time we arrived at Southampton docks, I thought Mary might die. She had become ill three days before arriving in Southampton and was losing blood. We were in an Italian Sitmar Liner, and the ship's doctor seemed bewildered by her condition. He sent a radio message to Southampton that an extremely sick mother-to-be was on board and, while I sat at her bedside, spent most of his time playing cards with shipmates.

The doctor who came on board in Southampton wouldn't let

Mary get out of bed. When I asked whether the baby would be all right, the doctor led me out of Mary's room. We sat down together, and she looked at me silently and gravely for a moment.

'Look,' she said, 'this could be very serious. Never mind the baby for now — we need to worry about your wife.'

The doctor had diagnosed a condition called placenta previa, which meant that the placenta nourishing our unborn child was in the wrong place inside Mary's womb, blocking her cervix. As well as being in the wrong location, her placenta had lost blood and might do so again, putting both mother and baby in danger. Mary was wrapped in blankets against the cold and carried by stretcher down the gangplank to a waiting ambulance. She was admitted to the Southampton General Hospital maternity ward, surrounded by newborns and their happy parents. Our child was not due for two months, and the doctors ordered complete bed rest. Southampton was 80 miles from London, but the doctors said even an ambulance ride was too risky.

Life stood still for four days. None of our plans mattered — no new house, no reunions with Mary's family and our old friends, no job. Everything was in limbo and I was a wreck.

'I feel fine,' said Mary. 'I'll lie here because they're telling me to, but honestly I feel normal. You can't just sit there for the next two months. Go to London and find a job.'

I had been in London 48 hours when a doctor called from Southampton. 'How soon can you get to the hospital?' he said. He sounded so anxious, I panicked.

'We need you to pick up your wife as soon as possible,' the doctor said. 'She's well enough to be discharged.'

It turned out the hospital had made a serious mistake. By the time I arrived back in Southampton, she had been moved from the maternity ward to an isolation room. Mary's illness had been misdiagnosed. She was suffering a serious bout of contagious food poisoning — salmonella. This poisoning had been the cause of her bleeding, not placenta previa.

The hospital had put into a maternity ward of vulnerable newborns a woman with a condition that could be fatal to them. For three days, proud mothers had allowed her to hold and admire their new babies. No wonder the doctor who phoned me had sounded desperate.

'They were really alarmed when they found out,' Mary said, as we drove to London. 'They thought I was going to kill them all.'

Mary recovered, and Martin was born on 9 January 1971. I did not see him for several hours; it was not yet customary for a father to be at the birth. When we met, I stroked his cheek with the outside of my left index finger. His skin was as soft as velvet.

———

The Sun was not glad to see me when I arrived in search of a job. Nick Lloyd, the news editor, gave me a few late-night shifts, but that was all. Lloyd was then 29 and starting out on a long newspaper career that would reach its peak with his editorship of the *Daily Express* and a knighthood from Margaret Thatcher when she resigned as prime minister in 1990. Lloyd was then at the height of a distinguished career. His newspaper had been one of Thatcher's most ardent supporters.

'I can't give you a full-time job,' he said. 'Larry doesn't want any more old *Sun* trade union militants. They're causing havoc.'

Larry Lamb, the new editor, was the prickly son of a Yorkshire colliery blacksmith. He had been a veteran of Cudlipp's *Mirror*, but was Manchester editor of the *Daily Mail* when Rupert poached him.

The Sun's trade union roots — dating back to the days when it was the *Daily Herald* — lived on among a significant number of journalists. Disputes with management were constant.

'But I'm not an old trade union militant,' I told Lloyd. 'And I started working for Rupert in Adelaide when I was fifteen.'

Lloyd paused when I told him this. I reinforced my case by sending him a note with details of my association with the new owner. I don't know what happened next, but within a few weeks I was on the staff.

By now, *The Sun*'s circulation was soaring — and Rupert's infamy was growing. In 1969, the *News of the World* published the memoirs of Christine Keeler, a model and 'party girl' whose relationship with John Profumo, the secretary of state for war, had forced his resignation.

As scandals go, the Profumo affair of 1963 had everything. It was a blend of juicy hard facts and wild rumour, with beautiful call girls, country mansion frolics featuring masked aristocrats, royals, and a love triangle that included a Soviet spy. It was the biggest political scandal of the 1960s, and a perfect story for the *News of the World*. The difficulty was that the paper published the Keeler memoir six years after the scandal, by which time Profumo was redeeming himself with charity work in the East End of London.

The newspaper and Rupert were eviscerated for digging up old dirt. There were angry denunciations in the House of Lords and from church pulpits — as well as among the Fleet Street rivals he had beaten to the story, and who were by now worrying that they had underestimated this interloper from Down Under.

Rupert, in an effort to explain himself, made the mistake of appearing on live television. He put his case to David Frost, then Britain's paramount TV interrogator. With a studio audience cheering him on, Frost demolished Rupert, who stormed out of the studio, allegedly hissing at Frost: 'You'll keep, David.'

Rupert said later that when he and his wife, Anna, left in his car that night they felt like heading straight for the airport and leaving town.

That was the early drama that inspired *Private Eye*, the satirical magazine, to award Rupert the immortal name of Dirty Digger.

Everyone knew by now that Rupert had come to Fleet Street to tear up the rules. Criticism never seemed to deter him. Like a punk rocker storming the stage of a Mantovani concert, he showed no respect to anyone.

The Sun that I returned to had joined the world of Murdoch and was a changed place. The easy life had ended. Long lunches and late filing had been abolished, and everyone had more work to do. There were fewer reporters and no longer a large contingent of specialist writers. On the old *Sun,* reporters expected to be assigned a story a day, maybe two, and sometimes none at all, but getting no assignment was a terrible feeling. Even now I get anxiety dreams that I'm sitting in a newsroom waiting to be sent on a job while everyone else is busy. At the new *Sun*, we were each given three or more stories a day.

There was no dallying in the pub over lunchtime pints. If you were given a story in the morning, you needed a good reason for failing to hand it in before lunch. To achieve this, reporters could be seen eating sandwiches at their desk, which was unknown in the old days.

The new newsroom overlooking Bouverie Street was tightly packed and spartan. In the space occupied by reporters, padlocks and chains secured a typewriter to each desk. A thief would have to be strong and poor because the typewriters were heavy and old, and pretty worthless.

I was soon caught up in the militancy that frustrated Larry Lamb. Strikes had become commonplace. We walked out over crazy grievances. Even the National Union of Journalists wouldn't support us most of the time.

We once stopped work when a reporter in the Glasgow office was sacked after he returned drunk from lunch, unzipped his fly, and exposed himself to female staff. This sounded to me solid grounds for dismissal, but we went on strike for almost two weeks. I couldn't pay the mortgage that month. But management refused to reinstate the Glasgow flasher, and we went back to work when they agreed to give him a payoff.

Striking journalists never prevented the newspaper being published. Senior editors could patch a newspaper together with agency copy. These editions weren't much good, but they thwarted the militants. Only print unions had the power to stop the newspaper going out, which made journalists feel like second-class strikers. Sometimes journalists would talk about physically preventing the newspapers from leaving the building. This never worked because it required confronting our brothers in the press hall, and they were tougher than us.

Malcolm Withers was our Father of the Chapel — a quaint old term for union leader — and he once urged us to lay in front of lorries to prevent them leaving Bouverie Street with their cargoes of newspapers. Attempting to lead the way, he sat feebly on the pavement with his feet in front of a lorry, wearing a suit and clutching a briefcase to his chest. Withers was a cautious kind of militant, whose plan fell apart when the lorry moved a couple of inches and he quickly withdrew his feet to let it pass.

Putting aside the mischief of militants, I had sympathy with old *Sun* people who had honest trouble adjusting to the redtop rowdiness. The new *Sun* was rough-edged and proud of itself. A typical self-aggrandising front-page description of itself in huge type was: 'It is the biggest, the brightest, the boldest, the very, very best.'

Television was still seen as the enemy of print, but Rupert became the first proprietor to use it to sell newspapers. These commercials were low-budget and it showed — not many retakes were allowed for a *Sun* spot. The frenetic, shouted voiceovers were like old-style fairground barking.

Their creator was Graham King from Adelaide. King was a 1950s pioneer of the Murdoch empire. He was promotions manager of Rupert's first television station, Channel 9. King was a genius at getting attention. When Rupert wouldn't give him a raise at Channel 9, he delivered socks with holes in them to his office every day, with notes saying he couldn't afford new ones, until Rupert relented.

Intentional or not, King's television ads were hilarious. They were also effective. Here's one about suburban 'swingers':

Scene:
Couple in a passionate kiss.

Voiceover: There's a whole new freedom in sex today ...
behaviour once confined to the free and easy world of the rich
is becoming more commonplace. How far can it go ...? *The Sun*
reveals that ordinary people who meet every day at work, or
even down your street, are taking this new sexual freedom for
themselves.

I helped write that *Sun* series and spent time with these wife-swapping 'swingers'. They didn't seem ordinary to me.

My neighbour in the newsroom was Keith Deves, a veteran of serious news. He had covered trouble spots in the Middle East as a Reuters correspondent; known Kim Philby before he was exposed as a Soviet double agent; and been shot in the leg with a Sten gun during a coup in Baghdad.

On *The Sun*, different work was required. Deves was sent to interview a Miss Whiplash at the house where she entertained clients. As he was leaving, Miss Whiplash stopped him. 'Wait, I've forgotten something,' she said, and opened a cupboard to reveal a naked and agitated old man, gagged and bound. 'Now calm down, judge,' she said. 'I'm only showing this nice man from *The Sun* newspaper around.'

Deves was perturbed. 'Was it really necessary to tell the poor old judge I was a reporter from *The Sun?*' he asked.

'Don't worry,' said Miss Whiplash. 'It's all part of his torture.'

The Sun's wild side gave it much of its commercial success, and the disdain of newspapers whose circulation it was stealing. But it ran many serious stories about politics, economics, industry, health, and crime. It was the combination of these two extremes that made it exceptional and successful.

For me, it meant a lot of weird work, and not what I imagined as a 15-year-old dreaming of life as a foreign correspondent. After a while, the silly-to-serious ratio of my assignments changed for the better, but I covered a lot of strange things.

I had to walk the streets asking bald men to talk about their sex lives. Research, very dubious research, had found that bald men had more sex. I gave up on that job when a huge man in a camel hair coat with a velvet collar chased me across the concourse of Euston station shouting, 'Sex life? I'll give you sex life. Come back here and I'll end yours with a bloody big kick in the balls.'

Other research, this time about people's willingness to accept charity, had me offering strangers £1 notes. This was interesting. Those who looked most hard up were least likely to take the money. The woman in hair rollers pushing a pram through a Brixton council estate looked terrified by the offer, but a man in a bowler hat on the steps of the Bank of England accepted it without hesitation.

A pioneering dating company, Dateline, had the idea of organising a package holiday of single people paired into couples by computers. I flew to Corfu with 60 excited lonely hearts. Whatever success technology has since achieved at playing Cupid, the Corfu experiment was not an encouraging start. This became clear when the 60-year-old widow of a Surrey accountant was introduced to her computer generated 'match' — a junior supermarket manager of 30 who lived with his mother in Bridlington. Their friendship did not blossom. The women were divorcees, widows, and unmarried women looking for fun, but the men were younger, shy and terrified. On the first night, a dozen men organised a chess tournament among themselves, forming a defensive circle in the bar that no woman managed to penetrate. The newsdesk was expecting a story about frolics on a romantic Greek island. My story demanded careful exaggeration to avoid disappointing them.

One story of mine was immortalised in a painting by Beryl Cook, a hugely popular artist whose work the art establishment of the time disdained. Linda Lovelace, the star of the porn film *Deep Throat,* wrote a memoir — *Inside Linda Lovelace* — that was so graphic its publisher was accused of obscenity at the Old Bailey. The jury reached a verdict of not guilty. The newspaper with my by-line — headlined 'Don't Crush "Sex Nut" Linda, A QC Tells Jury' — appeared in Cook's painting in the hands of a man on a crowded London underground train who appeared to be groping a woman passenger. I tried to buy the original, but its Swiss owner wouldn't part with it.

Sometimes the work could be serious and hilarious at the same time. Jeremy Thorpe was a 1970s Liberal politician alleged to have hired a hitman to kill his troublesome gay lover, Norman Scott, a former model. Thorpe was put on trial for conspiracy to murder; he was acquitted, but too late to save his career.

Scott had threatened to make public his claim to have been Thorpe's lover in 1961 when gay sex was illegal. At Thorpe's trial, it was alleged his friends hired a hitman to kill Scott. Although this was never proven to a jury's satisfaction, it was revealed that a man had driven Scott to Exmoor in 1975 and shot dead his Great Dane, Rinka. Scott claimed the man tried to shoot him, but that his gun jammed, allowing Scott to flee.

The scandal made Norman Scott a household name and he became a *Sun* 'buy-up' — the term for when a newspaper pays the main character in a big story for exclusive interviews. My photographer friend Arthur Edwards and I were appointed to be his minders.

Scott was completely open about his sexuality, which was not usual in the 1970s. He was also very fond of a drink, and since *The Sun* was paying to keep him safe from its rivals, he was drunk most of the time.

One night, the three of us were hiding away in Devon at a Barnstaple hotel and found ourselves in the dining room in the middle of a gathering of Church of England ministers. They soon recognised the notorious guest among them and gazed at him with disapproval. This irritated Scott, who drank even more and started to pull tongues at everyone he caught staring at him.

Arthur and I were already anxious when the bishop stood, with the clink of a glass, to silence his flock for the royal toast. 'Ladies and gentlemen,' he said, raising his wine, 'the Queen.'

Scott staggered quickly to his feet, clattering the glasses and crockery on our table and capsizing a bottle of claret.

The bishop froze and the room went silent as everyone turned their attention to our table. Scott was swaying severely, a beaming smile on his shiny red face.

'A toast for me?' cried Britain's most famous gay man to a room of gasping vicars. 'Oh, how kind of you all. Thank you so much. I should now like to make a few remarks in response.'

Arthur and I seized our charge, taking one arm each, and marched him from the room.

CHAPTER 12

Bombs, bullets, and a shaving cut

The bomb went off when we were halfway down the glass-walled fire escape of the Europa Hotel in Belfast. We were jumping the stairs two and three at a time. It was 1972 and Northern Ireland was plunged into the dark years of The Troubles; it was such an inadequate name — The Troubles — for a conflict that lasted 30 years and claimed more than 3,500 lives.

My colleague, Gordon Broome, was close to the glass. I was ahead of him, curled in a hedgehog ball in a windowless corner, waiting for the shower of glass. Broome gave a cry as he stumbled down the steps towards me, holding both hands to his skull. Glass had peppered his bald head with a hundred cuts, and blood was running freely down his face.

We weren't badly hurt — Broome needed a few stitches — just shaking uncontrollably and unable to hear each other for our ringing ears.

'What did you say, Gordon?' I was guiding him through the dust towards an ambulance.

'I said I swear I'm never setting foot in this fucking place ever again.'

I don't believe he ever did. Broome was always a reluctant visitor to Belfast.

The bomb was routine for Belfast, although on a personal level it was unsettling for us to discover it had been left in a car parked at the hotel, and we were running directly towards it. Tony Eyles, one of our photographers, had phoned from the lobby to say there was a bomb alert that looked serious. When he called, we ran for it; we would have been fine if we had stayed in the room where we were working.

That explosion injured 70, and seriously damaged the hotel and the neighbouring Belfast–Dublin railway station, but my story the next day in *The Sun* was just a couple of hundred words at the top of page two. It was on television only because the Europa was where the world's media stayed; blowing things up on our doorstep was an opportunity the IRA could never resist. Auntie Gladys in Liverpool saw me on the BBC leading Broome to the ambulance.

I didn't notice at first that I also had injuries, and blood was running down my face. I discovered this outside the hotel. Three women, one with a baby in a pushchair, had been laughing furtively at the mayhem and whispering to each other until they noticed me. One of them pointed: 'Oh, my God,' she said. The women fell into a guilty silence, and a soldier put a white wad on the cut and told me to hold it there. My wound was no more serious than the result of a clumsy morning shave, and was the only time I shed blood in the line of duty.

In 1972, so many bombs were going off in Belfast that reporters often didn't bother attending the scene. I was eating in the Beefeater restaurant at the Europa with Trevor Hanna, our Northern Ireland correspondent, and his wife Ann, when an explosion happened nearby. It didn't even interrupt our conversation.

It was a big bomb, but no one in the Beefeater restaurant flinched, except for me. Ann kept eating her smoked salmon and telling a story. I called the Army 20 minutes later to make sure no one had been seriously hurt. The newsdesk in London only wanted a bomb story if there were serious consequences. A sniper killing a British soldier warranted a few lines at most.

The Belfast Europa was famous for being bombed more than 30 times. When the IRA were preparing to attack, it was said they made two warning calls — one to the hotel and the other to a local glazier. The Troubles wrecked the Northern Ireland economy, but glaziers must have prospered.

Despite the attacks, the Europa was both a refuge and pleasure palace for the media, providing guilty insulation against the hardship everywhere else. In the evening, at the top of the building in the moody lighting of the Penthouse nightclub, you could survey the embattled city beneath, while cocktails were served by 'Penthouse Poppets' with high heels and long, stockinged legs, dressed to look like Playboy bunnies.

There was an atmosphere of defiant jollity as well as periodic excess, but the drunken jostling that sometimes took place in the early hours was never sufficiently energetic to be described as a brawl. Michael McDonough, a high-spirited *Sun* journalist, walked one night through the hotel's public places pulling decorative plants from their pots, and singing at each uprooting: 'Oops, there goes another rubber tree plant.' The manager, Harper Brown, had to be understanding. Without the world's media his hotel would go broke.

The Europa had a Graham Greene feeling of intrigue and danger, a mixture of apprehension and glamour, like a cold-climate version of the Continental in *The Quiet American*. The hotel was dominated by journalists, but also visited by curious strangers.

Trevor Hanna was a shrewd and burly man with the face of a

bulldog: square and big-jawed, with a slightly upturned nose. No one I knew understood Northern Ireland better than Hanna. Belfast born and bred, he would say, and he had evidently been toughened by the life. He was once in a dockside public house with cash for a newspaper buy-up when an armed gang emptied the till and took money from the customers. Hanna sat quietly at the bar as the drama unfolded and, when the gang had departed, reached into his sock, produced the buy-up money and announced: 'I suppose I'll have to get the next round in.'

He would guide me through the drinkers at the Whip & Saddle bar in the Europa, peering round over his glass of Bushmills, the Irish whiskey he favoured. 'Now, that lad in the brown suit there, he's here working for Army intelligence. And him at the bar, they say his son is a Loyalist gunman ... See that young girl in black? Now she has very, very strong republican sympathies.'

The Europa felt dangerous, but it was the only place for a journalist to be. Hanna told me always to put shoes under my bed so I could escape over the carpet of glass if a bomb shattered my window.

To keep his customers coming in hard times, Harper Brown employed a novel marketing technique, presenting his loyal visitors with a commemorative tie that was brown and imprinted with a golden E in the style of the Europa's logo. It came with a yellow certificate that felt like parchment and declared:

> Be it known that Leslie Hinton is authorised to wear the Belfast Europa tie which signifies that the owner was a valued guest during these unhappy days, as a memento of their stay and with the assurance that its owner will always be welcome back to enjoy the hotel, both during the present troubles and when peace returns.

A tribute such as that made it churlish to seek less risky accommodation. I treasure the tie as a medal, and the document as the closest I ever received to a citation for bravery.

Northern Ireland was my first complete escape from the trivial side of *The Sun*. I spent eight months there in the deadliest year of all The Troubles. During 1972, 479 people died, including 249 civilians, 148 British soldiers, and 70 IRA terrorists. All sides — republican, loyalist, and government — were scrambling for moral high ground, but there didn't seem much left to occupy among the grief and ashes and mutual wreckage.

Security forces would later curtail attacks on the city centre with a network of checkpoints and barricades, but that year everything was out of control and Belfast was a desolate place. At night it was deserted. A lone Chinese restaurant remained open through it all, serving excellent spare ribs that tempted us often to make the dark walk from the hotel. We never needed a reservation or saw diners who weren't other journalists.

The British Army arrived in Northern Ireland in the summer of 1969, after months of riots and shootings. Their role was to prevent violence between Catholics and Protestants, and at first everyone welcomed them, even serving them tea and biscuits in the Catholic Falls Road area of Belfast.

But as the violence went on and the IRA became more active, British soldiers became the enemy in the eyes of most Catholics. They were no longer seen as peacekeepers, but as enforcement agents of the Protestant-dominated government.

It did feel like a military occupation. Army patrols spaced themselves along inhospitable streets, tucking themselves for cover into the entrance of little terraced houses. Dark and ugly Army vehicles roared through the streets. At night, when your car lights illuminated one of these patrols, you were regarded with dangerous suspicion until you turned them off.

Roadblocks were equipped with spiked chains to be pulled across the road to shred the tyres of any car failing to stop. Belfast was not a city suited to fancy cars; high speed bumps outside sandbagged barracks and police stations were constructed to prevent drive-by shootings. They made it difficult to navigate the streets in a low-slung sports car.

An evening walk in the wrong area could end badly. I strolled ill-advisedly one evening near the Divis Street flats, a perennial stress point and favoured haunt of IRA snipers until the Army turned the top floor of the main tower into a fortified observation post. A squaddie spread-eagled me against a wall. Another, flat on the ground, aimed his rifle at me while I was roughly frisked. They were apologetic upon discovering my National Union of Journalists press card.

There were many victims in Northern Ireland, from innocent civilians to defenceless politicians and unarmed activists. British soldiers no doubt did bad things, and Irish Catholics surely had deep and powerful historic cause for their grievances. But the soldiers, most of all young squaddies, were in a unique way also victims. Many were teenagers from tough neighbourhoods all over Britain, where choices narrowed down to the Army or the dole. They were following orders in a conflict they couldn't fathom, trained as fighters, yet expected to act like understanding policemen. They were murdered with bombs and bullets, and captured and tortured now and then. The IRA tied cheese wire between lampposts in the hope of slicing a squaddie riding shotgun through his throat. No wonder the hatred became mutual.

One night, after the Army had exchanged fire with a sniper, I made the mistake of peering into the back of a vehicle where an injured soldier was being treated. His naked left arm was dark with blood. I don't know who he thought I was, but he threw himself at me, screaming curses before a captain and sergeant wrestled him to the back of the vehicle. The hate of the republican protesters was a familiar sight, but I had never before seen such unmasked fury from a British soldier. I think he wanted to kill me.

'Sorry about that,' said the captain. 'He's had a bad night. He'll face action for what just happened.'

'Please don't bother,' I said. 'Who can blame him?'

There were moments of humanity in surprising places. I was in the republican enclave of Andersonstown one Saturday afternoon as the Army and the police clashed with locals after a protest. I can't remember what the protest was about, or if it was about anything in particular, but rocks and petrol bombs were thrown, and the Army had fired rubber bullets, which were like propelled truncheons that would bounce through a crowd and cripple anyone they hit.

A soldier had been separated from his patrol and was standing in the front garden of a council house with his back to the front door, attracting a threatening crowd of men. He had no idea what to do. He didn't even raise his weapon, but just stood there in terror. He was very young, and his life was under serious threat.

'We can't do anything. They'll think we're plainclothes Army,' said a man beside me. I don't know who he was — plainclothes Army for all I knew.

As we stood there, a white-haired woman wearing a wraparound pinafore like my grandmother's opened the front door behind the trapped squaddie and shouted at the gathering mob in her garden, 'Stop it, the lot of you. He's a lad. Let him be.'

The mob on her doorstep was stunned long enough by her intervention to allow the old lady to grab the squaddie by the arm and push him out her garden gate, from where he fled to find his lost patrol.

It was an unnerving city for any newcomer. Elizabeth Riddell was an Australian writer and poet, a sophisticated woman who taught me which end of an asparagus spear to eat first. She contacted me through a mutual friend and asked if I would be her guide. I would receive such requests from time to time, but not from small, delicately framed poets in their mid-sixties.

Riddell was persistent in overcoming my reluctance to show her the bad side of Belfast. When I told her we might have occasion to run extremely quickly, she presented a pair of tennis shoes and offered to bet that she would be able to keep up with me.

I turned out to be a careless minder. On the evening I took Elizabeth out with me, we found ourselves standing at a wall with no retreat between the opposing forces of a solid line of advancing troops behind tall shields and an ever-growing group of young men and children who were hurling rocks and petrol bombs. We had been attracted to the scene by a theme tune of The Troubles. It sounded in republican Northern Ireland whenever a fight was coming. Women would leave their houses, banging dustbin lids on the pavements outside their homes, and blowing whistles. It was their alarm system to warn of arriving soldiers — they seemed to know before anyone else.

It was not a wise place to be, or even worth the risk; the London desk had no interest in an everyday Belfast skirmish. For Riddell, it was different; the moment provided perfect colour for the piece she wanted to write, and she leaned calmly against the wall making notes until the gap between army and rioters became too narrow. We negotiated with the Army, who allowed us to move behind their wall of Perspex after deciding that a tiny, elderly woman with a distinct Australian accent provided no threat.

Whenever I could find the excuse of a story that warranted it, I would escape by train to the peace and hospitality of Dublin. On my walk to the station, I would pass what must have been Belfast's most prosperous pharmacy, its success due to the flow of customers from the Catholic south, where in the early 1970s the sale of contraceptives was banned.

I once had to hurry back from Dublin to Belfast during a day of numerous bomb attacks. I took a taxi for the 100-mile journey and my driver slowed up at the outskirts of the city. 'I'm sorry,' he said. 'It's a bad day in there today. You'll need to walk. Even if I got home without a scratch, the wife would kill me for taking you.' No amount of money would change his mind and I walked the rest of the way to the Europa.

Terrifying as it could be, every journalist wanted to be there for the biggest stories. I remember my disappointment being safely home in England on 30 January 1972 — Bloody Sunday — when members of the Parachute Regiment shot dead 13 protesters in Derry.

The rotation of my life in 1972 was two weeks in Northern Ireland then one week at home. We lived in a silent, leafy part of north London, but after eight months of Belfast, I jumped when a garage door slammed. This experience put an end to the life I had imagined as an action-man journalist. I did not have a life-risking temperament. Winston Churchill once said: 'Nothing in life is so exhilarating as to be shot at without result.' That's nonsense, I promise.

I tried pre-empting my panic attacks by consuming large quantities of gin and tonic, but that was not a good idea; the gin didn't release stress so much as store it up, to be delivered all at once the next morning in the form of throbbing hangovers and depression. Alcohol has never been a stress reliever for me; I only enjoy it if I'm in a good mood.

Self-hypnosis helped me, but that's not exactly what I did. I would lie still on a hard surface and employ relaxation techniques I learned as an aspiring actor from the book *An Actor Prepares* by the great Russian actor and director Konstantin Stanislavski. In a chapter called 'Relaxation of Muscles', he writes: 'At times of great stress it is especially necessary to achieve a complete freeing of the muscles.'

Stanislavski's exercise involved identifying every area of tension in the body and slowly relaxing, starting at the head and descending. It was intended to calm overwrought actors, but it worked for me in Belfast. At the same time as doing this, I imagined the face of my sleeping baby, Martin, soft and free of care. These days, this ritual sounds like a form of yoga, but it continued to work when the stress of Belfast and other arduous places was replaced by business crises and executive politics. As the children became adults, I replaced their faces with those of my grandchildren.

Northern Ireland was the place to be for young journalists who wanted to make a name. Four of the names to emerge at the bar of the Europa in the year I began going there, 1971, were: Seymour, Dacre, Fisk, and Buckland.

Gerald Seymour was a bland young television reporter from ITN who became a successful author of bestselling thrillers. He was inspired by his Belfast experience to write *Harry's Game*, a frightening recreation of the darkness and terror of the early Troubles. He became a full-time writer, with many of his novels being adapted for television.

Paul Dacre was a 23-year-old from the *Daily Express* Manchester office who would become loved and hated by rival journalists, and politicians, as the editor of the *Daily Mail*. Dacre favoured writing colour pieces rather than hard news. He confessed to having an undeveloped sense of news, and it was easy to agree. He had eliminated this gap in his skills by the time we were together again a few years later working as correspondents in New York.

From his beginnings in Northern Ireland, Robert Fisk of *The*

Times, and later *The Independent*, covered probably more conflicts than any British journalist of his generation; he interviewed Osama Bin Laden three times.

The irrepressible Chris Buckland, bureau chief of the *Daily Mirror*, later covered wars and politics on numerous Fleet Street newspapers. The *Mirror* irritated the IRA so much they bombed its Belfast printing plant. Buckland's customary coolness was disturbed when he received a threatening call. 'We're watching you,' he was told. 'And by the way, the third step on the fire escape leading to your bedroom window needs fixing.' Buckland checked — his caller was correct.

Other careers flourished in the autumn of 1975, when the world's media invaded the tiny town of Monasterevin in the Irish Republic. The drama that attracted us was an irresistible combination of romance, riches, stolen masterpieces, and murderous intent.

The police and the Irish Army had surrounded a terraced white-stucco council house where two IRA members were holding hostage a Dutch businessman, Dr Tiede Herrema. Until being abducted on his way to work in Limerick two weeks before, Herrema had led a quiet life as the boss of a steel-cord factory.

The kidnappers were Eddie Gallagher and Marion Coyle, and they threatened to execute Herrema unless the Irish government released three IRA prisoners. One of the prisoners was Rose Dugdale, the daughter of a rich English family, who had been presented as a debutante to the Queen before turning away from her privileged life to become one of the IRA's most imaginative members, and one refined in her crimes. She burgled her own family home of silverware and art to fund the IRA. She bound and gagged a wealthy knight and his wife, and made off with their collection of masterpieces, including works by Goya and Gainsborough, and the only Vermeer in a private collection. Most dramatically, Dugdale helped commandeer a helicopter in Northern Ireland to drop bombs on a Royal Ulster Constabulary station in Strabane. Happily, they failed to explode.

The romance of this saga was that it happened for love. Rose Dugdale and the kidnapper Eddie Gallagher were lovers. When Dugdale was captured and sent to prison for her crimes, she was pregnant with Gallagher's child, and their son was delivered in Limerick Prison. Determined to liberate his lover and child, Gallagher had joined Coyle to kidnap Herrema and demand Rose Dugdale's freedom.

It didn't work. The Irish refused their demand, tracked down kidnappers and captive, and surrounded the house in Monasterevin. After two weeks, realising they were beaten, Gallagher and Coyle emerged one night into the glare of television lights and camera flashes.

Gallagher walked out between two men in plain clothes. 'Hey, Eddie, give us a wave,' shouted *The Sun* photographer Arthur Edwards. Gallagher paused fleetingly for his close-up, waved like a red-carpet film star, and smiled broadly at Arthur Edwards, who couldn't believe his luck.

Media had descended on Monasterevin like an occupying army. Journalists slept in shifts after the overflowing local motel ran out of beds. Big-spending newspapers and television operations accommodated their staff in caravans parked in boggy fields near the scene. *The Sun* acquired a nifty two-bedroom model in partnership with *The Times* — it was before Rupert owned both newspapers, and we made uneasy bedfellows.

On day two of the siege, a shaggy-haired radio journalist arrived in mud-coated boots at the door of our mobile stakeout, overloaded with heavy recording equipment. Jon Snow was working for the London Broadcasting Company, the country's first commercial radio station, which was a long way from earning respect from the rest of us.

'Any room for me?' he asked.

We turned Snow away. There was no space for a know-nothing stranger from a puny start-up without good contacts to make his presence among us worthwhile. He slept in a car for the next two weeks.

But Snow, the relentlessly cheerful son of a bishop, earned everyone's respect during the siege of Monasterevin by never leaving the scene, while the rest of us agreed shifts and headed for the local pub. He was also clearly not discouraged by our lack of regard for him; Snow went on to become a globetrotting ITN correspondent and then the enduring anchor of *Channel 4 News*.

Another emerging star of that story was a gleaming-eyed newcomer called John Ware, who had progressed from the now extinct *Droitwich Guardian* to become *The Sun*'s resident man in Belfast. Later, he went into television, and won awards and fame for his investigative reporting on the BBC programme *Panorama*.

By the time we met in Monasterevin, Ware had built an impressive number of contacts on his new beat. This made me, as well as him, look good in our daily reports. The information was excellent, rich in detail about what was happening in and around the besieged house. I never pressed him to name his source, but I was curious.

Halfway through the siege, the Gardaí, thinking everyone inside the house was asleep, sent two men to climb ladders at the back to see inside. The kidnappers, however, were awake and opened fire. Only one shot was fired, but that single bullet shattered an upstairs window and neatly removed a finger on the left hand of one Gardaí.

'Got a problem,' Ware told me the next day. 'My contact is in hospital in Dublin and won't be coming back.'

CHAPTER 13

Coward at war

It was my fifth year at *The Sun* and for all the adventures, enjoyment, and occasional horrors, life was becoming routine. With no clear next step, I was beginning to worry. After so long in the same job, in the same office, at the same desk, in the same country, I was getting itchy.

I had never set foot in the United States, the country I had dreamed of visiting since Jean, my cousin in Mississippi, began sending me 10-cent comics when I lived in Libya. The closest I had come was in 1970, when Mary and I sailed back from Australia along the Panama Canal. The canal was built by Americans and located at the time within a strip of US territory known as the Canal Zone. I met Americans there, but it didn't really count.

The Sun was the only Fleet Street newspaper without its own US correspondent. An aged veteran inherited from the old *Sun* had retired without being replaced. When I discovered editors were considering the appointment of a new correspondent, I thought I had built the credentials to be a candidate.

The obstacle to my ambition was a Northerner called Ken Donlan, who, as *The Sun* news editor, ruled my working life. Donlan was the most terrifying boss I ever had. Rupert made me tense, but Donlan made me afraid. He wasn't given to outbursts so much as silent menace. He had a death stare when angry that I recognised years later upon seeing Anthony Hopkins play Hannibal Lecter in *The Silence of the Lambs.* He was a short, fraught, muttering man whose face changed its shade of red according to his mood, or the duration of his lunch that day with Larry Lamb, the brilliant but bibulous editor-in-chief.

When I was out of the office, I tried to call in only at lunchtime, when it was most likely Donlan would be away from his desk. Before making a call where I had to convey unwelcome news about the success of my assignment, I would lie on my hotel room floor and do Stanislavski's relaxation exercises.

I was outrageous in my efforts to ingratiate myself with Donlan. I even tried appealing to his working-class roots by reviving my long-lost Scouse accent in the hope he might identify more with me. Nothing worked. He ignored me and continued to favour other reporters. His particular favourite was Iain Walker, whose own dour and unsmiling style must have connected with the boss. Walker could be fun away from the office, giving me grounds to suspect he adopted Donlan's manner at work as a cynical strategy to get ahead.

My first opportunity to cover a foreign assignment other than Ireland came when Donlan was absent. It was mid-summer — August 1973 — when the newsdesk number two, Tom Petrie, sent me to a bank siege in Sweden. Two armed men at the Kreditbanken building in Norrmalmstorg square in Stockholm had shot and wounded two police officers, and taken three young women and a man as their hostages.

Sieges were still novel events — this was two years before the IRA siege in the boglands of Monasterevin — and journalists arrived in hordes. We checked into a hotel in the square, spending hours outside the bank and cultivating senior police officers for information about what was taking place inside. We heard gruesome stories from them of rape and a threat to hang the hostages. We were told that the vault where they were imprisoned had become 'a virtual torture chamber'. But the story failed to live up to expectations.

After six days, when the police pumped gas into the vault to end the siege, we were ready to write many words on the unimaginable suffering the prisoners had endured. I had already alerted London of the graphic detail to come, when John Penrose of the *Daily Mirror* arrived in the hotel bar looking downcast. Penrose was an imposing figure, always smartly dressed, which was a tradition among *Mirror* men, probably because they earned so much more than the rest of us. But the usual brightness in his face was absent.

'The word is nothing bad happened to any of them,' he said forlornly.

To our surprise and disappointment, the hostages were telling a different story than the version conveyed to us by the police. Their captors, they said, were 'fine boys' who 'never harmed us'. Kristin Enmark, a 23-year-old hostage, said from her hospital bed: 'Don't harm the boys. They have been very sweet. We really had fun in there. We played poker and noughts and crosses, told funny stories and all the time we were treated all right.'

The police were astonished: 'Kristin's reaction is a real surprise. We heard some spine-chilling conversations from the vault.'

The Stockholm police psychiatrist was mystified, offering the explanation that the hostages must have blanked out the ordeal. 'If they were assaulted it is likely that they do not want to face the horror of the details,' he told us.

Many journalists felt thwarted, especially those such as Penrose and I. We had voracious tabloid appetites to satisfy, and had expected to serve up a tale of cruelty and horror. My tale of happy hostages and merciful captors, along with the psychological explanation of what might have happened, proved underwhelming in London. It was reduced to a short single-column.

But, whether or not the police had exaggerated their accounts, it was accepted that the mental pressure of their ordeal had caused in the hostages what became known as Stockholm Syndrome.

This term became standard in psychiatry, and the American psychiatrist Frank Ochberg was the acknowledged authority. This was how he explained it:

> The hostage is stunned, shocked and often certain that he or she will die. But then ... little by little, small acts of kindness by one of the captors evoke feelings deeper than relief ... a primitive gratitude for the gift of life, an emotion that eventually develops and differentiates into varieties of affection and love.

Hidden in that analysis, I saw parallels with the wildly swinging emotions that come with the fear of being fired by a tyrannical news editor. It's the only way to explain why I became fond of Ken Donlan.

Despite the disappointing outcome, my competence in Stockholm led to more important assignments. In the 1970s, reporting on aircraft disasters was a staple duty. It was the deadliest decade in history for commercial aviation, with 16,766 fatalities. In the worst year — 1972 — the Aviation Safety Network says 2,379 people died. By 2016, with many more aircraft carrying millions more passengers, the worldwide toll for commercial airliners was 325.

The aftermath I witnessed of one crash — the world's worst when it happened — was impossible to describe in full for the pages of a family newspaper.

I was on duty and starting a lunch of beef and roast potatoes at The Old King Lud in Ludgate Circus when the bar's phone rang. The call was for me. It was 3 March 1974. A Turkish airliner, bound for London via Paris, and with British passengers on board, had crashed outside Paris. The office had a helicopter — the flying bubble type — waiting at the heliport by the Thames in Battersea to take us there.

It was late afternoon when we arrived to a scene of overpowering horror. Turkish Airlines Flight 981 was an immense McDonnell Douglas DC-10, a missile weighing 200 tons, with 346 passengers and crew packed within its 170-foot fuselage.

The plane had come down at 500 miles per hour, and carved into the Forest of Ermenonville, 30 miles northeast of Paris. Like a harvester through a wheat-field, it had flattened everything in its path, reducing huge pine trees to stumps. It had been pulverised in the process, and only a couple of pieces of red-striped fuselage were intact among a lifeless carpet of human remains and wreckage.

No one survived and no body was found intact. Human parts were scattered everywhere and clothes were hanging in trees — a woman's blouse, a pilot's uniform jacket, a long black overcoat. What looked from a distance like red blossom on charred branches were human intestines. Searchers picked up body parts with spiked sticks, as if they were removing litter in a park. One held up to us a long brown scalp of hair. Six British models died in the crash.

Those sights revisited my dreams for years. Philippa Kennedy, a new young reporter who was with me, was white-faced and tearful. I tried to comfort her, but I think I felt just as bad.

The Sun published many pages on this story. Most of the dead were British passengers who had been forced to change flights because of a British Airways strike. The crash was caused by a faulty rear cargo door that blew off and wrecked the aircraft controls.

Back at the office, I was sprinting up the stairs for a night shift when I heard the low, silky voice of Arthur Brittenden: 'Les, Les, slow down.'

Brittenden was *The Sun*'s number three editor, an odd man out, tall and slender with the polish and deportment of a cavalry colonel, and perpetually unperturbed among the frequent frenzies of the newsroom.

'That was wonderful work,' he said. 'Any newspaper — tabloid or heavy — could have run your copy and been proud of every word. Wonderful work.'

I still felt miserable about what I had witnessed, but I was pleased by Brittenden's words. I knew by then that good stories and other people's misery were often not far apart.

I did not cover great conflicts, only minor disorders compared with Vietnam, the Middle East, and the brutal border of India and Pakistan. It wasn't by choice; I was never asked, but I also wasn't sorry. The occasional dangers and savagery I witnessed in other places easily exceeded my personal threshold for risk.

Thursday 8 August 1974 was my day off. I had gone that afternoon to a cinema in north London and was regretting my choice — a gruesome and silly film called *The Exorcist*. During an intense scene in which the blood-covered head of a devil-possessed girl was rotating on her body, much to her mother's distress, the film stopped and a loudspeaker called my name and instructed me to call the office urgently.

This was the way of things for news people before cell towers, mobile phones, and the magic of electromagnetic interaction. We had rules to follow: never go anywhere without making sure the office can reach you, not to a pub or a restaurant or a cinema. And when you are on the road, check in every hour in case something significant is taking place nearby.

The big international story of the moment was the imminent resignation of Richard Nixon, but a major sideshow was a crisis in the eastern Mediterranean. The month before, the military junta in Athens had engineered a coup in Cyprus with the objective of annexing the island. For the Greek colonels, this was a grave miscalculation. Greeks and Turks in Cyprus had a history of murderous conflict, and the coup handed Turkey a perfect pretext for intervention. It at once invaded Cyprus, claiming only concern for its minority population.

The Cyprus crisis was at its height the day I missed the end of *The Exorcist*. Iain Walker, *The Sun*'s number one 'fireman' — the first reporter to be rushed to every big breaking story — was being pulled off the Cyprus job after a near miss. A convoy of four cars had driven into a minefield as it carried Walker and others through the Turkish zone. Two mines had exploded, killing a BBC soundman, 33-year-old Edward Stoddart, and injuring five others, including a journalist sitting next to Walker.

Walker was so shaken by the experience, he asked to be relieved, and I was asked to take his place. I flew in on a Royal Air Force VC10 — commercial flights were suspended — and checked into the Hilton in the island's capital, Nicosia. The Nicosia Hilton was the media's HQ in Cyprus. Like the Europa in Belfast, it was the place travelling journalists had identified as home. These gathering places are not sentimental. We like the company, but most of all we want to know what everyone else is up to.

The hotel bar was crowded with staff from the big US titles — *Time, Newsweek, The New York Times* — and heavyweight international correspondents from Europe and Fleet Street. For many of them, Cyprus was a diversion from their main job of covering the Middle East; Beirut was 40 minutes flying time when the airport was open.

The fabled Don Wise, whose by-line I had known since I was 10 years old, stood at the bar, impeccably tall and slim in a pressed khaki safari jacket, looking like a Spitfire pilot or a French musketeer with his anachronistic curling moustache. Wise was an adventurer as much as a journalist. He was brave, witty, and sometimes hilariously crude — the most famous remark attributed to him was about the Vietnamese language. 'It's like the sound of ducks fucking', he is alleged to have said. He had attended almost every important conflict since the Second World War, when he was a serving officer and a prisoner-of-war on the Burma Railway. In a long career with the *Express* and then the *Mirror*, he had covered post-colonial upheavals from the Middle East, to Africa, to southeast Asia, and been wounded four times. Don Wise was an idol I didn't wish to emulate.

It was my first night in Cyprus, and I was overcome by the excitement and boozy fellowship of journalists with the kind of experience I no longer sought, but whose company still left me wide-eyed. I stayed too long at the bar.

The noise that woke me wasn't like a Belfast bomb. It was a sharp cracking sound, followed quickly by a heavy and repetitive thudding. As I went to the window of my hotel room, there was a mechanical roar so loud and so low that, pointlessly, I ducked. When I looked out, I saw flashing black shadows: Turkish jets were bombing the city, and retaliating Greek-Cypriot anti-aircraft guns were firing into the dawn light. There is nothing like the shriek of rocket-firing warplanes to amplify a hangover.

The hotel lobby was a rush of bodies. The carousing storytellers of a few hours before were now grimly preparing for a difficult day's work, some heading out alone, others forming themselves into the safety of groups.

Don Wise arrived with a huge Union Flag flapping in his wake. It was to be draped across his car to establish his neutrality. We could hear warplanes and gunfire, and see the rising panic of the hotel workers.

'Hey,' he called to me. 'Want to come along?'

'No thanks,' was my shameful reply.

That morning, Turkey had launched the second wave of its planned occupation. As bombers attacked military targets in the city and elsewhere, with a worrying lack of precision, infantry and columns of tanks were claiming new territory in the island's north. Ultimately, the Turkish zone would occupy more than 35 per cent of the island. To the Greeks, the invasion was an atrocity; to the Turks, it was deliverance.

I declined Wise's invitation because the Red Cross had declared the hotel a sanctuary area and it felt safer to stay where I was. The Red Cross designation proved academic, however, when several members of the Greek-Cypriot National Guard positioned themselves in the hotel doorway. I was 100 feet away when a Turkish rocket exploded by the main entrance, shattering the hotel's glass facade. It was then I decided that, with no reliable hiding place, I might as well take my cowardice onto the streets.

We had no way of filing copy from the city, so Walker, who hadn't yet left, agreed to head south to the British base at Akrotiri, where he could wire our story before the RAF took him home.

'Get the office to call Mary to say I'm all right,' I asked.

When the phone rang at home, Mary was seven months pregnant with Thomas, our second son. She was standing on a stepladder repainting a bedroom for him and listening to news of the action on the BBC radio programme *World at One*.

The UK had military bases on the island, but kept out of the fight, with orders only to protect British lives and defend the bases. British observation units placed themselves close to the invaders. We stood in trenches with them outside Famagusta watching dozens of tanks creeping eastwards through the dust, firing their guns towards no apparent targets. When a Turkish shell went awry, landing near the British observers, a major waving a white flag marched towards the advancing tank to berate a Turkish officer.

After the first explosive days, an uneasy ceasefire was declared, but the danger and tension were still intense. Crossing the no-man's-land Green Line dividing Greek and Turkish territory was a tricky procedure. Leaving the protection of the Greek zone did not guarantee a welcome from the Turks. For me, there was a particular difficulty. *The Sun* had fallen into serious disfavour in Turkey after Walker had written a vivid account of allegations of Turkish atrocities. Greek-Cypriot villagers caught in the first Turkish advance had told him terrifying stories of their ordeal, and *The Sun* had devoted pages to his account, describing the Turks in a large one-word headline as 'Barbarians'.

Sub-headlines included: 'My fiancé and six men were shot dead. The Turkish soldiers laughed at me and then I was raped'; 'The Turkish soldiers cut off my father's hands and legs. Then they shot him while I watched'; 'They shot the men. My friend's wife said "Why should I live without my husband?" A soldier shot her in the head'.

This story made *The Sun* the most loved and hated newspaper in Cyprus, depending on which side of the Green Line you were. The Turks were so furious that Greek-Cypriot authorities and the British military cautioned me about visiting the Turkish zone. I had no choice, but it was a tricky moment each time I presented myself to a zone officer who had the task of deciding who should be allowed to pass. The conversations invariably went the same way.

'Hello, I'm from *The Sun*,' I would say brightly.

'*The Sun*? You think we are barbarians. What are you doing here? You told lies about us. You are not welcome.'

'I didn't write that,' I would say. 'I had nothing to do with it. I have no knowledge to make me believe that the Turkish people are barbarians. I am here to understand what is happening and to tell the truth to our readers.'

In time, making the crossings became easier, but they reminded me often of their view that *The Sun* was guilty of a terrible injustice in allowing itself to become the victim of Greek-Cypriot propaganda.

Walker's story was the first contribution to what became a grisly contest by each side to establish the inhumanity of their enemy. Both sides produced persuasive evidence.

After *The Sun*'s 'Barbarians' front page, the Turks organised macabre day trips for the media to the sites of purported Greek atrocities. The worst of them ranks above Ermenonville as the most horrifying sight of my life. What we saw in Maratha, a village in the eastern Turkish zone, was more terrible than an air disaster because it was not an accident but slaughter.

Our mini-bus halted near the crest of a low dusty hill. Through the windows, we could see people wearing surgical masks, scarves, and handkerchiefs over their faces. Some were simply burying their faces in their raised, bent arms.

'You will want to cover your noses when we get outside,' a young Turkish lieutenant advised us as he tied a large white cloth around his head.

The air was hot and windless, and dense with the sweet stench of rotting flesh. One reporter began to retch, another returned instantly to the bus. An old woman dressed in black came towards us, staggering and wailing as a boy, no more than eight years old, his two small hands clutching one of hers, tried to take her away from where the lieutenant was leading us.

The bodies had been buried in the village rubbish dump for 20 days, we were told. When Turkey launched the second wave of its invasion, Greek-Cypriot nationalist gunmen had rounded up the Turkish villagers and shot them all. Turkish officers said 88 people were missing and they expected to find them in the dump.

Their remains formed a long, low mound, and had been exposed by a bulldozer that was now nearby with its engine running. They were stacked in seams, layer upon layer, and only partly covered with flesh. You could tell many were women, and could see the tiny decaying frames and skulls of children. Some bodies were charred, and we were told they were set on fire after being killed. A uniformed Turkish-Cypriot said he had arrived on leave from his post in Famagusta to discover his family had been murdered — six sisters, one brother, and his mother. Soldiers were picking with shovels through the pile like archaeologists, keeping the bodies as intact as they could.

Jon Akass, *The Sun*'s chief columnist, stood alone looking down on the scene. He had a pen in one hand and notebook in the other, but I didn't see him write. Akass had seen the aftermath of Aberfan, had reported from Northern Ireland, Vietnam, Biafra, the Congo, and other African wars. He had been at the Arab-Israeli War of 1967 and the Soviet invasion of Czechoslovakia. His piece next morning began: 'Maratha is the most dreadful place I have ever seen.'

The smell from that day was impossible to wash away. It was still there shower after shower, but I think by then it was only in my head.

I left Cyprus within a few days of seeing the Maratha massacre. My departure was not straightforward; there were no organised flights or ships. The concierge at the Nicosia Hilton appeared to be the best connected man in the city, and he promised Barry Came of *Newsweek* and myself a comfortable passage by sea to Greece in return for a substantial amount of cash. The dockside was a crush of refugees, many of whom were left stranded as our overcrowded ship sailed away. Refugees were crowded on every deck, sitting and sleeping without access to food, drink, or hygiene. Came and I became popular when word spread that we had a cabin with a bathroom.

That same year, I attended the revolution in Portugal. It was one of the century's most peaceful, and became known as the Carnation

Revolution. Crowds came into the streets with flowers, children pushed carnations into the barrels of guns, and the US government soon put aside its fears of a communist takeover. There were tanks in the streets, riots, and some people died, but my lasting memory was of the evening in Oporto, when I was hurrying to file after a town-square protest. Walking towards me as I raced down the street was Graham Greene, who loved to visit the world's troubled places. When I smiled at him, he smiled back.

These assignments gave me confidence. I was sure I was qualified to apply when I heard that Rupert Murdoch wanted someone from *The Sun* to join the all-Australian News bureau in New York.

Ken Donlan glared over his desk. 'You can forget about that, old boy,' he said. 'There's a long queue ahead of you for that job.'

CHAPTER 14

Rupert's raiders

It's a bad idea to put your self-esteem at the mercy of others. If your bosses have a low estimation of you, it's fatal to let their opinions creep into your head. It was clear I had to outflank Ken Donlan, who was obviously a lousy judge of talent. I had no prayer of getting to New York if I relied on him.

I first heard about the New York job while doing a good deed. Phil Rodwell was an Australian friend I'd shared a flat with when I was working at British United Press. He was at the BBC World Service then, but had returned to Sydney. I had good memories of Rodwell. We were both banned from our local in Kew Green after the landlord became convinced we were stealing those traditional big-handled English pint glasses — it was tempting, but the truth is we had been set up by a larcenous friend from Brisbane. When Rodwell wrote to say he was coming back to London, I said I'd help find him a job.

Murray Hedgcock was chief of the London bureau of News Limited of Australia that provided coverage for Rupert's Australian newspapers. He was the rigorous editor who taught me, as a 16-year-old, what a split infinitive was, and warned me against other grammar crimes.

Hedgcock had no opening for Rodwell, but told me of another that he knew would interest me. 'I bumped into Rupert on the stairs yesterday. They're looking for an extra body in the New York bureau. I suggested one of my people, but he said he wanted someone from *The Sun*.'

This information led me to approach Ken Donlan, only to be sent away burning with the injustice of his disheartening response. Realising I must enlist outside help, I wrote to friends and colleagues across the company. Mark Day had been a precocious copy boy with me in Adelaide, the brightest of us all, who became editor of Adelaide's *The Sunday Mail* at 26, and was by then editor of the Sydney *Daily Mirror*.

I drove home to Day the importance of my all-purpose versatility as a Brit with a deep understanding of Australia, who could provide coherent copy to the many titles the company owned. Day promised to speak to Rupert. I wrote to Murray Hedgcock, whose support I could count on, and to the New York bureau chief Peter Michelmore. I sent a note to Rupert, but heard nothing back. I didn't raise the subject again with Donlan; nor did I reveal what I knew about the vacancy to other reporters. I knew Donlan's first choice would be Iain Walker.

Four months went by without news. One afternoon, on my way to the lavatory, I passed Donlan's desk. He stood and followed me.

'About New York,' he said. 'You would have to agree to be there for at least two years.'

We stood at the men's room door to the sound of flushing urinals.

'No problem,' I said. 'No problem at all.'

'Ok. We'll sort the details in a week or so,' he said, and hunched his way back to the newsdesk. Donlan did not indicate any pleasure at giving me one of the opportunities of my life, which I took as conclusive evidence that my plan had worked and he had been thwarted from above.

It's important here to say that the act of going behind your boss' back is recommended only as a last resort, and with extreme caution. It's great if it works, but if it backfires you're in serious trouble.

I was invited to the inner sanctum of Larry Lamb, the fearsome editor-in-chief, with whom I had never exchanged a word. His office was away from the newsroom down a silent corridor of closed doors and clean, deep carpet. His large desk was strewn with page proofs, and none of the liquor bottles on the nearby table was full. Lamb was proud of his success; when Margaret Thatcher gave him a knighthood four years later, Lamb put a sign at his door, in type bigger than any front page headline, announcing: SIR LARRY LAMB.

Lamb told me I would earn $20,000 a year in New York, which was about the same as the prime minister received. This made me happy, but only until I discovered the crushing cost of living there.

In New York in 1976, I was the pauper of the Fleet Street Press corps. My peers worked on newspapers whose circulations *The Sun* was overtaking, yet they lived lavishly, claimed ridiculously fraudulent expenses without challenge, enjoyed the security of generous medical insurance, sent their children to private schools at the expense of their employers, and travelled with their families on regular office-paid holiday trips home. The harsh economies of Rupert's companies had been familiar to me since, as a 15-year-old in Adelaide, I was required to hand in a pencil stub before I received a new full-length one.

I did cheat the system travelling to New York. Larry Lamb's office booked my flight and did what they always did — which meant I flew First Class on British Airways. But it was a hard landing when I started looking for somewhere to rent for Mary and myself and our sons, Martin and Thomas. Manhattan was far too expensive, so I travelled the Metro-North commuter line to Westchester County and found a two-bedroom ground floor apartment next to a busy railway line. We had no furniture. After several attempts by me, the office agreed to loan me $800, to be deducted from my salary over two years.

Still, I bought a big American car — a five-year-old Chevy Caprice with two-tone green bodywork and an interior to match. It had an automatic transmission, air conditioning — which I hadn't even known existed in cars — and electric windows. It was 18 feet long, a two-door coupe, with a V8 engine that consumed 12 miles per gallon when driven with care. It was exactly like those gleaming, cruising cars I had yearned after as a nine-year-old in Tripoli while I waited for a battered Army lorry to take me to school. I lived the dream for two years before trading it in for a sensible Buick Skylark, a car as tame as its name.

Thomas was 18 months old and Martin was five, a finely spoken English boy whose accent was soon lost forever. They came to New York in 1976 and, more than four decades later, were still there. For them, the transition was painless, although Martin encountered early confusion as he worked to shed his accent. This was due to the Japanese pupils he sat by at elementary school. One evening, his right hand on his heart, he proudly repeated the lines he had learned for morning assembly: 'I predge allegiance to the flag ...'

For Mary, it was a culture shock too far. Stranded and friendless in alien American suburbia, at first she wept and then grew angry with me. I had chosen our apartment while she was still home in North Finchley sorting out our affairs there. As soon as the two-year lease was up, and once I had squeezed more money from the office, Mary moved us to an apartment on Roosevelt Island in the East River, across from Manhattan. This was where many Australians,

Brits, and junior diplomats from the United Nations lived with their families; Mary preferred the people and the lack of homogeneity. Our dark and compact new home did not impress Arthur Edwards when he came to visit. 'It's like a bleeding air raid shelter,' he said.

Although we couldn't afford to live there, Manhattan was the magical America I had dreamed of. I had read about it, I had seen and heard it in films a thousand times — the tall and eternal avenues, the 24-hour wakefulness. The brightness of New York, its vivid yellow cabs, took me by surprise — it must have been due to too many black-and-white films.

It looked the way I expected, but I wasn't prepared for the wild pace. Midtown was an incoherent frenzy, like a beehive poked with a stick, with everyone in a head-down hurry. Shop workers served you with unsmiling blankness — and that was at the best of times.

In a delicatessen on Lexington Avenue, I ordered a tuna sandwich. In London, it was a simple request, resulting in a thin layer of tuna inside two slices of pre-sliced white bread. But not in Manhattan.

'What kind of bread?'

'Err.'

'So what do you want? White? Sourdough? Whole-wheat? Rye?'

'Rye,' I said, having no idea what it was.

'What you having with the tuna? Mayo? Lettuce? Tomato?'

I was still thinking when the man behind the counter ran out of patience, along with the people waiting in line behind me.

'What's the matter?' he said, with a despairing look at his waiting customers. 'You never ordered a sandwich before?'

When I left a bar, unfamiliar with the local custom of tipping for a drink, the barman's farewell was hostile: 'Hey, you jerk. Don't bother coming back.' For the same offence, the man who had given me my first ever shoe-shine, shouted after me across the vast concourse of Grand Central: 'Fuck you, mister.'

I would soon learn to avoid violating these local customs; that waiters and barmen needed tips to live; that previously simple dishes — fried eggs on toast — were offered in more than one form; and that, once you understand them, there is a raw kindness in most New Yorkers.

Manhattan is an island of orderly joined-up villages, little communities repeating themselves mile after mile. Each has its Italian and French restaurants, its corner store bodega, its dry cleaner and pharmacy, and a shop that will repair shoes, or polish dirty ones. Any item — a pint of milk, a three-course meal, an evening dress in need of urgent pressing — will be delivered to your door.

E. B. White's brief masterpiece, *Here is New York*, describes it perfectly: 'Each neighbourhood is virtually self-sufficient. Usually it is no more than two or three blocks long and a couple of blocks wide. Each area is a city within a city within a city.' White's book was published in 1949 when New York was, in many ways, a different place. But for all its changes, his essay also understood the permanence. New York is a shape-shifter of destruction and creation, of vanishing streets and rising towers, eternally mutating its landscape and its population, digesting wave upon wave of immigrants of all colours and cultures into its swarming neighbourhoods. It is a masterwork that can never be completed. O. Henry, the great storyteller of New York, said: 'It'll be a great place — if they ever finish it,' and he died in 1910.

But, before White's time and through the years, the villages of Manhattan have endured, and discovering them cheered me up. I decided that the city owed much of its success to the comfort and protection these 'villages' provided against the swirling metropolis, and that one day I would become a Manhattan villager.

New York was not at its best when we arrived. It was virtually bankrupt, its infrastructure of roads and bridges was crumbling, and it was riding the greatest crime wave in its history. That year, 1622 people were murdered; in 2016, the number was down to 335.

A drive down Fifth Avenue, from the heart of stricken Harlem at 125th Street to Jacqueline Onassis's apartment 40 blocks south, was a 20-minute journey through the extremes of the American dream.

Central Park, Manhattan's green lung of more than 800 acres, was a no-go zone of muggings and rape; so dangerous at night almost no one went there. Women wore fake jewellery on the streets and carried Mace sprays in their handbags.

Times Square now is a blinding, round-the-clock electric light show of clean cafes and bright theatres. In the 1970s, it was seedy and dangerous, offering 'Live Nude Girls — 25 cents', and films such as *The Filthy Five* and *Wayward Girls*. Drug dealers conducted their business without discretion, and it was never wise, going home after a Broadway show, to wander down a lonely side-street.

Heading home towards Grand Central after work, I passed $10 hookers, patrolling the homebound tide in their towering heels, calling out entreaties — 'Come on. You can catch the next train.' It must have been a brisk marketplace; the hookers were always there.

New York City was full of stories. As for crime, the dread of being mugged was nothing compared with the permanent expectation of an IRA bomb. I witnessed only one criminal act in New York — a youth cutting through a chain to steal a bicycle on Central Park South. It was a heavy chain, cutting it took a while, and people walked past with hardly a glance as the thief laboured to break free his prize.

As for economic catastrophe, the challenges of New York paled against the crisis in Britain, where inflation had exceeded 20 per cent, unemployment was at its highest since the war, and the government had taken its begging bowl to the International Monetary Fund for a bailout loan that would be the biggest in the IMF's history.

There was angst in New York, but also a determination to overcome the difficulties. Britain was in the throes of a clinical depression: before leaving, I had the job of speaking to psychiatrists for a feature analysing the country's mental state. Their diagnosis was a nation on the edge of nervous breakdown. New York, by comparison, was a city of vitality and optimism; a sick patient convinced it would heal.

It was also America's bicentennial, 200 years since 1776 when the 13 American colonies declared independence. The country had been through tumultuous times, but by then the Vietnam War was over, Nixon had been forced from office by the Watergate scandal, and America was in the mood for a party.

Most important of all, this was Rupert Murdoch's new frontier, his foothold in America, and here I was.

The outpost of Rupert's American adventure was at 730 Third Avenue, an expressionless grey glass tower where we leased two floors. The building's main occupant was a sober operation providing pensions for members of the academic professions, which made the 19th floor where I worked easily the most overwrought area. Rupert's executive offices were upstairs. I only went there a couple of times — they were white and quiet and intimidating.

The 19th floor was where the action was. The News Limited bureau where I worked was a cluster of untidy desks and old typewriters. It looked like *The Sun*'s newsroom in miniature. A wall of beige filing cabinets separated us from our lively neighbour, *The National Star*. Rupert had launched *The Star* two years before. It was a manic weekly tabloid sold in supermarket checkout lanes, offering celebrity gossip of inconsistent accuracy, Kennedy conspiracy theories, tales of space aliens held captive by the government, and pages of psychic predictions foreseeing show business romances and divorces, as well as natural calamities and other disasters.

These two floors on Third Avenue were Rupert's New York universe. Three years before, he had bought two newspapers in San Antonio, Texas, but that was an act of restless opportunism rather than the acquisition of a strategic asset.

There was nothing else: no television stations, no big city daily, no film studio, no magazines, and not a lot of friends. Nor was there the contempt and obloquy he endured in Britain, at least not yet. Local newspapers hardly mentioned him, and when his unfamiliar name appeared it required explanation — he was 'the Australian-born international publishing baron'. Rupert was an outsider again, starting from scratch. It suited him.

The launch of *The Star* in February 1974 received modest coverage across three columns of *The New York Times,* which said its budget of more than $5 million was 'said to be the largest promotion budget in newspaper history'. *The Star*, it added, was 'for people who find their local dailies too intellectual'. It quoted Rupert: 'We're not interested in the publishing judgements of Madison Avenue or professors of journalism.'

At first, *The Star* was not the success Rupert had hoped for. Transplanted journalists from *The Sun,* who created the first editions under the leadership of Larry Lamb, hadn't taken much advice about American tastes. *The Star*'s first front page was a design riot that made *The Sun* look subdued. The main illustration was of Bruce Lee, the martial arts actor who had died the year before. A large comic-strip bubble from Lee's mouth offered four pages and a wall chart on Kung Fu, 'the craze sweeping the world'.

'It's a new kind of newspaper,' the front page boasted, and that was certainly true. The front page promised no actual news and the un-alluring main head said simply: 'Welcome To The Star, Folks.'

It failed to electrify the nation's supermarket shoppers, and Larry Lamb soon returned to London. Rupert briefly appointed himself editor and publisher, but by the time I arrived in New York, Roger Wood was in charge.

Wood was a Belgian-born Englishman who never renounced his Fleet Street habits in New York, even though his lunchtime absences would enrage Rupert. He was a senior editor on the broadsheet version of *The Sun* when I was a holiday relief. He had also been editor-in-chief of the *Daily Express,* and never challenged the widely held belief that when Beaverbrook sacked him he sent his money-savvy identical twin Victor into the office to negotiate his payoff.

Eventually, *The Star* would acclimatise and calm its display, if not its fanciful accounts of celebrity life and visiting UFOs. It copied the formula of London tabloids, where serious and frivolous material lived side by side, and appointed a Washington correspondent. It also ran a political column by Rowland Evans and Robert Novak, who were famous and respected US commentators. *The Star*'s circulation would peak at 5 million, and reliably deliver millions of dollars in profit.

Rupert's American empire would eventually develop into a traditional corporate behemoth, smooth-running and fairly well-behaved, but the pioneers who joined him at 730 Third Avenue were a wild bunch.

When Rupert acquired Dow Jones in 2007, a company advertising campaign was considered that characterised News Corp as a band of pirates and marauders. This idea was abandoned, but must have been inspired by Rupert's raiders of the 1970s. They were his American boarding party, an exuberant band of brothers, and a few sisters, who refused to learn the manners of New York media.

Steve Dunleavy, an Australian, wrote a raucous and angry column in *The Star*. The paper described him as 'Mr Blood and Guts', and his by-line included a photo of him with a bottle of Heineken. His escapades were company folklore. An early-shift office boy was reprimanded for calling an ambulance when he couldn't rouse Dunleavy as he lay beneath the City desk — he was merely recovering from the night before. A snowplough crushed his foot as he lay in a snowdrift outside Elaine's restaurant on the Upper East Side, leaving his female companion uninjured. He swam the channel at Chappaquiddick, where Mary Jo Kopechne died, to disprove Ted Kennedy's claim that riptides thwarted his effort to rescue her. Rupert both admired and disapproved of Dunleavy's life, but people went too far in describing Dunleavy as his 'alter ego'.

Neal Travis was Dunleavy's best friend and drinking buddy, and a former Murdoch star in Sydney. When he moved to Manhattan, he wrote racy novels and became first editor of the now world-famous Page Six column. His standard defence when challenged about the accuracy of an item was: 'Oh, please, you don't seem to understand. I'm writing a gossip column.' Travis was always leaving the company and coming back. Once, spotting Travis at a desk, Rupert told an editor: 'Not him again. I don't want him here.' But Travis had charm, and a moment after returning to his office, Rupert called the editor: 'I was a bit hasty. We should keep Neal on board.' Travis had rushed over to Rupert to express his joy at working for him again.

Australians and Brits enjoyed the fast life of 1970s Manhattan. Piers Akerman, called The Toad for no other reason than he rather looked like one, lived — as the euphemism goes — life to the full. The only adult brawl of my life happened when I insulted him in Costello's, a journalists' bar nearby, and he began pounding my chest. He was a short, un-athletic man and, although the blows of Akerman's tiny fists were slight and he meant no real harm, I helpfully fell to the floor and lay still until Freddie, the barman, threw him out onto 44th Street.

Ian Rae and I became close friends, even though he had a famously uneven temper and a larrikin streak he struggled to control. When I was news editor at *The Star* and he was editor-in-chief, Rae was once so annoyed with me that he chased me through our crowded newsroom threatening to kill me. Rae was known as The Pig, no one could say definitively why, and the staff looked only slightly surprised.

Another friend was Col Allan, a tall, stringy country boy from Dubbo in New South Wales, with unbridled self-confidence, a loud voice, and an intense social life. I enjoyed slight seniority over him, which Allan claimed I abused, landing him in the winter with cold jobs in Canada, while I monopolised Caribbean assignments. He was correct.

Peter Brennan, when he was chief of *The Star*'s Los Angeles bureau, would go missing for hours each day — he was writing a novel and never answered his phone before finishing that day's writing.

Phil Bunton, an outsized British sub-editor, owned two cats named Rupert and Dot — after Dot Wyndoe, Rupert's assistant. Bunton claimed his therapy after a difficult day was to go home and kick the cat called Rupert.

John Canning was a one-legged New Zealander who had contemplated the priesthood as a young man, but instead found his calling at the Sydney *Daily Mirror*. In high spirits, Canning was known to remove his leg and drink beer from it.

Others already established as members of Rupert's inner circle were relatively conventional. George Viles was an aggressive Australian executive. Working in London, he was called the 'Industrial Gorilla' after storming into a strike meeting at *The Sun* and threatening to fire the entire staff. Viles was first in the office, but by 5pm each day he was reliably leaning on a bar in the company of Paul Rigby and Curly Brydon. Rigby was an ebullient cartoonist already celebrated in Australia and Britain. He founded the 'Limp Falling Association', whose members would identify themselves by slumping suddenly to the floor, most often in bars. He once demonstrated this fall on national television in Britain. Brydon had been an Australian fighter ace during the war before helping run Rupert's businesses, peppered his conversation with aviation metaphors, and gave our roving boss the nickname that stuck for years — the Flying Doctor.

They weren't all oddballs, and there weren't many wasters. Among the couple of hundred inhabitants of 730 Third Avenue were serious and sober journalists, such as Ray Kerrison, a devout man and lovely writer; John Raedler, the solemn correspondent of *The Australian;* and Peter Michelmore, who was Australian but wholly Americanised after years living in New Jersey. Joe Robinowitz was a serious-minded young Texan who didn't realise he was being insulted when Kelvin MacKenzie, an Englishman then at the *New York Post,* addressed him repeatedly as 'you Texas toe rag'.

An early wave of American managers had already joined the company, led by Marty Singerman, a circulation executive from *TV Guide* who would rise to become chief of all US publishing. Marty became my mentor, and then one of my closest friends.

Many of these eccentric and determined misfits went on to great success. Col Allan was an editor-in-chief in Sydney and held the same job for 15 years at the *New York Post*; Akerman returned to Australia and gained fame as a dyspeptic conservative columnist; Dunleavy relished his notoriety as a *New York Post* columnist, was profiled by *Rolling Stone*, and, after gaining national renown on the *A Current Affair* television programme, helped Robert Downey Jr prepare for his role as an outlandish reporter in *Natural Born Killers*. Ian Rae became a leading Fox News producer; and Peter Brennan launched shows for Fox TV before breaking out on his own and creating hits such as *Judge Judy,* which won awards and made millions.

These Murdoch pioneers constituted the unstable chemistry of Rupert's early years in America. They were fiery, defiant, adventuring, boozy, and invincible in their own minds, imagining they were storming the beaches of American journalism, certain to overwhelm the opposition. They delighted in the pious disapproval of their American counterparts and retaliated with loud disdain of their new country's newspapers. It was a true clash of cultures, in which neither side could claim all the right. To the invaders, American newspapers were dull and its journalists smug and self-admiring. In return, Americans were aghast at Rupert's raiders, who they saw as raucous, reckless, and uncouth. There was evidence supporting both arguments.

But we newcomers were devoted to The Boss, and in the years to come most of us did pretty well whatever he asked of us. We moved from business to business, taking over newspapers, buying magazines, moving into television — and all the while professing not to give a damn what the rest of the media world thought. We didn't change American newspapers much, of course. Four decades later the pride of Rupert's American print properties was *The Wall Street Journal. The Star* had been cast off long ago, and only the *New York Post*, by then a tiny asset in a vast enterprise, remained. It was still in high spirits in spite of continuing losses and diminishing sales.

In the summer of 1976, America was still Rupert's empire of dreams. It was seven months after my arrival that he made his first serious moves.

First came the acquisition of the *New York Post,* a dull and struggling evening newspaper founded 175 years before by Alexander Hamilton. The seller was the heiress Dorothy Schiff, the *Post's* 73-year-old editor and publisher, who had bought the newspaper in 1939.

This was the time US media coverage of Rupert began to harden. Suddenly he became a 'brash millionaire' and newspapers gave details, not just of the supermarket *Star,* but also his newspapers in Britain and Australia and their appetite for scandal, sex, crime, and sport.

In this more hostile climate, Rupert began his effort to buy *New York* magazine and *The Village Voice*, two very different weeklies owned by the same company. *New York* was a slick magazine whose exaggeration of the glamour and sophistication of Manhattan appealed to a large readership. *The Village Voice* was a merciless arch-irritant of New York City power, choosing its victims from among a ready supply of dodgy politicians, company bosses, police chiefs, and judges.

The company was run by Clay S. Felker, a 51-year-old journalist from Missouri. He had created *New York,* and had become the darling of the city's best writers, including practitioners of 'New Journalism' — writers who applied 'literary' techniques to their reporting. According to critics, this technique meant that articles were not always completely truthful.

Felker had asked Rupert to become an investor in his magazines in the hope he would help him handle his troublesome board. He owned 10 per cent of the company stock, and needed allies. His talents as an editor were not, in his board's opinion, matched by a gift for fiscal responsibility.

If Felker had done some homework, he would have known Rupert was never interested in owning a minority share of anything. When Rupert, without informing him, bought other shareholders' stock until he owned 50 per cent of the company, Felker felt betrayed.

Rupert's arrival at *New York* caused uproar. Bereft at the loss of Felker, and appalled at their new owner's reputation, well-known writers swore never to work for a Murdoch publication. Editors walked out in an effort to prevent publication of his first edition — one fled the building with a bundle of copy. Rupert, with volunteers from News Corp, produced the edition without them.

This drama coincided with the launch of another film version of the King Kong story, and *Time* magazine adapted the film's poster to mark a real-life Manhattan invasion. On the cover, with hairy feet planted on each tower of the World Trade Centre, was a giant ape with Rupert's head. One gorilla fist waved a copy of the *New York Post*, the other clutched Clay Felker. The head said: 'Extra!!! Aussie Press Lord Terrifies Gotham'.

Rupert's reinvention of the *New York Post* into a noisy, emotional tabloid caused fainting spells among serious-minded custodians of American journalism. To Londoners or Sydneysiders, the *Post* was a typical tabloid — entertaining and sometimes over the top — but most American editors were horrified. To them, Rupert and his raiders were plague carriers.

What they regarded as an assault on cherished standards, Rupert saw as a business opportunity. He thought American newspapers were dull and distant, and that they cared more about Pulitzer Prizes than their readers.

He was right — few American reporters understood popular journalism — but he was also dismissive of pretty well all American newspaper people, and that was harsh. As a Brit, however, his prejudice served me well.

American editors never lasted until Ed Kosner came. When he was fired as editor of *Newsweek*, Rupert appointed Kosner to *New York* magazine, and he was still there when we sold the magazine 11 years later.

It was just as well Rupert did not need admirers. The *Columbia Journalism Review* described the *Post* as 'a force for evil'; Abe Rosenthal, executive editor of the *New York Times,* called Rupert, 'a bad element, practising mean, ugly, violent journalism'. Rosenthal predicted: 'He'll be out of town in a couple of years'. The *Chicago Sun-Times* columnist Mike Royko quit when Rupert bought his newspaper, saying 'no self-respecting fish would be wrapped in a Murdoch paper'.

When Rupert invited *The New York Times* to his Fifth Avenue apartment for an interview, the *Times* reporter recorded a prescient scene: 'As he spoke, his three small children scurried about in the apartment. The publisher's young daughter carried a portable tape recorder and played at being an interviewer of her brothers. The children would then gleefully replay the responses.'

Elisabeth was eight, Lachlan five, and James three.

CHAPTER 15

Johnny Rotten's leather jacket

America's introduction to Rupert Murdoch was a sideshow for me. I was on the road, having the time of my life. I didn't know I had entered the twilight of my days as a reporter. I had never wanted any other life, never wanted a big office — any office — and didn't dream of becoming a company boss. I didn't want the responsibility of thousands of employees and billions in revenue. I didn't even want to be an editor at any level, let alone in charge of an entire publication. I was quite a good reporter, if no superstar. All I wanted was to tell stories.

When my friend Mark Day became the youthful editor of *The Sunday Mail* in Adelaide, I had a dream that I had his job, and was walking through the office, panic stricken. We had no paper to print the newspaper, and in the dream it was my fault.

The thought of chairing a meeting or speaking to a large group filled me with fear. It wasn't nerves; it was morbid dread. Some people relished the rough and tumble of company politics, but it was too intense for me.

I'm not complaining about my move into management — I could

have walked at any time. I adjusted to the importance and power — and definitely the income — and enjoyed managing people more than I had expected. But it was an accidental career, and coming off the road in 1978, aged 34, was painful.

The New York bureau suited me. Peter Michelmore was technically in charge as bureau chief, but he thought *The Sun*'s editors were difficult customers and was happy for me to keep them off his back. His background was upmarket and he didn't understand the newspaper. As long as I provided London with a good flow of stories, I could be my own boss. I didn't have Ken Donlan or anyone else looking over my shoulder. Although I hankered occasionally to work on a 'serious' newspaper, I never grew tired of the insane range of topics that came with working for a redtop.

My first big assignment was the 1976 presidential election contest between Gerald Ford and Jimmy Carter. I swept across the country in trains and planes, and cheated to ensure that the small Michigan city, Kalamazoo, was my first out-of-town dateline. I filed the copy from Flint, 100 miles away, but couldn't resist the lyrical sound of Kalamazoo. It was an unattractive place, but composers of a certain era liked using the name in their songs.

Ford was a decent man. I had a couple of innocuous chats with him when he and his wife Betty stopped to talk when I was aboard his whistle-stop train. I don't know if he saw the three men mooning him as we rattled through a level crossing. The campaign was so hard on Ford that he lost his voice and Betty had to read his concession speech in the White House. When Mrs Ford wandered among us later, saying goodbye, her daughter, Susan, clung sobbing to her back.

Flying back to New York, I argued with an old guy who insisted I give up my seat for one of his party. The man was unfamiliar, but he had an entourage of five who treated him with excessive respect. I refused, telling him I needed to get back to New York. The man wandered off grumbling. The clerk behind the check-in desk at the airport had watched wide-eyed and silent. 'Do you know who that is?' he said. 'That's Walter Cronkite.'

I was a new boy and Cronkite was the face of CBS News. It dominated every other network, and he was the most famous journalist in the country. We sat across the aisle from each other without speaking.

Organised crime was a running story in New York. Mafia and gangland killings were commonplace. JFK Airport was a favourite dumping spot; bodies would often be found there, hidden in the boots of parked cars. The Mafia's preferred means of execution was a .22 handgun. When fired into the back of the head, its low velocity meant the bullet bounced around inside a victim's skull and could be counted on to inflict conclusive injuries.

Carlo Gambino was the most notorious Mafia boss in the country. I went to his funeral six months after I arrived in New York. The *Daily News* ran a classic, hard-bitten headline: 'Carlo Gambino Dies In Bed'. Gambino was said to be the inspiration for Marlon Brando's character in *The Godfather*. He was the leader of all the Mafia families — the boss of bosses. He died aged 74 of a suspected heart attack in his Long Island home, while lying in bed, watching a Yankees game on television.

The funeral was at the Church of Our Lady of Grace in Brooklyn. Gambino had been a benefactor, and hundreds of people were there, several with their faces covered. There were so many flowers it looked like a botanical garden had been uprooted. Thirteen black Cadillacs followed his bronze coffin. One uninvited vehicle was parked outside the church. The NYPD Organized Crime Control Bureau was there, taking photographs. When I approached one of them, he asked me fiercely to identify myself; I think my English accent exonerated me. Gambino had led his family for 20 years and had thwarted every effort the government made to deport him back to his birthplace in Sicily.

His successor, Paul Castellano, did not have a lucky reign. In 1985, he arrived for dinner at Sparks Steak House in Manhattan, and four men dressed in white trench coats shot him dead in the street. John Gotti had ordered the killing, and subsequently became Godfather. Sparks was across the street from the bureau, 300 feet from our building, and our favourite steakhouse. After the Castellano killing, it became even harder to get a reservation.

The Mafia held a curious fascination for New Yorkers. Law-abiding Italian-Americans enjoyed taking visitors to restaurants known to be Mafia haunts. Restaurant guides contained hints directing people to the most notorious establishments. It was easy to spot the gangsters by the excessive attention they received.

I often needed to go beyond the United States. Once, I spent three days travelling in a helicopter through the Sierra Madre mountains of Mexico with drug enforcement agents. They were spraying poison on the fields of farmers who had discovered that poppies were a better cash crop than beans. The destruction of their crops irritated the farmers; every so often they fired guns at the helicopters threatening their livelihood.

The idea of being shot at was not so unnerving as the moment the young Mexican rifleman next to me almost blew us up. We were returning to base and our chopper was awash with fuel leaking from a rubber pod that had carried reserves. Our gunman had spent the day uneventfully, staring down at the mountains with an ancient rifle across his lap, ready to return fire. We were ankle deep in fuel and dizzy from its smell when he lit a cigarette. The pilot leapt from his seat and extinguished the cigarette by clutching it in his fist. He returned to the controls of his veering aircraft yelling aggressively in Spanish and the careless young Mexican looked terrified. 'I told him

I was going to throw him out of the helicopter,' the pilot said.

I sometimes wonder if that was the closest I came to a violent death, but my children think it was the time they saw me surface from turtle watching in Barbados as a racing speedboat skimmed the top of my head.

Foreign correspondents regard it as a mark of distinction to be thrown out of a country for upsetting the local regime. It happened to me only months before my reporting life ended, but I did nothing intrepid to deserve it. In Eleuthera, a long, skinny island in the Bahamas, Prince Charles arrived with a 'mystery girlfriend'. This was important because Charles was still a bachelor and the tabloids judged every woman with whom he made eye contact a possible future queen. They were staying with a friend whose home was isolated behind acres of high brush, impossible to cross without getting lost. The photographer Burt Reavley came up with the piece-of-string technique of navigation. He bought several balls of string, tied the end of one to a tree beside our car, and unwound the rest as we tried to find our way to Charles' love nest. When the first ball ran out, Reavley attached a second one. But Reavley, a master with a camera, knew nothing about knots, and when the strings came apart we were suddenly lost in the hot and vast brown undergrowth of Eleuthera, without water or any means of establishing our position.

When we eventually found our way out, Reavley had another bright idea. 'We're going to pretend to go fishing,' he said.

We paid a man with a small blue boat to take us out to sea, and soon spotted Charles' hideaway. We drew closer, casting our unbaited lines into the choppy water while scanning the beach. We were 50 yards off shore when a Bahamian police officer came running along the sand towards us. He was carrying a pair of binoculars and a gun; he only pointed the binoculars at us, but still we decided to retreat.

We thought we were being discreet, but it's possible Reavley's huge telescopic lens gave us away.

That evening, as we plotted our next move over a bottle of wine in the hotel bar, we heard police sirens. Three officers appeared and a grave man with braided shoulders accused us of breaching the terms of our visas by employing a local man — the boat owner. He gave us 12 hours to leave the country. We thought it lame grounds for deportation, but we didn't argue much; it's not as if we were there on serious business.

There is a wary fraternity among competing journalists, especially foreign correspondents who spend a lot of time away from their offices and families. It can be lonely — the best foreign correspondents are often loners — but I never enjoyed waking up in a strange place knowing that there was no possibility of meeting even an acquaintance. I preferred company when I travelled.

A ghetto of Fleet Street correspondents had formed in and around the offices of the *Daily News* at Second Avenue and 42nd Street. It was a glamorous place to work before the paper fell on hard times and moved to cheaper digs in lower Manhattan. Its lobby was dominated by a gigantic globe and was the model for the *Daily Planet* where Clark Kent worked.

Costello's on 44th Street started as a speakeasy and had a long history of literary drinkers. When people told this history, they dropped the names of Hemingway and John O'Hara and great writers from *The New Yorker* such as A. J. Liebling and Joseph Mitchell. The walls of Costello's were covered by a James Thurber mural, which he allegedly painted to pay an outstanding bar bill.

By the time I became a regular, the drinkers were still illustrious, if not quite so celebrated. Big-name writers from Fleet Street dropped in, Jimmy Breslin was often there, and, for reasons I recall only dimly, Colleen McCullough, the author of a gigantic bestseller,

The Thorn Birds, asked me to dance one night even though no music was playing.

Two regulars were friends from Belfast. Chris Buckland, a cigar chewing, wisecracking *Daily Mirror* man from Burnley, was now the *Mirror*'s bureau chief in New York. He was hilarious company, compensating for his lack of height with a big personality and elevated shoes. Paul Dacre of the *Daily Express* was a shy, towering Londoner who conducted himself with the burdened seriousness of a man who might be in his fifties, even though he was only in his mid-twenties. Some called him pompous, but I gave Dacre the benefit of the doubt and decided it was how he coped with his natural reserve.

When Buckland died in February 2017 and Dacre and I were pallbearers at his funeral, an obituary said we had 'swept across America like three musketeers, funded by lavish expense accounts, travelling in hired planes and cars, always bent on outscooping one another, but invariably ending the day in the same bar.' It wasn't always so convivial, and Dacre and Buckland might have had unlimited expenses, but not me. But the three of us went thousands of miles together and enjoyed unforgettable moments.

Dacre and I once drank at the bar of the Hotel Jerome in Aspen, Colorado, with Hunter S. Thompson. We were there covering a murder trial, but Thompson was more memorable, even though much of what he said didn't make sense. We spent all night at a wild party at Studio 54, Manhattan's most untamed disco in the 1970s. Andy Warhol, Liza Minnelli, and Mariel Hemingway were there. A black panther was led on to the dance floor, but panicked and bounded off upon hearing the sound of the Bee Gees. We were there to ask Bianca Jagger if she was separating from Mick, and it must have been four o'clock in the morning before we could get her to talk. She insisted they were happy together, but we didn't believe it.

Buckland and I went to the tiny jungle colony of Belize in

ABOVE: Grandad Bruce.
This was a huge photo that
Grandma Bruce always hung
above the back room fireplace.

LEFT: Grandma Bruce,
aged about 20.

LEFT: Grandma Bruce (right) with scary Great Aunt Grace, outside 149 before the war. You can tell when because the iron railings are still there.

BELOW: Mum and Dad's wedding day, 8 June 1935.

ABOVE: Mum (left) her twin Gladys (right), and sister Emily in Grandma Bruce's back yard, 1947.

LEFT: Mum and her fierce eyes — military ID photo, 1953.

ABOVE: Just before Egypt at Catterick Camp, with Mum, Mal, and newborn Duncan, 1949.

LEFT: Blackpool with Dad (in his uniform) and Mal, 1946.

ABOVE: In Grandma Bruce's backyard, 1947, with sister Mal (right) and cousin Judith.

LEFT: Back in Bootle with an African suntan, 1955, with Duncan and Grandma Bruce, in her back yard.

BELOW: Boarding school in Hamm, West Germany. The only boy in the choir, 1956.

ABOVE: With Mum, Dad, Mal, and Duncan in Canberra.

RIGHT: Los Angeles, 1994. With Mary, and (from left) Jane, Will, Thomas, Martin, and James.

ABOVE: With a Beatle, London, 11 March 1969, the night before he married Linda Eastman.

ABOVE: With Rupert and Joe Robinowitz in Boston, 1982, at the time of the *Boston Herald* American takeover.

ABOVE: Johnny Rotten in Greenwich Village, New York, as he sandpapers his new leather jacket, 1978. *Photo: Joe Stevens.*

ABOVE: Johnny Rotten's prank — he draped me in blow-up sex dolls as I slept on his bed. *Photo: Joe Stevens.*

ABOVE: Apprehensive as Prince Charles and Rupert meet, March 2002, at commemoration of 300 years of the British newspaper industry. They were both very polite. *Photo: Max Nash, AFP/Getty.*

LEFT: With Gordon Brown in friendlier days, 19 October 2006, after service commemorating centenary of Newspaper Publishers Association. *Photo: Daniel Berehulak/Getty Images.*

ABOVE: With Prince Charles and Rebekah Wade, July 2007. He was our guest at the Police Bravery Awards and gave us the idea that night of doing the same for the military.

ABOVE: Rupert and me. *Photo: Arthur Edwards.*

ABOVE: Head to heads with the Commons Culture, Media, and Sport Select Committee, March 2007. *Photo: PA Images.*

ABOVE: The Queen and me. At a gathering of rival newspaper editors and executives, I told the Queen we had declared the occasion a demilitarized zone in her honour. She was amused.

ABOVE: Heading for the exit — leaving Rupert's London flat after resigning to him, 12 July 2011. *Photo: Oli Scarff/Getty Images.*

ABOVE: Rupert says hello to Dow Jones, 13 December 2007. Robert Thomson and I await our turns to speak. The Happy Holidays 'podium' did not match the mood of the room. *Photo: AP Photo/Mark Lennihan.*

RIGHT: With Kath on our wedding day, 11 May 2009, Marylebone.

BELOW: Life after Rupert. In Houston, 2013, on a long meandering drive from New Orleans to Santa Fe.

ABOVE: With the kids, New York. From left: Thomas, James, Jane, Will, Martin. *Photo: Arthur Edwards.*

LEFT: The closest I ever came to a citation for bravery — for loyalty to the Belfast Europa during the early days of The Troubles.

Belfast
Europa
Hotel

Be it known that

Leslie Hinton

is authorised to wear the Belfast Europa tie which signifies that its owner was a valued guest at the hotel during the period from the Summer of 1971 to the present date.

The Manager and his Staff present the tie in recognition of the loyalty of their guests to the hotel during these unhappy days. We hope that the tie will be worn with pride, as a memento of their stay and with the assurance that its owner will always be welcomed back to enjoy the hotel, both during the present troubles and when peace returns.

Harper-Brown
General Manager

August 1972

Central America when neighbouring Guatemala threatened to invade, claiming ancient territorial rights. Buckland arrived at the airport with maps and travel guides. 'I'm going to do some research,' he said, 'so I can file when we land.' After locating Belize on the map, he drafted his story. Next morning it was the front-page lead: 'By Gum! It's War', and the story referred to Belize as the 'chewing gum colony'. It was a good tabloid twist and made me gloomy, until I discovered Buckland's guidebooks were out-of-date. Disease had long since killed the trees that provided chicle, the gum ingredient that had been the backbone of the local economy. Buckland didn't mention it again, but no matter what he wrote, the subs kept putting the chewing gum back into his stories.

We took a Land Rover to the purportedly dangerous border, but the barbed-wire gate of the Guatemalan garrison was yawning open and a couple of soldiers snoozed in the shade. The captain in charge offered coffee, and invited us to meet his pet monkey, which was tiny with huge eyes and long black fur. We agreed to tell our offices they had sent us to a phony war and it was time to go home.

The craziest American road trip Buckland, Dacre, and I took together was the infamous Sex Pistols tour of January 1978. A few months later, we toured Canada with the Queen and Prince Philip. It was a neat juxtaposition of events, demonstrating the absolute extremes of British life.

I was glad we didn't have to choose which tour to cover. Watching traditional Ukrainian dancers entertaining Her Majesty on the Saskatchewan prairie could not compete with a Sex Pistols riot at Randy's Rodeo in San Antonio.

Sex Pistols concerts were invariably free-fire zones of flying objects — chairs, beer bottles, food, and even animal entrails. Their tour wasn't about music — what mattered was audience participation. Sid Vicious was delighted when a young woman struck him a mighty blow on the face. He sucked into his mouth the blood gushing from his nose and sprayed the crowd. He became gentlemanly, in a Sex Pistols kind of way, when security guards seized his assailant, instructing them: 'Get off her. This is great. Any cunt who bangs me across the face is a cunt I like.'

Buckland was a talented pianist. His favourite music was Chopin and the hymns of his childhood. He was no fan of the Pistols, but coped in his own way. During one performance, he leaned against a pounding six-foot speaker and fell asleep to the shouted lyrics of *Anarchy in the UK*. Buckland was an epic drinker at the time and we decided he self-medicated to render himself unconscious. Later, he gave up alcohol and stayed off it for the rest of his life, but in the years that followed he became hard of hearing. I blame the Sex Pistols.

Dacre's idea of a rave is a black-tie evening at Glyndebourne, so the Sex Pistols were torture for him. The sight of them on stage caused him more stress than petrol bombs on the Bogside. Dacre thought Sid Vicious was 'the most nauseating human being in the history of the planet'. To Vicious, this was an accolade, even though he was nothing more than a messed-up youth, who, in a more caring world, would have been sectioned and in medical care.

I had a beer with him one night in Memphis. He had an uncomplicated mind, inasmuch as I don't think it was ever filled with many thoughts. When he wasn't on stage, or pulling punky expressions because he knew he was being watched, his pasty face and small dark eyes would lose all expression. He was sweet natured and impressionable in the manner of an eight-year-old.

'How do you get your stories?' he asked me. 'Have you ever met people like the Prime Minister or the Queen?' He wanted to know how old I was, and how many countries I had visited. 'Wow,' he would say when I told him. 'That's so cool.' Of course, he might have been in a state of heroin-induced catatonia, but I like to think there were moments of truth when the lost boy he truly was showed through.

John Lydon — Johnny Rotten — was another matter. He was canny, brighter than Sid, and his punkish anger was not always an act. Lightning struck our plane when we were taking off from Baton Rouge, Louisiana, and there was a flash and a terrifying noise. It did no harm, but I decided it provided grounds for a joke. 'Hey, Johnny,' I said on the ground in San Antonio. 'You know what that was? That was a divine critique of your music.' That famous on-stage fire lit up in his eyes and for a moment, although it wasn't my plan, I thought I might have my page lead for the following day — 'Raging Rotten Takes Swing At *Sun* Man'. But, just as McCartney had a decade before, he disappointed me and let loose only a few rich curses and expressive hand signals.

It was no surprise when the group fell apart soon after the tour concluded. They looked bored with themselves by the end. The snarling had become automatic, the curses and gestures repetitive, and it was no longer shocking to see Rotten blow his nose on stage without the aid of a handkerchief. At their last performance in San Francisco, Rotten asked his audience: 'Ever gotten the feeling you've been cheated?'

I thought that was the last I would see of the Sex Pistols, which caused me no regret, until Joe Stevens called me in New York one Friday afternoon. Stevens was a rock music photographer who knew everyone, and, since I knew nobody, he had become my best contact during the Sex Pistols tour.

'Hey, Johnny's at my place,' he said. 'Want to come over for a drink?'

Stevens' apartment was in Greenwich Village above Arturo's pizzeria on the corner of West Houston and Thompson. Rotten was alone, wearing a leather waistcoat over a white t-shirt and thick, buckled leather bracelets on his wrists. I sat across from him beside a table stacked with empty Budweiser cans. He was paying close attention to a new leather jacket spread across his lap and did not look up.

'What do you want?' he said.

In his left hand was a folded piece of sandpaper; he was rubbing it hard against the jacket's polished surface.

'What are you doing?' I asked. But he ignored me, studying the coat's sleeves and collar, choosing carefully the spots to scour away the shine. It was a beautiful moment. Johnny Rotten, the king of punk and grunge, the emperor of scruff, the apostle of not giving a toss, was meticulously falsifying a brand new and expensive leather jacket with a piece of sandpaper.

'Why don't you go to a second-hand shop and buy a genuine beaten-up coat? And what's the shame of wearing a new one anyway?' I said.

He smiled at me with a look of weary scorn, as if acknowledging an unwelcome creature from an alien planet, and offered me a beer.

We went downstairs to Arturo's for pizza and more beer, which I paid for. Then I did something that impresses my children and grandchildren, and all their friends, more than anything I have done in my entire life. I went to CBGB's with Johnny Rotten.

CBGB's — or the Country, Bluegrass, and Blues bar — was a half a mile away in The Bowery. By 1978, it had outgrown its name and had become the world mecca of punk rock. We walked there with care through the slippery aftermath of a blizzard.

The bar was crowded and deafening. When Johnny Rotten and I arrived, hardly anyone took any notice of him. We pushed our way towards the bar through a sea of punks, and a few preppy onlookers dressed like me, and no one gave him more than an indifferent glance. It must have been a rule among punks to stay cool.

Rotten got talking to somebody, and I sat at the bar chatting to a group dressed in leather. Mostly, I talked to a convivial man with thick, dark-fringed hair. I don't remember the conversation except that it was friendly, but Johnny Rotten was amused at the sight of me deep in conversation with this intense-looking man.

'He's no fucking idea who he's talking to,' he said to Joe Stevens.

He was right — I had never heard of the punk band The Ramones, or Johnny Ramone, their lead guitarist. They were much more successful than the Sex Pistols.

Stevens told me: 'They always reserve a special section of the bar for the band and you just walked up to them and started chatting. You sat right next to Johnny Ramone.'

That night, I ended up back at the apartment above Arturo's, where I fell asleep on the spare bed. I awoke to camera flashes and Rotten's cackling. I have the photo — he had put two blow-up sex dolls on either side of me.

'Johnny said it would be a good idea to use them to blackmail you, but I think he was joking,' Joe Stevens told me later.

Next morning, I wondered why I had accepted Stevens' invitation, and why I was invited in the first place. The Sex Pistols were out of the news — if not for long. Stevens explained later: 'We were both out of money and starving, and I told Johnny you'd be good company.'

It was lunchtime on 12 October 1978 when I got to the Hotel Chelsea in Manhattan. It was already a place with a history: Welsh poet Dylan Thomas died there; Leonard Cohen sang sensually about his encounter there with Janis Joplin; Arthur C. Clarke wrote *2001: A Space Odyssey* while he was a guest. A familiar, shambling figure emerged from the main entrance, handcuffed and cursing, and flanked by two detectives. It was Sid Vicious, and upstairs in the bathroom of Room 100, a woman lay dead from a single stab wound.

I went there on a tip-off, and to my amazement no one else from Fleet Street was present. There were a couple of local camera crews and reporters, but no one else. In the age of universal, instant communication, I could never have been be so lucky, but news travelled more slowly in those days.

I knew there was a body upstairs and that Sid had been arrested as a murder suspect. But the police weren't identifying the corpse and none of the media there had any ideas. I went through the usual, now antediluvian, procedure. I walked to a pay phone in the hotel lobby and placed a reverse charge call to *The Sun*'s library in London. 'Can you dig out the Sid Vicious clippings and see if he has a girlfriend?'

After a few minutes I had an answer: 'The only name we can find is Nancy Spungen.'

Outside, I waited until the homicide lieutenant in charge was alone. He had already told me he couldn't tell me who the dead woman was.

'Am I going to be in trouble if I say the dead woman is Nancy Spungen?' I asked him.

For a moment he said nothing, then he shook his head. 'No, sir, you won't be.'

I couldn't believe my luck. It was the splash in the next day's *The Sun*: 'Sid Vicious In Murder Drama — Girlfriend is found stabbed in a hotel room.'

Not a single other Fleet Street newspaper had the story. I knew that when the first edition dropped in London, they would be scrambling desperately to catch up with me.

I sat in a bar — The Fleet Street — across from the office and waited. The first person to track me down was Paul Dacre. I have never since had greater pleasure in being cursed at, and Dacre was a vivid and original swearer. When he became the Editor of the *Daily Mail*, his morning conferences became known as the Vagina Monologues.

Big news is often bad news for other people. My small victory was a tragedy for others: for the spaced-out young woman probably killed by Sid Vicious, aka John Simon Ritchie, and for her family. Vicious was a crazy, lost lad from Lewisham, south London, and a little more than three months after his arrest, he was dead from a heroin overdose. He never stood trial. The mystifying legend of Sid and Nancy was born; there was something grotesque about the fascination with which people regarded their helpless lives.

That was my swansong scoop. After it, my life changed suddenly and forever. Within a month, I would be off the road for good.

By the end of 1978, Rupert was still unhappy with the mix of his executives at his number one American property, the *New York Post*. He had moved Roger Wood from *The Star* to be editor-in-chief, and wanted Steve Dunleavy, *The Star's* news editor, as city editor. The mercurial Ian Rae, who had been editor of *TV Week* in Australia, was given *The Star's* top job, but Dunleavy couldn't leave before his replacement as news editor was found.

'Mate,' Rae said, after taking me to a bar where no one we knew ever drank. 'It's time for you to move up in the business.' He wanted me to become his news editor on *The Star*.

I refused, point blank. 'I've only been doing this a couple of years,' I told him. 'I love it. There's plenty of people will do that job better than me.'

He kept trying over the next few days. Dunleavy, who was desperate to get to the *Post,* also put on pressure: 'It's a great job, mate, and they'll double your salary.'

'Steve, I'm not interested in sitting on my arse all day worrying about UFO invasions and who's screwing who on *Dallas*,' I said.

A week after that, it got serious.

'Rupert wants to have lunch,' said Rae. 'Larry Lamb is coming to town and we're taking him to Sparks.'

I sat at a table for five with Rupert, Lamb, Rae, and Ian's one-legged deputy editor, John Canning. In all the years I had known Rupert, it was the first time we had dined together. We talked about everything except the reason I was there.

We were at the restaurant door on our way out when I felt Rupert's arm around my shoulder. 'Les,' he said. 'I just want to thank you for helping out at *The Star*. I'm very grateful and I know you'll do a fine job.'

'You've got it wrong, Rupert. No way am I doing that job. I keep telling them, but no one will listen to me.'

Well, they're not exactly the words I used. What I said was: 'Oh, you're welcome, Mr Murdoch, you're very welcome.' Maybe a panel of psychologists could explain why I folded so quickly, but I guess being weak-kneed isn't a clinical condition.

The following Monday at 7.30am I was in my new office, with a view of 20 desks. In an hour, they would be filled with people waiting for me to tell them what do. It was what I'd always dreaded.

For years afterwards, even when I was a chief executive, I would have the same dream. It was late at night and I was sitting behind the reception desk of some faraway hot-weather hotel at the keyboard of a big beige Telex machine. In the dream, I was producing a paper tape of my story to file to London, and felt — I remember clearly — very happy. And every time, I would wake up to my real world of meetings on advertising revenue, or distribution contracts, and, now and then, a real-life newsprint crisis.

I miss it still: the liberating sense of not knowing what each day would bring, where I would be, or who I might meet; the hopeful way I always carried my passport with me, the rush and disorder of life on the road, the crazy variety of human life. I even miss you, Johnny Rotten.

CHAPTER 16

The psychic and the White House

We were at Lutéce, then Manhattan's most glamorous restaurant, with Jeane Dixon, America's most famous psychic and astrologer. Dixon wanted to share a secret with us.

Jeane Dixon must have liked Lutéce for its fancy reputation and cosy opulence; it can't have been for the food because she ate almost nothing, and drank only sips of Perrier water. That didn't stop her offering advice to its owner, the celebrated chef André Soltner. When she told him how to improve his pea soup, Soltner patiently took out pen and paper to record her recommendations.

Dixon leaned in to the table, clutching her Perrier in both hands. Phil Bunton, Ian Rae, and I leaned closer. 'I have a direct line to her bedside,' she said in a whispery conspirator's voice. 'I can call her whenever I wish. She plans her life and her husband's life around my advice.'

We were underwhelmed by Dixon's secret. She told us once that she gave psychic advice to the Pope, so we were naturally sceptical to hear her claim that she used her supernatural powers to help Nancy and Ronald Reagan.

We didn't tell Jeane Dixon she was nuts; she was too important for that. She might have been eccentric, but she was also a valuable asset to us, and besides, we liked her. After she had gone, we had a few more drinks, and laughed at her expense.

Millions of people across America had faith in Jeane Dixon, and a high concentration of them were readers of *The Star*. We had an exclusive contract with her, and whenever she was in the paper there was a colossal spike in circulation.

Dixon had built her reputation on the assertion that she had foreseen the assassination of John F. Kennedy. In a 1956 profile of her in *Parade* magazine, the interviewer wrote: 'As for the 1960 election, Mrs Dixon thinks it will be dominated by labor and won by a Democrat. But he will be assassinated or die in office.' Cynics called it a lucky guess, but Dixon used her remark to become a psychic superstar.

No one, least of all *The Star,* tracked the accuracy of her other predictions. Now and then, very gently, I would remind her of a prophecy that had not come true. When I mentioned her unfulfilled prediction that two Hollywood stars would divorce, she told me: 'The prediction was true when I made it, but their relationship improved soon after.' At the time of writing, her prediction that a descendant of Queen Nefertiti of Egypt would unite the world has yet to happen. She did tell me I would be promoted to a high position at News Corp, but I bet she said things like that to all her bosses.

Twice a year, executives from *The Star* would take Dixon to lunch at Lutèce. If Rupert joined us, she would ask him to say grace, and he would close his eyes, bow his head, and mutter a few kind words to God about Jeane Dixon and the food we were about to receive.

The astonishing truth about her did not emerge for years.

Donald Regan, who served as Reagan's secretary of the treasury and then chief of staff, revealed in a memoir that the Reagans had first consulted Dixon in the 1960s when he was governor of California. He said the first couple plotted their lives according to their horoscopes and the stars were consulted before: 'virtually every major move and decision ... made during my time as White House Chief of Staff.' Dixon's immodesty didn't allow her to confess that, at some point, the Reagans had decided her powers were fading and broadened their consultations to include other seers. I sat next to Donald Regan at lunch in the White House once and unfortunately he did not choose that moment to reveal his boss' secret

Working at *The Star* could be fun, but it was the netherworld of real journalism. It made *The Sun* look like *The Times* of London, and the story of Jeane Dixon's role as psychic consultant to the Reagans was the closest I came to a real scoop.

The Star was profitable when I joined. Millions bought it every week, most of them at the supermarket checkout where it competed with titles offering stories from an alternative universe. Their titles made them sound more respectable than they deserved: the *Globe*, the *National Enquirer*, the *National Examiner,* the *Weekly World News*. At their peak, these weeklies sold close to 10 million. They told stories of UFO fleets, and celebrity break-ups and romances that never happened. They wrote about famous people with 'terminal illnesses' who were still alive 20 years later; miracle cures for everything from arthritis to constipation; and high-speed diets that would starve to death anyone adhering to them. The most breathtaking was *Weekly World News*. Until it closed in 2007, it ran the most imaginative front pages anywhere in print: 'Abraham Lincoln Was A Woman!', 'Five US Senators Are Space Aliens'.

In comparison, *The Star* was mainstream. Medical advances were covered with care — Rupert liked stories about science. Stories about shipwrecks and improbable survival were also popular; every Midwest tornado season, we sent reporters to track down families with lurid tales of how lucky they were to be alive.

But we were not innocent. Tales of love and lust among the famous were not always impeccably sourced. We sometimes gave credibility to stories of alien abduction, or sent reporters to séances to conduct interviews with people beyond the grave. Images of Christ on slices of toast were always popular. *The Star* once ran a huge two-deck cover headline: 'Proof Of Life After Death'. The headline increased sales, but I don't recall any conclusive evidence in the story.

We organised a stunt with Uri Geller, the Israeli showman who purported to bend metal objects without touching them, and said he could communicate telepathically. His powers, he claimed, came from outer space.

I spent hours with Geller, and he was a convincing magician. Phil Bunton and I sat in the corner of a room as far from Geller as possible, and, when we created an image on a piece of paper, he instantly reproduced it. We flew him across the country — from New York to Los Angeles — and told readers to put out cutlery and other objects while Geller transmitted his metal-bending powers. We had hundreds of calls complaining about ruined knives and forks. Some threatened to sue for damages; our lawyers said they didn't have grounds.

In Rupert's first American television venture, *The Star* produced the pilot of a daily show. We worked with producers for months to develop a gossipy programme with all the qualities of the newspaper. The main on-camera talent was an un-telegenic Englishman, Robin Leach, who had a whining, high-pitched voice. In those days, English accents on television were rare. Only David Frost was well known. No one believed the show would work, and we had no success selling it. The competition that beat us was a similar idea entitled *Entertainment Tonight*. Thirty-five years later, *ET* was still on the air.

I had the job of telling Leach he was fired. He didn't take it well. He stood at the door of my office on his way out, and vowed: 'You will regret this. One day I'm going to be a big TV star.' Not long after, Leach became just that as presenter of *Lifestyles of the Rich and Famous,* a hugely successful show that ran for 10 years, making Leach a household name, and earning him millions. For years, every time we met, Leach would give me a wink. 'Told you so,' he would say.

After a while, the world of supermarket tabloids becomes a mind-warping place where your fantasy-reality equilibrium gets lost in the madness. I begged to be freed, but there was nowhere to go. I pestered my mentor, Marty Singerman, who was running the company's growing stable of magazines. 'Be patient,' he would say. 'Things are going to change. We're looking all the time at new opportunities.'

My complaints to Marty Singerman were at their height when the company began negotiations to buy the *Buffalo Courier-Express,* a 137-year-old daily that had fallen on hard times. Buffalo is on the shore of Lake Erie, next door to Canada and not far from Niagara Falls. Almost seven feet of snow is dumped on Buffalo every year, making it one of the nation's snowiest cities. I was sure many people loved Buffalo, but I knew it would be a disaster for us. Mary had thought Westchester County was a suburban wasteland — how could I expect her to cope with the frozen north of New York State?

'There could be a great job coming your way soon,' said Singerman, smiling at me happily. After months of pleading, how could I turn down Buffalo? And would my refusal doom me to more years of soothsayers, flying saucers, and the evildoing of J. R. Ewing?

Mum and Dad were visiting from Adelaide, and we drove them to Niagara Falls. They couldn't believe the power and the roar, or the rainbows in the misty spray. Mum was convinced the falls were going to suck in our boat and kill us all.

We found out later that, about the time we were touring the

Buffalo city centre, with Mary gazing silently out the window, the *Courier-Express* unions were voting against a Murdoch acquisition. They rejected the cost savings that were a condition of the purchase and said they didn't like Rupert's other papers.

'We voted to die with dignity,' one reporter said. In an act of suicide, the *Courier-Express* took its dignity to the grave — along with more than a thousand jobs — on 19 September 1982. Buffalo's loss was my lucky escape.

It was just weeks before Rupert found another newspaper to buy, this time the *Boston Herald American*. Boston was a city we knew and liked. The paper's owners, Hearst Corporation, were planning to close the newspaper unless they found a buyer. News Corp was quick to make a deal with Hearst, but once more the sale required the unions to accept fewer jobs and the introduction of new technology.

If the unions agreed terms, Joe Robinowitz, the 31-year-old assistant managing editor of the *New York Post,* would become editor-in-chief and I would become city editor, running the newsdesk. This put me several rungs below Robinowitz, but since it meant I could flee *The Star,* I wasn't going to complain.

'Go in there and see him,' said Rupert's assistant Dot Wyndoe, sitting outside his Boston hotel suite. 'He's in there by himself waiting to hear what's going on in the talks. He needs some company.'

Robinowitz and I joined Rupert in his darkened hotel room and spent the next 10 hours there gossiping, dozing, and plotting what we would do with the *Herald* if the talks were successful. He used his in-built world clock during the night, working out time zones and which of his executives in other countries would be awake to take a call. Andrew Neil, who was editor of *The Sunday Times* in London, wrote a book in which he accused Rupert of being a 'telephone terrorist'. I know what he meant; Rupert almost never sent memos, he just rang you. He could sound angry on the phone, and no doubt often was, but for the first time that night I saw him acting angry during calls, while winking mischievously at us.

After our overnight marathon, Rupert invited us to dinner. Robinowitz and I kept talking, delivering a torrent of ideas about what to do with the newspaper. I'm not sure either of us knew then how important it was to keep the initiative with Rupert; to make sure it never looked as if you were waiting for his instructions. Robinowitz and I simply wanted to make sure he knew we were full of ideas. It sounds obvious to act this way with any boss, but Rupert intimidated a lot of people. The dinner must have helped me because a couple of days later Rupert said I would no longer be city editor, but Robinowitz's number two.

The deal to buy the *Herald* reached the brink of collapse before Rupert and the unions agreed terms. Hearst had set a deadline, and when it passed they sent every employee home and prepared to shut down. It was five more hours before the last of the 11 unions was satisfied. I was ready to head back to New York, but instead, at lunchtime on 3 December 1982, we drank a champagne toast.

The media coverage of our Boston takeover was intense. It dominated television news for days and filled columns all over New England. The *Boston Herald American* had been close to death, and these were the days when communities had an emotional connection with their newspapers. When a newspaper's existence was threatened, it was as if a familiar friend was about to depart.

Newspapers are more common fatalities these days — some are dying, some just fading away — but even now there are moments when the best of them can search the soul of a city or a nation.

In our age of atomised communication, it is hard to imagine any form of media will ever again touch a community the way a newspaper could then.

———

It was shocking to move from *The Star* to a metropolitan daily. Until now, the most prominent American interested in my company was Jeane Dixon. Suddenly I was getting respect without doing anything to deserve it. First, a letter arrived from *Who's Who in America* informing me I was to be included in their next volume, and requesting my biographical details. I provided these details, of course, then wrote to tell Mum.

Then John Kerry came to lunch. He was 40 years old, the Lieutenant Governor of Massachusetts, already famously ambitious, but years from becoming the Democratic Party's presidential candidate and Barack Obama's secretary of state. It was Kerry who first exposed me to the blandishments of politicians. It happened hundreds of times over the years, but Kerry was my first. His visit coincided with a national debate about Reagan's support of a guerrilla insurgency in Nicaragua, which was seeking to overthrow the left-wing Sandinista regime of Daniel Ortega.

When we had finished eating, Kerry leaned back in his seat and put one hand on his oversized chin. 'Now, Les,' he said, with that look of phony earnestness that I was to witness in so many politicians. 'I would be fascinated to know what you think of our policy in Nicaragua.' I refrained from telling him that my most recent discussion about clandestine US policy had been with a conspiracy theory journalist offering proof that the air force had recovered aliens from a crashed spacecraft at Roswell, New Mexico, and preserved their remains in three Frigidaire freezers behind a Texaco gas station not far from where they perished.

A lot of people wanted to be friends with the *Herald*. There was a long procession of politicians — senators and aspiring senators, mayors and wannabe mayors — as well as an occasional bishop. The governor, Mike Dukakis, was in the office often as he built his campaign for the White House. Dukakis was a quiet man for a would-be president, and in the 1988 election to succeed Ronald Reagan, George Bush senior crushed him. Bush was aided significantly by Dukakis' attempt to toughen his image by staging a disastrous photo-op at the controls of an M1 Abrams tank, in which he looked more like Snoopy from Charlie Brown than a commander-in-chief.

The state's most famous living politician, Senator Edward Kennedy, was not a fan of the *Herald*. Kennedy had grown accustomed to generous coverage of his family from the hometown press, but his liberal policies did not align with the conservative views of Rupert's new paper. The *Herald* — and the *New York Post* — taunted Kennedy for years. Patrick Purcell, the *Herald*'s publisher, once attempted to make peace by coaxing Kennedy and Rupert to his house for a party, but they ignored each other the entire evening.

But Kennedy was the exception; most Boston politicians wanted to be friends. When we had the grand idea of redrawing the map of Boston by changing the names of a couple of streets outside our building and calling them 'Herald Square', the mayor Kevin White obligingly turned up to perform the unveiling. His successor, Ray Flynn, loved the *Herald* staff so much he sometimes came into the office on his way home from a bar and sang to the women on the office switchboard. When he was Archbishop of Boston, Bernard Law would come for lunch. He seemed a decent man, with the soft, celestial smile clerics so often practise, but he was forced to resign in 2002 for his part in the cover-up of child abuse by his priests.

It was the other way round with advertisers. They didn't care what journalists thought. The day after a joint appearance by Mike Dukakis and John Kerry, when our political reporters had rained down on them with tough questions, a big advertiser came to lunch.

I never had anything to do with advertisers before Boston.

'Your newspaper is crap,' he told us. 'It's been crap for years, and so far you guys aren't making it any better.'

As we began to retaliate, our advertising director silenced Robinowitz and me with a glare. 'Hang on,' he told our angry guest in a pacifying tone. 'You make some interesting points. But we are the new people in town so give us some time.'

It was the first lesson for me on the tricky frontier between journalism and business. Advertising is the lifeblood of most newspapers; circulation revenue rarely pays the bills. Our much larger rival, *The Boston Globe*, was hogging the ad market, and the *Herald* was losing money. We could be as tough as we liked on politicians, but it was wise to be gentle when meeting advertisers. Unless, of course, they tried to tell us how to edit the paper, or pressured us to be kind to their businesses — that was different.

The *Boston Herald American* was the first all-American newsroom I set foot in. I was the solitary Brit. Donald H. Forst and his senior editors were waiting to greet Robinowitz and me on our first day. They were straight out of the city room of a black-and-white film: big voices, jaunty smiles, and huge cigars gripped between their teeth. All the men seemed to have cigars. Alan Eisner, the city editor, didn't look comfortable with his — as though he were smoking it out of duty and solidarity.

Don Forst was the editor-in-chief. He was a short, wiry, bubbling New Yorker, and he owned the editorial floor of the *Boston Herald American*. He owned it like all powerful editors, through energy and will, and above all by always being there. The *Herald* men smoked cigars because Don Forst did. It was obvious they loved him as much as they feared the two cocky Murdoch interlopers who had just walked through the door.

Forst would not be staying, but there was no disgrace in that;

not many editors survive a change of ownership. He agreed to hang around for the transition, and was heroic as we set about disassembling the newspaper he had created. We never knew what he was thinking; he smiled like a man who knew things we didn't.

We shortened the name of the newspaper to the *Boston Herald*. It had changed from a broadsheet to a tabloid format a year or so before Rupert bought it, but to us it was tabloid in size only. We thought its headlines bland, its design flat, and that its copy was over long and rambling. We were never heartless enough to say that to Forst.

Still, the paper had more pep than *The Boston Globe*, the proud broadsheet that dominated the local market. *The Globe*'s bosses were a New England dynasty. The newspaper had been founded 110 years before by Charles H. Taylor, and ever since, a man with the same surname had held the job of publisher. *The Globe* looked down with scorn, from its mountaintop of power and profit, on our rough and struggling tabloid.

The Globe was excellent in many ways, but it was self-important, and its smugness got under our skin. We enjoyed taking shots at its pomposity and mistakes. Our editorials and columns were filled with jibes. When it put the wrong publication date on its front, we described it for weeks as 'The Newspaper That Doesn't Know What Day It Is'. We ran throughout the paper images of planet earth wrapped in rope with a caption saying 'We've Got *The Globe* on a String.'

It was enjoyable but sophomoric. We didn't know that *The Globe* cared much what we said, but it was therapeutic as we fought to chip away at its monopoly. We must have come across as zealous; *The Boston Phoenix*, Boston's answer to *The Village Voice,* called us 'Murdoch Moonies'.

We spent millions to increase circulation, introducing a game called Wingo. It was bingo, really, but for trademark reasons we couldn't use the word. Every household in greater Boston was mailed a bundle of Wingo cards, and every day readers had to buy the newspaper to see if their numbers had come up. When I arrived, circulation was just over 200,000. Three years later, it had reached 380,000. Soon after, publisher Pat Purcell had a celebration party when the *Herald* made its first annual profit in decades.

Robinowitz and I were working long hours and often seven-day weeks. We flew in reinforcements. Bill Ridley was an energetic colleague from London, and he became night editor.

Impatient with the pace of change, especially in our efforts to improve the paper's design, Ridley and I decided on drastic action. While Robinowitz was away on holiday, we spent hours adapting dozens of page layouts from the London *Daily Mail,* and distributed them to the copy editors — in America, subs are called copy editors. The *Mail* was Britain's best-designed mid-market tabloid, and its pages were complicated compared with the *Herald.* It wasn't the fault of *Herald* copy editors that they didn't understand tabloid layouts — no one had ever taught them.

Sir Harold Evans, a British editor as cantankerous in his old age as he was innovative in his youth, once said that changing a newspaper should be like surgery, that the patient must feel no pain. It is a wise doctrine that I ignored at the *Herald.* The editors executed their *Daily Mail* layouts and overnight we gave the newspaper a radical facelift.

Back from his break, Robinowitz was quick to call. 'Hinton,' he shouted, 'what the hell have you done with my newspaper?' To his credit, Joe didn't change a thing, but he made me promise not to do it again.

The learning was not a one-way street. Feminism reached American journalism before it took hold in Britain. I was behind the times when Betsy Buffington Bates, the women's editor, stood at my office door waving the proof of a two-page feature I had edited.

'You are not allowed to call grown women "girls" in the pages of the *Boston Herald*,' she said. 'It will be an insult to every adult female in the city.' I changed the story and headline according to Betsy's instructions and never made the mistake again.

In Boston, distant from the heart of News Corp, we were sometimes trapped in wider company catastrophes. I was in bed one morning listening to one of our radio commercials. It included the sound of Hitler's voice and the heavy thump of Nazi boots on the march. We were delighted to be sharing a worldwide company scoop by publishing the Führer's diaries. The phone rang. 'It's all bullshit,' said the marketing man from London. I could tell he was having trouble breathing. 'The diaries are a hoax. It's a total fucking disaster.'

Rupert would come to town sometimes. I learned a lesson on one of his early visits. 'How's it going?' he said, taking a seat next to me as I chaired the morning news conference.

'OK,' I told him. 'But it's a quiet day.'

Rupert scowled: 'There's no such thing as a quiet day. Some are more challenging than others, that's all.'

I never used that excuse again, or allowed anyone to make it to me.

Mary and I lived with our three boys — Martin, Thomas, and William — in Weston, a small town in suburban woodland, west of the city along the Massachusetts Turnpike. The only traffic jams were on Sunday mornings near the local churches. The day we moved in, neighbours arrived to welcome us with fresh-baked cookies. It was the kind of thing we had only seen on American TV shows like *Leave It To Beaver* or *The Adventures of Ozzie and Harriet*. The local school was packed for parent-teacher evenings and school concerts; in North Finchley in the 1970s, these school events were quiet and empty. In Weston, no one walked much; when we invited people to our home from the next street, they arrived by car. And we encountered the talk-to-anyone-anytime openness of most Americans and their readiness to chat to any stranger. In Britain, you could sit across from someone on a four-hour train journey and say nothing but 'goodbye' at the end of it. Most important, after six years of cultural decompression, Mary had acclimatised, and now even loved the suburbs. We lived in a clapboard house on top of a wooded hill and felt like Americans; we had become US citizens in Faneuil Hall near Boston Harbor, where pre-revolutionary patriots gave speeches demanding independence from Britain. A mischievous *Herald* photographer, Leo Tierney, took our photograph beneath a huge painting depicting a redcoat defeat.

I left the family alone in Weston when Hurricane Gloria struck Boston in September 1985. Hurricanes didn't often reach as far north as Boston, and Massachusetts was in a state of high alert. Mary drove me to the office. The Massachusetts Turnpike was deserted apart from emergency vehicles. She dropped me off and returned to the house. Martin was 15 then, Thomas was 10, and Will was 5, and while they hid in the basement with their mother, listening to the hurricane, I was at my desk at the *Herald* selecting dramatic photos and stories for the newspaper.

Back home, trees in our yard were blown down and a section of the roof went flying down the street. It wasn't too bad, but when I heard their stories of crashing trees and winds that rocked the house, and could see how frightened they'd been, I thought that the job sometimes twisted my priorities. It wasn't the last time I felt that way.

As my third anniversary in Boston approached, I knew it was time for me to start another escape campaign. I loved Boston, and we had developed serious talent among our journalists, but the city was on the sidelines of big media. Now that I was snared in the executive world, I wanted to keep moving.

Marty Singerman was now the boss of all American publishing.

He was one of the first Americans to be counted by Rupert as an equal alongside his loyal Australian business team. Singerman knew I was restless yet again, and invited me to New York for dinner.

What happened at that dinner and soon after was the perfect example of the haphazard culture of News Corp, and how it was possible to benefit, or suffer, from its hit-and-miss randomness.

Singerman was already my mentor. He was a strong executive, 18 years older than me, and he was taking a special interest in my future. He wanted to sound me out. How I would react if I were offered the editorship of *The Village Voice*?

Of all the positions I had imagined, that one was not on my list. It was the publication Rupert liked least of all in the entire company. *The Voice* was New Corp's black sheep — a radical alternative periodical that paid no attention to the views of its proprietor. Marty didn't spell it out, but I knew what was happening. Rupert wanted an ally to change this mutinous weekly to his liking. But I knew that making me editor was a fatal idea, and that a tamed version of *The Village Voice* would bore its readers and quickly sink without trace, probably taking me with it.

I had never turned down a job before, and felt gloomy and ungrateful on the plane back to Boston. I had pressed Marty Singerman for an opportunity and he had offered me one. But a few months later, after Rupert rid himself of *The Voice* by selling it to a pet-food magnate for $55 million, Singerman called with another offer: would I become editor-in-chief of *The Star*?

First *The Village Voice,* now *The Star.* There could not have been two publications in all the United States that were more distant. *The Village Voice* was a fire-eating crusader, hip chronicler of Manhattan's underground, champion of gay rights, tormentor of the rich and powerful — and *The Star* was, well, *The Star.*

Maybe I should have been flattered; I was certainly confused.

What kind of a life plan was this? I took the job, even though more time at *The Star* was not a heart-lifting prospect.

My second spell at *The Star* lasted 18 months. We tried making it more of a magazine, calming the layout and content in the hope advertisers would like it better. We had limited success in coaxing new advertisers, and managed one pioneering technological achievement.

Prince Andrew was to marry Sarah Ferguson in the summer of 1986, and AT&T was promoting a new high-speed technology to transmit colour photos by satellite. Alistair Duncan, the picture editor, persuaded AT&T to demonstrate it free of charge, and they agreed to transmit photos of the Fergie-Andrew wedding from London to New York. We beat our competition with colour photos of the wedding and saw a big lift in sales.

It doesn't seem much now, in the age of FaceTime with the grandkids, but in 1986 Rupert was impressed: 'Your magazine looks fabulous this week,' he told me. 'I can hardly believe it.'

CHAPTER 17

Pissing with Picasso

I felt pretty good in my new fawn seersucker suit. It had cost $60 at the Moe Ginsburg discount store in the Flatiron district of New York City. I wore it for the first day of my new job, along with one of the $6 defective Arrow shirts I routinely bought at a downtown street stall. I wanted to look my best.

I had spent three years in Boston before moving back to edit *The Star* from offices in a suburban Westchester business park. Now, I was in Manhattan — the centre of the world — newly in charge of Rupert's stable of glossy magazines.

Carl J. Portale was not impressed when I arrived at the Madison Avenue offices of *European Travel & Life*, a periodical aimed at the very rich. Its mission was to reach that touching part of the American psyche that is dazzled by anything more than a century old. It did so by presenting a flawless fantasy of Scottish castles, Tuscan villas, and an idyllic rustic life of wine, fresh bread, and pure air, as if the entire European continent were embalmed in a perfect past.

Portale was the magazine's publisher. He was born to the role. His skin had a Mediterranean hue, and his slicked-back hair was black with matching streaks of white at each temple. His dark-blue suit was creaseless, with the tiny hint of sheen, and his silver tie had a broad knot; the kind I had never been able to master. As we shook hands, he raised his chin and peered at me down his Roman nose.

My appointment as executive vice president of Murdoch Magazines was a jolt. I had always been a newsman, living with the immediacy of newspapers and news agencies. Now, most of the publications I had to work with were glossy monthlies, including *Elle* and *Premiere*. There were just two weeklies: *New York* and *The Star,* the twilight zone tabloid I knew so well. With these exceptions, my new world was an unrushed one. It could be intense, even fiery at times, but no one was ever in a hurry.

For the first time, I had the task of overseeing the business as well as the journalism. This was a challenge. I was suddenly in charge of a multi-million-dollar enterprise without ever before having looked at a balance sheet.

Rupert had surprised me again. In the autumn of 1987, he called me to his oval-shaped office at the *New York Post*. It was in a dirty-white slab of a building that sat anonymously in downtown Manhattan in the shadow of the FDR Drive. According to office lore, it had been anonymous since the previous owner, Dorothy Schiff, removed the *New York Post* sign for fear a disaffected reader would take a shot through her office window. This made sense because the FDR offered a perfect line of fire and an easy getaway.

'Welcome to super management,' Rupert said, and announced my new salary, which was agreeable but not lavish.

I had never worked with people like Carl Portale. I moved into an office next door to him and he took me into his care, advising me I needed to look the part when visiting clients. They represented, he said, the world's most desirable hotels; they were purveyors of expensive fashions, jewellery, and high-end European cars. The Moe

Ginsburg suit I was so proud of wouldn't do at all. He took me to his Italian tailor on the 15th floor of a building on Central Park South. 'Three decent suits for this young man, and don't overcharge him,' he ordered.

Other colleagues joined in. Julie Lewit-Nirenberg, the sleek publisher of *Elle*, disapproved of my shirts and their wayward collars. She recommended an expensive substitute, and told me to use collar stays. I had thought those plastic strips were part of the retail packaging. A stylist at the magazine told me to wear long socks to avoid the unacceptable exposure of skin when I crossed my legs at meetings. Ed Kosner, editor and publisher of *New York* magazine, explained that seersucker suits were strictly for summer, to be worn only between Memorial Day and Labor Day.

The dress code at *The Star* had not been so demanding. No one cared about my shaggy dark-green coat or brown plastic boots lined with faux fur, or the happy yellow pom-pom ski hat I wore on cold days. My briefcase was a Sloan's Supermarket bag. It wasn't much different at the *Herald*, where I kept a tie on the back of my chair in case someone important came to lunch.

If genetic coding links all journalists, those working for fashion magazines and supermarket tabloids are at opposite ends of the chain — although *Elle* staffers did snatch up the free copies of *The Star* that were left in piles around the building.

At *Elle,* looking chic was essential. Black dominated the tribal costume, with added semaphores of taste such as the H buckles on Hermes belts; Chanel's interlocking Cs; the Gucci strip; and the golden LV monogram. Accessories were commonly layered around necks and wrists, and there was subtle disapproval of those who didn't get it quite right, who overloaded the accessories, or clashed their colours, or fabrics.

After I took the job, we launched *Mirabella* with the doyenne of Manhattan fashion magazines, Grace Mirabella. Her chiming accessories acted as an early-warning system when she prowled the office. At *Elle* and *Mirabella*, I developed an inconvenient work-related condition — a sneezing allergy to strong-smelling perfumes.

Grace Mirabella was one of the best-connected journalists on the Manhattan social scene. Dinner parties at her Upper East Side brownstone were full of notable people. I met Donna Karan there, just as she was hitting the big time; Peggy Noonan had gained renown for the speeches she wrote for Ronald Reagan; Tom Wolfe sang Christmas carols — and I saved the company millions of dollars after meeting Carl Icahn.

Icahn was already a billionaire and famous for his forceful takeover tactics. He had gained control of Trans World Airlines (TWA), so it seemed polite to show respect for his success. I asked the kind of question sure to flatter a towering tycoon: 'When you acquire a company, what is the first thing you do?'

He smiled. 'I fire all the procurement people,' he said. 'Not because they're crooked or taking kickbacks, but if they stay in the job too long they become friends with the people they're buying from. They play golf together, they go to shows. That softens them when they're renewing deals.'

Soon after my conversation with Icahn, we were negotiating to renew a multi-year printing deal. I put the company's most cantankerous finance executive alongside the regular negotiators. He was a stranger to the people we were buying from, and he was tough. We reduced our costs by $90 million.

The least fashionable member of the *Elle* staff was also its most important. Regis Pagniez was the publication director, and he dressed in a simple shirt with an old V-neck sweater. Sometimes, but not often, he combed his grey hair. He had spent years in the superficial atmosphere of fashion, and I suspect most of its rituals bored him. He cared only about shapes — a handbag, a silk scarf, a face.

Pagniez could crop a picture so that a simple shoe looked like a beautiful sculpture. It was wonderful watching him work; he would select a shape or a photo that he knew was right, but no words could explain, only the sight of it on the page.

Elle was a 50-50 venture with the French publisher Hachette Filipacchi, and Pagniez made it an instant success, which caused brief but satisfying anxiety at *Vogue*. He was a perfect example of how exasperating the best creative people can be, and a lesson for me in dealing with them. I worked with many: art directors who stormed off after mild criticism; columnists who went into hysterics when a sub-editor invaded their fine prose with a clumsy comma; editors who sulked after a gentle rebuke about an underplayed story or an oversized headline. But in my entire career, no one compared with Regis Pagniez. Any challenge provoked in him a wild Latin tantrum. We had many arguments. Didier Guerin was my French counterpart in the joint venture and once had to jump between us as Pagniez reached for my throat.

Pagniez's boss, mentor, and defender was Daniel Filipacchi, chairman of Hachette Filipacchi magazines and a legend in France. He had started as a *Paris Match* photographer and made many millions in media. He also had a vast and renowned collection of surrealist art.

I once complained about Pagniez over lunch at Filipacchi's country house near Paris. Filipacchi gave me an understanding look. 'Certainly, Regis is a prima donna, but he is brilliant also, and worth the trouble he causes. Companies must always burst with imagination, and they need people like him.'

It was good advice. I repeated his lecture many times to orderly minded executives struggling to cope with crazy creatives. All the same, I was secretly relieved in 1988 when we sold back to Hachette our 50 per cent share of *Elle*.

But I did not forget Filipacchi's wisdom, or my visit to the toilet down the long corridor leading from his dining room. The walls of his home were covered with paintings, and that included the bathroom. There was an eye-catching blue abstract low on the wall to the left of the toilet where I stood. It was a perilous position for a valuable work of art, easily within splashing distance. I mentioned it to the waiting butler as he led me back to the dining room.

'Yes. It is a Picasso, sir,' he said.

The job did have variety. Glossy magazines dominated the group when I arrived, but we brought it down to earth by buying *Soap Opera Digest*. This came with the rights to an annual awards ceremony for soap operas. Within a few weeks of watching the high fashion parades in Paris of Gaultier, Givenchy, and Chanel, I was in the ballroom of the Beverly Hills Hilton applauding winners from classic daytime soaps such as *The Young and the Restless* and *One Life to Live*.

John B. Evans was president of Murdoch Magazines, and theoretically my boss. He was a brilliant, quixotic Welshman and an important figure in the history of News Corp.

Evans was a recovering alcoholic and drug addict, and always eager to share the details of his struggle. He had spent years crewing private yachts in Europe and the United States before becoming a classified advertising salesman at *The Village Voice*. In a company tolerant of quirky characters, Evans rose to become publisher of *The Voice*, then president of its magazine division.

As a manager, he was haphazard and restless; too distractible to spend time on detail, and with a propensity for madcap ideas. But in his search for excitement, Evans gave the first warning of the thing that would threaten News Corp's newspapers more than anything before.

In the late 1980s, when Tim Berners-Lee had yet to become famous for creating the World Wide Web, Evans began warning of the dangers of a dull sounding thing called 'electronic publishing'. He became a digital apostle, the canary down the mine who sensed the changing atmosphere that would demolish the business model that for generations provided riches for the owners of print.

He told us that the end of days was coming for any business that depended on 'smearing ink on crushed trees'. In the future, he warned, everything would come to us on screens and these screens would become mobile. They would act as 'butlers', organising our lives with calendars, and access to banks and restaurants. They would also, he said, provide customised news, tailored to the interests of each user.

He took groups of us to the pioneering Media Lab at the Massachusetts Institute of Technology in Boston, where its founder Nicholas Negroponte issued terrifying predictions. The coming age would offer instant and absolute communication, he said, and fresh news would no longer be delivered in lumbering trucks.

When Microsoft was still the spear-point of new technology in the early 1990s, Evans arranged a visit to its Seattle HQ, and we flew there with Rupert. After signing an agreement to keep their secrets, Microsoft told us they had purchased electronic rights to *Funk & Wagnalls Encyclopedia* and were going to compress its entire contents onto a single CD-ROM — a disc that looked like the one that transformed the music industry. This disc would be searchable by typing 'keywords' on a computer keypad. Its contents would include sounds and images; at the touch of a few keys, you could see a bird and hear its song. This vast, magical, almost weightless encyclopaedia would be called Encarta.

Microsoft gave us a glimpse into the future, and while CD-ROMs were not the future for long, we knew that the information business was heading for an upheaval. But it was only a hint of what lay ahead, and we left Seattle uneasy but not yet alarmed.

When I went to Murdoch Magazines in 1987, digital media was not a threat, but new technology was already changing the industry. Software that produced magazine pages quickly and cheaply had lowered the cost of entry, and the market was crowded. Magazines, like most newspapers, earn their profits from advertisers. With only so much advertising money to go around, the competition was intense.

Having moved to the business side of media, I spent a lot of time with advertisers. Apart from Portale's instructions on the dress code, there were other rules. When meeting advertisers, it was important not to wear or carry a competitor's product. Wearing a Hermes scarf to a Chanel sales meeting was never a good idea, nor was drinking a Diet Coke in the company of a Pepsi marketing director. Once, when Ralph Lauren came for lunch with Rupert, an advertising executive handed us Ralph Lauren ties. 'Be sure to wear them. He will notice.' I found an old Lauren sports jacket in my closet and wore that, too. It might have helped. Back at his office, Lauren told his marketing team: 'I want to advertise in that magazine every week.' Unfortunately, it was a monthly, but we liked his attitude.

It is dangerous to appease advertisers when they complain about editorial content. When *New York* magazine was working on a long profile of Calvin Klein, and the writer Michael Gross was asking penetrating questions about Klein's personal life, all Calvin Klein advertising was pulled from the magazine. They were spending about $1 million a year, so it was a big deal. I took one of Klein's partners for a long lunch and he gave me an ultimatum: fire Michael Gross or lose the ad revenue. I have always found threats like this easy to handle; if we capitulate to one advertiser, others would soon try the same trick. I told Klein's partner what he could do with his $1 million a year ads, and the lunch came to an abrupt end. Gross continued writing for us, and Calvin Klein returned to the magazine, but not before we lost millions.

Years later, when I was running Rupert's British newspapers, the Korean company Hyundai was starting to gain a foothold selling its cars in Britain when *The Sunday Times*' motoring writer Jeremy Clarkson gave one of their new models a scathing review. He added that no country whose citizens 'ate dogs' could ever make a decent motorcar. Hyundai threatened to pull its advertising from all News International newspapers unless there was an apology. I told our panicking sales executives to let the Koreans know that Clarkson was the country's most popular motoring writer and that over-the-top remarks were part of his brand. I also told them to assure Hyundai that the company had no opinion on the Korean tradition of dog eating. They kept advertising. The hard reality was that the pages around Clarkson articles were prime real estate for selling cars.

At Murdoch Magazines, it wasn't just the intense world of advertising that was new to me; there was also The Numbers. I had never seen a balance sheet, or a profit and loss statement, or heard terms like discounted cash flow, or accretion. Most journalists think they're the only people in the business who matter. They aren't interested in what goes on behind the scenes in the less obvious or visible parts of publishing. I know because I was like them.

Now, I had to cope with it all: advertisers, printing contracts, marketing budgets, distribution costs, paper prices. These were all areas where numbers ruled, not words. Numbers had never been my friends. The grades and comments on my school mathematics reports were painful. The stories numbers tell are stubborn and unchangeable; you can't add a flourish, as you can with words, at least not legitimately.

For some clever people, numbers live and breathe. Rupert loved and understood numbers. It was always fun to see him show off in meetings, scratching billion-dollar figures on a pad with his green pen, working out if deals made sense. He might have made bad decisions now and then, but it wasn't because he couldn't count. I never saw him use a calculator.

I worried about numbers, but Marty Singerman calmed me down. He was one of the few who could match Rupert when it came to mental calculations. 'It's common sense, just common sense,' he would say as he guided me through my first profit and loss statement.

He was right. Any business comes down to this: the proper balance between spending and earning; increasing revenue while controlling costs; how much actual cash the business earns; whether customers are being charged enough; and whether debtors pay up on time.

In making acquisitions, you need, simply, to understand the business and be confident that you can make it worth more than you're paying for it. Mostly, it is about the talent who will come with the purchase; the most valuable assets go home at the end of the day, and that doesn't always need to include the bosses. Will the new people be easy to work with and fit into the company's personality and style? If it's a business with a new idea, is their intellectual property safe — patented — or easily copied? How crowded is the competition? If it is crowded, will our purchase accelerate the target company's chance of success?

In deciding whether to buy a new company, other calculations come into play, but the final decision is more abstract than any mathematical equation. There is a natural tension between 'ideas people' and 'numbers people', but they need each other. Numbers keep a creative business grounded, but ideas make it fly. You can't rely too much on piling statistics into a computer when the most important currency is ideas, and everything depends on those quirky, mercurial, undependable readers.

A good idea can overwhelm every cautious accountant's gloomy spreadsheet — but a big financial mistake can bring disaster. In the summer of 1988, News Corp agreed to buy Triangle Publications, publisher of *TV Guide, Seventeen* magazine, and the *Daily Racing Form*. The price was close to $3 billion. It was the biggest acquisition in the history of US publishing.

TV Guide had a weekly circulation of more than 17 million and was the trophy of the deal. For decades, Rupert had imagined owning it; long ago, he had acquired a copycat publication in Australia, *TV Week*.

This acquisition was the high point of the biggest spending spree of Rupert's career. In the 1980s, he spent billions buying TV stations across America, as well as the 20th Century Fox film studio, Triangle Publications, and more newspapers in America and Australia. Rupert didn't like waking up in a town where he didn't own a newspaper.

At the time of these deals, interest rates were low and banks saw Rupert as a safe bet. In 1987, he unlocked a river of new profits to service more debt when he won a year-long conflict with British trade unions whose shakedown tactics had strangled his newspapers and the entire industry.

These were high-stress years. I remember the day we closed the Triangle deal and handed billions to publisher Walter Annenberg. We were waiting in a motel near Triangle's HQ in Radnor, Pennsylvania. Lawyers and finance people were working the phones in an ill-lit conference room, organising the wiring of cash to Annenberg's banks. Rupert was standing in the lobby with me and a couple of others, talking about what we would do when we walked into Triangle's huge offices to take over the business. Here was the tough and invincible mogul on the brink of another mega deal. But then I saw a red smear on his fingers, staining the white handkerchief he had taken from the breast pocket of his jacket. He had picked at the cuticles of his fingernails until they were bleeding.

At the time of the *TV Guide* deal, Rupert had built his company with debt instead of selling equity. He never wanted other shareholders to threaten his control. But in 1990 a global recession hit and interest rates began rising. The mountain of borrowed cash that had fed News Corp's spectacular growth turned into a potentially fatal trap. The company's share price plunged as details emerged of the debt — it had reached more than $7 billion — and free-lending banks became afraid News Corp could not meet its obligations.

At the time, News Corp was also losing £2 million a week on a risky new start-up in Britain. Sky was the satellite television service Rupert had launched against the country's broadcasting duopoly — the BBC and competing ITV commercial channels. But Sky faced the competition of another newcomer — British Satellite Broadcasting — and the two were beating each other to death.

The debt crisis was the existential threat of Rupert's career, far more dangerous than the phone-hacking scandal 20 years later. The company owed money to more than 140 banks, and it faced the immense and potentially impossible task of persuading every one of them to keep its debt and extend the repayment terms. A single bank's refusal risked triggering an exodus by them all, and that could mean the company's liquidation.

Bringing round these anxious bankers involved the most important show-and-tell in the company's history. Executives of every bank were assembled in London and New York to be persuaded that, for all its overload of debt, News Corp was profitable, growing, and a sure success. Our life-or-death mission was persuading them to cut us some slack. Whatever fear I had of public speaking, that experience cured it. Nothing would ever compete with the tension of those days in the autumn of 1991. When we appeared first in the City of London in a steep-tiered auditorium, with a sea of sceptical faces looking down on us, it felt like the Colosseum.

Never again in the business would so much be at stake. The debt drama was a brutal experience for Rupert. His life's work was on the brink of ruin. He called me at home one Sunday night to talk. It was a wandering, inconsequential conversation, just gossip and a discussion of the day's news. We spoke only briefly about the banks.

His voice was low and drained. He was famous for inexplicable, long silences during phone calls, but this time the silences were longer than usual. After a long pause, he said: 'How are you doing? You sound tired. Are you tired?'

Actually, I felt fine after a relaxed weekend, but I didn't want to tell him that.

'Yes, I'm exhausted,' I said.

'Me too,' he replied, with relief.

The author William Shawcross, in his 1992 biography, gives a graphic account of Rupert about to place a make-or-break phone call to the president of a Pittsburgh bank. Everything was at stake. This bank was the last holdout; News Corp could disintegrate if it refused to roll over its $10 million debt, and Rupert had to stop them.

Ann Lane, a Citibank vice president, was Rupert's chief adviser during the crisis, and she told Shawcross:

> It's not a pretty sight to see a great man like that. He was so vulnerable. One phone call could mean the end of his whole life's work ... But my job was not to show panic. My job was to keep Rupert calm and focused ... He didn't wig out. He was visibly shaking, but he didn't go crazy. He wasn't hyperventilating.

That Pittsburgh bank came through, and News Corp survived the debt crisis, wounded but pretty well intact. The banks were happy when Sky stemmed its cash drain by merging with its competitor and forming British Sky Broadcasting. But they also demanded the company raise cash by selling assets.

The company sold 8 of the 10 magazines I was managing, including *New York,* the city's leading weekly; *Seventeen*, since the 1940s, America's most popular magazine for girls; the film magazine, *Premiere*; *European Travel & Life,* the high-end bi-monthly peddling its illusory image of the old countries; and *Soap Opera Digest*. The two remaining were *Mirabella* and *TV Guide*. *Mirabella* was struggling to break even (it still hadn't when sold to another buyer four years later), and *TV Guide*'s circulation was declining in a losing battle against local newspapers that were providing more detailed TV listings. It was no fun being required to help with the sell-off.

John Veronis, the New York media broker behind many of America's biggest deals, was hired to help. He produced a string of interested buyers and I had to explain the business to them. The ultimate buyers surprised me. K-III Communications was an offshoot of the New York investment firm Kohlberg Kravis Roberts. They saw our titles as a trophy asset for the magazine group they were building, but they didn't seem to know anything about magazines. After our first meeting, I felt my time had been wasted. I'd spent more than an hour answering their questions — and they were pretty basic questions. 'These people will never buy,' I told John Veronis. 'They know nothing about what we do.'

But Veronis had made millions knowing how to sense a good prospect. 'I think you're wrong,' he said.

I turned out to be both wrong and right — wrong to dismiss them as buyers, but right that they didn't understand the business.

'Looks like we've got a deal with K-III,' Rupert said. 'But there's a catch. If they make the purchase, they're going to make it a condition of the sale that you go with it. They need you to teach them about magazines.'

By now, I was president of the magazine division — John B. Evans had been given an assignment in London — and until that moment the plan was to put me in charge of US publishing, replacing Marty Singerman, who was due to retire. This group included the magazines we were not selling, *TV Guide* and *Mirabella*, as well as newspapers in Boston and Texas, the *New York Post*, and a highly profitable company that inserted cents-off shopping coupons in Sunday newspapers.

'Go with them for a couple of years,' Rupert said. 'You'll make a lot of money, and I promise that a job will be here for you when you come back.'

I wasn't happy.

'I don't mind making money,' I told him, 'but I would sooner make it working for you.'

But I couldn't refuse and expect Rupert to forgive me. The magazines were the bulk of a $600 million deal (we were also selling them the *Daily Racing Form* newspaper) and News Corp needed the cash. It was 1991, and 32 years since I first worked at the company. I was enjoying how it continued to grow and change, and felt dismal at the prospect of hanging out with the K-III people. They were a joyless group set on turning around the magazines in a few years and selling them at a big profit for themselves. It's a popular and reasonable activity in all areas of business; it just didn't excite me. There was not much choice, however, so I continued with my meetings and tutoring. But as the deal looked stronger, I stopped being so enthusiastic in my efforts to help them, and that probably explained what happened next.

'I've great news,' said Rupert one morning. 'Stan has got you out of the deal. You're staying.' Stan Shuman was a partner at the investment bank Allen & Co. He was part of the negotiating team and a good friend, and he knew how badly I wanted to stay.

The magazine sale was a painful retreat for Rupert. He had built his name as an innovator and conqueror whose empire only expanded. Now he had been forced to sell a business he wanted to keep, and he blamed himself. He was miserable about it.

He organised a dinner for the departing executives, about 50 of them, and we sat in his office early that evening discussing what he would say to them. He wanted to be sure to have a grateful remark for every individual in the room. He put down his pen at last and looked silently across his office, in the direction of a wall of television screens.

'I feel like I've let them all down,' he said.

CHAPTER 18

Down the Fox hole

There was an unreliable rhythm to life with Rupert. Sometimes he called several times a day, asked you to lunch, laughed at your jokes, seemed fascinated by everything you had to say. This experience felt great, especially for newcomers and rising executives; they thought the boss had admitted them to his inner circle.

Old timers, seeing new executives dazzled by this best-friend treatment, considered them Rupert's 'flavour of the month'. They knew it was unlikely to last because Rupert's true best friend was always The Business. When the infatuation ebbed and another dazzling objective or person caught Rupert's eye, there would be knowing looks as the bewildered and abandoned executive agonised over what he or she had done wrong.

I became good at providing therapy to executives and editors who suddenly felt out in the cold. Sophisticated people would come to me, wounded because 'Rupert hasn't called me for more than a month.'

My response was always the same: 'Lucky you.'

I had been there, too. But experience made it easier to handle; it even became a relief when yet another moment in the sun had come and gone.

It was the way Rupert operated and an occupational hazard of working for him. The secret was to never take it personally; he was oblivious to hurt feelings. He was like a visiting comet, and the mysterious astronomy of Rupert made it impossible to know when he would appear and how long he would stay.

Rupert's style, and his power over people, meant his was not a regular multinational, with tidy layers and streamlined channels of process. It became more conventional when it was very big, but that wasn't the style of company that helped him triumph.

Maybe News Corp was a personality cult. It didn't occur to me when I worked there, which might be the proof itself. Rupert's attention was the drug of choice for certain needy executives. He could also be a tyrant, but big business has never been short of tyrants and not many earned the intense devotion he did.

Maybe he has what's known as 'charismatic authority'. The term was created a hundred years ago by the German philosopher Max Weber. In an essay analysing styles of leadership, Weber wrote of charismatic authority as 'the wholly personal devotion to, and a personal trust in, the revelations, heroism, or other leadership qualities of an individual.' These qualities, Weber said, were possessed by successful demagogues, warlords, and even prophets. Whether or not Rupert belonged in the company of warlords and prophets, he certainly possessed for a lot of people a special power to engender loyalty and obedience; when he had you in his beam he was impossible to ignore and difficult to refuse.

The most unfortunate time he turned his light on me was in the late autumn of 1992 when I was in New York, running the American publishing operation of magazines and newspapers. Marty Singerman had retired as planned, but luckily for me had agreed to remain as a consultant.

The group had been diminished by the forced sell-off during

the debt crisis, but it was still substantial, and I was enjoying myself. Then Rupert started calling me.

For the first time, he had gained total control of the Fox operation in Los Angeles. Barry Diller, a Hollywood veteran with a powerful personality and a long record of success, had left to set up his own business. Diller and Rupert had not worked easily together; power sharing was not a compelling concept for two men so accustomed to having their own way.

I was with them in a meeting once when Rupert made a mildly dismissive remark about 'you Hollywood types' and Diller pounced like an alpha beast protecting its territory.

'This is our town and these are good hard-working people,' he said, glaring at Rupert.

Diller had an entertaining repertoire of glares and his top lip curled dramatically when he was angry. There was a bated silence. No one took any notice when I tried getting back to business. Rupert didn't say a word. He just threw down his pen and sent it bouncing down the long table. The meeting soon ended.

Diller was only two years older than me, but he was a formidable figure in LA. At first sight, he looked mild — bald and short, with a mottled, relief-map complexion — but he was fierce and shouty, and people treated him as they would an unexploded bomb. Rupert held him in wary awe. 'He's smart as a barrel of monkeys and as tricky,' he said. But Rupert was strategic and patient — most of the time — and chose his battles with care; he might have backed off that day, but he hadn't succumbed.

A year after that bad-tempered meeting, Diller was gone and Rupert had a free hand to — as he put it after every purchase — 'change the culture'. Diller and Rupert got along much better when each was running his own empire.

Each time he acquired a business, Rupert became manically

restless until making it his own, sweeping aside old practices and purging executives he didn't like, which was usually all of them.

For weeks, he had been calling me almost every day from LA, sometimes twice a day. The conversation was never about the companies I was running. He only wanted to talk about Fox and his problems there.

I knew my unplanned life was in for another change. Just like my army dad, I went where I was sent, and most of the time it worked out well. Far-off generals had moved me round the world as a boy, now High Command was on the phone each day, and these conversations were leading somewhere.

Eventually, in his low, matter-of-fact mumble, Rupert revealed himself. 'I want your help,' he said, and asked me to take charge of Fox's television station group and its news operation. The group was nationwide, a big and profitable unit with stations in the largest American cities. I had zero experience of the television business, but Rupert already knew that. I was astonished by the offer, but couldn't resist it.

I knew it was a risk, but what was the worst that could happen? If I had refused every job that scared me, I would never have gone anywhere. Sure, I could be fired, but every job worth having comes with that risk.

My colleagues in New York were full of congratulations about my Fox appointment. But they treated me with the tempered good cheer extended to a friend who has been assigned to cover a dangerous war. No welcoming calls came through from Hollywood. Maybe I shouldn't have been surprised. With Diller's departure, the West Coast had become even more suspicious of News Corp. Fox and News Corp were clashing cultures, and it was dawning on LA that there could only be one winner.

My new boss was Chase Carey, the Fox group's chief operating officer, but I didn't hear a word from him until he telephoned me at home the evening before my appointment was to be made public. 'You'll have a problem doing this job if you're not an American citizen,' he said. American law had required Rupert to become a citizen in the 1980s in order to acquire his first television stations, but I had never heard that citizenship was required to manage them. Not that it mattered.

'I've been an American citizen for seven years,' I told Carey. He sounded thwarted, and ended the call without an encouraging word. Carey was a decent man, but never fulsome; his extravagant, curling moustache gave a misleading hint of flamboyance. But even for him it was odd, and I felt uneasy.

But I had been in charge of new acquisitions before. I was accustomed to cold welcomes and false smiles. I was good at this by now; I knew how to win over people. That's what I thought.

I refused to let Carey's call bother me. We were off to Hollywood, and a celebration was required. I called Mum and Dad in Australia and put them on a plane to Hawaii, where we all stayed for a week in adjoining oceanfront rooms at the Kahala Hotel in Honolulu. We had a great time, once Mum recovered from the shock that a boiled egg cost $8. At the end, Dad, who was in his eighties by now and still didn't show his feelings much, told me in that 'h' dropping manner that I'm ashamed to say once embarrassed me: 'Cor, it's the best 'oliday I ever 'ad.'

———

We were both new in our jobs when I was invited to Bill Clinton's White House in the winter of 1993. I thought it would be a friendly visit, but I was wrong. I didn't meet Clinton — that happened a couple of years later — but went to the West Wing to meet George Stephanopoulos.

He was 32, and newly installed as the White House director of communications. He did not greet me warmly. 'You responsible for that so-called news show called *A Current Affair*?'

I was, I agreed.

'That show is a complete disgrace,' he said.

A Current Affair was a daily half-hour news show, and the pioneer of 'tabloid TV' in America. The sober establishment of American network news hated it. To them, *A Current Affair* was the creation of a demolition squad sent from the underbelly of journalism to swing a wrecking ball through their high ethics and fine taste. This was not an entirely invalid point of view.

The show provided an unabating diet of celebrity gossip, salacious trials, messy divorces, gruesome murders, state executions, and evil cults. It ran strange small-town stories: a sheriff who videoed himself and his wife having sex had carelessly handed the tape into his rental store; a high school principal was suspended for showing his pupils pornographic films; the annual Fainting Goat Festival in Marshall County, Tennessee (the goats were a local amusement because they fell over when startled due to a congenital disorder).

Above all, *A Current Affair* liked tales about famous people in deep trouble. For its producers, the emergence of a young, handsome, and wayward head of state was the perfect running story.

'Fox should be ashamed of itself,' Stephanopoulos said, and stared at me, waiting for a response. One of his short legs was crossed high over the other, so I faced the slightly worn sole of his new left shoe.

'Please explain to me why we should be ashamed?' I said, and Stephanopoulos duly obliged, pouring out his grief over the 'scurrilous, gratuitous, ridiculous' lies he claimed *A Current Affair* had told about his boss, William Jefferson Clinton.

'The president is not happy. None of it's true, and your people know it's not true.'

'An awful lot of Americans are not so sure about that,' I countered. 'This is a legitimate story and they are entitled to cover it.' I knew I sounded sanctimonious; I meant to.

Clinton had astonished most of us by riding to the White House through the storm of accusations that began in early 1992 when Gennifer Flowers, a government worker from his home state of Arkansas, claimed she had been his lover for 12 years. Other allegations added to a persuasive body of evidence that the would-be president might not be a model husband in an ideal marriage. The scandal was in a lull by the time I went to the White House, but *A Current Affair* had not gone quiet enough for the energetic new communications director.

'You cannot expect this administration to take seriously a media company that broadcasts this kind of garbage,' he said.

I didn't respond to that, but felt chastened as I walked from the White House. Had the programme gone too far? Had we made an unnecessary enemy of a new and popular president?

Some of the Fox political team had been with me at the meeting, including the relentless and famously well-connected reporter Niles Lathem. 'Don't worry about it,' Lathem told me. 'He's still doing it. He sneaks out of the White House at night to see women.'

I couldn't believe it. 'How could he still be seeing other women after his entire life almost came to ruins over Gennifer Flowers?' I asked. 'He would have to be completely mad to still carry on like that.'

Lathem smiled at me, and raised his arms in mock surrender. 'Ok,' he said.

Taking flak for *A Current Affair*'s wild ways was a small part of my job. The Fox-owned stations I managed were in big cities: New York, Los Angeles, Chicago, Dallas, Houston, and Washington. I flew so often among them that American Airlines gave me a medal: a Million Mile card.

We also had a tiny station in Salt Lake City, Utah, where the programme director was an energetic young woman named Elisabeth Murdoch. Rupert wanted his kids in the business, and while they progressed disproportionately quickly, they started at the bottom.

Almost all programming created by the television stations was local news. The Fox network provided evening primetime; programmes like *The Simpsons*, *X Files*, and *Beverly Hills 90210* had driven the network's success and made it a serious challenger to the long-established big three — ABC, NBC, and CBS. Syndicated programmes purchased from outside production companies filled most other time slots. These were daytime talk shows, and old sitcoms and dramas sold as repeats at the end of their network runs.

A Current Affair was a Fox-produced show for sale to any buyer — at its most popular it was broadcast five days a week in 150 cities. It was handed to me to oversee because it qualified as a news show. I also suspect no one else at Fox wanted anything to do with it.

When I arrived in Los Angeles, News Corp was growing its reputation as a colonising multinational, seizing properties across the world. Fox was still a restive new territory, and News Corp's wild streak worried people. In particular, they disliked the tabloid antics of the *New York Post* and *The Star*. When my appointment was announced, trade publication headlines called me an 'Ex-Tabloid Editor'. The Fox people hated that.

News Corp didn't entirely deserve its rowdy reputation. It also owned the publisher HarperCollins, as well as more staid titles like *TV Guide*, *The Times* of London, and the *Times Literary Supplement*. But *A Current Affair* was regarded as a tabloid Trojan horse, and, for all its success, Fox treated it like the delinquent child in the family.

The show was produced by transplants from Rupert's tabloid print operation; cheerful subversives who saw it as their mission to teach American journalism how to touch the masses with torrid scandal and heart-warming 'human interest' stories. Many were Australians and they hung their national flag on the office wall, like a territorial claim.

When he was still at Fox, Barry Diller stood at a management conference in Aspen, Colorado, and complained that *A Current Affair* and the company tabloids were contaminating 20th Century Fox. He claimed box office stars would think twice about working for a studio associated with newspapers that trashed the lives of their friends, and might one day trash them.

But Rupert liked the show. He had always thought American journalists were self-absorbed and elitist, and *A Current Affair* was his television antidote, another of his attempts to cater for a neglected market.

His favourite line to queasy journalists was: 'You worry too much about what your next-door neighbours think.' I knew what he meant. As editor-in-chief of *The Star*, living in a Westchester County enclave of lawyers and bankers, groups at house parties ignored me when I told them what I did. Later, when I ran more 'respectable' magazines and newspapers, and my name appeared in *The Wall Street Journal* and *The New York Times,* I ignored their eager dinner invitations.

When Rupert had an instinct about something, it was hard to change his mind and risky to try. In Britain, when a singing contest called *Pop Idol* was a hit, Fox stonewalled his efforts to create a US version, convinced that a reheat of out-of-date talent shows would never work. When Rupert got his way, *American Idol* became one of the most successful shows in history and ran for 15 years.

Prone to gloating, Rupert called the network president after *American Idol*'s huge opening. The president was sitting triumphantly in his office, surrounded by bouquets and gifts of champagne, soaking up the praise for a success he had resisted. Rupert's call upset him so much, it was said he went home unwell.

Developing TV shows is a risky and expensive business. There was high anxiety every year in the spring when the new season was planned. In those days, before the upheaval of cable and online streaming, networks presented almost all their new shows in the autumn.

Each new season was a casino bet. Networks spent hundreds of millions of dollars every year developing and testing new shows. The hit-to-flop ratio was high, but when one worked — as it so spectacularly did with *The Simpsons* and *American Idol* — Fox would make a fortune, and the network president would become a hero. But network presidents are like football managers — too many missed goals and bad calls will get them fired.

I displayed no gift for spotting good shows. New pilots were shown each year to a panel of insiders. We spent days watching them in a darkened room. I once saw a pilot with a preposterous storyline about UFOs, aliens, and mad government conspiracies. It looked like a sure-fire flop to me, and I was foolish enough to say so, but *The X Files* was a worldwide hit and ran for 10 years.

When we watched the opening of a new late-night chat show starring Chevy Chase, I told Rupert and the others how much I enjoyed it. They gazed at me in silence, as if I were crazy. The show was a flop and cancelled after five weeks.

Decisions on films were difficult, too. At a management conference in 1986, we saw a preview of a James Cameron film, a grisly thriller in which disagreeable extra-terrestrials slaughter the crew of a spacecraft. It was not a good choice for an audience composed significantly of elderly board directors and their wives. There were shouts of horror, and people fled the room at the sight of an alien dismembering an astronaut. Barry Diller feared he had a disaster on his hands, but he had chosen the wrong audience — *Aliens* was one of the year's biggest grossing films.

Diller told me later: 'You can do all the market research you like, but the only truth is at the box office.'

I was in a meeting when Peter Chernin, then head of the 20th Century Fox film studio, was enthusiastically telling Rupert about a new James Cameron creation; yet another film about the sinking of the *Titanic*. Rupert was sceptical. 'That doesn't sound much good. Everyone knows how it ends.'

Chernin persisted. 'It's more than that. It's a great love story,' he said.

Titanic became the highest-grossing film of all time, the love story between the characters played by Leonardo DiCaprio and Kate Winslet at its heart. It remained number one for 12 years until another Fox-backed James Cameron film, *Avatar*, was released in 2009.

One challenge for me was raising Fox's profile in news. Long before it happened, Rupert was determined to challenge the monopoly of CNN with a Fox news channel. Others at the company, convinced CNN was unbeatable, kept managing to talk him out of it.

In 1993, he told me to prepare a business plan for a news channel, and I put together a team of news and business development executives. A couple of weeks later, he called me at home one Saturday. 'Ease up on that for now until you hear from me again,' he said. Three years later, Roger Ailes created Fox News. I didn't have Ailes' vision of what a news channel should be; his gold dust idea for stridently right-wing programmes didn't occur to me. Even if it had, I could never have brought Roger's heartfelt verve to the task.

Rupert also wanted to challenge CBS's *60 Minutes* with a weekly network news magazine. I worked on this project with Van Gordon Sauter, one of the great characters of television news. He had a billowing white beard and loved bow ties, broad braces, tweed, and telling old jokes in his booming baritone.

Rupert liked Sauter because he had the right kind of enemies. He was forced out as president of CBS News after crusty veterans like

Andy Rooney and Bill Moyers complained he was too down-market. According to Moyers: 'Tax policy had to compete with stories about three-legged sheep, and three-legged sheep won.'

In reality, Sauter was a serious journalist who understood the importance of mixing light and heavy news. He had also become convinced that traditional network news shows were dull, indistinguishable from each other, and therefore doomed. Rupert agreed: 'They look like they were produced by journalists from the same dumb journalism class.'

But we found it impossible to hire the best news talent away from the established networks. They thought moving to Fox was too much of a risk, and they were probably right. They agreed to meet us all the same, of course — then leaked the meetings to their bosses to leverage better contracts and higher salaries. Katie Couric was a star at NBC when she agreed to have breakfast with us. She told us where to meet and was waiting for us, beaming over a cup of coffee. The diner was directly beneath the NBC offices and the place was full of her colleagues. Her bosses knew about the meeting before our eggs arrived.

Occasionally, Sauter and I went on the road together, chasing big stories. This didn't always work out well. In 1993, when Michael Jackson was first accused of child abuse, we drove to his Neverland ranch, north of Los Angeles. It was a French-style chateau in the middle of a fun fair, with a Ferris wheel, a merry-go-round, a petting zoo, and eerie statues of children.

Jackson's father, Joe, met us in a shrine-like room with walls plastered with framed gold discs and photos of his son. He wasn't convinced when we told him it would be a good idea for Michael to tell his story on our Fox news show.

We were invited to talk more over lunch by a man with a colossal girth bursting out of his bright and vast Hawaiian shirt. Beautiful young women were attending to him, placing a napkin across his lap, pouring his wine, and putting food on his plate with great care. They took no notice of us. The man told us he was one of Michael's closest friends and when I made a remark that indicated a shred of doubt about his friend's innocence, he exploded in a wild rage about the injustice and the cruelty of the world. He then produced a huge knife and waved it close to my face, before plunging it with both hands into his food-stacked plate, showering us with crockery pieces and his chicken enchilada. Van and I bolted from Michael Jackson's Neverland without our interview.

We called our news programme *Front Page*, which didn't seem such a retrograde title in 1993. It was aimed at younger viewers, with hyperactive graphics and zippy editing that turned out to be ahead of their time. On-air reporters were young enough to be children of the *60 Minutes* anchors. One was Ronald Reagan Junior, the ex-president's son.

The show did not flourish, however, and David Corvo, the executive producer, was convinced the Fox hierarchy was killing it by neglect. 'No one is going to watch a news show on a Saturday night,' he said. 'And the promotions people are ignoring it. We don't have a chance.'

Everyone knew a news programme was a hard sell — even big successes took time to develop an audience. The problem was that entertainment experts, with no understanding of news, led the network. They didn't have the interest to give *Front Page* enough time and support. Entertainment programmes offered quicker rewards; successful sitcoms and dramas won ratings quickly, delivered instant revenue, and provided job security for people at the top.

Andrew Neil, an abrasive Scot who had recently been a successful editor of *The Sunday Times*, led our second attempt at a news magazine. Rupert regarded Neil with a mixture of admiration and irritation. Neil had developed a high profile, and Rupert never liked his executives getting too much publicity. Once, when the *Financial Times* interviewed me and the paper filled an entire section front with my headshot, a sharp phone call followed. Neil was good on television and radio, and appeared a lot — to the point at which his fame as a talking head was competing with his reputation as editor of *The Sunday Times*.

'He should stay in the office and edit the bloody newspaper,' Rupert would grumble. But what Rupert saw as a failing made Neil a good choice for Fox: he was a successful British editor, enjoyed being on television, and was free of what Rupert thought of as hidebound traditions of American journalism.

Neil would be the show's executive producer and principal talent on-air, but it was agreed he needed a co-anchor. American viewers, or at least producers who pick the talent, care more than Brits about the appearance of their presenters. No one doubted Neil's commanding presence and quick mind, but he was not going to make an impact with striking good looks. A female co-anchor would enhance the show.

The choice for this job was book publisher Judith Regan. Regan had her own imprint at HarperCollins, but she wanted to be on television, and Rupert agreed to give her a chance.

I had never met anyone like Judith Regan because there can't possibly be anyone else like her. Regan would talk to anyone, even people she hardly knew, about the excruciating personal details of her life. It felt sometimes like she was dictating her own scandalous memoirs right there in my office. But she was an oddball with a gift for picking books that would sell millions in the mass market. I thought Neil and Regan were a bright and edgy couple, both clever and driven, but with different approaches to news. Neil was more serious and Regan a little racy; she once worked on the *National Enquirer*.

The first hint of trouble for the show came early. A couple of

LA executives met Neil in his midtown Manhattan offices and were concerned about his accent. 'We'll need subtitles if he goes on air,' one of them told me. 'In Oklahoma, they'll think he's talking another language.'

'They'll get used to it,' I said. 'America is full of immigrants. Foreign accents are everywhere.'

'Not on nationwide television delivering the news,' he retorted.

In the autumn of 1994, Neil and his team brought the pilot of their show to Los Angeles. It was called *Full Disclosure*, and the pilot had a strong mix of stories: a celebrity interview, a piece on the intrigues of international money laundering, and a compelling murder case. It was rough — they knew that — but it was a promising audition of what they could do.

Rupert said he liked it, and, as impatient as ever, asked about a quick launch. No one among the retinue of network chiefs in the room echoed his praise. No one openly disapproved, but they all knew — as did I — that it was more effective to argue in private if Rupert was about to make a mistake.

His parting words to Neil were encouraging: 'Congratulations, and thanks to everyone for their hard work.'

Neil and his team were triumphant as we walked away down the long corridor from Rupert's office, past the film posters marking Fox's past triumphs. He took me by the arm. 'Let's find somewhere to celebrate,' he said.

'Slow down, Andrew. We didn't get the green light,' I told him.

'Sure we did. Rupert loved it. He's told us he wants a quick launch.'

I shook my head. 'Don't be so certain. This isn't Fleet Street. It's not as simple here as being thanked and congratulated by Rupert.'

The green light was never switched on. The network people complained about Neil's accent and Regan's on-air stiffness, and the plan was abandoned. I still think the real problem was that the people who dominated Fox didn't understand news. Maybe they were right, maybe Fox's future fortunes were in buzzy young shows and not serious news; certainly the network flourished, but 20 years later, after a couple more attempts, Fox remained the only big network with no prime-time network news show.

Regan shrugged it off. She went back to publishing bestsellers for HarperCollins until she commissioned a book in which O. J. Simpson was to give a theoretical account of how he 'might' have murdered his ex-wife and her boyfriend. Soon after, she was fired after an allegation of anti-Semitism. She sued and received an undisclosed payment — some reports said $10 million. Within a few years, she was publishing again as Regan Arts.

Andrew Neil, however, was enraged and I couldn't blame him. Rupert asked him to work on his new idea — a nightly late news show — but Neil refused. 'I've had enough. I need to get back to London while I still have currency there,' he said.

Neil was accustomed to the uninterrupted authority and sure hand of the Rupert he knew from print. He went back to London and wrote a lively memoir that he called, in tribute to his failed adventure, *Full Disclosure*.

'I grew to resent that one man could have so much effect on me,' he wrote. His supreme revenge was to reinvent himself as the go-to 'authority' on Rupert — and, ultimately, as the best political interviewer on British television.

CHAPTER 19

Lost in Hollywood

Brentwood Park, north of Sunset Boulevard in the Westside of Los Angeles, was an untroubled world. The only people walking the streets were short and tough Latinos carrying gardening gear into the grounds of other people's homes. Not much broke the silence but the palm-filtered wind and the hum of expensive cars and quiet motors that opened the gates to mansions. The walls and shrubbery hiding these houses were so high and impenetrable that even the desire for privacy became part of the ostentation.

Our next-door neighbour was O. J. Simpson. We met in our back garden the day he said I was the worst tennis player he had ever seen.

The house we had rented in North Bristol Avenue was huge. The guesthouse at the bottom of the garden was the size of our clapboard colonial in Westchester County. Joan Crawford had lived across the street with Douglas Fairbanks Junior; Marilyn Monroe was found dead a short drive away; up the road was the house where Steve McQueen would get drunk and throw beer cans into the yard of his neighbour James Garner; one of our favourite places to eat was the Brentwood Country Mart, where Steven Spielberg had Saturday brunch with his kids.

That was how people talked. They littered their conversation with the names of famous people they lived near or saw in their local stores. It was hard to avoid the habit when Mel Gibson was at the next table at dinner and you were surprised he wasn't taller, or Meryl Streep walked into the local diner with a baby on her hip, just after you had been in the barber's chair next to Harry Morgan, the gruff old colonel from *M*A*S*H*. Or when Mary came home from the gym downhearted after half an hour on a treadmill next to Cindy Crawford. Or that my young son Will's new school was a few hundred yards from the Viper Room in West Hollywood, where River Phoenix dropped dead on the sidewalk from a drug overdose.

In any other town, estate agents talked to house hunters about local schools and when the roof had been replaced, about new electrics, and refitted bathrooms. But in LA salespeople dropped names to add value. 'This is Tony Bennett's house ... Deborah Kerr stayed in that guesthouse ... Chevy Chase's bathroom sinks are this high because he is six-foot five ... William Wyler, the director of *Ben-Hur*, lived here. Check out the old film clippings on his projection room floor.' Even our real estate agent was connected; her husband was Patrick McGoohan, who starred in the cult TV series *The Prisoner*.

The house we chose was grand, but also a little ramshackle, which is why we could afford it. The owners were rich and either proud of it or possessed of an ironic sense of fun; outside the double garage where they had kept their Rolls-Royce, a gigantic dollar sign was etched into the driveway. As well as the oversized guesthouse, it had a wine cellar, a poolroom, a cocktail bar, a maid's apartment, a swimming pool, and a floodlit tennis court.

O. J. Simpson was not our only strange neighbour; the saddest sight at Halloween was of a young boy handing out candy from a table just outside the tall locked gates of the mansion where he lived — alone except for the family security guard.

O. J. Simpson's house was at the back of ours, an even fancier place on North Rockingham Avenue. I didn't need to understand American football to know Simpson was one of the country's most loved celebrities. He was a Hall of Fame football great, with a successful second career as an actor in comedy films. For years, I had seen his broad, easy smile in car-rental commercials for Hertz.

The owners of our house were such good friends with Simpson they put in a gate to connect their gardens. When one family had a party, guests would spill next door to use both tennis courts and basketball hoops. I found out about this gate while playing tennis with my son Thomas one Saturday morning. Tom and I were not a pretty sight; my hand-eye coordination was terrible, and he was no natural at ball games. Several balls had sailed aimlessly over the 15-foot fence into O. J.'s property, and I had just missed a second serve, when the sound of slow, heavy hand clapping came from beneath the big willow drooping over the path to the guest house door.

'I never in my life saw such an awful game of tennis. You are the worst.' We walked towards the big figure in a white t-shirt and grey shorts that was visible through the limp branches and shook hands. 'I'm O. J., your next-door neighbour,' he said.

His face was so open, warm, and familiar I had to fight the urge to treat him like an old friend.

We chatted about tennis, the neighbourhood, and football at the college where Thomas was a student. O. J. said his football career had wrecked his knees, and Tom was pleased to be comparing football injuries with the great O. J. Simpson. He said we should use his pool and tennis court whenever we wanted, and to help ourselves to the food and beer in his poolside refrigerator.

We were 40 minutes under the willow tree with O. J. Simpson, and for 20 of those minutes he was the charming, funny character people loved. But then the cheerfulness drained from his face, his smile disappeared, and his eyes went empty. We sat like reluctant psychiatrists, listening as this familiar stranger poured out his heart.

He was, suddenly, nothing like the man millions thought they knew. He was desperately anxious that we understood his pain, repeating himself constantly. He looked away from us, with an unfixed gaze, until we began to think he had forgotten we were there. He had loved his wife, he said, but she had left him. They were divorced and he missed his children. Now they were going to try to be a couple again. Nicole was going to move back in, but keep her apartment.

He didn't sound sinister; he sounded lost and haunted in the way people can when their lives go wrong. After a while we weren't listening, just waiting for a moment to escape. When we finally left him there, still standing under our tree, Thomas summed up our conversation. 'That was fucking weird,' he said.

We lived for months on the fringes of the O. J. drama, thinking only that a famous man with a messed-up life lived next door. He was friendly enough. Mary wanted to buy a bicycle for my birthday and O. J. told her the best place to shop. She liked him. 'He's not that bright, but he's beautiful and nice,' she said. His kids came round to play with ours, running around the garden and jumping in the pool. Jane, my daughter, went to the same pre-school as their youngest. We went next door to a pool party. Thomas watched O. J. play tennis with Bruce Jenner long before he became Caitlyn.

Then his housekeeper started coming to our house to sit in the kitchen and cry and talk about the arguments O. J. and Nicole were having. 'They're going to kill each other,' she said, but we knew it was only a figure of speech.

One day, O. J. sat on our front deck talking about how he

was struggling to make a success of being back with Nicole. One problem, he said, was his housekeeper — Nicole hated her. 'They can't be in the house together. They're always fighting,' he said, 'Can you give her a job?' When we said we couldn't, O. J. went door to door in the neighbourhood, looking for someone to employ his troublesome housekeeper.

On Sunday 12 June 1994, we took Jane for a dance performance at the local school. She wore a pink tutu, and, in an early act of single-mindedness, decided firmly against going on stage to perform. We waited hopefully in the auditorium for her to appear, a few rows ahead of the Simpson family, whose eight-year-old daughter Sydney was also dancing. O. J. was there, but he sat apart from Nicole. It was the last time they were seen together in public.

I heard the news next morning in the KTTV Fox newsroom, which was beneath my office in Hollywood. It's nothing to be proud of, but double murders involving famous people are inclined to pep up a newsroom. Big news and blanket coverage is easier to organise than piecing together a string of smaller stories and trying to make them seem exciting. Everyone from advertising sales people to news anchors loves it when lots of people are watching.

Shortly after midnight, Sukru Boztepe, a neighbour drawn to the scene by the wails of a dog, found the bodies of Nicole Simpson, aged 35, and her friend Ronald Goldman, a 25-year-old waiter. They had been stabbed outside Nicole's apartment, two miles from Simpson's house. Sydney and her six-year-old brother Justin were asleep inside.

While the news was breaking, a convoy of television vans laid their deep track marks in the perfect green verges of Brentwood Park, and sprouted satellite dishes, ready to tell the story to the world. Over-groomed television reporters struggled for the best angles for live shots, and photographers, cameras clattering at their necks, competed for the most promising spots to position their aluminium ladders around the high hedges of O. J.'s estate.

For weeks to follow, the rough and ugly outside world arrived to violate the precious serenity of Brentwood Park. The theme parks of California — Knott's Berry Farm, Disney Adventure Park, Universal Studios — had a competitor. It was 360 North Rockingham Avenue, and this show was free of charge.

The rowdy, untidy, picnicking, camper vanning, beer drinking, rap blaring, plump, and happy proletariat — the 'rubberneckers' and 'looky-loos' — trampled flower beds and littered streets with McDonald's wrappers. The convention was to call these people ghouls, and I admit they were hard to take, but there was something wonderful about seeing the citizens of Brentwood Park, in all their prim conceit, with the real world camped on their doorsteps.

Many of our neighbours had not liked the Simpsons. They didn't like Nicole's 'common' ways — her tight dresses, how she bathed topless by the pool while other mothers were setting up for a school party in their garden. After the trial, they lobbied the local school principal to ban the Simpson children for fear O. J. might appear.

The spectacular climax of the O. J. drama came five days after the murders. The White Bronco Chase was an early reality TV event that brought America — and much of the world — to a standstill. When Simpson vanished after learning he would be charged, police who were tracking his cell phone found him on a freeway near his ex-wife's new grave. A flashing fleet of black-and-white Los Angeles police cars soon caught up with him and began a slow pursuit.

There were so many cars it looked like a comedy chase in a buddy cop film. A thudding fleet of television news helicopters beamed pictures to a watching world, and Domino's Pizza reported a record night for home deliveries.

It was an out-of-body experience for the Hinton family, looking down on our own world with millions of others as O. J.'s Bronco made its weirdly safety-conscious left turn at our corner driveway, creeping along Ashford Street past our back gate and into O. J.'s drive. The world's most famous car chase ended right next door.

On the day of the chase, we had begun moving out of North Bristol to a more modest house we had bought in Santa Monica. It was the best-timed relocation ever.

Our last O. J. moment came with a poignant visit to our dry cleaner, with O. J. in jail and the country arguing about his guilt. The dry cleaner was a solemn Indian. 'It's so sad,' he said. 'Their clothes are still hanging there, next to each other, and no one is ever going to pick them up. What should I do?'

We took two particular memories with us when we left that sprawling Brentwood Park mansion. The other was more terrifying.

Six months before the murders, on 14 January 1994, at 4.30am, the house shook so hard it felt like I was on a speeding train that had jumped the tracks. Our home shook and tilted violently; it felt as if everything was about to crash down.

Later, we were told the LA earthquake lasted 10 to 20 seconds, depending on where you were, but it felt like forever. None of us was hurt; the heavy framed picture above Jane's sleeping head miraculously stayed in place, and, when getting dressed in the dark, I cut my feet on mirror glass. But the quake cracked walls, shattered mirrors, brought down a chimney, and scared me more than anything since Belfast and Cyprus.

I felt that old reflex to get to the office, just as I had when Hurricane Gloria swept through Boston and I left the family home alone. In Brentwood, a power blackout had killed the motor that opened our garden gates, trapping my car inside. I found a set of pliers under the kitchen sink and loosened the rusted nuts and bolts that held them shut. I drove to work slowly, peering ahead for fissures in the road. Families dressed in nightwear stood in small groups in their front gardens, afraid of their own homes. Fires flickered through cracks in sidewalks, and the air was filled with wailing alarms and sirens.

The Northridge earthquake was a huge natural disaster, killing 57 people and injuring more than 8000. Apartment buildings collapsed, roads and freeways crumbled, buildings were destroyed or later condemned. Many gas mains caught fire, and dozens of Santa Monica's famous little beach houses jumped off their foundations.

I had never before seen a city, previously so rich, safe, and at peace, go into clinical shock. There were dozens of aftershocks in the following weeks and the larger ones didn't just scare people, but sent some into real, ashen panic. People who could afford to, left town. An executive I worked with spent hours talking his wife out of moving back to the Midwest with their children.

Kids could be cooler; during one heavy aftershock when Jane, three, and James, six, our fourth son, were watching cartoons, they went without a word — and without taking their eyes off the screen — to sit under the pool table until it passed. 'They told us to do that at school,' said James.

This post-traumatic shock surprised me. The people of LA didn't talk about earthquakes much, considering they lived on a fault zone and there were well-developed theories that something apocalyptic would one day happen. Occasional tremors bothered them less than me; everyone knew the ground moved all the time, and that most motion was so slight it wasn't even felt.

But Northridge was too serious and threatening even for a newsroom to take any secret pleasure in it. It was unusual and lethal, and the moment when reality finally crashed through abstract theory. The city settled down in time, but its citizens knew they had been through a dress rehearsal for what everyone called The Big One.

While this was going on, and the earth was literally moving

under my feet, I was feeling uneasy about how things were going at the office.

'Les, the boss wants to talk. Put on your crash helmet, love.'

I was visiting New York, and Rupert was in LA, when Dot Wyndoe called me.

Dot started working for Rupert about the same time as I did. She managed his life for more than 50 years and no one worked so closely with him for so long. He had secretaries and assistants in Sydney, London, New York, and LA, but Dot went with him everywhere.

The mystery of Dot was that she never seemed agitated, no matter what was happening. I don't know how she felt, but even when things were really, really hectic, all she ever did was roll her eyes and sigh. And her hair was never out of place, ever.

More than anyone, Dot knew how tough things could get. She had tracked me down and was giving me a warning.

I don't think she knew that I kept a helmet in my office for years to lighten bad moments. It was a toy G. I. helmet to which I attached a large plastic razor blade. I put the helmet on when I knew Rupert was calling in a bad mood. The razor was to slash my wrists when he went over the top.

'What the hell are you doing in New York having long lunches with bloody Andrew Neil when you should have been here on the lot for that meeting?' he said. Sometimes Rupert pretended to be angry, but this was real, loud, high-pitched fury.

Neil was in New York working on his network news magazine pilot. Technically, I was overseeing the project — managing Neil was about as easy as caging clouds — and that was why I was in Manhattan.

I had no idea what important meeting it was that Rupert claimed I had neglected to attend. I was also pretty sure it had not slipped someone's mind back in LA to let me know about it. Subversives were at work at Fox and they were beginning to get the better of me.

I had arrived at Fox 18 months previously, leaping over others with years of knowledge and experience. All I knew about the television industry I had learned in a few weeks of desperate all-night reading. I was an unwelcome alien, and some were out to make life difficult for me.

The hard lesson in this experience is a simple one: don't let people stick around if you can't trust them. It's pretty obvious, really — at Fox I gave the wrong people the benefit of the doubt. But it was a mistake I never repeated, and from then on I advised every rising executive: 'You are now in charge of people, some of whom think they deserve your job. Give them a period of grief to adjust to the new reality, but if they haven't come around in a few months tell them it's time to move on.'

But it was too late then for firing people, and I wasn't going to hang around waiting to be fired myself. So when Rupert called to protest about my lunch with Andrew Neil, I knew it was time to do something.

'Rupert, this is fucking ridiculous,' I told him. 'You have no idea what's going on. I'm not going to discuss it on the phone. I'll fly back and see you in LA.'

For years, a few of us had a joke about our fantasy 'Fuck Off Funds'. When we had enough money in the bank and if life was unbearable, we would go to see Rupert:

Knock-knock (on Rupert's office door).

Yes, Les?

Rupert. Fuck off.

I phoned Dot and she booked me in for a meeting four days later. That morning, I went for a long run through the flat streets of Santa Monica, past the quake-ruined beach houses, weaving around the sleeping bodies of the homeless in the palm-lined park overlooking the beach. I ran down to the long pier that reminded me of Blackpool and Southend.

Life here was sunny and easy, even if the business was fierce. The worldview of LA County is warped by its show business reputation. It has a diverse economy — healthcare, technology, fashion, education — but the glamour and bursting ego of Hollywood washes over the whole town, catching pretty well everyone in its thrall.

It's a brutal business keeping America enchanted with good films and television, and the competition was not often friendly. Hollywood's best acting happens at the Academy Awards every year when everyone pretends to love each other.

One of Hollywood's biggest producers, who worked in both television and films, once told me wearily over dinner: 'People think the television business is savage, but movie people are worse — they're horrible. They lie and cheat, and they do it while smiling in your face.'

The intensity consumed so much of people's time and energy they didn't want to talk much about the world outside, about big issues and other countries, not like people in New York and London.

Rupert's morning habit astonished his LA executives. One of them told me: 'Do you know he gets all the papers — the *Los Angeles Times*, *The New York Times*, *The Wall Street Journal* — and he reads them all?' No wonder they cared so little about a news magazine or 24-hour news.

Before our meeting that morning, Rupert had sent David Evans to measure my mood. Evans was an Australian and the latest outsider to be at Rupert's side at Fox. 'He's worried that you're going to quit,' he said. I smiled and said nothing, but it did feel like the end of the road. Staying at Fox was impossible. I didn't want to leave News Corp, but couldn't think of an equivalent job that might be available. I wasn't sure I wanted one. I had imagined following the script of my

'Fuck Off Fund' fantasy, but by now I was only angry with myself.

After 25 years, I could count on a decent payoff. I was ready to go back to New York and build up from there, outside the company. It had been a wonderful run, but I was never on top of the job at Fox, and I was unhappy.

We sat at the bottom of his office, opposite each other on cream-coloured sofas. Rupert reserved his sofa chats for visiting VIPs, or difficult moments like this. He is famous, when a tough personal topic needs addressing, for avoiding the point, and freethinking about the world's problems and unconnected company issues. That's not what happened this time.

'I've been laying awake worrying about this,' he said, straight away. Whenever he had a problem, Rupert said it kept him awake.

'Well, that's been a shared experience,' I replied.

He lectured me sternly about how to manage big problems and deal with difficult people. 'Sometimes when you have a problem you have to drive through it, crash through the wall. If other people make life too difficult, if they're getting in your way, you have to fire them. Why didn't you just fire someone?'

I shrugged. I knew by now he was right. I had planned to list my grievances, but knew they would sound lame. I was beyond trying to explain myself. 'Maybe I should have, but this hasn't worked out for me. I'm sorry I couldn't make a go of it,' I told him.

Rupert sank into thought. Always when this happened his bottom lip pushed out, his eyes closed slightly, his head slumped forward, and his face crumpled. Anyone interrupting him at moments like this was sure to be ignored.

'Look,' he said eventually. 'You must trust me. I want you to stay with the company. Things are changing in New York. I might want you to run HarperCollins. I'm not sure exactly when, but it could be soon.'

'Really?' was all I could think to say. I had walked defeated in his office moments before and now he was talking about putting me at the top of one of the world's biggest book publishers.

'Take the family back to New York, and we'll sort things out,' he told me.

I flew alone to New York. Our three youngest were mid-term and we had to sell the Santa Monica house. I was given a small office on the floor beneath Rupert. We went together on a couple of visits to HarperCollins when Rupert was being briefed on the business. It was clear no one at HarperCollins had any idea what Rupert had said to me. While I waited, he filled my time with random tasks.

Mirabella, the magazine we started in 1989 with Grace Mirabella, was still struggling. I reviewed the business and recommended it should close if we couldn't sell it. David Pecker, a New York publisher, added *Mirabella* to his growing group, but five years later he gave up on it, too. At *TV Guide,* the chief executive was not working out, and I knew exactly how he must have felt when I asked for his resignation. I also organised the launch of a new magazine; Rupert had wanted for a long time to own a right-leaning weekly — he admired British magazine *The Spectator* — and asked me to plan one. Any new publication needs the right editor and Bill Kristol was keen on the idea. Kristol had been known as Quayle's Brain when he was chief of staff to George Bush senior's vice president, Dan Quayle. It was a title intended more to insult Quayle than compliment Kristol, but Kristol was very bright. When we met to decide a name for the new magazine, I thought I had a great idea. 'Let's call it the *American Standard*,' I said.

The pundit Fred Barnes, who would become Kristol's deputy, shook his head. 'American Standard is a company that's famous for making toilets.'

We agreed it was a bad idea to have a name that was urinated on by millions every day, and decided instead on *The Weekly Standard*.

Before any change at HarperCollins, something else happened.

When Rupert called my New York office, Mary was on her way to Los Angeles airport for a weekend of house hunting in New York.

He sounded urgent: 'Can you come up now?'

Rupert was holding some papers when I arrived, and walked to his desk as he told me: 'Don't faint, and please don't refuse me. We've got big problems in London. I need you to go back and run the newspapers.'

I was almost speechless. How could I have got this lucky?

'Rupert, there is no job in the entire company I would enjoy more.' I told him.

CHAPTER 20

Fleet Street RIP

When the Great Fire of London ravaged Fleet Street in 1666, printers and publishers had already worked there for more than 150 years. In 1976, when I left for New York, it was still the palpitating heart of the newspaper industry; a village locked inside a great metropolis, with its own distinct culture, rhythms, and familiar faces. Each morning, lorries jammed the warren of alleys to deliver huge rolls of the paper that is the raw material of Fleet Street's daily alchemy; arriving blank and lifeless, and leaving at night reincarnated by the drama and trivia, brilliance and dross, outrage and entertainment of the British national press.

Twenty years later, when I returned to London, Fleet Street had become an archaeological site, a newspaper ghost town even as it bustled with new purpose.

Old newspaper temples today are protected, like the pyramids. Their facades are frozen in time, almost, but not entirely, stripped of their original identities. *The Daily Telegraph* building, grey stone and mighty pillars, stands in all its glorious art deco ostentation. Its gilded two-faced timepiece hangs above the street, the clock tower of a lost village. The building's identity, once displayed across its front in glorious Gothic, is gone. The only clues are in the sculpted facade: the two winged messengers above the main entrance fly away with the news, and two sculpted faces represent Past and Future. 'Past' is grim and beaten, 'Future' open and hopeful.

The Telegraph's shining neighbour is Fleet Street's slinky lady-in-black, the glass and chrome-trimmed *Express* building. Inside, still intact, is the manically lavish lobby, a glittering folly of gold and silver, its gigantic tableaus of Empire an everlasting testament to Beaverbrook's idea of patriotism, and possibly his state of mind as well. This lobby must embarrass the new tenants, Goldman Sachs; heavy grey curtains hide it from the street.

Between these two giants sits the proud, but respectfully small, bay facade of Mersey House, once the London home of the *Liverpool Echo*, the newspaper that announced my birth.

Engraved plaques in the pavement commemorate dead pioneers, and newspapers that are lost, or shadows of their former greatness: *The Daily Courant*, the *Standard*, the *Express,* the type designer William Caslon, and Charles Dickens, who wrote as 'Boz' in Ye Olde Cheshire Cheese pub. One plaque depicts Space Invaders, an early kill-or-be-killed computer game in which waves of jagged-edged aliens attack the player. It was put in place to commemorate the arrival of the computer technology that ended the era of linotype machines and hot metal. Now, it is an unintentional metaphor for the digital destroyers that would descend on the industry that built Fleet Street.

Life is no less febrile, and lights still burn into the night, but the new citizens of Fleet Street talk obscurely of 'discounted cash flow', of 'accretion and dilution analyses', and 'affirmative covenants'. The talk of 'upside collars' and 'downside collars' has nothing to do with fashion, and 'goodwill' does not mean precisely that. This is now the world of big money, of mergers and acquisitions, and the language coming from these buildings will never again touch the masses. Bankers and lawyers are the citizens of Fleet Street now; it was once a world of words, but now money does the talking.

For me, a visit to Fleet Street is like wandering through a mirage; it's not what it seems and never will be again. Physically, much of it is intact. I pass many of the same buildings walking east from the Strand, past the ornamental spires and arches of the Royal Courts of Justice. The surviving pubs and wine bars are as inviting as ever, but the drinkers inside are strangers.

A fierce dragon in the middle of the street, flying high on a plinth, still guards the City of London border, but nearby, the Wig & Pen Club, once a haunt of lawyers and journalists, is a Thai restaurant. El Vino, the ancient wine bar, thrives, but I hardly went there; it was the officers' mess of Fleet Street, and down-table youngsters were not welcome.

As the road bends near Bouverie Street, you get the same unaltering glimpse of St Paul's Cathedral. On the right is the narrow, red-painted facade of The Tipperary pub. It was the local for *The Sun* and the *News of the World,* but their nearby offices are now the headquarters of Freshfields Bruckhaus Deringer, a multinational law firm, and the conversation in the 'Tipp' is more sedate.

Ye Olde Cheshire Cheese still draws crowds. A public house has stood on the same site since the 1500s, and the Cheese itself was built soon after the Great Fire. Its ceilings are blackened by pipe and cigarette smoke, and its sloping timber floor makes guests unsteady even before their first drop. Journalists drinking in the Cheese once jostled for room with Ben Jonson, Dickens, Conan Doyle, and P. G. Wodehouse. Now its unruly farewell parties are for bankers and lawyers off to globalising jobs in Tokyo, Hong Kong, and New York.

In 1976, no journalist worked more than 50 yards from a pub.

From seven o'clock in the evening, it was a safe bet who would be in each of them. Each newspaper had its favourite bar and its share of notorious drinkers. Journalism was a thirstier trade back then. Drink and dissolution felt like a prerequisite, and I arrived in 1965 at the age of 21 as a happy apprentice. The old hands were role models and even their bad habits were desirable. Pubs were study halls where veterans conducted barstool seminars, spinning yarns of great scoops and dangerous travels. The tuition fee was a round of drinks.

These days, now and then, in places like the Cheese and El Vino, white-haired groups can be seen among the brisk new habitués. If they look out of place, it is because they are. They will be the frail old nostalgics of Fleet Street on a pilgrimage of remembrance. They approach the bar more slowly and less often. Sometimes they sit in silence, with recollecting smiles.

Often, they will have taken an ambling walk from St Bride's Church, where the father of Fleet Street, Wynkyn de Worde, set up his print shop in the churchyard more than 500 years ago, before St Bride's was destroyed in the Great Fire and rebuilt by Wren. Fleet Street may have been a godless world, but journalists will always crowd pews beneath the wedding-cake spire of St Bride's for funerals and memorials. Today, outside St Bride's, a crude notice of red letters announces: 'The world-famous Journalists' Church'. It has become a tourist trap.

In their day, heavy drinkers were the heroes of Fleet Street. The lost productivity that resulted was seen by companies as an unavoidable cost of business, and an occupational hazard for the journalist. A man too drunk after lunch would be sent home to sleep it off. He might — or might not — be given a mild chiding next day. When *The Sun*'s news editor Ken Donlan found a reporter snoozing at his desk, he attempted a reprimand. 'Drunk again, Mike?' he asked.

'Are you, Ken?' came the reply. 'I've had a few myself.'

Heavy drinkers who could still do the job would carry on for years until their health failed. Many of my peers died in their fifties and sixties. Others would crash and burn quickly. These were serious casualties, who would sneak out for a morning Bloody Mary or two, or return at closing time for the overnight shift with a hidden bottle of Scotch. I went on a royal tour with the Queen and Prince Philip, and no one was sober after a six-hour flight from Vancouver to the Bahamas, but one reporter was so incapable his rivals filed his copy to London. Fleet Street had its own support system for its alcoholics.

In the 1960s, I worked with a brilliant but deeply troubled and alcoholic reporter whose perfect copy the sub-editors rarely altered. A decade later, a shuffling old-looking man stopped me on Fleet Street. I recognised him at once, but his raincoat was torn and tied by thin rope, his long hair and beard unwashed, and sticky tape held together his wire-rimmed glasses. He was looking for money and I gave him some, but Barrie didn't know who I was. He could not yet have reached his fortieth birthday.

Heavy drinking was a habit that came from the top. Ruth Dudley Edwards writes about this in *Newspapermen,* her dual biography of Hugh Cudlipp and Cecil King, the odd couple who made the *Mirror* newspapers great. The papers, she says, were 'produced on an ocean of alcohol ... Visit Cudlipp before 11am and you would be offered a beer (unless it was a day of celebration, when there would be a champagne conference at 10.30).' After 11, Cudlipp would open a bottle of white wine; lunch was 'aperitif, wine, brandy'.

The *Mirror* was not alone. Rupert would fume when he surprised imbibing executives sitting together in the office of Larry Lamb, *The Sun*'s editor. Lamb had learned his trade and drinking habits at Cudlipp's *Mirror.* For years, Rupert railed against 'those bloody Fleet Street lunches', and once the company was safely removed to

Wapping, he put in place a strict prohibition. This ban never worked as well as he thought; executives kept secret stores in their offices, which I pretended not to notice.

This prohibition was at odds with the rest of London. The growing New York tradition of dry lunches had yet to leap the Atlantic. I was still Rupert's strict enforcer when John Major, the prime minister, came to Wapping for lunch in February 1996. The night before, the Provisional IRA had blown up a double-decker bus in the West End. The device had gone off too soon, killing the bomber and injuring eight. We were sure Major would be too busy at Number 10 to come to Wapping, but he did. Walking into our dining room, his first words were, 'I am in serious need of a large gin and tonic.'

It was no time to recite company rules. 'I can imagine you are. Right away,' I replied.

The problem was there was no known gin bottle within 500 yards, although, in reality, there were probably a secret dozen. While I kept the prime minister entertained with sparkling water — 'Have I caused a problem asking for gin?' — Marianne Krafinski, my assistant, hurried to the local Morrisons supermarket to return breathless with a bottle of Beefeater. From then on, we had plenty of alcohol for visiting VIPs.

Newspaper people today certainly drink less. They may use less evident intoxicants, but it is not so easy to tell. When *The Sun*'s editor David Yelland dreamt up a tabloid gimmick involving the purchase of a drug-sniffing dog, there was anxiety among some staff when it visited the editorial floor.

Despite all the mourning for the lost spirit and community of old Fleet Street, it was a sick place by the time I left for America. Newspapers had stayed there too long, trapped by greed, mismanagement, and torpor. Fleet Street would have become the industry's tomb, had it not escaped.

Fleet Street was not just a thoroughfare, but also a neighbourhood. Every newspaper, in the local labyrinth of backstreets and beyond, belonged to Fleet Street. In the 1970s, it was being eaten away by the mad avarice of over-powerful unions. For years, feeble newspaper managers had enabled these unions by yielding to ever more ruinous demands.

The unions rejected every effort to introduce new technology, reduce manning, and increase profits — in some cases, simply to allow newspapers to become profitable. While these methods were being adopted around the world, unions were binding UK newspapers to production practices that were a century old. Reporters sat at ancient typewriters when desktop computers could save time and expense, bypassing clunky mechanical practices. Printing plants were trapped inside an ancient, congested city when new technology could transmit pages to distant press sites.

It was a natural reflex for unions to protect jobs, but they didn't only resist new technology. The unions practised extortion against pliable management. Many printers didn't even work the days they were paid; workmates would sign them in while they stayed home or worked shifts at other newspapers. The power to hire rested entirely with union leaders, and jobs were passed from father to son. Salaries were huge; the men who cleaned the reporters' room at *The Sun* earned more than reporters.

The unions exploited bitter competition among newspapers, picking them off one at a time. If a strike closed one paper, others increased their print runs to steal readers, forcing the newspaper under attack to surrender to the latest demands. This fatal cycle went on for years.

There were dubious sidelines. For years, I did my Christmas shopping in newspaper production areas, which would be turned into bargain basements selling everything from clothes and cosmetics to electric kettles. I never asked about the provenance of these goods.

By the time I went to New York, a turning point was approaching in the history of Fleet Street, and its fate would be rewritten by an epic confrontation. In 1981, exhausted by shakedowns, the Canadian Thomson Corporation, owner of *The Times* and *The Sunday Times*, decided to quit Fleet Street. After fighting union rapacity for years, Thomson had staged its last stand in 1979, suspending publication for almost a year rather than surrendering to union pressure. When the strike ended in another union victory, non-striking journalists, who had been paid throughout the dispute, staged their own walkout demanding higher salaries. This was when Thomson left town, and Rupert bought their struggling titles to become Britain's biggest newspaper publisher.

The same intractable union demands confronted Rupert, but he had a plan. In January 1986, when more than 5000 production workers walked out in yet another dispute, he moved his entire newspaper production to a fortified new plant in Wapping, in the East End of London.

For months, the plant had secretly been made ready with the modern technology unions had scorned for years. The 5000 he left behind in Fleet Street were suddenly jobless and furious. They and their supporters lay siege on Wapping. There were many nights of violence and hundreds of injuries before the unions agreed a settlement and the pickets went away. The siege of Wapping lasted for 12 months.

Other newspaper groups watched this drama from a safe distance, but when Rupert prevailed they followed in his footsteps. One by one, they threw off their shackles, joined the late twentieth century, and left behind the neighbourhood and traditions of Fleet Street.

Wapping was a great drama of Margaret Thatcher's struggle against trade unions. She had changed the law to diminish their powers, and protected Wapping with a strong police presence that ensured the plant remained in operation.

But the dispute left a bitter taste, and the left's loathing of Rupert and News International had abated only slightly eight years later when Rupert introduced me to Wapping in May 1995.

———

We drove around the turrets and battlements of the Tower of London, turned left onto The Highway, and headed into Wapping. Long ago, this was a rowdy seafaring village, the haunt of sailors, fishermen, footpads, and smugglers. Royal Navy press gangs prowled the pubs, kidnapping drunks to fight for king and country. Local entertainment was provided beside the Thames at Execution Dock where crowds gathered for the hanging of mutineers and pirates.

But the excitement had drained out of Wapping long ago. The thriving docklands economy had perished after the Second World War, and its great riverside warehouses had been transformed into flats and offices. The Wapping siege had been the most dramatic event since the London Blitz.

This was my first glimpse of the place the entire country knew as 'Fortress Wapping'. Until now it had been the flickering backdrop on American television news, the scene of surging crowds and charging police horses.

It was not a sight to lift the heart. The building was massive, with a cold and Soviet blandness, and was encircled by tall fences topped with barbed wire. It looked like a penitentiary. Speed bumps slowed the approach of our green Daimler and guards lifted the barrier quickly when they recognised Rupert. Other vehicles were searched at random.

The building had been designed as a factory to print newspapers, and architects had failed in their attempts to give it the appearance of a successful company's headquarters. The most recent effort when I arrived was an unfinished £2 million entrance lobby designed to impress the parade of cabinet ministers and other important visitors. It was attached to the original factory, with floors of chocolate-coloured marble, and enclosed by walls of glass. When finished, escalators swept guests between tall palms and indoor fountains pungent with chlorine. It felt like checking into a Midwest Marriott hotel. Rupert didn't like it either. Within a few months, he also appeared to have forgotten who had built it, and accused me of squandering £2 million. When I told him he was pointing the finger at the wrong person, he grunted: 'Bloody waste of money.'

The offices of *The Times* titles challenged every standard of decent working conditions. Journalists were housed in a narrow listed building next to the factory. Napoleonic prisoners-of-war had built it as a warehouse for barrels of rum shipped to London. It was fitting in a way. *The Times*, established in 1785, was about 20 years older than the building, but this cannot have given much comfort to the twenty-first century trustees of a historic newspaper. There were few windows, and rain bouncing off the modern corrugated roof drowned normal conversation.

The executive suite I inherited was so lavish I felt I needed an appointment to be there. I spent several years in it, but when the managing director left and wasn't replaced, I moved next door to his more modest space and turned my old suite into meeting rooms.

My introduction to Wapping was fleeting. Rupert wanted to show me the scene of one of the triumphs of his career. It was Saturday, and whenever he was in London on a weekend, his favourite pre-dinner ritual was to visit his Sunday editors. These visits were unannounced, but never unexpected; when Rupert was in town, his arrival at your door was never a surprise.

We paid a hasty visit to the *News of the World*, thriving in 1995. Its editor was Piers Morgan, then aged 30. Piers wouldn't be in the job for long, but none of us knew that. He ran through his big stories for the next day's paper and Rupert nodded non-committally. Piers had become editor a year before, and already showed a talent for notoriety. The British Press Complaints Commission had admonished him for publishing a photograph of Princess Diana's sister-in-law at a rehab clinic. She was the wife of Diana's younger brother — Charles, Earl Spencer — and the photograph was a clear invasion of her privacy. Rupert had taken the unusual step of publicly rebuking Piers, declaring, 'the young man went over the top'. In private he admonished editors all the time, but I don't remember another occasion when Rupert did it in public.

'He's a very bright man,' said Rupert as we left. 'But he can be a bit reckless. Keep an eye on him.'

Rupert would later express his view more colourfully: 'The trouble with Piers is that his balls are bigger than his brains.'

In the old rum warehouse, we visited John Witherow in his brick-walled office at *The Sunday Times*. Witherow was as taciturn and considered as Morgan was chatty and impulsive. He belonged to the school of editors who stayed in the office and produced the paper, avoiding the tempting glitz of the television sofa and the overseas seminar. In this, Witherow and Paul Dacre of the *Daily Mail* were brothers; both shackled themselves to their desks for many successful years. These were the editors my mentor and guide at News International, Sir Edward Pickering, loved. He was still working in his eighties, and had taught a young Rupert Murdoch subbing skills on the *Daily Express*. 'Pick' scorned editors too frequently absent from their posts,. 'An editor's job is to stay in the attic and edit,' he would say.

Having presented me with this vast enterprise, Rupert took me off to dinner. And for two hours I listened. We sat among white-clothed tables in the empty silence of a hotel restaurant near his St James's flat. It was the kind of place where the old head waiter wore a stiff collar and tails. I suspected the menu hadn't changed since Dickens was alive. This is why it was empty, and why Rupert chose it for our chat.

He laid out the problems at Wapping and was as frank as ever in his criticism of people and their mistakes. The place was stagnating, the workers were unhappy, and a deep antipathy had developed towards the bosses. Above all, the staff in the production departments — the historic source of most woes — were beginning to agitate. The Labour Party, after years in the wilderness, had been resuscitated by Tony Blair and already looked set to win the next general election. We were certain, should they win power, they would loosen the controls Thatcher had imposed on the unions.

The unions were back at the gates, literally, but this time they were wielding recruitment pamphlets instead of rocks. Wapping was the print unions' crucible, where Rupert had crushed and humiliated them. Their defeat had released a gush of profit now being used for expansion in the United States, and the unions' return to News International would be a catastrophe for the company, and, as the new boss, a disaster for me.

These circumstances helped Mary and me focus on family matters. The job of running News International was notoriously tricky and the mortality rate of bosses was high. I was to become the fourth chief executive in five years, and I was taking the job at what seemed to be the most dangerous moment since the siege.

When one predecessor, Bruce Matthews, died, an obituary said: 'The court of Rupert Murdoch is much like the court of Henry VIII. Men and women are promoted to positions of great power only to be felled on the royal whim, either because they cease to be useful or because they threaten to gain more fame than the monarch himself. Bruce Matthews was Murdoch's Thomas Cromwell.'

That might have been a harsh judgement of Rupert, but I had to be realistic. Based on history, my chances of long-term survival were about equal to that of a subaltern in a First World War trench. When the Hollywood executive Peter Chernin had been promoted at Fox, he sat down his children and told them that one day their dad would be fired, but there would be no disgrace in it. In fact, Chernin spent many years as Rupert's deputy before deciding it was time to go.

We prepared for a short stay. We placed our two youngest children, James and Jane, into London's private American School in St John's Wood. After moving them from city to city — and now to a strange country — at least we could keep them in the same education system.

Rupert can be casual about turning the lives of people upside down. He did it to me a few times, but the move to London was completely unexpected. We were happy to be out of Los Angeles and looking forward to New York. We had lived in the United States for almost 20 years, and three of our five children had been born there; the two eldest moved with us to New York aged just 18 months and 5. We had become US citizens a decade earlier. We were an American family.

Mary took the news of London imperturbably. She had become accustomed to a life of perpetual motion. Will, our third, was 16 and at high school in Los Angeles. We worried he wouldn't want to move to a country where he had never lived. He chose to stay behind at boarding school, and leaving him was hard on Mary and me. His two older brothers, Martin and Thomas, had jobs in New York.

When we moved to London in August 1995, the family saw it as a short-term foreign posting. I was still in the job 12 years later.

That night at dinner, Rupert warned me what to expect. I would be in charge of a company responsible for one-third of the country's national newspaper sales. He said I should prepare for an onslaught of flattery from politicians, Royal Family acolytes, company bosses, and every civic leader with a cause to promote. As well as flattery, complaints would pour my way from important people annoyed at the way they had been treated in our pages.

'Don't get too close to these people,' he said. 'In a few years, they'll probably offer you a knighthood. Be careful about accepting it.'

He talked about something else that night that I believe is a key to him. He talked about how often he had been underestimated. As a young man, he said, others dismissed him because of his age and inexperience. It had been the same whenever he arrived somewhere new.

Rupert didn't reveal to me — then, or ever — any complicated secrets to his success. He repeated what he often said. He was willing simply to work harder than anyone else. But that night, alone in our restaurant, I saw him wistful. He had long ago lost the underdog's ability to surprise and subvert. Never again could he be the little guy with not much to lose and so much to gain — the upstart with impossible ideas and boundless self-conviction.

In 1969, when he was seeking to buy *The Sun*, he arrived in the lobby of the *Daily Mirror* headquarters in Holborn Circus on his way to see Hugh Cudlipp. He walked up to a wall graphic showing the International Publishing Corporation's newspaper circulations. The *Mirror,* Britain's biggest seller at more than 5 million, towered above the limping *Sun*. Rupert unpinned the two ribbons tracking the newspapers and reversed them, putting *The Sun* at the top of the scale.

'That's what is going to happen', he told Stephen Catto — the hereditary peer, Lord Catto — the banker who helped Rupert make his foothold in Britain.

'I didn't know where to look,' Catto told me years later.

Later that year, Hugh Cudlipp, the IPC chairman, turned the pages of the first edition of the new tabloid version of *The Sun,* raised a glass of champagne, and told his team it had nothing to fear. Cudlipp soon knew he had made the mistake of his life.

This story repeated itself often, and each time Rupert became the big guy — in Sydney, in London, in New York, and in Los Angeles — he went looking for the next unconquered world, searching for a new place to be underestimated.

Rupert had been his own kind of revolutionary and overthrown giants on three continents to become the biggest giant of all, an authentic colossus. But I think he missed the life of a long shot, and that all his success had drowned a little of the original man.

CHAPTER 21

Wappingworld

Looking down the long boardroom table, I counted four lords, one baroness, and three knights, all murmuring among themselves. When I called the meeting to order, an instant silence resulted as they turned their gazes towards me.

I'm still embarrassed by how much pleasure this memory gives me. I had thought of my parents and imagined my mother's pursed-lip pride as her son sat at the head of that important table, chairing the quarterly meeting of Times Newspapers Holdings Limited.

Twenty years before, these people would have intimidated me, but America — for all its imperfections, so irrepressible, so full of unruly ambition and self-belief — had inoculated me against the old class divides of Britain. Peers of the realm and people with hyphenated names no longer represented a superior species. The men and women at the table were interesting, and mostly clever, individuals, that was all. The few who affected old, high-born manners looked out of date. The best among them was Ralph, Lord Harris of High Cross, the economist who inspired Margaret Thatcher, and his father had been a London tramways inspector.

The Times board, whose duties included protecting the two editors from managerial interference, was a constant problem at News International. This was because so many people suspected it was toothless. Six independent directors had the power to agree the hiring and firing of an editor. The flaw in this part of the arrangement was that, no matter what the independent directors thought, no self-respecting editor would stay in a job where they felt unwanted by management, and no management could be expected to tolerate an editor it considered to be no good. But that didn't mean these directors were impotent. Some rightly saw their presence as a nuclear deterrent, and understood the damage they could cause by publicly complaining that management was dictating policy to an editor.

But *The Times* board was far from top of my list of worries when I arrived in London. We needed to fix a faltering and unhappy company. Also, as Rupert had warned over dinner, I had to deal with the tides and currents of a high-profile job. Keeping a low profile was easier in America, but Britain was a smaller pond and I was a bigger fish. Uncomfortable references to me appeared in rival newspapers. Newspapers that didn't like Rupert — that would be every one he didn't own — described me in unappealing ways. I was his hitman, consigliore, henchman, capo, or, divinely, his 'representative on earth'. Paradoxically, for all the antipathy towards us, every industry crisis seemed to arrive at our front door. Within weeks I had to decide the fate of the Press Association, the country's premier news agency, which had existed since 1868. An alliance of newspaper groups, dismayed by the cost and quality of the PA, was supporting an effort to replace it with a new agency called UK News. I was besieged by rivals imploring us to join them. These rivals had a good argument against the agency; its coverage had deteriorated at the same time as it put up prices. The newly appointed editor-in-chief was desperate when he came to my office. 'We're on the brink,' he said. 'I know I can fix the place, but I need time.' Paul Potts was an old friend and a talented editor. He had taken the PA job after quitting as deputy editor of the *Daily Express*. I decided against ditching the PA and Potts went on to rebuild Britain's oldest news agency as editor-in-chief and chief executive, with many of its would-be destroyers becoming significant shareholders. Six years later, the official history of the Press Association — *Living on a Deadline*, by Chris Moncrieff — recorded the details of the company's existential crisis. There was, it said, 'a key figure in PA's survival without whom the modern PA probably would not exist ... it was Hinton who had saved the day'. It was nice of them to say so, but in truth I was too busy with other things to think clearly about the drastic action of killing off an institution.

There were activists outside the gates of Wapping, and employees within, who believed the company was ripe to re-unionise. At a Westminster cocktail party, a union official smiled narrowly at me. 'We're coming back, you know,' he said. Our journalists were picking up the same message among trade union officials and Labour MPs.

Trade unions provided Labour's lifeblood of cash, as well as millions of votes. They wanted to be free of the restraints Thatcher had imposed, and Labour had promised, if it won the election, to reinstate powers that could allow the unions to force their way back into Wapping.

But unions were no longer at the heart of News International's problems. The threat from them was symptom not cause. We were desperate to keep out the unions, but our problems were home-grown.

———

Bill O'Neill had been Australian, in every way — a laconic, soft-spoken, country style of Australian, even though he grew up on Sydney's North Shore. By the time we worked together in Wapping,

O'Neill had been body-snatched by the spirit of Texas. He wore sharp-tipped snakeskin boots with Cuban heels, heavy turquoise and silver rings, string leather ties, and Western-style jackets decorated with curved and pointed piping. It was cowboy business attire. O'Neill remained laconic as he morphed into a Texan, but became more Gary Cooper than Paul Hogan. He even had a rolling, just-off-a-horse gait, but only since he broke a hip running for a train in icy Poughkeepsie, 2000 miles from his home in San Antonio.

Wapping was in trouble, and when Rupert made me boss, he sent Bill O'Neill ahead with his knuckle-duster rings to clean up the place. O'Neill was the sheriff of Wapping, gliding through its corridors, nodding to passers-by, leaning here and there on the wall to talk, fingers slipped into the horizontal pockets of his trousers. No one knew Wapping better than him, and no one was a better peacemaker. He was the chief negotiator who settled the Wapping dispute in 1987 and then became friends with his trade union counterpart, Brenda Dean. They dined together regularly to share war stories, like respectful old generals who had made peace. O'Neill was one of my heroes.

Wapping was a peaceful place in the years following the dispute. New technology had made the newspapers far more efficient, employees felt secure and fairly treated, and bosses were delivering good profits to News Corp's New York headquarters. But a few years before I arrived, there was an economic downturn. Consumers stopped spending and companies stopped marketing; big declines in advertising revenue mean trouble for newspapers. When managers get lax in good times — and this happens a lot — they are forced to take painful action when business dries up. This is what happened at News International, and by 1995 there were so many layoffs that Friday became known as Black Bag Day — you needed the bag to empty the contents of your desk.

O'Neill was dismayed by what he found. The company was boiling with anger and resentment. In personal papers donated to Warwick University, he writes: 'Morale was in the basement and distrust of senior management extreme.' O'Neill was convinced the company would lose a union ballot in a landslide.

When Richard Stott became editor of *Today*, one of News Corp's three dailies, he was shocked at what he found. Stott had been editor of the *Daily Mirror*, and in his memoir *Dogs And Lampposts*, he writes of his arrival in 1993: 'For years we envied News International their management [but] I was amazed to find excesses ... inefficiency, overstaffing, and indiscipline long since eradicated at the *Mirror*.' Evening print runs, he said, were 'rarely managed without some form of disaster'. It was so bad that Stott suspected print workers were sabotaging the presses.

O'Neill's advice to me was clear. 'You must act quickly. You've got to be seen and heard,' he said. 'They've got to believe things have changed.'

We decided on a company road show to all our big offices, travelling from London to Merseyside, Manchester, Glasgow, Peterborough, and Dublin. Every employee was invited to hear from the new team. A fancy, portable set was built to serve as a backdrop for each appearance. A giant screen came with us to display optimistic video and slides, with numbers laying out the company's strengths and difficulties.

The first session was mid-afternoon in the vast newsprint warehouse in London. Hundreds of seats were placed among newsprint reels stacked to the ceiling. The detail of our presentation doesn't matter much now; the important point was to make people feel involved. We told them as much as we sensibly could about our financial performance, growing costs, opportunities, and threats, remembering whatever we said would surely leak. This kind of open session seemed years later to be a natural thing to do, but in the

1990s many companies didn't care so much about keeping the mass of their workforce informed.

But it was only one small step. The plant was a factory building with rudimentary office space that had been added as an afterthought. The building had 'levels' instead of floors, like a warehouse — I was on Level Six. When Wapping was at war and everyone was in the trenches, no one gave much thought to comfort in the office. But that was years ago and now there were unending complaints. It was not a thoughtful management that spent millions on a gaudy lobby and the splendid office suite I inherited, while crowding people into tiny, windowless offices.

Doug Flynn was an animated Australian chemical engineer who had stumbled into newspapers. Flynn had joined News International a year before me and was about to quit when I arrived, fed up with his bosses. He had a tempestuous Irish streak, but a quick and logical mind, and I promoted him to be my number two. We worked together through the toughest years at Wapping, before he left the industry and went off to make millions in outside businesses, too restless to spend any longer as a second in command.

'This place is a fucking dump,' he told me soon after I arrived. It was only a slight exaggeration. We decided a gesture was needed, and Flynn developed a plan. We bought a new building next door and moved *The Times* and *The Sunday Times* out of their rundown rum house. We began to renovate office space everywhere else. It took a couple of years, but spirits were lifted just by the knowledge it was happening.

The road show became an exhausting annual event. We also introduced a regular workforce opinion poll, the results of which were not always comfortable reading. Thousands came to 'family days' at the plants in London, Merseyside, and Glasgow, with food stalls and games, and exhibits where parents showed children what happened where they worked.

We had an annual retreat with members of the Staff Association Consultative Council, who had been elected by employees. These could be boisterous meetings. At our 1999 session, some of the council were determined to shut down the plants on New Year's Eve so everyone could celebrate the millennium. It was a terrible idea, and out of the question. We were newspaper people, I told them. The arrival of the new millennium was historic. How could we not have newspapers with the date 1 January 2000? It was our duty to record the moment. Thousands would keep our newspapers as souvenirs.

There was silence when I finished, but they knew I was right. One of the Liverpool members stood at the back. 'That means you'll be working that night too, right?' There was no escape.

'You got me,' I said. 'I will be now.'

And so, on the night of 31 December 1999, I wandered the Wapping plant with nothing to do but show my face while the rest of the family reunited more than 3000 miles away in New York.

Showing my face was always a good idea. It's amazing what you discover by leaving a lonely desk. There are always unpleasant secrets that executives keep to themselves. Hyman Rickover, the admiral who developed nuclear propulsion for the US Navy and who had a formidable reputation for hard work and high standards, said: 'Always use the chain of command to issue orders, but if you use the chain of command for information, you're dead.' It was advice I commended to everyone.

The discontent faded over the years, but it would be overdoing it to say Wapping became an industrial paradise. Jobs were lost when projects failed, or economies demanded it. Digital began to squeeze our profits, managers made dumb mistakes, and badly treated employees won grievances. We were like every other media company struggling into the new millennium. But there was never a serious effort to bring back the unions.

In his book, Richard Stott gives me the credit for this. He says my 'more relaxed, informal, and accessible style kept the unions out of Wapping. But for Murdoch it had been a damned close run thing, too close for comfort.'

It was hard work and I don't remember often feeling relaxed. But Bill O'Neill, the shrewd, soothing sheriff of Wapping, deserved much of the praise. There is an old saying that you can get anything done so long as you don't care who gets the credit. It was a corny epigram until I worked in Wapping with O'Neill. I didn't meet many like him in Hollywood. All he wanted was to do the job and head out of town, back to Texas.

———

When it came to swinging elections, politicians in Britain gave newspapers too much credit. Naturally, no newspaper tried hard to disabuse them, but it was mostly nonsense that the press determined election results. Two years after Neil Kinnock lost the 1992 general election, and after the death of his successor, John Smith, Tony Blair was reshaping the Labour Party. In 1997, he swamped the Conservatives, winning his party more seats than ever before. No newspaper campaign would have changed the 1997 result. After 18 years in government, the Conservative Party's own blunders and internal fighting had reduced it to a nervous wreck.

But Blair and his inner circle were taking no chances. Nor were the Conservatives, for that matter. They still placed value on *The Sun*'s support and worked hard to maintain it as the 1997 election approached. My first invitation to Number 10 Downing Street was for a party hosted by John Major, but it was the American guest of honour I most remember.

An invitation to Number 10 makes an impression. Walking

through the tall black gates guarding Downing Street, towards that blackened Georgian symmetry, is like entering a sculpture you have known all your life. Most of the time, you don't even need to knock on the towering entrance, with its patent leather sheen; as you approach, it magically opens. I walked for the first time through that front door in November 1995, up a staircase lined with portraits of past prime ministers.

Guests were crowding around in happy-eyed anticipation. Downing Street staff offered drinks with looks of blank routine. A hand squeezed my elbow. 'Come on over and meet the president,' said John Major, and the Prime Minister of the United Kingdom led me across the great drawing room to meet the President of the United States.

Bill Clinton was standing with his back against a fireplace. Hillary Clinton looked sullen on a gold sofa, surrounded by other women. Major pressed me into the tight group around Clinton, so that I was standing to his left. 'Hi,' Clinton said with his famous blue-glow beam. We talked about Northern Ireland, Europe, and his Rhodes Scholar days in Britain in the 1960s.

All the time, Clinton was leaning on me, not just touching shoulder to shoulder, but leaning. If I had suddenly moved, he would have lost his balance. It's an unusual feeling being leaned on like that by the world's most powerful man. I discovered seven years later that it was not a unique experience. The American journalist Joe Klein, in his book *The Natural: the misunderstood presidency of Bill Clinton*, writes about bowling with Clinton in New Hampshire. 'At times, as we stood there, waiting for our balls to return down the alley, he'd lean up against me — a strange feline sensation; he needed the physical contact.'

Before the 1997 election, when Blair came to lunch with *The Sun*'s editors, he knew he was not among friends. Rupert may have been softening towards him, but key people at *The Sun* were not convinced.

Stuart Higgins, *The Sun*'s hyperactive editor, hated the idea of supporting Labour. He would wake me at home in the early hours with emotional pleas to reject Blair. Trevor Kavanagh, the urbane political editor, thought it was a terrible idea. So did Chris Roycroft-Davis, the chief leader writer. Roycroft-Davis never adjusted to the change; when Rupert walked into his office a few days after *The Sun* endorsed Labour, Roycroft-Davis sprung to attention. 'Good morning, comrade,' he said, with a salute.

At lunch, these men put Blair through an intense grilling. As Blair answered their questions, he cast glances towards his aide Alastair Campbell, checking on his reaction. To express approval of his boss's performance, Campbell responded with almost imperceptible nods. A former political editor at *Today*, Campbell had left News International when Blair became leader. He was a blunt adviser and a fierce advocate to the media. He admired his boss, but never flinched from confronting him. I never heard another adviser interrupt the prime minister with the words: 'Tony, that's total bollocks.'

In his final weeks as opposition leader, Blair, Rupert, and I had dinner with our wives. Blair wanted a discreet venue, so they came to our house in Hampstead. It was a last-minute plan, and Mary went out for off-the-shelf Marks & Spencer meals and supermarket wine. 'I hope we haven't put you to any trouble,' Cherie Blair said.

'Not at all,' I replied, 'all we had to do was microwave it.'

Blair responded amenably that evening to whatever Rupert said, and slickly changed the subject whenever the European single currency and other tricky matters arose. The single currency was always an issue. David Blunkett came to the house for dinner when he was home secretary and kept waving at Rupert with a €5 note he had pulled from the breast pocket of his jacket.

As the Blairs walked away down our garden path that night, Rupert said: 'I like him. She's a bit odd, but I like him.'

Soon after I arrived in London in 1995, Campbell had come to visit me with another close aide to Blair, Peter Mandelson. They were two of the principal architects of the New Labour revival that would return their party to power. They were an unusual couple. Mandelson smiled in a way that made it feel risky to smile back. He looked away when he spoke. Campbell had an air of incipient anger and when he smiled, his stony eyes did not always join his mouth. I did not detect much warmth between them.

They came in friendship, however, because Mandelson made a surprising proposal. He offered to help us remake Rupert's image, which, he said helpfully, could do with 'improvement' in Britain.

Labour's great rebranding had been to substitute its militant red flag with a moderate red English rose. Mandelson took part in this rebranding, but the rose was Neil Kinnock's idea.

'I hope you're not going to propose a rosebud,' I said. I had never heard a more ridiculous and self-serving proposition.

At Mandelson's request, I arranged a discreet lunch with Rupert in one of the private townhouses connected to The Athenaeum Hotel in Piccadilly. Towards the end of the meal, Mandelson subtly suggested Rupert might make a donation to the Labour Party. After he had gone, Rupert was thoughtful. 'Maybe I could give Blair a private donation,' he said.

'Do you honestly believe Labour would keep quiet about you giving them money?' I asked. 'There'll be a photo of the cheque in *The Guardian* within 24 hours.' We quickly decided it was a bad idea.

The pre-election charm of Labour lost its intensity in the years after Blair took occupancy of Number 10. Blair saw us frequently. He was usually cordial, but sometimes the meetings were tough. On one occasion, I was at Downing Street with Rupert, and, after talking for a while with the visiting Australian prime minister, John Howard, we left the grand formal rooms and took a small lift to the Blairs' rooms on the top floor.

The flat was modest and chaotic in a family home kind of way. The lobby was cluttered with toys — their youngest son Leo was still a toddler. In the compact living room were two sofas on either side of the fireplace, and Blair's guitar rested in a corner. Rupert and I sat tightly together on one sofa opposite Blair.

I got an uneasy sense this was not going to be a regular chat when Blair's three most senior aides walked into the room and took up position beneath a window to our left. Jonathan Powell was Blair's chief of staff, a patrician looking man whose oldest brother, Charles, had been an adviser to Thatcher. Weirdly, the brothers pronounced 'Powell' differently. Sally Morgan was a baroness with cropped reddish hair, and another of Tony's inner circle. Alastair Campbell looked mischievous.

We were four feet apart across a coffee table when Tony launched into an attack on *The Sun,* rattling off a list of stories he thought unfair or inaccurate. I had never seen him so fierce. What was interesting was that he directed none of his attack at Rupert. It was the perfect moment to give him a piece of his mind, but he left Rupert untouched, aiming all his ire at me. I became Rupert's proxy while he sat right next to me without saying a word. In the car heading out of Downing Street, Rupert put a reassuring hand on my knee.

'You handled yourself very well in there,' he said.

'Thanks for your support,' I replied.

Sometimes the meetings were more amusing. I was in Downing Street for dinner with Rupert and his sons Lachlan and James. Blair and his wife were the only people with us, apart from the inevitable Campbell. The discussion became heated as the evening advanced and James, agitated by his father's opinions on Israel, began swearing loudly and freely. After he had used the words 'fuck' and 'fucking' a dozen or so times, I became uneasy. I know the feeling of being attacked by adult children who think they know everything, but we weren't at home sitting around with a few beers.

Cherie looked startled, but Blair and Rupert appeared unfazed. Afterwards, we went for a further drink at a hotel bar. James had cursed only three or four times before the barman instructed him sharply to mind his language. The tycoon's son had no privilege here — what had been tolerated at the dinner table of the British prime minister was too much from an anonymous drinker in a swanky London saloon.

Cherie Blair could be free with her advice. Sitting beside me at a dinner in 1998, soon after Stuart Higgins had departed as *The Sun*'s editor, Cherie was forceful in recommending a successor. The only person for the job, she insisted, was Rebekah Wade. I told her that Wade — later Brooks — was 30, had only recently become Higgins' deputy, and had yet to prove herself.

Mrs Blair sometimes sought favours. She asked me to give her eldest son, Euan, a summer internship at *The Times*. 'He thinks he wants to be a journalist,' she said. 'Please talk him out of it.' Euan spent a few weeks working on the sports section. There is no record of him having any further association with the media.

The hostility between Tony Blair and Gordon Brown was the perpetual backdrop of Labour's reign from 1997 to 2010. Before Labour's victory, Blair and Brown came together to Rupert's flat to drink wine and talk of their plans should they become Downing Street neighbours. They came across as a perfect double act, seamlessly united, sitting side by side in the vast living room, echoing each other's words. Their relationship was strained even then, but it would be years before it unravelled so completely and so ruinously for their party.

Brown had, in 1994, been seen as the natural successor to then Labour leader, John Smith, who died of a heart attack in May that year. But others thought differently, and Blair himself was convinced he was the party's best hope.

By the time of the 1997 election, with Blairism at its height, the pair had reached an uneasy but genuine truce. Brown's later, intense malice was rooted in his belief that Blair betrayed a promise that he would stand aside in order to give Brown a shot at being prime minister. In the early years, both blithely denied their relationship was troubled, but not many people were fooled and in the end they stopped pretending.

When the tension between them was at its height, Blair invited me one evening to his flat. It was just before the 2003 Iraq invasion and Blair had never been under more pressure. I had never seen him so careworn. The bright-eyed, election-winning boyishness had drained away. I remember the bottle of wine he opened was corked. He made no attempt to fake his feelings towards Brown and waved his hands furiously towards the ceiling. 'He has no idea what it takes to do this job,' he stormed.

I asked him why he hadn't fired Brown: 'Why have you lived all these years with a disloyal deputy?'

'You don't understand,' he said. 'It was never as easy as that.'

He had always been afraid that Brown would become his open enemy on the backbenches of Parliament. There were a significant number of MPs who preferred Brown, or thought they did. Many people got caught in the crossfire between Brown and Blair, including me.

Invitations to spend time with Brown were frequent. He asked me to breakfast at Number 11 Downing Street, the chancellor's home, with Terry Leahy, chief executive of the supermarket chain Tesco. Leahy was a Liverpudlian, too, and Brown wanted us to lead a project to revitalise the city. It might have been a good idea for Leahy, but I wasn't getting hooked into working on behalf of any political party.

Just as we were leaving, Blair came bouncing down the stairs. It looked like a well-timed arrival, and Brown's face fell as he greeted us. But Blair gave me an icy smile. I think until then he thought I was his ally. I was never again invited for a quiet drink at Number 10.

Brown stayed close to News International as Blair's reputation was shredded in the gruesome aftermath of the Iraq invasion. Even after I had gone back to New York, he would call to vent about one political problem or another, especially if News International papers were giving him a hard time. Brown and I had a connection in our poor eyesight. He had lost the sight of his left eye to a rugby kick when he was 16, and, like me, had suffered retinal detachments in the remaining useful one. We talked about the difficulties and the possibility of blindness we had both faced. Brown was an odd mixture of brooding ill temper and a jollity that much of the time seemed artificial. His laugh seemed more decided than spontaneous. He was a decent man but devoid of the natural charm possessed of the most successful politicians, in particular Tony Blair.

After the Blair years, when a chain of events shattered the relationship between Rupert's newspapers and Labour, it was surreal that they had ever been so harmonious. I didn't discover until years later how distasteful the job of befriending us had been for some New Labour leaders.

Alastair Campbell had joined Rupert's *Today* newspaper from the *Daily Mirror* in 1993, leaving the following year to work as Blair's press secretary. He was appointed chief engineer in Labour's effort to gain *The Sun*'s endorsement, but his published diaries suggest he found the task painful.

Writing of a dinner in January 1997 attended by Blair, Rupert, and me, in which there had been a difference over the European single currency, he sounded disgusted: 'It was faintly obscene that we even had to worry what they thought.'

After another Number 10 dinner, he writes: 'I felt frustrated that we had to pander so much.' And of another occasion: 'He [Blair] felt there was something unpleasant about newspaper power and influence.'

I also discovered the motivation behind the 1995 visit to my office by Mandelson and Campbell when Mandelson offered to help polish Rupert's image. Campbell writes: 'TB saw Murdoch and Les Hinton at Murdoch's flat ... He felt that Murdoch personally liked him but Hinton was not so sure ... TB wanted me and Peter M to see Les again soon.'

The relationship between Blair and Rupert may have been born out of self-interest, but it became a true friendship that lasted beyond Blair's Number 10 days, long after the support of newspapers mattered to him quite so much. Their friendship ended famously and bitterly in 2013 when Rupert divorced his third wife, Wendi, amid suspicions she and Blair had been lovers. Five years later, Blair's many denials had failed to renew it.

In 2007, soon after Gordon Brown had become prime minister, Rupert asked me to meet him in Sicily. I gave Blair and Cherie a lift to Sicily in Rupert's Boeing 737, and we took a helicopter to his 184-foot sailing yacht, *Rosehearty*. It was a social meeting of two fond friends; I had never seen Blair seem so relaxed and unweighted with worry. He seemed happy to see the last of Westminster. Whatever plans he had upon leaving Downing Street in 2007, I wasn't surprised he decided against following the route of predecessors who went to the House of Lords. He told me once: 'I would sooner have my testicles nailed to a passing train.'

Blair and Rupert talked for hours, and went alone together on a long Mediterranean swim, two distant pinheads in the waves as security men tracked them with binoculars. Cherie was in a buoyant mood. The issue of feminism came up over a deck-top lunch and I remember her calling me a 'caveman'. She might have been joking, but I couldn't be sure.

We spent time on James Murdoch's smaller, faster yacht, and Blair stood happily at the helm for more than an hour with a look of childlike glee. I remembered, over those few days, the occasion 10 years before, when Blair came alone to Rupert's flat. As Blair and I were leaving, Rupert walked us to his door, talking about flying in his plane the following day to the Caribbean, where he would spend a week on his yacht. Rupert often talked this way, about his houses and boats and what kind of private jet he might buy next, in the casual way others talk about adding a kitchen extension, or leasing a new car.

Blair looked over his shoulder at me, raised his eyebrows, and smiled. I was never sure what that smile meant — whether he was indicating his disapproval of such ostentatious wealth, or revealing his envy of it.

CHAPTER 22

Twilight

At home one night, a grainy photo arrived in my email inbox. I could tell it had been taken at an expensive Mayfair bar. Four people were grinning happily, each with champagne glasses raised towards the camera, as if they were toasting me.

This photo was an act of defiance by the four senior editors at Wapping: John Witherow, Robert Thomson, Rebekah Wade, and Colin Myler. I had mounted a purge of editorial spending and this was their retaliation. It did not indicate an eagerness to cooperate, but that was no surprise. It was not easy working with worthwhile editors. Most of the good ones were serious pains. They could be subversive, secretive, self-important, and petulant in response to the smallest criticism. But in the golden days of Wapping, everything revolved around them.

There are essential executives in every department of a newspaper. Pressrooms will print and bundle millions of newspapers every night; the circulation teams deliver to more than 50,000 retailers; advertising pays the bulk of the bills. But during my time in London, the other managers complained constantly about editors. Production and circulation bosses bemoaned missed deadlines; advertising executives agitated about the unsatisfactory location of their clients' important ads, and the editorial content that had offended them; finance people sent me notes about excess spending and overstaffing. They also protested, now and then, about the high-handed manner of their insufferable peers on the editorial floors. But they knew that editors were the real engines of the newspapers; that it all meant nothing without the scores of stories and thousands of words they generated every day.

Editors were not discouraged from regarding themselves as the nobility of News International. Rupert believed there was never a shortage of able business managers, but that talented editors were the most difficult executives to find.

Behind its monolithic, jailhouse architecture, Wapping was a loose federation of publications, all wary of one other and sometimes quarrelsome. There were not only the redtops and broadsheets — so different they published in their own dialects — but also the lettered cloister of dishevelled poets and critics at *The Times Literary Supplement,* and the academic enclaves of *The Times Education Supplement* and *Higher Education Supplement.*

Each of the big newspapers kept a jealous score of comparative marketing and editorial spends. They also double-crossed each other over exclusives. The *News of the World* once stole an expensive book serialisation from *The Sunday Times* office. *The Sun* overheard a *News of the World* scoop in the men's room and beat their neighbour to the story.

Most of the newspaper industry didn't like News International. The siege of Wapping was their liberation as well as ours, but Rupert had embarrassed his meek opponents by breaking both his chains and theirs. The carnivore, it was said, had liberated the herbivores.

We didn't expect much affection; we were the hovering 10-tonne gorilla in their lives. Other media didn't like us either. Sky TV was shattering the snug duopoly that dominated British broadcasting, and Rupert was forever antagonising the BBC by branding them a market-warping, state-sponsored monopolist.

It wasn't surprising News International had so much bad publicity. Media is the vocal chords of a free society, and just about every media property we didn't own was lined up against us.

How much it damaged the image of our newspapers was something else. Measured by the millions of readers and increasing profits, we were definitely keeping our customers happy. The fact that we sold so many copies — one in three of every national newspaper people bought was one of ours — was used to support claims that we were over-powerful. For us, it was a point of pride.

Our market share had not been achieved by buying already successful titles, but through beating the competition. *The Sun* was dying when Rupert bought it in 1969. Twenty-five years later, on a good day it was selling more than 4 million copies. *The Times* was acquired in 1981 and lost money well into the new millennium — even some of Rupert's harshest critics give him credit for supporting it.

For all the hostility, Wapping was a thriving world of gale-force personalities and abounding self-confidence. We didn't know back then that twilight was coming. We didn't know that the triumphant age of newspapers would quickly begin to fade, that the industry freed by one wave of technology would be besieged by another, and that my photo of four grinning editors would become a treasured souvenir of the days when piddling spending reviews felt like a crisis.

The electronic squeal of dial-up internet was the herald of a shattering revolution, but in 1995 it could be heard in only 1 million British homes. There were warning signs — Rupert and I had seen Encarta, the paperless encyclopaedia miraculously stored on a plastic disc, and John Evans, our canary down the mine, had predicted a challenging future for news that was printed on crushed trees. We knew it was a threat, but never imagined what would happen.

We still lived in an all-paper world, and talked with only casual curiosity about the World Wide Web. In the summer of that year, Microsoft launched its Internet Explorer. At News International, we were fascinated by the novelty of office-wide email.

Twenty years later, the empires of print were creaking super-tankers, left behind in the spray from a sleek fleet of algorithm-fuelled speedboats. Old media had been like a pyramid, with a few at the peak broadcasting to the masses beneath. But technology had turned the pyramid upside down. Now anyone with a 5oz mobile has infinity at their fingertips.

Wapping was at the pinnacle of the pyramid in the 1990s. Each of our newspapers was growing, with new magazines and extra sections. *The Sunday Times*, a pre-digital goldmine of classified advertising, turned its newsprint supplements into glossy magazines and dwarfed its main rival, *The Observer*. *The Sun* and the *News of the World*, with slick magazine inserts and beefed-up sports coverage, extended their leads until their redtop rivals became distant stragglers. *The Times* bundled more sections into its Saturday edition and saw its circulation grow. In a heart-stopping leap in 2003, *The Times* became a tabloid and found thousands more readers. We had toyed with the idea for years, planning to try it with our Ireland edition. But we always feared the damaging disapproval that could result from the Murdoch press turning a great newspaper into a tabloid. When *The Independent* led the way, we pulled out our old dummies and followed them in a few weeks.

Our editors were famous, and sometimes notorious. Kelvin MacKenzie drove *The Sun* to success, but also alienated an entire city. In 1989, MacKenzie chose to believe South Yorkshire Police's accounts of the behaviour of Liverpool football club fans in the aftermath of the Hillsborough disaster, which killed 96 people. The claims — including that drunken supporters stole from the dying — have long since been discredited, and *The Sun* has apologised, but the city has never forgiven either MacKenzie or the newspaper. The enduring bitterness — almost 30 years after the tragedy — was not easy to understand. Nations who lost millions of people in wars had restored diplomatic relations with their old enemies in far less time. My children, without ever living there, had been Liverpool supporters all their lives and it puzzled them as well. Kath told me it was foolish to be seen carrying a copy of *The Sun* when we were in town, so I wrapped mine inside *The Times*. When I first got the London job, it was six years after Hillsborough, and I was briefly hopeful my local credentials could help heal the rift. I went to Liverpool with Stuart Higgins when he was editor and met club executives and family representatives. The club in those days wanted a good relationship, but the families were too angry. It might be mystifying after so many years, but you can't challenge their right to be angry, given the grief and malign deceit they suffered.

By the time I arrived in 1995, MacKenzie had left, which was a lucky escape for me that had nothing to do with Hillsborough. He was known to lock his office door to keep business executives at bay. When editors were selling newspapers, they got away with things like that.

MacKenzie's successor, Stuart Higgins, was a flesh-and-blood version of the newspaper he edited. He was excitable and sentimental, and his feelings were as readable as a headline two inches deep. He was also a folk hero among his staff — I never knew a more popular editor.

Higgins and Piers Morgan were creatures of Kelvin MacKenzie's *The Sun*. They must have hero-worshipped him because both absorbed his personality and mannerisms: the swagger, the loud cocky voice, the biting put-downs. Morgan in particular was a simulacrum of his maverick mentor — just younger, taller, and, at the time, thinner.

It was a blow when Morgan walked out of his job at the *News of the World* three weeks after I started. His idol MacKenzie had moved to the Mirror Group and wanted Morgan to edit the *Daily Mirror.* Morgan at the *Mirror* got into such a bitter feud with Higgins' successor, David Yelland, that they fought it out in the pages of their newspapers.

Yelland was the most unsuitable editor in *The Sun's* history. He was a broadsheet man trapped at a tabloid and screaming to escape. He didn't stand a chance in his feud with Morgan. Piers was a world-class — a Kelvin-class — insulter, and Yelland didn't possess the tabloid genes to retaliate. Yelland had alopecia and appeared constantly in the *Mirror* as the Mekon, the bald, green monster out of Dan Dare comics.

Yelland's revenge was savage. When the *Mirror* became embroiled in allegations that its financial journalists were guilty of insider stock deals, Morgan became a suspect, but never faced charges. Yelland put the story on page one, again and again, so infuriating Morgan that he cornered me at a party and threatened to kill my family. 'I know where you live,' he said. In his volume of diaries, *The Insider,* he confesses how he felt the morning after: 'I disgraced myself ... It was Sonny Corleone without the brains or the charm.'

Rebekah Wade had worked for Morgan in features on the *News of the World*. She was an Olive Oyl lookalike in those days, tall and skinny with her mass of red hair tied tightly back against her scalp. Wade became Phil Hall's deputy when he succeeded Morgan as editor. Hall took great care with his appearance. He favoured Italian suits and sometimes sat at his desk reading page proofs while wrapped in a new-fangled electric device like a heart monitor that was alleged to firm abs without exercise.

Hall had a haul of personal stories. The Archbishop of Canterbury once told him he bought the *News of the World* in order to find out what his staff was up to. On one occasion, Hall was house hunting and found himself in the home of a former prison governor who explained he was obliged to sell up after the *News of the World* had written a sensational story about his prison. Hall kept his own counsel.

It was Hall who exposed the author and politician Jeffrey Archer for perjury during a libel trial. He was sentenced to four years in prison. At the time, Archer was running to be London's first mayor and Rupert was thinking of endorsing him in *The Sun*. I waited until the last minute to tell Rupert about the story. 'Oh. Poor Jeffrey,' was all he said.

Rebekah Wade succeeded Hall as editor of the *News of the World*, before becoming editor of *The Sun*. Her cool, determined deputy, Andy Coulson, followed her at the *News of the World*. Both would later become world famous.

The broadsheet editors were more sedate. Peter Stothard would glide dreamily through the office. His high chin and the haughty droop of his eyes could intimidate those who didn't know him well enough. During Stothard's decade, *The Times* began its radical reshaping, with an enlarged Saturday edition, a magazine, and its first timid flirtation with a tabloid format. When Stothard moved on to edit *The Times Literary Supplement*, with his knighthood for services to journalism, Robert Thomson, an enigmatic Australian from the *Financial Times*, replaced him. Thomson was famous for his unfathomable demeanour, presumably adopted during his years as a correspondent in the less scrutable societies of China and Japan. His staff puzzled to penetrate his real meanings and thoughts, although, on the rare occasions he lost his temper, they would be vividly evident. John Witherow of *The Sunday Times* was the most in-the-office, heads-down editor. He was also tough. Witherow once asked his sports editor: 'Alex, what do they think of me out there?'

'They think you're a complete cunt,' came the reply.

Witherow beamed: 'That's fantastic.'

On the fringe of the editors were the marketing people, whose job was to please editors by enhancing sales with giveaway promotions and snappy television commercials. Ellis Watson, the most exuberant among them, had the inexplicable habit, when he was over-excited, of rugby tackling people. He once sent Rupert's son-in-law, Alasdair MacLeod, flying across my office. I was grateful that day for the over-thick executive carpet. One of Watson's promotions, offering rock-bottom holiday flights, was such a terrifying success that I found him tearfully calling airlines to charter extra aircraft, filled with dread that he did not have enough seats to meet demand.

There were difficult times, and missteps. *The Sun* filled its front page with the story of a video purporting to show Princess Diana and her adulterous lover, James Hewitt, cavorting together inside Prince Charles' Highgrove estate. It was an elaborate hoax.

In a moment of madness, *The Sun* also ran a topless photograph of Sophie Rhys-Jones on the eve of her wedding to the Queen's son, Prince Edward. There was a huge outcry. Buckingham Palace described it as an act of 'premeditated cruelty' and the Press Complaints Commission called it 'reprehensible'. We ran an apology next day, complete with a cartoon showing the editor, David Yelland, in chains as he was led to the Tower.

The Sun lost sales after both these mishaps. No government need worry about regulating the press: readers do a fine job of punishing its mistakes.

Well-meant campaigns sometimes had unintended consequences. The most infamous was during Rebekah Wade's editorship of the *News of the World*. The paper published dozens of photographs of known paedophiles in an effort to persuade the government to allow parents to know if a child-abuser was a neighbour. The campaign provoked shocking incidents: in a Welsh village, a woman paediatrician found the word 'PAEDO' scrawled on the wall of her home; in Manchester, a brick was thrown through the window of an innocent man. *The Daily Telegraph* ran an editorial headlined 'Rebekah gets her riot' after a paedophile fled his Portsmouth home in the face of a stone-throwing mob of 150 people who also set fire to an innocent woman's car.

High and lows blended together over the years, and those long-ago days seem like a bliss of big sales and high profits — a time when Wapping was at its most successful.

The special difficulty of working at his newspapers was that Rupert really did know more about the business than anyone else. By the 1990s, he was the victorious old warrior of Fleet Street, interfering, argumentative, convinced of his point of view, and loving every detail of the job of putting out a newspaper.

He could spot a poor photo crop, or a careless headline, or a badly inked page, or a clunky story mix. He knew how to write a picture caption, which is not a straightforward skill, and an editorial, and he could sketch a clean layout. He didn't like layouts to be too tidy: they look too still, he would say, and a newspaper should look urgent, as if put together in a hurry. Large 'reverse heads' — black blocks within which white headlines appear — also annoyed him. He had a mysterious loathing of curly serif type in headlines. Serif fonts are traditional in heavies like *The Times* and *The Wall Street Journal*, and where there is an outbreak of sans serif headlines in their pages, that's Rupert's imprint.

He would debate with a printer the technicalities of operating a press, discussing manning, paper quality, and press speeds. He would spring awkward questions on executives with commercial responsibilities: How much does this newspaper cost per page —

which meant the total cost of paper, editorial, and distribution. How much is Ford spending each year on advertising? How does our advertising-to-editorial page ratio compare with the competition? What's the year-over-year circulation of the Irish edition? It was important to know these things, but a mistake to bluff when you didn't because Rupert often knew the answers to his own questions.

The sense that he was connected to everything was almost universal across the company. This had been true when the company was smaller, but even as it exploded in size, and it was impossible for him to know it all, the mythology of Murdoch perpetuated the idea he was all-seeing and everywhere.

Rupert played the part, lived the legend, but he also built an efficient management machine that freed him to burrow down into the company wherever he chose: to solve, or create, any crisis; or to dedicate himself to a single project.

He left others to oversee those parts of the business that didn't much interest him. The book publishing division was not a passion and he occasionally considered selling it. One of his businesses made large profits printing and distributing supermarket discount coupons to American Sunday newspapers. Its boss for years, Paul Carlucci, rarely heard from Rupert. But when Carlucci became publisher of the *New York Post,* a newspaper that lost millions a year, Rupert was on the phone almost every day.

Rupert folklore, apocryphal or not, was handed down through the years. There was young Rupert the prig, protesting at suede shoes in the office — 'We don't belong to a bloody jazz band!' — or his attempt to ban office beards, only to face a rebellion on *The Australian* sub-editors' desk when every member grew one. There was Rupert the tyrant, who so terrified an underperforming classified advertising manager that he would secretly re-run the same pages — unpaid — to keep the boss happy. One Sydney editor hid beneath his desk whenever Rupert arrived, crying, 'Run for it, the great sacker is on the way.' There was the boss with mystical instincts who visited the site of a new press facility in San Antonio, studied the new concrete foundation that was under construction, told the gathered architects and engineers that it did not look level, and turned out to be right. David O'Neill, one of the company's brightest technicians, told me the story, and he was on the scene.

Rupert enjoyed these stories himself. His favourite was about the Manhattan cab driver who told Rupert about his brother's high-paid job in a Melbourne pressroom where he had almost nothing to do. The pressroom was, of course, owned by News Corp, and the luckless managing director soon had his angry boss on the phone. Rupert told that story with glee for years.

This feeling of his presence ran deepest in the places he built from nothing. In Australia and Britain, he felt a closeness to his businesses, an emotional ownership that was not the same everywhere.

His charismatic authority was an actual aura in these places. Old hands were his agents, undaunted loyalists spreading the word of their wonderful lives with Rupert, recalling small moments in his presence and seeming blessed to have been victims of his ire. They had tales of his furies and mistakes, but for them every transgression faded away in the burning light of his cleverness and energy. Like party commissars, they guarded his reputation, correcting the careless frankness of newcomers and internal dissidents.

At a meeting in Sydney, when I raised the matter of Rupert's mortality, the man in charge of Queensland looked thunderstruck. 'Mate,' he said, straight-faced. 'I don't think we're allowed to be talking about things like this.' I started to smile, then realised he wasn't joking.

People spoke guardedly about his off-duty quirks: the altering colour of his diminishing hair; the diet fads; the personal trainer he took everywhere; and the *feng shui* man who appeared during his marriage to Wendi Deng, prowling the Wapping plant, placing 'lucky' objects everywhere and denouncing colour schemes, desk positions, and the choice of office plants.

The *feng shui* man told me to remove a tree in the boardroom. 'It will create conflict,' he said.

'Good,' I told him. 'A little boardroom conflict is an excellent thing.'

The *feng shui* man's magic did not prevent the living-room ceiling collapsing at Rupert's refurbished London flat. It fell harmlessly but noisily in the middle of the night, when Wendi and her two children were safely in bed. A few days before there had been a gathering in the living room of the News Corp board and senior executives. The architect told me the ceiling was very heavy. 'It would have broken everyone's neck,' he said.

We wondered at Rupert's appetite for work. His life merged work and play so closely that in his mind there seemed to be no difference. In 1999, Rupert married Wendi Deng aboard his yacht *Morning Glory* as it cruised the Hudson River off Manhattan. As I went ashore in the early hours of Saturday, he took me by the arm. 'You will not be hearing from me for a month,' he said. 'I want to spend time with Wendi, and read.'

Back in London, fewer than 48 hours after his pledge, Rupert called from his honeymoon villa in the hills of Tuscany. Two days after that, having assembled the team he requested, I was on board his Gulfstream jet heading to Italy to talk business. For three days we talked, hiked, and dined, taking a break when Rupert disappeared each day with his trainer to challenge the local curves and peaks on a racing bicycle. Ten days after that visit I was on the plane again, with a different group ready to brief him on other topics. Wendi's forbearance impressed us all.

The prospect of Rupert's presence had a visible impact on those who worked for him. At executive meetings, when I announced Rupert was coming to town, there would be a physical reaction, a wave of sighs and mutters, a shiver through the room as everyone shifted in their seats, or rearranged their papers. I knew how they felt. It was a mixture of dread and thrill, and I was not exempt from it.

When I arrived in London, a large portrait of Rupert was hanging in the boardroom, positioned to the right of my chair. He was wearing a blue suit and had been captured in a businesslike pose, peering sharply into the room. It was one of those painted Mona Lisa gazes that followed you everywhere. After a few weeks, I banished Rupert to the downstairs lobby where visitors could enjoy his grim welcome.

I was luckier at Wapping than my predecessors. Rupert was absent often, busy developing his US television business and Sky, and struggling to grow in China and India. This gave me more space and safety. Thirty years after the company's arrival in Wapping, no one had come close to the 12 years I lasted.

Absent or not, the small businessman in him wanted to know everything. Each business division delivered to him a weekly financial report. Ours alone ran to 30 pages, meaning that each Wednesday he received scores of pages outlining the corporation's worldwide performance. Gathering and printing these reports was an internal publishing operation that occupied dozens of people. He couldn't have read it all, but always read some. Thursday was the day to be prepared for a telephone ambush, when he would seize on obscure issues: an increase in the percentage of paper waste on the presses, a slip in retail advertising rates, overspends in editorial or marketing.

In meetings, he went easy on junior people; he must have seen how terrified some were. When I included bright juniors in lunches with him, I was firm. 'Don't just sit there. Speak up, or you won't be invited back.' Without this threat, they were likely to sit dumbstruck by his presence.

With senior people who displeased him, he could be savage. I witnessed more of these moments than I suffered, and they were never a pretty sight. He would often ask, when one more beaten executive walked limply from his office: 'Did I go too far?' Usually the answer was yes.

I consoled over drinks more than one tearful editor. He went too far with me now and then, and I wish I could say I became accustomed to it, but that wouldn't be true. Sometimes he knew he had gone over the top.

I flew once to New York with an idea I loved and, it turned out, he hated. The idea wasn't so important as the argument we had. He kept telling me it was a rubbish idea and I kept telling him it wasn't. It was pretty unpleasant. When I was leaving the office to fly back to London that night, he wouldn't let me go. 'Don't go tonight,' he said. 'Let's have dinner.' We went to a Greek fish restaurant on the West Side with Wendi and didn't talk business at all. Next day, he told me to go ahead with my idea.

Not too far from now, talk of Murdoch the newspaperman will be misty history. When I arrived in Wapping — and the company's first faltering footsteps onto the web were more than a year away — no one knew he would be the world's last newspaper tycoon.

The old press titans were already fading away. These dynasties began their rise around the turn of the twentieth century when high-speed printing, the first mass media, was at the frontier of information technology. They were famous: Northcliffe, Rothermere, and Beaverbrook in Britain; Hearst, Pulitzer, Ochs, and Sulzberger in America; Packer and Fairfax in Australia.

The age of the press baron yielded to a mightier generation of information moguls whose technology would swallow the world and make newspapers puny. These pioneers — Bill Gates, Mark Zuckerberg, Jeff Bezos, Steve Jobs — would unleash an infinite torrent of information and entertainment that would crowd every moment of our lives and make human attention the world's most precious commodity.

When newspapers got round to launching websites in 1996, they had no coherent strategy. There was so little fear or understanding of the web, they offered content free of charge, following the geek mantra that 'information wants to be free', along with the woolly assumption that advertising would sustain their businesses. *The Wall Street Journal*, in an almost solitary act of sanity, made the decision to charge its users.

High-priced journalism — the product of generations of inherited experience and tradition — was sucked into a vast electronic maw, to be purloined and distributed to millions, unpaid and often unacknowledged. The internet was a digital vampire, draining the lifeblood of the press and stealing its profits. Tiny start-up 'news' sites and giant search engines sold low-price advertising alongside newspaper journalism they paid nothing to produce.

As consumers became accustomed to getting their news free and abandoned newspapers, advertisers naturally followed them. By the time the industry came to its senses, it faced years repairing the damage — if it ever could.

But the dilemma for newspapers went deeper than the decision to give its content away. Economically, a newspaper is a manufacturing and distribution business with huge fixed costs. It needs thousands of tons of paper, printing presses and buildings to house them, and fleets of trucks to distribute bundles of hard-copy news.

Free online news sites swept into the market with nothing to lose. They had cheap and instant distribution, and tiny fixed costs compared to newspapers. They were able to deliver profits with advertising alone, while charging advertisers far lower rates than print could afford.

Newspapers hesitated because they were in a trap. Migrating into low-profit digital would undermine their traditional high-cost, high-profit operations. They would cannibalise themselves, and, while readers and advertisers abandoned print, they would still have to carry the burden of costly printing presses and physical distribution.

No amount of business school theorising about the virtues of permanent renewal and creative destruction can factor in the emotional challenge, or the human difficulty. So, while newspapers edged along, riding two horses, hoping against reason that the threat might not be so great as they feared, freewheeling digital ate their businesses.

I can tell this story with more clarity now, but I was lost in the fog as much as anyone. As a corporation News Corp had long ago diversified across different media and countries: Rupert first invested in television in 1958. But for newspapers, digital wasn't just another thief of people's time. It wasn't a version of radio, television, and film that was competing for human attention by providing more vivid forms of information and entertainment. It wasn't a competitor at all. It was a substitute.

Once-great companies crumbled as they struggled to learn profitable new tricks. Rich, multimedia parent corporations ran out of patience. Time Warner, Tribune Media Company, and News Corp-Fox reviewed the growing wreckage and washed their hands of properties that once gushed profits but were now becoming liabilities. They followed the unsentimental laws of commerce, exorcising a decimated industry that investors feared was approaching the end of its days. Rupert could not bring himself to put his beloved print properties up for adoption and leave their fate with unknown investors; he satisfied shareholders, and Fox executives, by separating

News Corp and Fox, and maintaining the same family shareholding of both.

These castaways with their life-threatening wounds were left to navigate away from their disintegrating foundations, to reinvent themselves or perish. Time Inc, with limited resources, splashed out to buy internet enterprises such as MySpace, then, in a search for safety, made a deal to sell itself to another big magazine publisher, Meredith. Tribune, like a grandmother at a rave, renamed itself tronc, inc — for Tribune online content. News Corp — Rupert's publishing operations kept the name when they were divorced from Fox — invested in real estate websites, radio, and arcane online advertising technology.

At the turn of the millennium, we were sufficiently optimistic about print to persuade Rupert's board to approve a £650 million spend on three new printing plants. It might have been the last big pressroom construction project in the western world.

In 2006, when these great press halls were nearly complete, Rupert flew with a group of us to Japan as part of a continuing study of what many newspaper people were still calling 'new media', as if it were nascent and unthreatening.

'We've got an extra passenger,' said Rupert. 'We're bringing along the man who owns Blueberry.'

'BlackBerry, Rupert,' I said.

The world was spinning faster than we knew. Within 10 years, the pioneering BlackBerry smartphone, once every sophisticate's mobile choice, was itself outclassed and outdated.

CHAPTER 23

Damsel in distress

'There's a lady on the phone wants to speak to you. Says she's Princess Diana.'

I had been in London a few weeks when my assistant Marianne Krafinski, a tough and worldly native of Queens in New York City, called from her desk. She was used to crackpot calls, but handled them with care since telling a croaky-voiced man to 'Piss off' when he claimed to be Rupert Murdoch.

'No, no — it's Murdoch here,' said Rupert, who didn't sound himself, having just come round in hospital after a general anaesthetic.

The anxious, whispery voice on the phone was unmistakably Diana. She said she hoped I was enjoying my new job, but quickly came to the point. Photographers were making her life unbearable, and she didn't know what to do.

'They follow me everywhere, every day. I can never escape. They hide in bushes and behind trees. I can never go anywhere without them following me. Can you help me, Mr Hinton? I'm a damsel in distress.'

I offered sympathy, but no practical help. I told her these

photographers were paparazzi, that they didn't work for newspapers, and were beyond our control. I told her that Jacqueline Kennedy Onassis had been the target of obsessive media attention for 30 years, and that she was the new Jackie: every publication and television network in the world wanted her image.

'I understand that, but it doesn't help me,' she said. Diana wanted to meet for lunch to talk more, but I declined her invitation. I knew that Diana was sophisticated in dealing with the media, that she lunched with editors, leaked to trusted reporters, gave aid to sympathetic authors, flirted with photographers one moment and raged at them the next. She had regularly outwitted Royal Family spin doctors, sworn enemies since her separation from Prince Charles three years before.

But mass media had in some ways lost control of itself. Technology had spawned an uncountable army of wannabe photojournalists. Rich newspapers and magazines were ready to pay a lot of money for compelling images, wherever they came from. These newspapers could profit from the work of the paparazzi without being responsible for their behaviour. It was an unhealthy mix, and this was before the advent of the internet and online news.

Once, taking a photograph, developing a print, and wiring it to potential customers, was complex and expensive. Now it was simple: buy a camera and a laptop and you're ready to distribute photographs anywhere in the world in minutes. Anyone could join the paparazzi, and a relentless horde followed Diana because they could earn thousands — tens of thousands — for the right photo.

Diana tried thwarting them. Arriving at the gym, she walked with her face to the wall and her back towards the photographers. She wore the same clothes day after day in an effort to date and devalue the images. She pleaded in tears to be left alone. Nothing made them give up the chase.

At lunch in Park Lane, London, with Peter Stothard, when he was editor of *The Times,* she said: 'When we leave they will be hiding everywhere.' She was right. Cameras emerged from behind trees, walls, and parked cars as she appeared.

Publications worldwide created the market, but none paid better than Fleet Street. Diana photos had become the paparazzi's daily cash crop.

I last saw her at *The Sunday Times* Christmas party in 1996, dressed in red, chatting and charming, and relaxed, ironically, because at a Fleet Street party she was truly safe from tormenting cameras.

The following summer on Sunday 31 August, my bedside telephone woke me soon after 1am. Phil Hall, the editor of the *News of the World*, said Diana had been in a car accident in Paris. Her companion, Dodi Fayed, was dead, and Diana was in hospital. I drove to Wapping.

It is a paradox how calm newsrooms can become when something momentous happens. Murder and disaster are daily events, but when no expression of alarm, anger, fear, or grief can do justice to what has happened, a tense and almost speechless calm occurs. This was how it was that night in the *News of the World* and *The Sunday Times.*

Phil Hall came towards me as I entered his newsroom. His walk was unhurried and his face looked as it usually did, clench-jawed and unexpressive.

'We're hearing she's dead,' was all he said, and led me towards Stuart Kuttner, the veteran managing editor, who was leaning against a cabinet of newspaper files, looking at the ground with one hand against his face. He had been on the phone to an aide to Prince Charles.

'I asked how she was,' Kuttner said. 'He told me it was as bad as I could imagine. It's pretty clear she's dead, but he wouldn't say so.'

Photographs of the accident began arriving. One showed a flash-lit image of Diana in the back of a wrecked Mercedes. The car door was open and she looked upright and calm, without any evident injury. How could she be dead? Was our contact wrong? We knew we had to wait for an official confirmation before the presses could run.

Word arrived that paparazzi on motorbikes were chasing Diana's car when it crashed, and police had arrested photographers at the scene. I remembered that call from Diana — 'I'm a damsel in distress' — and walked to my office to sit alone in the dark. Stuart Higgins, the editor of *The Sun,* called me. He was crying.

The *News of the World* editors had prepared a front page. The headline — 'Diana Dies In Paris Crash' — was wrapped around a photo of the wrecked car. I looked at it for a moment, then took a piece of paper and wrote: 'Diana Dead'.

I handed it to Hall. 'Everyone is asleep. A lot of people will find this out when they see the Sunday front pages, which is something that almost never happens any more. Let's tell them the simple fact. Why not make that your entire front?' He agreed.

When her death was announced, the presses did not stop until Sunday lunchtime, many hours later than usual. I had woken our production and circulation executives, alerting them to stock extra newsprint and to prepare for days of big print runs. The prospect of big sales is often a cause for celebration, but not that night.

Rupert was in London and I called him with the news at 5.15am. There was no point waking him sooner, but I didn't want him finding out from anyone but me.

In the aftermath, both the Royal Family and the tabloid press were cast as villains. When grief demonstrated by the Royal Family failed to match the public mood, Diana's death created one of the biggest crises of the modern monarchy. Mourners had laid an immense carpet of flowers outside Kensington Palace, where Diana lived, but two miles away the flag above Buckingham Palace flew at full mast. The Queen stayed 500 miles away at Balmoral Castle, her summer retreat in Scotland.

Diana's admirers had seen their princess banished by the Royal Family after her divorce from Prince Charles, now they believed her death was being treated with cold indifference. Wrenched into reality by public anger, the Queen returned to London to address the nation, pledging to 'cherish her memory', and the Union Flag at last flew at half-mast above the palace.

Diana's brother Charles, Earl Spencer, accused the press of having blood on its hands. His funeral oration was angry: 'A girl given the name of the ancient goddess of hunting was, in the end, the most hunted person of the modern age.'

It was quickly clear, however, that Diana's paparazzi pursuers had not caused the crash. The driver, Henri Paul, a 41-year-old Frenchman, was drunk and travelling at twice the speed limit when his car plunged into the column of a tunnel near the Seine.

But it was still a terrible time for media. Although the pack of bike-riding photographers did not hound Diana to her death, she died as they sought yet again to cash in on the woman they treated as a commodity. And Fleet Street, while it did not bear guilt for her death, knew it had laid siege to her life.

With demands rising for laws to restrain the press, newspapers competed in a fever of self-exculpation to cleanse themselves of responsibility. The *Daily Mail* announced a ban on the purchase of paparazzi pictures. The *News of the World* was followed by the entire industry when they made freelance photographers sign agreements to abide by the industry code of conduct.

The chief watchdogs of self-regulation went into action. Lord John Wakeham, chairman of the Press Complaints Commission, toured Fleet Street editors, pressing for remorse and change. Sir David English, former editor of the *Daily Mail,* was chairman of the Editors' Code of Practice Committee, which wrote the self-imposed rules of conduct for newspapers. His statement acknowledged a problem while skirting smoothly over anything sounding confessional: 'The tragic death of Diana, Princess of Wales, has focused unprecedented public attention on press intrusion, harassment, and respect for privacy.'

Wakeham and English swiftly put in place new industry guidelines to guard against the relentless pursuits that Diana had suffered. Promises were made to protect Diana's schoolboy sons, William and Harry. Photographers stayed away when William and Harry attended Eton, and a press blackout was agreed when the Army deployed Harry to Afghanistan.

But still the paparazzi plague endured. In January 2007, there was a rush of speculation that Prince William would propose to Catherine Middleton on her twenty-fifth birthday. The result was a Diana-scale paparazzi hunt; television was full of images of Middleton fleeing the mob that laid siege to her Chelsea flat. It was an alarming echo of 1997. I spoke to the editors and announced publicly that we would refuse to buy any paparazzi photographs. I knew our rivals would follow us — we were the country's biggest newspaper group and they didn't have a choice. The siege ended instantly. Next morning outside Kate's home there was only a lone and disappointed ITN camera crew — there to film the pap marauders.

In 2015, Diana's grandchildren, George and Charlotte, became new victims. Fleet Street had stopped buying paparazzi photos of the royals, but foreign media were unquenchable and the digital age meant demand had increased incalculably. Prince William, now 33, and his wife, Catherine, accused photographers of hiding in car boots, and using other children to lure their toddler son within range of their cameras. The pursuit fell back when Kensington Palace warned the paparazzi they risked being mistaken for terrorists and shot.

The relationship between monarchy and media — even the best-behaved media — is born of mutual need. The Royal Family understands the importance of marketing and public relations. The mission statement for their enterprise is potent — 'Duty' — and its intended return on investment an eternal franchise with incomparable working conditions.

Although every Briton is a financial subscriber to this venture and can never opt out, the people still have the power to destroy it. Far more than revenue, the important currency for this operation is public approval.

The monarchy was a peculiar institution to me when I returned from America. It defied any rational explanation, served no evident practical purpose, and yet was indispensable in the minds of most of the country. Pressed to explain what they loved about it, and why it mattered in a mature democracy, people would grow irritated, as if they had been challenged about an embarrassing personal habit they could not understand or control. The monarchy seemed just that — an emotional habit offering some deep comfort for which no justifying logic was required. The monarchy casts a spell over Britain.

But this spell must be kept in working shape. Public approval needs constant nourishment, and customers need value for money; but the monarchy is an enterprise that can't afford to look too anxious to please. Dignity and restraint are central to the equity of the brand; there must be no vulgar exploitation. Exposure in print and on screen is essential, but advertising is obviously not an option. The Royal Family is forced to work with the unruly British media because it is an unavoidable route to market, the conduit to its all-powerful customer base.

This uneasy collusion between the royals and the media was never in its history more important to the Royal Family than after Diana's death. There had been rocky years since the breakup of his marriage, but now Charles' popularity was lower than ever; one poll rated it at 20 per cent. Even the Queen was under pressure.

With Charles, there was good reason. In a 1995 television interview, Diana famously said: 'Well, there were three of us in this marriage, so it was a bit crowded.' The country knew what she meant. The publication of a racy mobile phone conversation between Charles and Camilla Parker Bowles, recorded in 1989, had caused a sensation.

Charles wanted to marry Camilla, but Diana's death, five years after her separation from Charles, had blown a crater in the road to Camilla's rehabilitation. In the autumn of 1997, it was impossible to imagine the country would ever accept her as their new princess and future queen.

My car arrived at the blue-canopied entrance of The Ritz Hotel in Arlington Street just off London's Piccadilly. It was the spring of 1998, the National Osteoporosis Society was having a charity dinner, and the hostess had invited me.

'Hello, I'm Camilla,' she told me, unnecessarily. 'You'll be sitting next to me.'

Camilla Parker Bowles' face opened into a big smile of bright teeth and pink gums. Two fan-shaped patterns of lines appeared above each cheekbone. Her blue eyes were small and sharp, and given added dimension by circles of thin black liner. Her hair was upper-class Farrah Fawcett, two golden wings sweeping away from her cheeks. Her handshake was country-girl strong.

We were at a private fundraiser for 40 or so people. Camilla sat me to her left at a table for eight. On her right was the trim and meticulous Italian fashion designer, Valentino. His face was tanned, waxen, and as still as a celebrity mask in a souvenir shop window.

'I'm terrified,' Camilla said, leaning close to me. 'I have never in my life had to make a speech until now.' Beneath the table she showed me her notes, neatly folded, sitting at the top of her open handbag.

Across the table was the author William Shawcross, an acquaintance since he published a biography of Rupert in 1992. He and Camilla had grown up together in Sussex. 'I had such a crush on him when we were young,' she whispered. 'He's so good-looking.'

Camilla's speech lasted only three minutes and was an obvious ordeal. It was oddly moving seeing her struggle to contain her nerves, the speech notes shaking in her hand. She was driven by strong and invisible feelings; in that leaked mobile phone conversation, she had told Charles: 'I'd suffer anything for you. That's love. It's the strength of love.'

This love had made her Britain's most hated woman. It was too dangerous for her even to be seen with Charles. In the popular imagination, Camilla was a scarlet woman, the marriage wrecker who had broken the heart of a fragile princess. Newspapers sometimes reflect public opinion and other times inflame it, but there was no doubt that the public loathing of Camilla had become a real and threatening thing.

But Charles' determination to marry Camilla was non-negotiable. It led to one of the most extraordinary feats of public relations in royal history.

Charles and his aides were convinced the British people could grow to accept Camilla. The first step was persuading the media, and I was an early victim of their efforts. It worked on me — she had an open and uncomplicated charm — but the redemption of Camilla still looked to me like a dangerous high-wire act as I left that night, with a long way to fall for the two principals.

My Ritz invitation had not been made casually. The court of Prince Charles got to know me first, to make sure I was 'safe'. The 31-year-old son of a Middlesbrough bricklayer was an unlikely emissary, but Mark Bolland had the smooth bearing and flourish of an old-fashioned courtier. He was a reincarnated Georgian attendant without the powdered wig.

Bolland was Charles' deputy private secretary, and his mission was to persuade the media that his boss and Camilla were a lovable and loving couple. *The Daily Telegraph* may have overstated his importance in calling him 'the real power behind the future King of England', but it had the right idea.

Bolland was not popular in the various courts of the Windsor family. Competing courtiers suspected him of leaking damaging stories to enhance Charles' image at the expense of other family members. Certainly, he did not play by old rules. Royal staffers were world-class obfuscators, but Bolland knew intuitively how to get the media on his side. He was the master of tantalising indiscretion — whispered nuggets for gossip columnists, tip-offs on upcoming celebrity knighthoods, and sometimes more. These morsels never put his core objective at risk, but drew closer to him the people he needed in order to achieve it.

Bolland had trained well for the task. Before joining Charles, he was director of the Press Complaints Commission. When newspapers were unfair, inaccurate, or cruel — which was often — the PCC was the field hospital where victims took their wounds to be redressed. After four years in the job, Bolland had seen the best and worst of newspapers, and knew the best and worst of journalists.

Bolland took me to dinner in 1996, soon after taking his job with Prince Charles, and before Diana's death. The rehabilitation of Charles and Camilla was already a challenge; he had no idea how hard it would become.

For our meeting, he picked a place to impress. Mayfair's cheerful name belies its aloofly opulent, overdressed, and curiously soulless personality; and Harry's Bar was one of Mayfair's most desirable venues, a private dining club where the prices were ridiculously high, and the chairs and tables uncomfortably low. Its founder, the perfectionist entrepreneur Mark Birley, shortened the legs of all the restaurant's furniture to make space for a huge, dominating chandelier that he loved.

Harry's Bar was where Bolland took me for his subtle vetting of me, to decide whether I would be useful to his mission, or an obstacle. He knew Rupert disliked royalty and inherited privilege, and had noted along with many others how this view contradicted his own dynastic determination to have his children run the company he created. Bolland was keen to know how closely I followed my boss' lead.

Fleet Street covered the spectrum in its support of the monarchy. *The Independent* proudly ignored them most of the time, while the *Daily Mail* offered its readers cheap souvenir crockery marking every royal moment. Rupert was too pragmatic to impose his own republican instincts, but was not displeased when his newspapers went on the attack.

By the end of our meal, Bolland understood that I was more bemused about royalty than hostile, and, above all, recognised that most readers approved of the monarchy. He was keen to get Charles and Rupert together for lunch, but I told him that was a bad idea. Rupert thought Charles dull and 'lightweight', and cranky in many of his views.

Bolland's task of rehabilitation was sidelined by the tragedy of Diana's death, but he was diligent in keeping in touch with me and other Fleet Street bosses. By the spring of 1998, when I had dinner with Camilla Parker Bowles, his campaign was in full swing again.

In November 1998, the Queen staged an epic party at Buckingham Palace for Prince Charles' fiftieth birthday. Tony Blair and Margaret Thatcher were there, along with Charles' show business friends — Spike Milligan, Stephen Fry, and Jimmy Savile. The Hobbit-height figure of the 98-year-old Queen Mother wandered among the guests. The Queen and Charles stood on a dais before two gold and crimson thrones. He called her 'Mummy', and the Queen offered her son a champagne toast, but nothing so informal as a birthday kiss. In the state dining room, a tuba-euphonium ensemble, Tubalaté, had not chosen an ideal repertoire; they played the theme from *Mission Impossible*.

Editors and media executives were invited to Buckingham Palace, but not Camilla, not yet. She appeared later that week at another birthday event not attended by the Queen. It was a banquet at sixteenth-century Hampton Court Palace, 12 miles southwest of London. Camilla was present, but Charles was not her escort. They sat at a careful distance, diagonally apart at the top table, within sight but well beyond touching distance. Again, Fleet Street was flattered with invitations. We were far away, at the bottom of a long table, but close enough to bear witness.

Camilla was eased into the spotlight at other opportunities. Whenever she and Charles attended the same private events, Mark Bolland made sure newspapers knew. Images appeared on front pages of the couple arriving and departing separately, but not yet together, and never close enough to be captured in a single frame.

With these perfectly orchestrated overtures, Bolland and his team played the country and the media towards the main event. It happened on the steps of The Ritz Hotel on 29 January 1999, at a birthday party for Camilla's sister, Annabel Elliot.

When it finally came, it was studiously informal and understated. There was no happy-couple pose and no cooperative pause to help photographers frame their shots. There was no eye contact between them, and no touching. Charles walked first down the hotel steps, with Camilla immediately behind, a prosperous middle-aged couple on their way home after an evening out.

Within seconds, they were in a car and gone. But scores of photographers had been positioned across the street, and the lightning storm of cameras was so intense the British Epilepsy Association appealed to television channels not to broadcast it for more than five seconds.

Britain had at last seen Camilla and Charles as 'a couple', but there was no shock and surprise, or horror. The public, without knowing, had been cleverly eased towards the inevitability of the moment.

These joint appearances were repeated, but sparingly, until the bravura moment of Bolland's public relations master class. On 7 February 2001 the Press Complaints Commission held a party to celebrate its tenth anniversary. It was an occasion that deserved no more than a modest drinks party, but that's not what happened. Bolland's partner, Guy Black, had succeeded him as director of the Press Complaints Commission, and together they turned this minor celebration into an epic.

Charles and Camilla were there, as was Prince William, pink-cheeked and uneasy, at the first public event with his future stepmother. Charles' two brothers, Andrew, the Duke of York, and Prince Edward, arrived, and there were a score or more celebrities, as well as citizens, whose complaints the Press Complaints Commission had satisfactorily adjudicated.

One newspaper said the royals had been lured into the lions' den and emerged unscarred. William, who was 18, said he was grateful to have been left in peace during his recent gap year. Charles praised the editor of the *Daily Mail* for his crusade against genetically modified food, and urged him to keep it up.

Mark Bolland looked pleased with himself. It was his victory lap, and he quit his job with Charles the following year. Given his impatience with palace apparatchiks, and how skilfully he undermined them, it was a miracle he lasted five years.

Charles and Camilla were married in a civil ceremony in Windsor in April 2005. By the time of their tenth anniversary, they were an accepted couple. Opinion polls revealed a tolerance, if not yet love, for Camilla. Charles had recovered from near-disaster, but his popularity was already yielding to the next generation — to William and Catherine, and Prince Harry. For a business whose objective is an eternal brand, the monarchy looked to be in robust condition.

Concerns about the media, and its power, had reached the top of the Royal Family. Following the turmoil of Diana's death, and during Camilla's rough passage to public acceptance, I was invited to Buckingham Palace for lunch.

My host was the Lord Chamberlain, the senior officer of the Royal Household, its chief executive officer, whose job had existed since the Middle Ages. In 2000, the position was held by a former Conservative MP, Richard Luce.

Never was duller food served in a grander setting: dry mashed potatoes, overcooked cabbage, and blackened lamb. Since the Lord Chamberlain was eating from the same kitchen as the Queen, I guessed she had a bland palate.

Luce belonged to the patrician school of mannered men of old power. This kind of man is disappearing, along with their cut-glass accents, but still bear themselves with a raised-chin formality. They have the habit of standing stiffly, with one hand in their jacket pocket, while stroking their ties with the other. It's upper-class semaphore practised by Prince Charles and his father, and widely copied.

Lord Luce was fishing for my opinion on the mood of Fleet Street. In 2002, the Queen would mark her Golden Jubilee — 50 years as monarch — and he wanted to know how I thought the media would react to a national celebration.

This was a time when post-Diana wounds were still unhealed and the dot-com bubble had burst, casting a gloom over the economy. Luce was worried about the hangover of grief and anger, and the risk of looking extravagant at a time of economic hardship. Would Fleet

Street, and in particular, News International, disapprove?

Luce knew Rupert was not an avid royalist, but it was still astonishing that the confidence of the Royal Family had reached such a low ebb that they needed to conduct media focus groups.

I thought widespread antagonism in the media was unlikely, and told Luce so. The usual unwelcoming and anti-monarchist noises would come from *The Guardian* and *The Independent*, and from columnists in other papers, including ours, but I could not imagine broad hostility towards a national celebration.

He listened in silence, and thanked me. A few months later I was invited back to repeat what I had said; by that time, I was even more certain he had nothing to worry about.

The Golden Jubilee was celebrated throughout the Commonwealth. The Queen visited 70 British cities and towns. In New York, the Empire State building was lit in purple, blue, and gold. In a climactic weekend, a pop concert in the palace grounds was watched live by 12,000, and by a further 1 million on giant screens outside.

Brian May, the guitarist from Queen, stood on the palace roof riffing wildly through *God Save the Queen*. The event was televised around the world and declared the most watched pop concert in history, with 200 million viewers.

The Golden Jubilee was a spectacular success. It was also clouded with sadness for the Queen; her younger sister, Margaret, had died in February of that year, and her mother the following month.

But Luce was still fretting about media. In his memoir *Ringing the Changes*, he says the media were: 'exceedingly gloomy and pessimistic ... rather assuming that the public was not interested'. He clearly dwelt on the negative stories because positive ones far outnumbered them.

Sitting in the palace gardens that weekend, after walking through throngs in The Mall and the parks, it was hard to imagine what he or the palace had ever worried about. For all its travails and missteps, the Royal Family's spell over Britain was unbroken. Eleven years later, when Prince George was born, a poll showed that three quarters of the population expected him one day to be king.

CHAPTER 24

No thanks, Rupert

For the third consecutive Sunday afternoon, my telephone rang. It was Rupert again. It was the autumn of 2007, and once more I was caught in his headlights.

After years of dreaming, and four months of intense and tricky negotiations, Rupert was buying Dow Jones & Co. It was a huge information operation, with global print and digital interests, and annual revenues of more than $2 billion. But the real object of Rupert's desire, the pin-up in Dow Jones's portfolio, was *The Wall Street Journal*, the newspaper he had wanted for more than two decades. He had once told me he wanted to run it himself. 'I would make myself publisher and let other people manage the rest of the business,' he said.

The deal was due to be completed before the end of that year, and Rupert wanted me to leave News International, move to New York, and take the job of chief executive. Dow Jones was Rupert's holy grail — or at least, his most recent one — and running it would be high profile, high pressure, and high paid.

I told him I wouldn't do it.

For more than 40 years, I had zigzagged back and forth from three continents. I was pulled around the world in the tailwind of Dad's military life, and then I had hitched myself to the wagon train of Rupert Murdoch's ambitions. I had found it exhilarating — there was nothing I would have changed. But I had had enough.

I had been in London for 12 years in a demanding, sometimes exhausting, job. For nearly 20 years, I had managed large divisions of News Corp — magazines, television stations, newspapers. I had been 'in harness to Rupert', as a fellow veteran, Andrew Knight, would say, for almost my entire career.

I had also just come through the most personally painful period of my life. After 35 years of marriage and five children, Mary and I had separated in the spring of 2004. She had travelled everywhere with me in Rupert's wake — 11 relocations among six cities, in three countries. My work had dictated the geography of her life and our children's.

The decision to separate had been mine, and I had moved into a flat a mile away from our family home in Hampstead. The three oldest were adults and in America, but James and Jane were teenagers and still at school. It had been hard on everyone, but three years later, although Mary was still angry, we were at least on an even keel.

In 2007, I was living with Katharine Raymond, who I had first met at a Labour Party conference. *The Sun*'s political editor, Trevor Kavanagh, had introduced us, but I had no memory of it until Kath reminded me. The second time we met, years later, I wondered how I had forgotten. Kath was a clever, dark-haired, blue-eyed Liverpudlian. The daughter of a joiner and a librarian, she was born three miles south of Bootle, but 23 years after me. With Kath, I was happy in a way I had never expected to be and, at the age of 63, beginning to imagine there might be other ways of life.

Kath mattered more than another big job; besides, she had her own career and ambitions. Brought up in working-class Liverpool, her father had been a trade unionist and a socialist, and she had inherited his passions — joining the Labour Party as a teenager and ending up as a special adviser in Tony Blair's government. In 2007, she was working at Number 10 as a member of Gordon Brown's policy unit, and being encouraged by the prime minister to seek election to Parliament.

Rupert's job offer was, of course, appealing, even though I no longer felt the need to prove myself. I enjoyed being the boss, but deep down I still missed journalism, and always preferred the intense immediacy of the newsroom to the insulated corridor of the executive. Another big job didn't matter enough to uproot Kath and upset her plans, and I was going nowhere without her.

But still Rupert kept calling.

These calls were not a complete surprise; he had been plotting his Dow Jones bid for months, and had talked to me about it often. When the terms of the deal were agreed that summer, I was part of the first News Corp group to visit the company headquarters in downtown Manhattan. Ten of us spent a day in the company boardroom with a dozen apprehensive Dow Jones executives.

As well as explaining the business to us, the Dow Jones managers were enduring personal auditions in front of their prospective future employers. It's not hard to work out from Rupert's body language who fails to impress him. He rarely tells someone when he thinks they're talking rubbish — especially when he doesn't know them — but he has a skill of simply disconnecting. More than once that day, his face glazed over, leaving me and others to continue the conversation, while he studied the notes in front of him. He could do the same to long-time executives; it was unfailingly disconcerting.

That night, he took us to Scalinatella, an Italian restaurant in a basement off Third Avenue, where we pooled our judgements. It would have made painful listening for some of them as we discussed, dismissed, and crossed names off our mental list of 'keepers'. Danny DeVito, the comedian and actor, looked on curiously from a nearby table.

I gave in to Rupert on the fourth phone call. The previous weekend, Kath had unexpectedly told me I should take the job. Until then, she had said nothing, only listened as I talked. I told her several times that I had spent enough time running big businesses, that I didn't want to go back to America, and that News International would be my last job as a chief executive. I didn't say she was the main reason I was turning down the job, but Kath is no fool, and that Sunday she sat beside me on the bed as I put down the phone, having once again declined Rupert's offer.

'Why don't you do it? It'll be hard work, but exciting and we'll have fun for a few years. Besides, admit it, you're bored here. What have you got to lose?' she said.

Kath had seen little of America, apart from occasional trips with me to visit my sons, and a month-long tour of American prisons when she was working at the Home Office. When I told her this wouldn't have provided her with a proper perspective of the country, she had replied: 'You learn a lot about a country from its jails.' I knew that America's had horrified her.

'But what about you?' I asked now.

'Don't worry about me. I'm happy to go. I can turn my back on British politics for a while. It might even be a good idea,' she said.

Shortly before Brown became prime minister, Kath and I had taken him and his wife, Sarah, for dinner at Le Caprice, a smart restaurant tucked away in a dead-end street in St James's. Kath, prone to sudden attacks of enthusiasm, had poured forth a stream of policy ideas on drug abuse and violent crime. After three years at the Home Office she had developed a range of odd passions. Gordon pulled out a notebook and began scribbling in thick felt pen. They talked for ages while Sarah and I chatted more sedately. The following day he phoned to ask her to join his policy unit at Number 10. She had accepted, but with a measure of reluctance.

She had spent four exhausting years as an adviser to David Blunkett through his three Cabinet positions at Education, the Home Office, and Work and Pensions, and was now building her own, more easy-going, portfolio. As well as writing occasional comment pieces for the *Evening Standard* and other newspapers, she was working as a freelance political consultant, and the flexibility — and the money — appealed to her. Returning to government felt like dressing herself up in chains again. Besides, she was suspicious about Brown's job offer. 'I think he's trying to please *you*,' she told me. 'I might be useful to him on policy, but he's more interested in keeping News International close than he is in reforming equality laws.' I told her she was too modest, and paranoid.

Soon after going into Downing Street, Kath began to worry about Brown's state of mind. He had started on a high. The unanimous vote of Labour MPs propelled him into Number 10 after Blair's mid-term resignation, and early polls showed a surge in popular support. But his first weeks had been hard going. All politicians dread uncontrollable 'events', and the summer of 2007 had plenty of them. Extensive flooding across Britain, terrorist attacks in London and Glasgow, and the gangland murder of a child in Liverpool all contributed to the chaos. Kath thought Brown was a brilliant and original thinker, but one evening after another stormy day, she told me: 'I think the strain's beginning to show. He threw a telephone at someone today.'

Brown had been in a foul mood that morning when Kath walked into his office. He had been reading the newspapers and they were not treating him well. When another official arrived late for the meeting, he kicked his office wall in a fury, leaving the latecomer in tears.

Brown's intemperance became the gossip of Downing Street. He once grew so angry with a harried secretary who was slow to type his dictation that he lifted her from her chair to seize control of the keypad himself. Even as chancellor of the exchequer, his flashes of temper were famous.

But Kath also found him disorganised, limited in the range of policies that kept his interest, and said he often failed to complete the more boring work in his overnight red boxes. She was also disappointed, considering Labour's vaunted advocacy of women in politics, to find herself the lone woman in Brown's 10-member policy unit.

The next time Rupert called, I was less emphatic in my refusal. He could hear my new hesitation and pressed hard. 'I've got to make a decision,' he said. 'Are you going to take the job or not?' For the first time he named two other candidates he was considering. 'You're my first choice, but I need to know soon.'

I told him we should meet, and on the evening of Sunday 7 October 2007 we sat together in the same small hotel where we had dined 12 years earlier when he first took me to Wapping. It was Kath's birthday and we had spent the weekend in Norfolk, walking the freezing fens and bird watching, talking about the possibilities of Dow Jones and New York. She waited for me a street away at another hotel while Rupert and I talked.

Our meeting didn't take long. He produced paper and a pen and began writing numbers. I periodically invited him to increase these numbers, and sometimes he did, but not always.

Rupert said he wanted me to sign a five-year contract. It would be the first time in 48 years that I would have a written employment agreement; it was the same for many of Rupert's early executives. This informality ended as the American operation grew, but by that time I had been there so long tenure was on my side, and Rupert had a reputation of being a generous sacker; more than once, I proposed a settlement for a departing executive and he instructed me to improve upon it. I had imagined working full-time three more years before putting together a portfolio of more varied and less demanding jobs. But five years was a solid guarantee going into a challenging job.

With the deal done, Rupert, Kath, and I headed for dinner at the home of Rupert's daughter, Elisabeth, and her husband Matthew Freud, in Notting Hill. It was a big, white-stuccoed house, overlooked by a block of council flats, with many rooms and levels, and the scene of some spectacular and occasionally wild parties. That night, there was only a small group gathered at a table in the kitchen.

Matthew was wearing his standard expression of permanent pop-eyed surprise. He was one of London's most successful PR operators and a perennial schemer whose mother once told Kath: 'We knew he would end up either a millionaire or in prison.'

Elisabeth, for all her drive, success, and practised toughness, was a naturally warm woman whose face in quiet moments would soften to the point of seeming almost needy. Born in Australia, raised mostly in America, now a dedicated Brit, her American accent was thinning with the years.

Also at the table was Rupert's younger son James, 34, who always radiated a fierceness and absence of self-doubt that was either innate or an act, I could never decide. He had made shareholders happy and his father proud as CEO of Sky TV. Rebekah Wade — soon to be Brooks — was there, with her sharp, measuring eyes; and Charles Dunstone, a family friend, and to me always a plump, sweet-natured man and great company. However, since he had built a billion-pound company, Carphone Warehouse, from savings of £6000, I doubt I had the full picture of him.

Even at family gatherings, Rupert's presence brought tautness to the atmosphere; he was always the patriarch his children were anxious to impress. For outsiders, it could sometimes be awkward to watch, but that night I paid no attention to the usual tensions.

I spent the evening in a daze of excitement and doubt, feeling the familiar thrill that came with another big Murdoch move, relishing the drama and challenge, and the power and attention as well. But I was worried about Kath. She might have appeared cheerful to everyone else that night, but by now I recognised her brave face. I knew she would have preferred a quiet evening at home, discussing our plans. Besides, she disliked this sort of dinner party, and wasn't fond of all the guests. She had once told James Murdoch to 'watch your manners, Mr Murdoch' during one of his famous sweary rants.

She was leaving behind her whole life for a place where she knew no one but me. She also knew she had triggered the decision, that it would not be happening but for her. I think, consciously or not, she had tested me, that at first she feared I would find the offer irresistible and accept it whether or not she came with me. Once she knew I would never leave without her, I think she made her sacrifice in place of the one she knew I was ready to make.

Excited as we were, we had to keep our news secret for two months, until the Dow Jones deal was formally closed and News Corp took possession. I told the children in New York — they had been keen all along for me to come 'home' — but Robert Thomson and I shared the secret alone at News International. After five years editing *The Times,* Robert would become Dow Jones' 'publisher', in practice the editor-in-chief. He was another veteran of New York, having spent four years as US editor of the *Financial Times.*

A few at the top of the company knew in advance of our appointments, and Kath told her boss she would be leaving at the end of the year. Brown was surprised. He had been prime minister only six months. 'I thought you were going to stay and become an MP,' he said. He sent me his congratulations, but Kath knew he was anxious about who would take over at News International. Kath's resignation coincided with the fatal decision of Brown's political life. Three days before my 7 October deal with Rupert, Brown had been at Kath's birthday party at the Shoreditch House club. He presented Kath with a gift from their son John — a toy windmill that flashed lights and played music. The evening was buzzing with the expectation he would call a general election; most of Brown's staff were sure he would. But on Saturday 6 October, as we walked the Norfolk coast near Cley next the Sea, expecting Kath would be submerged for the next month or so with the campaign, Downing Street sent her a text saying the election was off. Brown, who had been struggling to decide, appears to have been spooked by news that an opinion poll would appear next day in, of all places, the *News of the World,* predicting a decisive Labour defeat. The front page next day took credit for Brown's retreat: 'News of the World POLL KILLS ELECTION.'

———

The acquisition of Dow Jones and *The Wall Street Journal* was not popular with everyone at the top of News Corp. By 2007 the company's centre of gravity had shifted away from print. The new money-spinner was television, in particular US cable and the company's share of British Sky Broadcasting. It had been a healthy transition from one media to another, a transition many newspaper companies failed to achieve, but that hadn't made it less painful for inky-fingered old hands. They saw the Dow Jones bid as a last hurrah for the industry upon which Rupert had built his fortune.

It was made with a shrewder motive than the simple purchase of a famous newspaper. *The Wall Street Journal* was a global brand with a peerless reputation. It had positioned itself online more cleverly than any competitor, determining from the start that its journalism was too good to give away. Beyond the newspaper, there was a range of promising digital assets, most of them in the growing business-to-business sector.

All the same, there were strong reservations about the deal from some. Peter Chernin was Rupert's number two and a Hollywood veteran who spent much of his time running the Fox operation. When he called, I thought it was with congratulations, but the first thing he said was: 'You must be crazy taking that job.'

We were definitely paying what business people euphemistically describe as a 'full price'. Rupert's offer of $60 a share was a 67 per cent premium on Dow Jones' trading price, and valued the company at more than $5 billion.

The bid needed to be high to make sure it broke through the resistance of the family that had controlled the company for ninety years. The business was started in 1882 by Charles Dow, Edward Jones, and Charles Bergstresser. Clarence Barron bought the company in 1902, and upon his death control passed to his stepdaughters, Martha and Jane. Barron's son-in-law, Jane's husband, a depression-prone lawyer named Hugh Bancroft, became boss in 1928, but killed himself five years later.

By the time of our bid, the company had gone through years of change and expansion. It owned a wide range of publications including *Barron's,* a weekly for sophisticated investors, and *SmartMoney* magazine, a down-to-earth guide to personal finance. There was also the *Far Eastern Economic Review,* the weekly *Financial News* in London, one-third of the Moscow business newspaper *Vedomosti*, and a chain of local newspapers in seven American states. An array of digital businesses included Marketwatch.com; Factiva, a worldwide aggregator of news and data; the business and finance news agency Dow Jones Newswire; a dozen or more operations providing high-speed data feeds and corporate governance information; and the Dow Jones Industrial Average, the world's most famous stock market index.

For the Bancrofts, a rich and secluded clan of Boston Brahmins, control of Dow Jones — in particular, *The Wall Street Journal* — was a point of family pride, even though it had been years since a Bancroft was in charge. Rupert's takeover generated uproar among the usual suspects. It was a familiar chorus of hostilities that had built over decades among thwarted rivals, cast-off editors, and everyone else disaffected by his style of journalism, politics, and business.

The pundit Bill Moyers, a charter member of the Rupert Haters Hall of Fame, represented the most extreme outrage. 'Rupert Murdoch is to propriety what the Marquis de Sade was to chastity,' he said. 'When it comes to money and power, he's carnivorous — all appetite and no taste. He'll eat anything in his path.' Of the Bancrofts, he said: 'Like Adam and Eve, the parents of us all, [they] are tempted to trade their birthright for a wormy apple.'

The Economist said *The Wall Street Journal* was the media version of Rupert's 'trophy wife'. Leslie Hill, a Bancroft family member who opposed the deal, mourned 'the loss of an independent global news organization with unmatched credibility and integrity.' James H. Ottaway junior, who became a director and shareholder upon selling his newspaper chain to Dow Jones in 1970, was the loudest internal critic. 'Dow Jones is not for sale, at any price, to Rupert Murdoch,' he said.

There was uproar almost every time Rupert tried to buy a newspaper, and the hostile climate was familiar to him. He had won and lost many battles: he tried to buy London's *The Observer* in the 1970s — failed; *The Buffalo News* — failed; the *Boston Herald* — success; *Chicago Sun-Times* — success, but only after a bitter struggle; *The Times* of London — success after another struggle.

For him, it was just the conqueror's latest campaign. But for the insulated Bancrofts it created a nightmare of family tensions, tearing them between their self-perceived heritage as guardians of a great institution, and the allure of a cash pot for the family in excess of a billion dollars. As the deadline for signing the deal approached, the family patriarch, 76-year-old William Cox junior, went into diabetic shock and was taken to hospital. The Bancrofts resisted Rupert's overtures for three months before enough of them surrendered to the money, and the pressure of other shareholders. Thirty members of the family shared $1 billion.

Two years after the sale, Jim Ottaway crossed the ballroom of a charity event for the Committee to Protect Journalists to introduce himself to me — and take back his words. 'I feared the worst and it didn't happen,' he said. '*The Journal* is excellent, much better than I believed it would be under Murdoch. And you made investments that would never have happened under the old ownership.'

I think he came offering peace, but his apology made me angrier than ever that people like him were sucked in by the worn-out anti-Murdoch theology that we were not worthy of the responsibility of running a world-class newspaper. By then, I had purged Ottaway's name from the local newspaper chain Dow Jones had acquired from him. It was called Ottaway Newspapers, but I gave it the bland new title Local Media Group, thus sparing Jim Ottaway the ordeal of having his family name associated with an acquisition he fought so hard to prevent. It was an act of pure spite, but I didn't feel guilty.

The news of my appointment broke in the first week of December and the office Christmas party in London turned into a farewell. A life-size cut-out of me was positioned at the entrance. I was presented later with a photo album with pictures of every guest standing next to 'me', and brief messages from each. James Murdoch, who was adding News International to his portfolio of responsibilities, wrote:

'Big shoes, mate.'

My farewell gifts included a huge, bright oil painting of *The Sun*'s newsroom, with its main characters plainly identifiable. It hangs on the wall of our London flat.

Within a few years this painting would look like a rogues' gallery — or, at least, a gallery of alleged rogues — of close friends and good colleagues who were about to experience some of the most difficult years of their lives.

CHAPTER 25

Barbarians in the elevator

It was a cold winter afternoon — Thursday 13 December 2007. From the window we could see the vast, heartbreaking hole where the twin towers of the World Trade Center once stood; one of the biggest stories *The Wall Street Journal* ever covered had happened across the street.

The sight of it had personal meaning — nothing in the context of that horrifying day, but a nightmare for my family. Thomas, my second son, was working as a freelance photographer and ran to the scene from his Greenwich Village apartment. When the towers collapsed, and it was clear many were dead, it was three hours before we knew Thomas was safe. Mary, at home in Hampstead, stared helplessly at the television; I wandered the office in a daze; Martin was at work as a television news producer; and William, still at college, sent a family email that somehow got through to me: 'Is anyone there?' The two youngest were at school and oblivious. Thomas lost most of his camera equipment running from the first collapsing tower, and found himself with police and fire officers unable to escape behind a plate glass window in the lobby of *The*

Journal building where I now had an office. A police officer fired his handgun to shatter the glass that trapped them. 'When he did,' said Thomas, 'the cops and fire officers ran straight towards the second tower. I'll never know how many of them died.'

Rupert, Robert Thomson, Gary Ginsberg — the News Corp communications chief — and I were waiting to appear before the massed staff of *The Wall Street Journal.* The four of us were in a small room on the eleventh floor of the Manhattan headquarters of Dow Jones, in the World Financial Center near the southern tip of the island.

While Ginsberg chatted cheerfully, the rest of us were pensive. We had heard that Dow Jones shareholders, meeting in a Manhattan hotel, had formally voted to support the sale of their company to News Corp. Some of the Bancroft family were reported to have been in tears as the vote was announced.

I had never been involved in an acquisition that seemed to mean more to Rupert, but he was taking it coolly, reading notes on a couple of sheets of paper that were folded to fit in the pocket of his dark-blue suit, repeating quietly to himself the words he was about to deliver to thousands of anxious new employees.

The newsroom two floors beneath was packed, and offices across America and the rest of the world were hooked up by telephone — Hong Kong, Singapore, London, Beijing, and scores of others in more than a hundred countries. After an eight-month onslaught of critical publicity, the people waiting to meet their new ruler must have felt as if Genghis Khan had entered the building. We went down to make our appearance. 'We're the barbarians in the elevator,' I said. Rupert gave a wry smile without looking up from his notes.

The dense crowd were silent as we walked among them. I was shocked at the condition of the newsroom; it was austere and in disrepair, with a ragged blue carpet and worn-out furniture, its low ceiling bearing down on us.

In the tradition of newsroom speeches, no special effort had been made for our appearance; there was nothing so formal as a podium to elevate the speaker. The common vantage point for any newsroom address, however important, is the top of a desk, but Rupert was 76 and, fit as he was, perhaps no longer sufficiently nimble to clamber onto one. Four green-and-white boxes of printer paper had been arranged in a neat square and someone indicated to Rupert he should stand on them. The design on these boxes was not in tune with the mood of the room — 'Happy Holidays', each said, next to an illustration of a jolly snowman.

Rupert didn't speak for long. He acknowledged that everyone was nervous and recognised the high standards *The Journal* had achieved, but added pointedly: 'If anything, you'll find we set a higher bar.'

'But I hope it's a day of excitement,' he said. 'Because it is a new day in the history of this company. We've come here to expand it, to develop it, and, where possible, to improve all of its products.'

He finished with a smile and a hint of menace. 'You'd better get back to work, and make sure you're not scooped tomorrow.'

At Dow Jones the morning after Rupert's speech, I arrived early at my new corner office. At my door was a bagful of baseball caps, t-shirts, and other items bearing *The Wall Street Journal*'s brand. A note was attached: 'Good morning and welcome to Dow Jones,' it said. It was signed by a woman who was among the executives to be fired over the next few days. The ugliest part of the first few weeks of an acquisition is the dismissals. You can't be a boss without firing people, and you can't be a good boss if you ever get used to it.

I asked dozens of senior people to resign over the years. Many hundreds more departed because of decisions I made, or enforced for Rupert. I cut costs, closed publications and businesses, pushed out editors and executives, always convincing myself it was for the greater good of the company and its remaining employees.

At Dow Jones in the first few weeks, a swathe of senior people departed. Rich Zannino, who had been CEO for two years, went immediately, but he knew Rupert would want his own person in charge. Others followed Zannino, including the publisher, and the heads of legal, finance, marketing, and human resources. The most senior survivor on the business side was Todd Larsen, a tall, thoughtful former Booz Allen consultant with deep family roots in media — his grandfather was Roy E. Larsen, Henry Luce's right-hand man from the dawning days of the Time Inc. publishing empire. Todd was to become my number two.

Getting to know senior people in those first weeks, I told myself to follow the same rules and routines I had in every new job: remember it's high pressure adjusting to new bosses, so be wary of first impressions. Nerves can conceal talent, and glib confidence can disguise a fraud; pay attention to the quiet ones, encourage them to speak. Jump on anyone who derides the ideas of others, even if they are dumb — great things often come from uninhibited, free-flowing conversations.

On my first day, an earnest, white-haired man arrived in my office. He was Joe Cantamessa, a former FBI agent now in charge of the company's worldwide security. He was here, he said, to discuss my safety. I would have a personal driver who would carry a gun at all times, he told me, and the car in which he would drive me contained special security features.

Already unnerved, I followed him to the underground car park and opened the back door of a black Lexus. 'This is in case of emergency,' he said, lifting the top of the armrest in the back seat and pointing to a red button. 'You press it if someone tries to abduct you.'

When you activate the silent alarm, he said, Dow Jones security would be alerted and instantly begin tracking the vehicle through a device hidden inside the car.

'If this happens, we will also call the car phone. It will appear to be a normal call from your office,' he said. 'If you are in difficulty, you will use a secret phrase which we can agree on now. It must be something inoffensive to your abductors, but if you say it we will know you are in trouble.'

I decided my secret sentence would be: 'Remind me later to work out my weekend plans for next month.' At least, it was something like that; as the years passed, and I cruised uneventfully around New York City, the details of my coded cry for help grew foggy.

The prospect of being kidnapped in Manhattan did not seem high on the list of life's risks. There were more banal but real hazards; no armed driver or panic button helped on the day a careless driver ran a red light and crashed into us.

Joe Cantamessa also inspected the townhouse we had rented on East 65th Street. Given our neighbour was David Rockefeller, one of the richest people in town, it must have been among the city's safest blocks. Rockefeller was 92, the last surviving grandchild of the nineteenth-century industrial baron John D. Rockefeller, and his huge house sprouted security cameras. There were often police cars outside, and a retinue of nurses and bodyguards accompanied him whenever he faltered past our door on his walking frame.

Cantamessa terrified Kath with demonstrations of how easily our new home could be broken into, and explained he had refined his own burgling skills at the FBI, where one of his duties was to break into homes of mobsters to install bugging equipment. Kath didn't argue when he offered to install a range of devices to keep us safe.

This concern for security stemmed from a terrible event six years earlier. In January 2002, five months after his colleagues had watched an act of war from their office windows, Daniel Pearl, a reporter for *The Wall Street Journal*, was kidnapped and beheaded in Pakistan by Islamist militants connected to Al-Qaeda. He was 38 years old. His only child was born four months after his murder. The grief, anger, and fear Pearl's death created was still profound when I arrived at Dow Jones, and, apart from the exaggerated precautions extended to me, Dow Jones undertook serious work to heighten the safety of its staff in troubled areas around the world.

Dow Jones had about 6000 staff, including more than 2000 journalists who worked in the most peaceful and prosperous countries on earth, as well as some of the most dangerous and deprived. Most of the journalists concentrated on business and economic news, but *The Journal*'s definition of these subjects was broad. Despite its name, *The Wall Street Journal* never looked at the world from the elite perspective of Wall Street or the City of London.

Bernard 'Barney' Kilgore, the son of an Indiana school superintendent, was the acknowledged creator of the modern *The Wall Street Journal*. More than any member of the Bancroft family, he had driven the newspaper's success and crafted its down-to-earth approach to business news. Kilgore's ideal newspaper was straight talking, and as accessible to the small car dealer in Tulsa as it was to the boss of J. P. Morgan. He crusaded for plain English and sent sharp missives whenever he was unhappy. Richard Tofel, in his Kilgore biography *Restless Genius,* quotes one of his most famous: 'If I see 'upcoming' in the paper again, I'll be downcoming and someone will be outgoing.'

Tofel says Kilgore treated readers as if they were interested but not necessarily experts. He told his journalists to write not only for bankers, but also for the 'almost infinitely more numerous bank depositors'.

'Financial people,' he said, 'are nice people and all that, but there aren't enough of them to make this paper go.' Business news, Kilgore decreed, 'embraces everything that relates to making a living'.

Forty years after his death in 1967, aged only 59, Kilgore still had a saintly reputation among veteran staffers. My granddaughter, Samantha, was at school with Kilgore's, and when their class visited *The Journal*, it was as if a little Dalai Lama had arrived.

But Rupert wanted a newspaper that stretched far beyond business, and we increased the foreign and political pages as well as adding lifestyle news and a solid Review section to a fattened Saturday edition. We also launched a glossy magazine — *WSJ* — that eventually became a monthly. In digital, we deepened the website, added hours of video, and in 2010 created an iPad edition — a novelty at the time, and very successful with readers.

A new daily section — 'Greater New York' — increased our sales in the heartland of *The New York Times,* which gave us great pleasure. We enjoyed watching our vendors, in their *The Wall Street Journal* livery, handing out free copies on the doorstep of *The New York Times* Eighth Avenue headquarters.

We added more space to the opinion section. To many American conservatives and libertarians, *The Journal* opinion section was a temple of clear thinking. To liberals, it was a constant bugbear. Rupert had a few quibbles about its policy positions; unlike *The Journal,* for instance, he supported stronger gun control laws, but he was proud to be associated with its outlook on almost all other matters.

In common with other US newspapers, journalists at *The Journal* exist in two divisions. There are two editors — one in charge of news, the other of the opinion pages — who report independently to the publisher. Opinion was run by Paul Gigot, a snowy-haired veteran whose editorials, whether or not you agreed, were the most deeply researched and cogently argued of any American newspaper.

The relationship between news and editorial was polite, but never warm. Many news journalists did not share the conservative views expressed in editorials, and opinion writers regarded their news colleagues as being, on occasion, too soft and liberal. The relationship between these two sides was not aided by the difference in the quality of their offices; the editorial department enjoyed comfortable cloisters on the corporate floor, far superior to the threadbare news space downstairs in steerage.

The opinion section of *The Wall Street Journal* website expressed its principals clearly: 'The *Journal* stands for free trade and sound money; against confiscatory taxation and the ukases of kings and other collectivists; and for individual autonomy against dictators, bullies, and even the tempers of momentary majorities.'

The Journal editorials had not endorsed a presidential candidate since a bad experience in 1928 when it declared Herbert Hoover, 'the soundest proposition for those with a financial stake in the country'. *The Journal* editors had second thoughts eight months after Hoover became president and the Wall Street market crash of October 1929 triggered the Great Depression.

Every acquisition brings surprises and crises, but we had no idea of the nightmare ahead when we took over Dow Jones. Days before the handover, we were presented with a budget packed with rosy expectations. We also had our own ambitious and expensive plans.

The first bold idea was Rupert's. He wanted to stop charging users to access *The Wall Street Journal* website. In 2008, website pay-walls were an unfashionable concept, but from the launch of *The Journal*'s first digital edition, customers had been required to pay for full access.

All News Corp's other newspaper websites were free to use, and almost everyone in the industry thought pay-walls were a bad idea. The belief then was that advertising would pay for everything. Rupert was spending a lot of time with digital experts and they were telling him the same thing.

But subscription revenue at *The Journal* had reached $60 million a year and was growing. Robert and I didn't want to give that up. The entire Dow Jones executive team hated the idea of knocking down the pay-wall, and I organised a meeting with Rupert so they could tell him so. It did not go according to plan. They knew he was determined to drop the pay-wall, and no one was brave enough to stand in the path of an oncoming Rupert Murdoch. The only person to speak up was the head of digital. When Rupert asked him what he thought he replied in a shaky voice that going free was a 'great idea'.

Robert and I exchanged a despairing glance, but stayed quiet — as ever, it wasn't a good idea to argue with Rupert in a room full of newcomers. My approach with Rupert, and every direct boss who preceded him, was to say: 'You are the boss. I will do as you wish. But before you decide, it's my job to make sure you understand my side of the argument.' This was especially necessary with Rupert. On a couple of occasions, when things went wrong, he told me: 'You should have made me listen.'

I went through the numbers with him later and told him that, while we could change our minds at any time and drop the pay-wall, it would be hard to bring it back once we had killed it. He relented. Within a year Rupert, Robert, and I were like missionaries, making speeches all over the world about the foolishness of newspapers giving away valuable content.

By then, the economic crash of 2008 had crushed the world and shredded the business plan we had inherited at Dow Jones; many millions of dollars in advertising had evaporated. It was a brutal time for all businesses, but particularly hard on newspapers already squeezed by the relentless drift of readers and advertisers towards digital.

For Dow Jones, in addition to lost advertising, we faced pressure from the clients of our business service divisions — banks, big investment funds, and private equity — who cancelled their contracts or demanded better terms.

We had already achieved millions in the savings that come when big companies merge. We had integrated back office functions such as finance, legal, human resources, and purchasing — News Corp was one of the world's biggest newsprint buyers and *The Journal* shared the discounted prices. We closed 9 of the 17 print plants Dow Jones owned, and instead made deals with local newspapers whose dwindling sales meant they had hours of spare printing capacity. We raised almost $1 billion by selling the Dow Jones Industrial Average business, and the company's share of a European indexing business, STOXX Ltd. We also froze all salaries for two years.

The crash was painful for Dow Jones, but it was also the biggest economic story since the Great Depression, and we were now publishers of the world's most respected business newspaper. Interest was so intense that *The Journal's* audience kept growing even as we increased prices to readers and online users.

Other 'general interest' newspapers were making ever more desperate cuts — closing overseas bureaus, firing staff, and reducing the size of their newspapers. In Detroit, newspapers stopped making home deliveries for four days every week; they couldn't afford the petrol and trucks.

The New York Times cut pages and fired journalists in the biggest cutbacks in its history. To help it through the crisis, the Times Company raised $225 million by selling and leasing back part of its Manhattan headquarters and accepting a high interest — 14 per cent — loan of $250 million from the Mexican billionaire Carlos Slim, with warrants allowing him to convert the loan into shares.

Rupert, having already spent $5 billion, urged us to press ahead with our expansion. With our enlarged print edition more competitive in general news and features, we mounted circulation drives in the biggest markets, including Los Angeles and Chicago, promoting our added coverage at the same time local newspapers were cutting theirs.

Within two years, *The Journal* was the country's biggest selling newspaper, with print and digital sales exceeding 2 million, surpassing the perennial bestseller, *USA Today*.

When the recession was at its deepest, the trade newspaper *Editor & Publisher* reviewed the devastated state of publishing company stock prices. It calculated that, had Dow Jones remained independent, its stock would be trading around $9–11, compared with the mid-thirties price range when News Corp made its bid of $60. News Corp might not have timed its purchase ideally, but it was the saviour of Dow Jones. The old management would have been forced into far more brutal cutbacks. News Corp, with its deep pockets and grand plans, saved hundreds of jobs and kept the company intact.

Before the worst of the recession, we had committed lavishly to move the entire operation out of its dismal downtown premises to new offices at the News Corp headquarters on Sixth Avenue, near the Rockefeller Center.

It was, without doubt, the finest newspaper office News Corp had ever built. The heart of the existing Sixth Avenue building was gutted and hundreds of people displaced to neighbouring buildings to make room for us.

The News Corp headquarters was forever restructuring to accommodate new businesses. It could get confusing knowing who was where. One facilities executive took advantage of this by carving out his own secret apartment, which he stocked with wine and food from the executive kitchen. He was caught one morning, wearing a dressing gown as he picked up the morning newspapers, by the early and untimely arrival of his boss.

Most of the time, journalists are a conscientiously cynical breed and only very occasionally visibly pleased. But many of them were gleeful the day we popped champagne to celebrate the escape from our drab downtown workplace. At the democratic new *Journal,* most private offices were eliminated, and those that remained were denied window views, allowing everyone to share the rare direct daylight of high-rise Manhattan.

At the heart of the newsroom was a huge, horseshoe-shaped desk surrounded by giant screens. It looked like the NASA control centre or the Starship Enterprise. Walls of video displayed news and market numbers. Radio and television studios were constructed to feed websites and our syndicated radio bulletins. In a glass-faced office overseeing it all, sat Robert Thomson, like a taller, thinner Captain Kirk.

Four months after the acquisition, Robert had moved from the job of publisher to that of editor-in-chief. Marcus Brauchli had resigned. Brauchli was a gifted journalist — within three months, he became executive editor of *The Washington Post* — but a new owner can be impatient, and an old hand can have difficulty making desired changes. Brauchli had been at *The Journal* for 20 years. Rupert had always wanted Robert as his editor-in-chief, and Brauchli knew it.

His resignation didn't please the 'special committee' that News Corp had agreed to put in place to protect editors from management interference. The committee's five members — two academics and three senior editors recalled from retirement — knew nothing until Brauchli had quit. They complained bitterly — and publicly — they had been deliberately kept in the dark.

Brauchli was emphatic that there had been no management meddling while he was in charge, saying in his resignation statement: 'the new management scrupulously has avoided imposing any political or business viewpoints on our coverage and rigorously has enforced the code of conduct.'

Still, the committee felt they had been poorly treated. I made a public apology and promised to act with more care in future.

In selecting Brauchli's successor, we followed the rules meticulously. We nominated Robert and the committee invited him to appear before it to scrutinise his qualifications. It was surprising how nervous Robert was as he went off for his interview, dressed in his best tight-fitting Zara suit, black skinny tie, and lethally-pointed shoes. Rupert and I were more relaxed, sitting with glasses of white wine at the quiet bar of a Turkish restaurant in 47th Street next to the office, waiting for him to return from his interrogation. He joined us after a couple of hours, still apprehensive — 'I think it went okay' — and drank his first glass quickly, which was unusual for him. The committee's verdict was unsurprising: 'News Corp has made an excellent choice.'

With Robert in position, the pace of change quickened. Excellent though much of it was, *The Journal* sometimes moved at a stately pace. Robert decried the months spent on researching and writing the paper's 'long reads'. 'It's like the gestation of a llama,' he complained — that's 11 months. He ordered more and shorter stories for modern, time-pressed readers, and revamped the newspaper's static design. And Rupert, having forgotten his dream of becoming publisher himself, told me I was to become publisher as well as CEO.

Running Dow Jones involved a lot of dry but important work: subscription pricing, printing contracts, advertising rates, web strategy, headcount reductions, potential acquisitions, potential disposals. It was grinding and unglamorous most of the time, but satisfying as the company slowly came through the crisis and *The Journal* grew stronger.

There were also unforgettable moments — encounters with dozens of important people, a procession of fame and power. This happens with all great newspapers, but I had never worked at one with such a global reach, or with so many powerful people eager to talk to its editors.

These meetings are dotted through my calendar. I met Benjamin Netanyahu, Israel's cold-eyed prime minister, in a fortified Manhattan hotel in July 2010, and found him chilling in his readiness to bomb Iran's nuclear facilities.

In September 2008, I sat with Asif Ali Zardari, Pakistan's president, as — close to tears — he talked about the legacy of his wife Benazir Bhutto, who had been murdered in a bomb attack nine months before when running for election as prime minister.

I listened to General Pervez Musharraf, sitting forlornly in *The Journal* offices as he spoke of his life in exile. In the medieval machinations of Pakistani politics he had been forced to quit to avoid impeachment and been replaced by Zardari. I talked to Rwandan president Paul Kagame, the tall, bony-faced, incongruously soft-spoken head of a conquering rebel army who rose to be his tiny landlocked nation's president. To some he was its saviour; to others he was a smart-suited tyrant.

I met General David Petraeus at the height of his military career when he was a potential presidential candidate; he arrived with his gold-braided retinue to talk of the fighting in Afghanistan and Iraq.

I knew Harvey Weinstein slightly from parties at Rupert's. He greeted me one evening in the lobby of the News Corp building on Sixth Avenue as I was leaving the office. He was on the way to a *New York Post* reception. 'I always accept a *New Pork Post* invitation,' he said, with a little laugh. 'Got to stay friends with Page Six.' This exchange took on more significance in 2017 when multiple allegations of sexual assault rained down on him.

I was wandering through the office one morning, deep in thought, when someone grabbed and pumped my hand. 'Good morning,' said George W. Bush, with that familiar tight-lipped smile. 'Have a good day.' He was on his way to Rupert's office to discuss his memoirs.

I remember the free-market apostles of *The Wall Street Journal* Editorial Board giving a hard time to Hank Paulson, the US secretary of the treasury, after the Federal Reserve contributed a $30 billion loan to rescue the Bear Stearns investment bank as it was about to be swept away in the financial crisis. Paulson protested it was done to forestall a worldwide financial meltdown.

And I remember listening to Bill Gates as he slumped languidly in a swivel chair, bulky zip-up sweater under his jacket, making smart observations in the computer geek dialect that relies so heavily on the word 'super' — super-smart, super-exciting, super-cool. He spoke with oddly self-effacing pride of the good his charitable billions would do around the world, and I wondered whether he was becoming the first emperor of an age of philanthropic imperialism.

Early in February 2010, Steve Jobs came to the office to demonstrate his latest creation — the iPad. An Apple advance guard warned against shaking his hand. Jobs had undergone a liver transplant and was avoiding all risk of infection. But as he stepped towards me, gaunt in his uniform of black turtleneck and jeans, he reached out his hand to grasp mine. He impressed me hugely — not least because when I had trouble operating my device, the iPad's creator gave me his personal tuition. Jobs left behind a half dozen of his new devices for us to develop an app for *The Wall Street Journal*. But the security-obsessed genius imposed conditions: we had to keep them padlocked to a table in a windowless room with no more than six people given access to them.

I found myself upstaged by mighty people. The day I was due to speak to the Association of American Publishers, they asked me to put back my speech due to the early arrival of another speaker. I sat at the side of the platform and listened to Bill Clinton talk brilliantly on books and life for almost an hour before surrendering the podium to me. 'Your turn now,' he smiled. As I pronounced on the arcane challenges of the digital world, the audience drained away.

At dinner on Central Park West, a slick and self-important man in his thirties held court about the promise and change that was coming to his homeland. I told him of my happy childhood days in his country. 'Please accept my invitation to visit,' he said. 'You will be my guest. We will visit together where you lived as a child. I know the road. It will be an honour to greet you.' I declined the invitation to Libya from Saif al-Islam Gaddafi, heir apparent to his father, Muammar Gaddafi. Libya did not fulfil young Gaddafi's promise.

Kath and I went to the apartment of the PR guru Peter Brown for a dinner he was holding for Tony and Cherie Blair. Brown apologised to Kath in advance for the seating plan. 'You are next to Bobby,' he told her. 'He's charming, but very quiet, and has difficulty making conversation. I'm afraid he will be hard work.'

Barbara Walters, the American broadcaster, nodded in understanding. 'Just so long as I'm not sitting next to him,' she said.

Kath handled this by encouraging her silent neighbour's appetite for vodka martinis, and pretty soon Robert de Niro was expounding loudly to Tony Blair about the failings of America's public education system.

These were the moments that relieved the toil behind the scenes as Dow Jones was mired in the recession.

There were also trips around the world, both enjoyable and numbing. I am happy never to repeat the suffocating formality of meetings with government officials in Beijing, sipping green tea, listening to their vapid droning, longing to escape. After I quit, I took Kath back and we saw the real Beijing, wandering lost through the city streets, drinking cheap beer and eating spicy backstreet food.

I went across America, and across Europe, and to India, Japan, Singapore, Hong Kong, and Australia. These trips were exhausting, packed with back-to-back meetings, lunches, speeches, and dinners.

Sometimes I failed to keep up the pace. I arrived in Hyderabad, India, in December 2009 to make a speech to the World Association of Newspapers. The speech contributed to our crusade against free newspaper content online. I talked about the hardship confronting print — 'algorithm and blues' — and warned against the internet's false prophets — 'beware of geeks bearing gifts'.

Pleased with my speech, I sought out old colleagues for a reunion drink, putting from my mind the important midnight conference call I had with Rupert and a dozen News Corp executives. When midnight arrived — by this time I had not slept properly for 24 hours — I linked in to the call and settled on my hotel bed, the receiver resting by my ear. It was 45 minutes later when the text message chirp on my mobile woke me. It was apparently the latest of a series I had received from Robert Thomson and Rebekah Brooks: 'Wake up. Rupert's asking you a question'; 'Wake up ... We can hear you snoring'.

I had answered most of Rupert's questions with heavy breathing. 'I think we've lost Les,' he had said. Awake again, I made minor contributions before Rupert wound up the call. 'You can go back to sleep now,' he told me.

In Tokyo with Rupert, we were swept into the city in a caravan of black limousines. The cars sped along within inches of one another until Rupert's, at the head of the line, braked sharply and ours smashed into it. Robert, a former Tokyo correspondent, married to an elegant Chinese woman, and so steeped in the ways and manners of the East that he could seem like an Asian trapped in a Caucasian body, whispered instant advice: 'Whatever you do, when we stop, don't get out of the car and check the damage. This is a deep, deep humiliation for our driver, crashing into the car of such a famous and important man.'

I obeyed Robert's instruction, but of course Rupert hadn't been privy to it. He leapt from his back seat to check what had happened, running his hand across the dents, beaming at our adventure. Robert, fearing for our stricken driver's wellbeing, spoke to him in Japanese, using soothing tones and making many bows.

By 2011, I had been running large companies for a quarter of a century. I had signed a five-year contract that would expire at the end of 2012, when I would be approaching my sixty-ninth birthday. By then, I would have been in full-time employment since I was 15 — for 53 years. I told Kath that, even if asked, I would not continue as a full-time executive; that it was time, finally, to ease up and put together that portfolio of part-time work.

But my plans for a tidy retreat would soon be in ruins. Five years before, when I was still executive chairman of News International, a *News of the World* reporter, Clive Goodman, had pleaded guilty to hacking into the mobile voice messages of members of Prince Charles' household. When Goodman and his accomplice, a private investigator, were sent to prison, many people, including me, believed the case was closed. We were wrong. Back in Britain a bomb was ticking.

CHAPTER 26

Thirteen days in July

Burford is an ancient Cotswolds town of honey-coloured cottages on the edge of the tame curves of the River Windrush in Oxfordshire. The hills surrounding Burford are softly contoured and covered by a patchwork palette of greens, as impossibly perfect as a computer-generated image from a Hobbit film.

At Burford's heart is a priory with a long history of tranquillity, prayer, notoriety, and power. By 2011 — behind its Jacobean veil of towering chimneys, sharp gables, and golden masonry — the priory had joined the twenty-first century. It was now the seat of modern influence, as well as dubious modernity; the Gregorian chants echoing through the old chapel came from an iPod, and the candlelight dancing on the altar walls was battery powered.

A rich and important couple owned Burford Priory. She was building her own reputation beneath the shadow of her family's name; he was a world-class practitioner in the business of important connections. Since their marriage 10 years before, his public relations business had prospered; his wife's family was one of the best-connected on earth.

Elisabeth Murdoch was 42 and Matthew Freud 47. They were what facile headlines describe as a 'golden couple', and the evening of 2 July 2011 would be the social apex of their life together. That weekend, they staged an epic party in the grounds of their new home. The couple had spent millions refurbishing the Priory, and they wanted a housewarming for the ages.

But the party would also become an unintended farewell for a powerful axis of British life. That night, we danced on the brink of a cataclysmic chain of events that would shatter this world and the lives and friendships of many guests and hundreds of others. It would also see the death of a 168-year-old newspaper with the biggest circulation in the English-speaking world.

The Freud-Murdochs were famous for their parties, although they were really his parties. Liz Murdoch's career had been measured, impossibly, against the success of her father's, but now she was making her own way in the television industry. Freud, however, depended on his reputation as a party giver. It was a tangible asset of his public relations business, and the Murdoch brand gave it immense added equity.

Freud mixed people for a living. His magic ingredients were politicians, celebrities, big-money business people, and journalists. His business idea worked best in London because of the kind of town it is. He had tried the formula unsuccessfully in the United States. The people he needed were spread across a continent and centred in Los Angeles, New York, and Washington DC. They were much harder to shepherd together. In Britain, London is the cross-pollinating heart of power.

An invitation to a Freud-Murdoch party was an assembly bell for these people. Politicians need to meet other powers. They also need to maintain support — and Murdoch support mattered to them. Journalists like mingling with people who make news, but they are also susceptible to seduction, some more than others. Freud was good at seduction, really good; he selected his journalist guests with care. The celebrities were easy; he had started his career as a show business PR, and they liked and trusted him.

The final, crucial ingredients were the actual money earners — corporate clients. They came from less glamorous worlds: the soft drinks business, supermarket chains, clothing stores, and chocolate makers. Freud introduced them to power and glitter, and they lined up to pay him for it. His company did important, duller, work for them, but this was the shiny bait that made it fun to be his client. Where else could a supermarket boss listen to Sting, strumming out a midnight song? Or watch Mick Jagger on the dance floor, towered over by his 6-foot 3-inch then-companion, L'Wren Scott? Or see Tony Blair chatting to Bono? And they could count on a sighting of the ultimate tycoon whenever Rupert Murdoch was in town.

I stood with George Osborne at his first Freud party, before he became Britain's chancellor of the exchequer, and well before he turned newspaperman himself. There were Labour government ministers there, too; the guest lists were carefully ecumenical.

'We're just Freud's props,' I told him. 'The important people are the paying clients. Just wait until he brings over some business big shot from PepsiCo he wants to impress by introducing you.'

Five minutes later, Freud appeared. 'George, I want you to meet the chief marketing officer of PepsiCo Europe,' he said.

Osborne gave me a quick smile, but he also played the game, exhibiting intense interest in all the marketing director had to say. The geeky stiffness of Osborne's public image was a political handicap, but also misleading — in fact, he could be charming and entertaining company, and was famously fond of good wine.

Freud had spent years as a collector of important people, and the gathering on 2 July 2011 would be his climactic work. Bono was there, as was the actress Helena Bonham Carter and her then husband, the director, Tim Burton. Lily Allen the singer was there with her husband, and many other celebrities wandered the elegant gardens.

There were politicians of all hues: Michael Gove, then education secretary; Ed Vaizey, the minister responsible for media policy; David Miliband, the former foreign secretary, who had been beaten by his brother Ed to the Labour Party leadership and was indiscreet that night about his brother's suitability for the job. Sitting on my left was Douglas Alexander, who had been a youthful cabinet minister in the defeated Labour government.

Media was there in force: Mark Thompson, then director general of the BBC (Rupert loathed the BBC, but it was an important customer for his daughter's programmes); Piers Morgan, with his rowdy social style, even more ebullient at the start of his CNN days, which would not end well; Jeremy Clarkson, the chain-smoking, blunt-talking television personality and columnist; Jon Snow, who liked to tell people his left-leaning Channel 4 News was *The Guardian* of the airways; Robert Peston, a former *Financial Times* journalist who had become a famous face on BBC News. Peston's closeness to some at News International, including managing director Will Lewis and corporate affairs director Simon Greenberg, would later lead to speculation that he was being spoon-fed selective stories about the phone-hacking scandal to show the 'Murdoch machine' in a positive light.

Kath and I arrived with Rebekah Brooks and her husband, Charlie; we were guests at their Chipping Norton home. Brooks and I were already feeling the heat of the phone-hacking affair, but I could never imagine what was to come.

Rupert was not at the party. Maybe he had unavoidable business; maybe he was kept away by certain names on the guest list, or the growing tensions with his independent-minded son-in-law. Freud often displeased Rupert, not least when he appointed himself family spokesman and gave *The New York Times* candid views of Roger Ailes, then head of Fox News: 'I am by no means alone within the family or the company in being ashamed and sickened by Roger Ailes' horrendous and sustained disregard of the journalistic standards that News Corporation, its founder, and every other global media business aspires to.'

Present or not, Rupert's aura was the lure for many of the guests. The Freud-Murdochs were his social ambassadors in London. Prime Minister David Cameron was a regular visitor to Burford, but he was also absent that night. His communications director, Andy Coulson, had resigned six months before. Coulson had been editor of the *News of the World* when phone-hacking was going on at the paper, and doubts were growing despite his denials.

The deep-pocketed clients bathed in the excitement, and Freud was exultant in tight leather trousers — fractionally too tight — marching guests through his vast new home. Someone said it had 22 bedrooms.

We represented that night the component parts of British life at the top: rival politicians, competing company bosses, warring television moguls, and enemy editors. It was a summit meeting, a high gathering of the New Establishment, a sea of shiny-faced excitement on a hot summer's night, and, for all our clashing interests, there was a wary camaraderie, a fraternity of self-importance, that held us together. We were all happy participants in this tournament of egos.

This group is permanent yet ever-changing. CEOs are fired, editors fail, politicians come and go, but the caravan keeps moving forward, leaving behind its casualties. Rupert's summer party in London had been an annual magnet, but 2011 would be the last for years. Within three years, the marriage of Matthew Freud and Liz Murdoch had ended. The Murdoch light had faded in the social world of London, and no one knew if it would glow so brightly again.

But when we drove away from Burford in the early hours of Sunday 3 July — Rebekah and Charlie, Kath and me — we didn't know that the ground was already moving beneath us and a force was heading our way that would change our lives forever.

The very next day — 4 July, Independence Day — I browsed the news sites at home in our London flat. *The Guardian* was leading with the story that *News of the World* reporters had hacked into the voicemail of a 13-year-old Surrey schoolgirl after she had disappeared in 2002 on her way home from school. Mushroom pickers discovered Milly Dowler's body in woods six months later.

This was the latest in months of gathering allegations that phone-hacking had spread far beyond the actions of Clive Goodman and his accomplice, Glenn Mulcaire. Of all the accusations, it was by far the most serious; the story horrified me.

That night, Kath and I were having dinner with my old Fleet Street colleague, Chris Buckland, and our friend Kay Burley of Sky News. Buckland had worked on Fleet Street's biggest newspapers, including the *News of the World*, and was shrewd about media and public taste. He had a relentlessly cheerful personality, but that night he was as gloomy as me.

'This is very bad,' he said. 'The masses don't care so much about the voicemails of royal flunkies, politicians, and celebrities — but the mobile of a murdered schoolgirl? If this is true, people will be really angry.' Kay Burley, tuned as ever to the public mood, agreed. Until then, the story had animated mostly the tight and self-immersed world of media and politics. Media covers itself to an extent far exceeding any general interest, and the arcane twists and personality wars of politics fascinate politicians — and journalists — far more than everyone else. But everyone understands crime and tragedy and grief, and the hacking of Milly Dowler's phone would be the detonator for a much bigger explosion.

Kath and I flew back to New York the next morning, but by now I was seriously worried. What exactly had been going on at the *News of the World* all those years ago?

———

Eight days later.

The Range Rover turned so sharply into the narrow street that I was pushed hard against the leather-lined passenger door. We drove too quickly between Georgian terraces towards a modern building of flats; its sharp black-and-white geometry jarred amid the settled architecture.

When photographers waiting at its entrance saw our car they came towards us with their cameras raised. We took another swerve into the basement car park. Bodies thumped against us and lenses clattered on our windows. I had experienced the press pack hundreds of times, but this time I was the prey.

I stood alone in the small elevator taking me towards the penthouse that was Rupert Murdoch's London home. I had been there many times but this was the early afternoon of 12 July 2011 and Rupert's great creation was in the throes of a corporate nervous breakdown.

It had been eight days since *The Guardian*'s disclosures about Milly Dowler had turned phone-hacking into a national outrage stretching far beyond the tight circle of media and politics. Suddenly, the *News of the World* was to be closed, and rivals and politicians were describing Rupert's company as a 'mafia'.

Rupert had called me in New York the night before, highly agitated, saying he wanted me in London. 'I want you here to walk around the News International building with James and me,' he said.

I thought this was a curious reason.

Kath and I took an overnight flight and I phoned his office from Heathrow Airport. 'The boss says go home, get some sleep, and come into the office in the morning,' I was told. Two hours later I got another call. There had been a change of plan. 'He would like to see you now,' I was told, and a car had been sent to collect me.

Inside the flat, I walked up the wide, luxurious staircase towards Rupert's living room. He was slumped forward in a chair. His elbows rested on his knees and the fingers of his old hands were locked together. His head was drooped and still.

He looked up at me as I walked in and for a moment he didn't speak. His heavy glasses had slipped down his nose; his jaw was slack and his mouth slightly open. The familiar intensity in his eyes had given way to an empty gaze.

'This is the worst day of my life,' he said. He looked so ill and tired my first impulse was to soothe him, to keep him calm.

As I had guessed, he did not want me to walk the building with him after all. I don't know whether he changed his mind overnight, or whether he couldn't bring himself to discuss the real reason on the phone, but he had decided to accept my resignation. When I had tried to offer it six days before, he refused. 'No, I'm not pushing anyone under the bus,' he had said. 'I spoke to Tony Blair last night and he said that every time he pushed someone under the bus he regretted it.'

But something, or someone, had changed his mind. Rupert asked me to stay in my job until a replacement was found. He was so distraught, I knew he wasn't thinking straight. I told him it made no sense for me to stay on and I refused. In all the difficulties I had seen him go through, I had never seen him so distressed; he seemed almost on the edge of panic. I never forgot his seeming calmness at the height of the debt crisis, when there cannot have been more at stake, standing silently before those anxious bankers while he calmly fastened the jacket of his double-breasted suit, addressing them without a quiver of nerves in his voice. But hacking had a deeper impact. Maybe it was tougher because he was older, maybe seeing his son James at the heart of the trouble made it more personal, or maybe, for the first time in his life, he simply didn't know what to do.

The car was in the basement waiting to take me home.

'Don't drive so quickly through those photographers, Damian,' I told the driver. 'It's not a good time to knock anyone down. There's nothing wrong with a few pictures.' The newspapers and television bulletins had plenty of shots of me being driven away looking dazed.

Kath and I flew back to New York, and pieced together the events of the last eight days. Four days after the Milly Dowler story broke, Rupert called me from a conference in Sun Valley, Idaho, to tell me the *News of the World* was to be closed. I was speechless. Its style was loud and sometimes cruel, but it sold more than 2.5 million copies. What clear-thinking company would fire millions of customers? The *News of the* World had been published for 168 years. Hundreds of innocent people would lose their jobs because of the criminality and stupidity of a few. It was a desperate move. It was also foolish to imagine sacrificing the newspaper — and its staff — would quell the public outrage whipped up by politicians and Murdoch rivals. Better to ride the storm, lose sales and advertisers for a while, and then rebuild. It would not be long before Rupert admitted closing the paper was a mistake born of panic. He toyed later with the idea of resurrecting it, if not as a newspaper then as a website, but by then he could not generate much enthusiasm among his shell-shocked London team.

It was during the call from Sun Valley that I first attempted to offer my resignation. He refused, but two days after that conversation I began getting the strong sense that either Rupert wasn't so sure that I should stay, or others in the company disagreed with him. A Reuters story appeared online with the heading: 'Could Murdoch deputy Hinton take the fall?'

This was the first article I had seen suggesting I should be fired. The rival media pressure had reached a pitch of merciless glee, but it had been concentrated mainly on London and on James Murdoch, in charge of News International since I left in December 2007, and on Rebekah Brooks, by now chief executive of the company.

The same day, I received an email from Andrew Edgecliffe-Johnson, the London-based media editor of the *Financial Times*. Under the subject line 'Can we talk?' it said:

Les,
People are briefing that you'll be 'sacrificed', and I'll probably have to write something sooner rather than later (probably tomorrow morning for Monday's paper) ... If there's any way to hear your side of the story, I would very much like to.

Andrew

This shocked me. I had clear views on how well — or how badly — the crisis was being handled in London, but I had spoken to no one about that or about phone-hacking, and I wasn't going to start now. I replied:

Andrew,
Thanks for getting in touch but I am not going to be saying anything.

Best
Les

Edgecliffe-Johnson came back with a second email:

Sorry to hear it, but I understand.

Again, for the avoidance of any doubt, we are currently planning a front page story saying pressure is growing within News for you and others involved in the 2007 initial inquiry to take the blame.

Best wishes,
Andrew

It was now clear that the 'briefing' was coming directly from News Corp. All large organisations have their own versions of what politicians call 'spin doctors': PRs and media spokespeople. Occasionally, these people go too far, but it's most likely they are acting according to the wishes or direct instructions of their bosses.

The following day, as Kath and I were on a bus returning from a family weekend in Long Island, I received a text message from *The Guardian*. Someone — no names were given — had told them I had seen an internal company report providing evidence of widespread phone-hacking at the *News of the World*. I had no idea what they were talking about — unsurprising, as it became clear that no such report existed. I didn't respond, but I was beginning to feel beleaguered. My messages to executives in London to find out what was going on went unanswered.

The next day, one theme dominated the front pages of *The Guardian* and the *Financial Times*. 'Murdoch's top aide faces new questions on hacking scandal' said *The Guardian*; and in the *FT*, 'Focus on Dow Jones chief Hinton as Murdoch takes charge of hacking crisis'.

According to *The Guardian*: 'Les Hinton, Rupert Murdoch's

lifelong lieutenant and closest advisor, faces questions over whether he saw a 2007 internal News International report, which found evidence that phone-hacking was more widespread than admitted by the company ...' This 'report', it said, comprised a collection of emails that had been discovered and sent to the police by executives who 'recently' joined News International. '*The Guardian* understands that Hinton was among five NI executives who had access to the report.'

The *Financial Times* story ran along similar lines. 'Les Hinton, chief executive of Dow Jones, is being blamed by people close to News Corp, for failing to get to grips with the *News of the World* phone-hacking scandal when he was in charge of Rupert Murdoch's UK newspaper group. Mr Hinton, a loyal Murdoch employee for 52 years ... could become the most senior casualty of the crisis, his friends fear, deflecting blame from James Murdoch, who runs News Corp's European operations, and Rebekah Brooks, chief executive of News International, which publishes Mr Murdoch's UK papers. "Les will be sacrificed to save James and Rebekah," one person familiar with the company said. "It happened on Les's watch," another added: "James was not even a director of News Corp at the time."'

There was no mistaking that senior people inside the company were going to a lot of trouble to stitch me up.

I had, of course, been running News International when phone-hacking took place at the *News of the World*. I was not responsible for, nor had I known about, the secret pay-offs to victims the company had later made, and I wasn't responsible for the management of affairs as they flew out of control. But hacking had happened — in the time-honoured, quitting-letter phrase — 'on my watch'.

I had already offered Rupert my resignation, which he had refused. So why the unattributed attacks and press briefings? It looked like others were forcing the spotlight on to me, and pressing their point with Rupert, to protect themselves. It was beginning to feel like a fight on an overloaded lifeboat.

When I challenged Rupert, he blamed 'out-of-control public relations people'. At no stage did I believe he was behind it. Management by leaking is a tacky and cowardly technique, and never his style. When Rupert wanted to fire people, he sat them down and did it.

No one at News International had asked me about the damning 'internal report' that I was supposed to have seen, nor was it ever produced in evidence to a select committee, or by the prosecution in the long-drawn out court cases that followed. It didn't exist. The closest thing to a 'report' turned out to be a collection of previously unseen emails discovered on file at the firm of lawyers, Harbottle & Lewis, employed in 2007 by me and other executives to explore allegations of phone-hacking. Years later, the full story of these missing 'toxic emails', and how they were overlooked by the lawyer charged with examining them, would be revealed.

The newspaper coverage of me during this uproar was not entirely unkind. Conrad Black wrote a comment piece in the *Financial Times* headlined: 'Murdoch, like Napoleon, is a great bad man'. In it, he said: 'It is unlikely that Mr Murdoch, his son James or Les Hinton committed crimes (Mr Hinton is a very decent man).'

The power of Black's testimonial was somewhat diminished by the fact he wrote it from a prison cell. He was serving three years for mail and wire fraud and obstructing justice, crimes committed while he was running a newspaper empire.

Back in New York, after initially wanting me to stay until a successor was found, Rupert was suddenly impatient for me to announce my resignation. Perhaps there was a view from some within the company that my going would take the pressure off; that it would draw a line under events. If so, it was a vain hope. It wasn't me who was in the gun sights of politicians and rival media groups, and my scalp was incidental. They were after other prey, as the coming weeks and months would show.

I told Rupert I needed more time to talk to my family and to reach agreement on a separation settlement. At the same time, I prepared my resignation letter, with the help of Kath and two sympathetic senior executives, Robert Thomson and Mark Jackson, the Dow Jones general counsel.

My letter said: 'That I was ignorant of what apparently happened is irrelevant and in the circumstances I feel it is proper for me to resign ...' I added that there had 'never been any evidence delivered to me that suggested the conduct spread beyond one journalist'. But I ended with a personal note to Rupert: 'I want to express my gratitude to you for a wonderful working life. My admiration and respect for you are unbounded. You have built a magnificent business since I first joined 52 years ago and it has been an honour making my contribution.'

Rupert published his statement: 'Les and I have been on a remarkable journey together for more than 52 years. That this passage has come to an unexpected end, professionally, not personally, is a matter of much sadness to me ... his great contribution to News Corporation over more than five decades has enhanced innumerable lives, whether those of employees hired by him or of readers better informed because of him.'

By Friday evening — 15 July 2011 — it was time to leave the office for the last time. Mark Jackson, who was a close friend as well as a good colleague, arranged for my emails to be sealed and my office files locked away. 'You will thank me for this, I promise,' he said. 'We've got to eliminate any possibility you could be accused of tampering with documents or deleting emails.'

Jackson also recommended an attorney — it was an unpleasant surprise to realise I needed one. Chip Loewenson of New York law firm Morrison & Foerster became a friend, and his team, including the London-based Kevin Roberts, would guide me faultlessly through the storms that followed.

A few colleagues had gathered in the News Corp executive dining suite, where the staff kindly opened bottles of seriously good champagne. Robert Thomson asked me to visit his office. As I left his newsroom, there was a burst of applause.

It was a Friday, and that night we drove to our house in Bridgehampton, Long Island. Robert Thomson, his wife Ping, and their two sons, Luke and Jack, joined us for the weekend. Rupert called my mobile a couple of times. I know he was worried about me, but I felt overdosed with sympathy. I think I was more wounded than I realised and wanted to push him away. He sent me an email:

Les, I can't wait to see you to tell you of my feelings. Your letter is generous as well as dignified and speaks volumes about your loyalty and integrity. Excuse not writing more, but I'm more than exhausted at the moment. Love to Kath.

It was a bright, wide-skied weekend, and we did our best to put it all aside. The unknowing innocence of the children made it easier — Ping and Robert's energetic two sons and my grandchildren, Samantha and Dylan, who had arrived with Martin and his wife, Stephanie.

The house was on the edge of a lake, and our telescope was fixed on an osprey across the water, feasting on a fish we had watched it catch. Deer were grazing on the far bank. Thomson had taken a phone call and walked back out to the deck where we sat with our drinks. 'It was Rupert,' he said. 'Rebekah has been arrested.'

No one spoke. We looked at each other, and we looked at him. Robert gave a sad-eyed smile: 'It's amazing that Rebekah gets arrested and we just sit here in silence,' he said. We were all in a state of shock saturation.

Later that Sunday, we heard that Sir Paul Stephenson, the Metropolitan commissioner and Britain's most senior law officer, had quit over the police handling of phone-hacking. The next day, John Yates, the assistant commissioner and nationwide counter-terrorism chief, also resigned. After defending the original police investigation, he was later forced to admit it had been, 'a cock-up'.

Two days later, Rupert and his son James appeared before the Culture, Media and Sport select committee. Rupert was contrite, telling them: 'This is the most humble day of my life.' He also said: 'I worked with Mr Hinton for 52 years and I would trust him with my life.' Soon after that, a man in the audience pushed into his face a paper plate covered with shaving foam, and his wife Wendi became the hero of the moment when she took a fierce swing at the attacker.

With the headlines, accusations, and wild rumours showing no sign of abating, Kath decided we should get away from it all and took me out of town to a lonely country inn in the Connecticut woods. Rupert called, still sounding shaken and full of concern. 'I'm fine, honestly,' I told him. 'Please don't worry about me. Rebekah is in a much tougher spot than me — take care of her.' Kath, seeing me white and tense on the phone, put a piece of paper in front of me. On it, she had written: 'Remember, you don't work for him any more.' She produced that same piece of paper often in the following weeks.

John Nallen, News Corp's deputy finance chief, called. 'I need to ask a favour,' he said. 'Can we please pull from the settlement our agreement to provide you with an office?'

The company was worried because a New York website had discovered I was to be provided with an office for a year, where I could work with my assistant, Marianne Krafinski. It didn't make much difference to me, but I wondered at how badly shot everyone's nerves were if they were worried about the potential image problem of giving me a transitional office. The real issue was Marianne. She had been with me for 26 years, travelling wherever I was posted. She needed to stay employed by the company for another 18 months to qualify for a full pension. 'Just promise me Marianne keeps a job,' I told Nallen. He promised, and she did.

Kath had banned me from reading newspapers or watching the news — 'I'll let you know what you need to know.' For several weeks she censored everything, but periodically gave me a carefully vetted good-news package.

I was allowed to read an editorial in *The Wall Street Journal* headlined 'News and its Critics' which said: 'In nearly four years at the Journal, Mr Hinton managed the paper's return to profitability amid a terrible business climate. He did so not solely by cost-cutting but by investing in journalists when other publications were laying off hundreds. On ethical questions, his judgment was as sound as that of any editor we've had ... Mr Hinton was at the helm when we again became America's largest daily.'

The Journal's special committee, appointed to guard the newspaper against management interference, said in a statement: 'No journalist at Dow Jones has even whispered to us before or since Mr Hinton's resignation that he pressured him or her or condoned or promoted journalistic misconduct.'

Michael Gross, a star writer at *New York* magazine when I ran it two decades before, set himself apart from the 'surge of *schadenfreude*' felt by some at my departure. 'I felt sad,' he wrote, and told the story of my refusal to fire him in the face of a demand by Calvin Klein bosses who so hated his profile of Klein that they pulled their advertising from the magazine.

Kath also showed me, surprisingly, an interview with Nick Davies. Davies was *The Guardian*'s chief anti-Murdoch obsessive, which is a hotly contested title on that newspaper. Davies is a man driven by cranky ideas about media and capitalism that are about as coherent as an anarchist's rant just after he's hurled a brick through a McDonald's window. Still, he spent years unearthing the hacking story and the cat-and-mouse doggedness of his work deserves to be acknowledged.

Davies said in an interview in American *Ad Age:* 'There were some people who were clearly going to have to resign before the Milly Dowler story, but it went beyond that — Les Hinton, for example, in New York. There was no pressure on him to resign, but somehow there was this kind of contagion of panic.'

The New Yorker was driven to rhyme. In a protest against the 'sexist' attention paid to Rebekah Brooks' curly red mane, it wrote a poem to my hair, 'Every Follicle, Diabolical':

Les Hinton's hair
Will not behave
It grows and flows
A silver wave
Les Hinton's hair
Will not comply
With orders that
Come from on high
Les Hinton's hair
Has its own mind
It only acts
When it's inclined
It's shiny, ruthless
Debonair
It's everything
Les Hinton's hair.

Ben Greenman
The New Yorker © Conde Nast

I framed that one.

I had scores of phone calls and messages from friends and old colleagues all over the world. I read the messages over and over for comfort.

Hidden away in our woodland sanctuary, making tentative travel plans, I didn't understand until later what an all-encompassing storm was loose. After a cautionary conversation with my US attorneys, I decided not to travel to London for a while to permit the hysteria to fade. It made me feel like a fugitive, even though I had done nothing wrong. But Kath was insistent: 'Everyone has lost their heads over there. Don't risk it.' So she flew to London for a good friend's wedding while I hid away in Manhattan.

There was a quiet lake in the grounds of our country hotel. It was just after dawn, lazy and cool before the heat of the day, and I sat there with mingling feelings of freedom, fear, and disbelief. Thirteen days had altered my life forever. I had long ago made my personal bargain with the restraints and rewards of working for a personality like Rupert. I never felt immune; I had seen the casualties pile up over the years. But I never thought it would end for me like this, as a castaway in a hurricane.

While I was free of the bonds, I had also grown accustomed to status and security and, for all its fierce pressures, the comfort of life inside a huge, raucous, relentless organisation. It may be overweening, but it was daring and inventive as well. It was an institution, and now I was de-institutionalised. I could sit there beside the water as long as I wished. There were no crises to calm, no faltering executive to rebuke, no struggling new editor to hearten, no clashing egos to soothe.

But what a mess it was. Kath was being tough and brave, but I knew she was distraught and angry, and that the kids were, too. Mal and Duncan were emailing anxiously from Australia too distant from events to sort the hysteria from the facts.

A few ducks were dabbling for food on the glassy, green surface of the lake. Among them was a blue-winged teal. Teal are glorious birds; small with white crescents beneath their rich-blue bills, speckled brown chests and brilliant flashes of blue when they spread their wings. Suddenly, a red-tailed hawk swept down and seized the teal in its talons. For a while, the duck struggled on the lake's edge beneath its killer's grip, but slowly succumbed, until it was still, and the hungry hawk began plucking away at its morning meal.

I have always felt there should be a metaphor in the sight of that beautiful, helpless creature and its feasting predator, but I couldn't nail it. I guess it would have been something about how much luckier I was than the duck.

CHAPTER 27

Meltdown

The *News of the World* phone-hacking affair was about much more than the reckless behaviour of journalists who betrayed their trade and helped kill a newspaper. They wrecked their own lives, and those of many others, but their actions also set off a chain of events that eventually dwarfed their deceit, even their criminality, and boiled up into a monumental legal, political, and media hyper-drama. Unwittingly, they created a monster of unstoppable anger, grief, paranoia, and hysteria that gave old enemies, and new, an unexpected and unprecedented opportunity to attack Rupert Murdoch, his politics, and his newspapers.

The affair had been ebbing and rising since August 2006 when reporter Clive Goodman and Glenn Mulcaire, a football player turned private investigator, were arrested for phone-hacking. When the case went to court in November of that year, both pleaded guilty. Sentencing was deferred until January, when the judge, Mr Justice Gross, described their conduct as 'reprehensible in the extreme'.

He gave each a short prison sentence. Goodman and Mulcaire had apparently hacked more than 600 times into the voicemails of senior employees in the household of Prince Charles and his sons, William and Harry. In addition, Mulcaire admitted to hacking into the phones of others, including the model Elle Macpherson and the publicist Max Clifford.

Mulcaire was a hacking aficionado. In their early years, mobile phones were sold with a common four-digit passcode. Unless new owners created their own unique passcode, listening into other people's voice messages was easy — anyone could dial the number and enter the default code. Even when someone had created their own passcode, Mulcaire could usually discover it. He would call telephone companies masquerading as a forgetful customer; or he would use software, available on the internet, that made it possible to bypass some passcodes completely.

As the court case later showed, Mulcaire and Goodman's scheme began to fall apart in November 2005. The paper had run two gossip items by Goodman — one revealed that Prince William had seen a doctor about a knee injury; the other that a television reporter covering the Royal Family had loaned the prince broadcasting equipment. While William was wondering how the *News of the World* could have obtained this information, a couple of his courtiers noticed their voicemails were displaying as old messages before they had listened to them.

The police were called in, and due to the importance of the complainants, Scotland Yard assigned its counterterrorism squad to the case. It's possible these elite officers thought the task an unhelpful distraction from their main job. London was on high alert after four jihadist terrorists had murdered 52 people in July that year, followed two weeks later with a further attempted attack.

Nine months later, Goodman and Mulcaire were arrested. Many people — myself included — assumed that, after so long, these two arrests were the culmination of a painstaking investigation.

Goodman's desk had been searched; papers had been removed, and Goodman and Mulcaire interviewed at length. No one else had been arrested, or charged. It appeared that they had acted alone.

When Goodman and Mulcaire went to prison, the police closed the case and returned all their resources to the main task of tackling terrorism. I thought the curtain had been drawn on an embarrassing and painful episode for the *News of the World*.

I fired Goodman, and gave him a year's salary, telling him in my letter of dismissal that the payment was for his 'many unblemished, and frequently distinguished, years of service ... and in recognition of the pressures on your family.' This was true, but I was also over-generous. I soon wished I hadn't done it.

At the same time, Andy Coulson resigned. He was close to tears as we sat in my office. I hadn't asked him to go — in fact, I thought there was no need. He had told me he knew nothing about phone-hacking, and I believed him. I believed him for years.

By 2007, Coulson had been editor of the *News of the World* for four years. He was a demanding boss, but mostly popular. I considered him a gifted newspaperman, and still do. I was proud to have recognised his talent and advanced his career. Colin Myler, a former *Daily Mirror* editor-in-chief who was then based in America as deputy editor at the *New York Post,* agreed to come home and take Coulson's place.

In an effort to repair the damage, I called Prince Charles' principal private secretary, Sir Michael Peat, a silky Old Etonian. Coulson had already publicly apologised on behalf of the paper, as reported in *The Guardian* the day after the guilty pleas of Goodman and Mulcaire. I apologised to Peat on behalf of the company, and offered £100,000 to any charities nominated by Princes William and Harry. It was a token gesture given the scale of intrusion, but Peat was gracious in accepting both the offer and the spirit in which it was made. Unfortunately, by 2011, with Peat no longer at the palace, both the apology and donation appeared to have been forgotten at News International and Clarence House. *The Times* gave great display to a story about Prince William complaining to James Murdoch and Rebekah Brooks that he had never received an apology. Murdoch, the newspaper said, was 'shocked' at the news. I wished someone had checked with me.

In the summer of 2007, Prince Charles was guest of honour at the annual Police Bravery Awards, an event *The Sun* sponsored in support of the Police Federation. Rebekah Brooks and I greeted him in the lobby of the Dorchester Hotel in Park Lane, seating him at our table. He was impressed with the evening and suggested that *The Sun* stage a similar event for the military. We did, and *The Sun*'s Military Awards became an annual event. I thought we had made peace with the palace, and steadied the ship at the *News of the World*. But the real trouble hadn't even started.

Shortly after receiving my note firing him, Clive Goodman had sent an angry letter dated 2 March 2007 to Daniel Cloke, the human resources director, accusing the company of unfair dismissal. He also claimed that *News of the World* editors knew about phone-hacking, and alleged 'other members of staff were carrying out the same illegal procedures'. Goodman said his case would be supported by copies of his email exchanges with several executives over a 16-month period.

I asked Cloke and Jon Chapman, the company's legal director, to join with Colin Myler, the new editor, to investigate Goodman's claims. None of these three men had any conceivable reason to hide wrongdoing. Chapman and Cloke had nothing to do with editorial operations, and Myler was new at the paper.

They interviewed everyone Goodman had named, and reviewed around 2500 emails, but came up with nothing to support the allegations. To reinforce the independence and thoroughness of the investigation, I asked Chapman to hire an outside law firm to conduct a further review.

Chapman appointed Harbottle & Lewis, a well-established media law firm, and forwarded them the emails, including a batch that went beyond the dates specified by Goodman and had not been previously examined. The email review was led by the firm's managing partner, Lawrence Abramson, who subsequently wrote to Chapman confirming he had found no evidence of criminal activity.

It would be eight years before it became clear that Abramson had made a terrible mistake: he had missed crucial emails, not seen by the News International team, that contained evidence of wrongdoing. These were the so-called, and now infamous, 'toxic emails' mentioned in court cases, criminal trials, and countless news stories. They referred to 'lifting quotes from tele' and 'turning mobiles.' In another, Goodman wrote about actions that could land 'me, you, and the editor in jail'. In one exchange, Coulson gave Goodman permission to pay £1000 for a palace phone book containing the phone numbers of the Royal Family and their staff.

It was a disastrous mistake by Harbottle & Lewis, and one with serious and irreparable repercussions for their client, News International.

A paralegal helping Abramson had flagged the emails for his attention, warning him against sending his proposed letter to News International. 'I cannot say that I agree there is no evidence,' she wrote. But Abramson didn't read her note, or the email attachments she had sent him — a failure that led him, in 2015, to appear before the Solicitors Disciplinary Tribunal charged with unprofessional behaviour.

He offered a litany of excuses: it had been 'probably the busiest week' of his life; he needed to complete outstanding work before taking his children on holiday; he was 'juggling, trying to keep everything in the air'; he flew to Athens to see his club, Liverpool, play in the Champions League Final, and in the chaos outside the ground, his ticket was snatched from his hand, requiring him to watch the game in a bar; his return flight that night was delayed; he didn't get home until 10 o'clock the following morning; his secretary was away and the temporary one unfamiliar with his work; she mislabelled the paralegal's vital message and so he overlooked it. Everything that could go wrong for him apparently had. Even Liverpool lost 2-1 to A. C. Milan — I witnessed the defeat myself, in the stadium with my two youngest children, James and Jane.

Despite his excuses, the tribunal ruled that Abramson's errors were 'major in nature and caused consequences which were there for all to see'. For his 'genuine, major but inadvertent oversight', the tribunal ordered him to pay a fine of £20,000 and £15,000 in costs. The tribunal was forgiving: 'his misconduct was a single episode in a previously unblemished career'.

I found it difficult to feel charitable, thinking of the consequences of his 'busiest week' and how different life might be, for me and many others, if he had read the emails instead of sending his lack-of-evidence note.

In 2007, it would be another four years before the truth was known. *The Guardian*, the BBC, and others would write extensively about the 'smoking gun emails'. Tom Watson MP, a member of the House of Commons Culture, Media and Sport select committee, claimed it was a 'fantastical notion' that executives hadn't known about the emails, and said the company had misled Parliament. Chris Bryant, a Labour frontbencher, accused News International of 'a massive cover-up', claiming it was 'inconceivable that the senior management of News International did not know about this. It is quite clear that Parliament has been lied to.'

When the truth was finally uncovered during the Abramson tribunal, it went almost entirely unreported. Labour's fiery critics — MPs such as Tom Watson and Chris Bryant — had nothing to say. The truth must have been too inconvenient.

With the evidence to the contrary lost in Harbottle & Lewis' files, we told Goodman in 2007 that his claims were without merit. He immediately pressed forward with a claim of wrongful dismissal.

Companies regularly settle wrongful dismissal claims to avoid bad publicity and the time they take up. Our initial intention was to fight it — I thought we had a strong case — but after looking at the details, our lawyers said we should agree a settlement. The company had apparently failed to follow statutory disciplinary and dismissal procedure — this made Goodman's firing automatically unfair, and gave him the right to appeal at a public hearing. Mulcaire, in turn, claimed the amount of work he had done for the *News of the World* gave him the rights of a member of staff. Legal advice was we could lose both cases.

Common sense said they both deserved instant dismissal for gross misconduct and — legal technicalities aside — that we were entitled to kick out the pair of them. But I agreed we should avoid the risk of defeat and the probability of painful, if unfounded, public allegations, and we settled both cases.

By the end of 2007, I wasn't thinking about phone-hacking at all. It had been a difficult interlude for everyone involved, but I had put it out of my mind. I was in New York buried in the complicated makeover of Dow Jones and *The Wall Street Journal*. My memory wouldn't be jolted until the morning of 9 July 2009.

Kath and I had planned it as a happy day. We had married quietly two months before, but this was the day of our wedding party. We had hired Hertford House, a grand building five minutes from our London flat that had become a gallery, the Wallace Collection. We loved wandering its rooms. It was left to the nation by the family of Sir Richard Wallace, the illegitimate son of the fourth Marquess of Hertford, and contains a beautifully eclectic collection of Old Masters, antiques, furniture, and porcelain.

We invited 100 family and friends. Kath's mother Angela and a merry troop of her Liverpool relatives were there. All five of my grown children came from New York, with spouses and partners, and my two grandchildren, Samantha and Dylan. Dylan, aged three, looked uncomfortably splendid in a blue suit and bright yellow tie.

But that morning's edition of *The Guardian* had taken the shine off things. 'Revealed: Murdoch's £1m Bill For Hiding Dirty Tricks' said its front, across two page-wide decks. The lead paragraph was chilling: 'Rupert Murdoch's News Group Newspapers has paid out more than £1m to settle legal cases that threatened to reveal evidence of his journalists' repeated involvement in criminal methods to get stories.'

The biggest payout, it said, had been a settlement in 2008 of £700,000 to Gordon Taylor, chief executive of the Professional Footballers' Association, who had received the money after signing a 'gagging' clause preventing him from talking about the case.

A photograph of Rupert, Rebekah Brooks, Andy Coulson, and myself dominated two pages of further coverage inside. We were sitting solemnly in the pews for a memorial service at St Bride's, Fleet Street's parish church. I would grow sick of that image; it became the default photo used to illustrate scores of stories.

The Guardian quoted an unnamed police source saying that officers had found evidence that reporters hacked into thousands of mobile phones, including those of cabinet ministers, MPs, celebrities, and sports stars. It ran photos of the actor Gwyneth Paltrow, the cabinet minister Tessa Jowell, the TV chef Nigella Lawson, the mayor of London Boris Johnson, and the comedian Lenny Henry.

The first person to greet Kath and me at the Wallace Collection was not an invited guest. Jon Craig of Sky News was there with a camera crew, looking for an interview. Craig was the first of many, and the media cluster that grew through the evening discouraged some guests from attending. Andy Coulson sent his regrets by text, and Tessa Jowell phoned Kath with her apologies.

Our guests included politicians and party operatives from Labour and the Conservatives, and friends from most Fleet Street newspapers. They were enjoying themselves — politicians and journalists take delight in a crisis when they are merely witnesses. Senior politicians in particular live in a minefield of catastrophes waiting to happen; their glee at the troubles of others must be a relief reflex that comes with surviving another explosion.

It was a worrying article, but *The Guardian* had stalked News Corp for years and had overplayed other stories against the company. This latest was a dramatic read, but looked thin and depended heavily on unnamed sources. I was also sure that someone would have told me about such a massive payoff. Rebekah Brooks, there that evening, agreed. No one had told her, she said, and she doubted it was true.

But Kath was not so ready to dismiss it. 'Even if *The Guardian* has jazzed it up, they can't have invented the whole story. They would have to be sure about the details of a payment as huge as that,' she said.

As I prepared to make my speech, she took my arm, kissed my cheek, and whispered: 'No jokes about this — it isn't funny.'

The Guardian story ran for three days and the hacking saga came back to life in the news. Parliamentary hearings were convened, and politicians and critics accused News International of a cover-up. But Scotland Yard decided not to reopen its investigation. The assistant commissioner John Yates said: 'This case has been the subject of the most careful investigation by experienced detectives ... No additional evidence has come to light. I therefore consider no further investigation is required.' The Director of Public Prosecutions, Sir Keir Starmer QC — later a Labour MP — agreed with Yates.

Andy Hayman, who was assistant commissioner in charge of counterterrorism when the palace made its complaint, wrote in *The Times* about the original 2006 investigation: 'This was not the time for a half-hearted investigation — we put our best detectives on the case and left no stone unturned as officials breathed down our neck.'

It seemed conclusive. But there was something I didn't know, and that Yates and Hayman did not at that time reveal. When the police had searched Mulcaire's home, they had taken away and stored 11,000 pages of notebooks and papers in bin bags. They had never properly examined them. This turned out to be a big mistake. It might have been incompetent, but I don't believe it was sinister. The anti-terrorist police assigned to the job believed they had more important things to do, and it's likely they made a time-and-cost decision based on the logic that the jailing of Goodman and Mulcaire would have brought phone-hacking to a dead halt; the job of police forces is to prevent crime and that doesn't necessarily mean catching every criminal. However, in 2012 when events required them to take another look, Mulcaire's papers provided abundant evidence of hacking, and led to dozens of civil cases and several criminal prosecutions.

But in July 2009, in the face of an emphatic police response, and without solid evidence against others at the newspaper, the story receded. But the number of civil court actions mounted, with more and more people suspecting their phones might have been hacked.

The Guardian, meanwhile, had stalled in its effort to find a smoking gun inside News International. With no new leads, editor Alan Rusbridger phoned Bill Keller, executive editor of *The New York Times*, hoping to excite his interest.

Rusbridger's call was well timed. The long-running war between News Corp and *The New York Times* was at its hottest. Days before, we had announced that *The Wall Street Journal* would go into direct competition with *The New York Times* by launching a daily section called 'Greater New York'.

Rupert enjoyed battling *The New York Times* and having fun at the expense of its chairman, Arthur Sulzberger. His admired father and predecessor had been nicknamed 'Punch' by his staff; Arthur was known as 'Pinch'.

Psychological warfare between News Corp and *The New York Times* had gone on for decades. The *New York Post* took constant personal shots at 'Pinch'. Even *The Wall Street Journal* joined in by illustrating, with part of Sulzberger's face, a story about 'men with feminine features'.

The new 'Greater New York' section in *The Wall Street Journal* was a direct assault on *The New York Times* when it was at its weakest. The 2008 recession had cost the newspaper millions in advertising.

Keller seized the opportunity that Rusbridger's call gave him. Within three days, three staffers from *The New York Times* arrived at *The Guardian*'s London office. *The New York Times* was cutting costs elsewhere, but these reporters were given all the time they needed to get their story. It was almost six months before it appeared. It wasn't in the main paper, but in its Sunday magazine — giving it more room for detail and speculation. The cover, dated 1 September 2010, was presented in tabloid style with a vivid red slash of a headline across a photograph of Princes William and Harry: 'Tabloid Hack Attack!'

The paper had spoken to a dozen *News of the World* reporters who claimed that the hacking of mobile phones was pervasive — and that Coulson knew about it. It also named three journalists, giving the report greater strength than the nameless quotes that had appeared in *The Guardian*. The hacking story had legs again — and this time it was running on both sides of the Atlantic.

The Metropolitan police held their ground, despite calls from politicians for a judicial inquiry into the mishandling of the investigation. 'We remain of the view that no new evidence has emerged to justify re-opening this inquiry,' a police statement said. 'Independently, the Crown Prosecution Service, leading counsel, and the director of public prosecutions reached the same conclusion.'

But this time the inaction did not last long. By the end of 2010, as News International found itself fighting further civil actions, the company began its own internal inquiries. This was when William Lewis, News International's managing director, found the 'toxic emails' that had been lost at Harbottle & Lewis.

Lewis' discovery flipped a switch within the company. Some at News International appear to have jumped too eagerly to the conclusion that these emails had been covered up in 2007 by the then-management. I realised later that the emails must be the 'internal report' someone from News International had inventively told *The Guardian* I had seen. I was baffled that no one among News International's team of diligent investigators appears to have questioned Harbottle & Lewis about them. No one asked me if I were aware of them; I would have said flatly that I was not. Without discussing them with me, News International's investigators handed these explosive emails to the police. The Met, meanwhile, had remembered the bin sacks of papers it had removed from Mulcaire's home, and reopened its inquiry in the face of 'significant new evidence'. In the following months, Ian Edmondson, the *News of the World* head of news, was suspended; Andy Coulson quit his job in David Cameron's office; and three *News of the World* journalists were arrested on suspicion of hacking.

By now, the crimes of phone-hackers — and the misery of their victims — were becoming lost in a drama that encompassed political parties, police, media companies, and a band of baying crusaders demanding new laws to keep the press in check.

But the most ferocious attacks on Rupert and News Corp came not from the victims of hacking, or from the police, but from the Brownite faction of the Labour Party.

CHAPTER 28

Draining the swamp

There was a history of hostility between the Labour Party and Rupert, dating back at least to the Wapping siege and *The Sun*'s fierce support of Margaret Thatcher and its equally fierce opposition to socialism. But that was before the party's conversion to 'New Labour' under the moderate leadership of Tony Blair. During the Blair years, the relationship was mostly cordial; two later events were central to understanding Labour's new animosity.

Within four months of resigning as editor of the *News of the World*, Andy Coulson accepted the job of director of communications for the Conservative Party leader, David Cameron. The *News of the World*, along with *The Sun*, had supported Labour for ten years and now an influential former editor, who was still close to the company, had switched sides. Coulson's hiring came in the final days of Blair's reign, four weeks before he resigned, and his appointment disturbed Labour's new leadership.

Then, in September 2009, when Labour was still in government but struggling under the unsteady leadership of Gordon Brown, *The*

Sun finally abandoned the party, and switched its support to the Conservatives.

Brown was furious at the manner in which *The Sun* turned against him. Warming up his party for a general election, he had made a powerful and well-received address to the Labour Party conference in Brighton. 'We are the Labour Party and our abiding duty is to stand. And fight. And win. And serve,' he thundered.

It was stirring stuff, and Brown was pleased with his performance. But his post-speech heart rate had scarcely returned to normal when he received news of the front-page headline in the following day's *The Sun*. It said, simply: 'Labour's Lost It'. A supporting subhead went on: 'After 12 Long Years In Power, This Government Has Lost Its Way. Now It's Lost *The Sun*'s Support Too.'

It was a sneak attack and timed to deliver maximum damage. Brown had spent years making a friend of Rupert and there was a genuine fondness between them. Rupert liked Brown; he thought he was cleverer than Blair and admired his unshowy, blunt style. Brown's father had been a Scottish church minister, as was Rupert's grandfather. This shared history was important to them both. 'Gordon has a Calvinistic approach to life, and there is a lot to be said for it,' Rupert once told *The New Yorker*.

The timing of *The Sun*'s declaration seemed more malice than the paper's typical mischief-making. Both James Murdoch and Rebekah Brooks had become close to Conservative leader David Cameron, whose former life as a public relations executive made him more palatable company than the awkward and often spiky Brown.

But soon after that front-page shock, *The Sun* delivered another: 'Bloody Shameful' was the main headline. The supposed 'shame' was that Brown had written a letter of sympathy to the mother of a soldier killed in Afghanistan and misspelt the soldier's name.

The story was deeply unfair. Brown was partly sighted; aides sent emails to him in extra large font, and when he spoke in the House of Commons, the despatch box was stacked with books to bring his notes closer. Every newspaper knew that Brown wrote clumsily with a thick-tipped pen — and that apparent spelling mistakes were often nothing of the sort. It was a low blow and Brown is said to have snapped over the story.

Rupert said later that he received an angry call from Brown in which Brown said: 'Your company has declared war on my government and we have no alternative but to make war on your company.' Rupert, observing Brown's mood during the call, said: 'I don't think he was in a very balanced state of mind.'

Brown's response to this accusation was emphatic: 'This call did not happen. This threat was not made. I couldn't be unbalanced on a call I didn't have.'

What's fascinating about these two statements is that they were both made under oath in 2012 in front of the so-called Leveson Inquiry, which was ordered by a beleaguered and weakened David Cameron, by then prime minister, into the 'culture, ethics, and practices' of the British press.

It's impossible to be sure whether either committed perjury — or which was simply forgetful — but before they testified I had heard several accounts from company insiders of a conversation in which Brown threatened Rupert.

Whatever he did or didn't say in a phone call, Brown was intent on serious damage when he rose from the backbenches of the House of Commons during a debate about phone-hacking in the summer of 2011. News Corp, he said, had 'descended from the gutter to the sewer ... The tragedy is that they let the rats out of the sewer ... they marched in step, I say, with members of the criminal underworld ... this criminal media nexus [was] standing side by side with criminals against our citizens.'

It was shocking stuff, and it surprised me. In many conversations with Brown over a decade — during private dinners, at the theatre, after Goodman and Mulcaire had gone to prison — he never once hinted at any concerns he harboured about the ethics or propriety of News International. If the prime minister thought the company was 'in the gutter', he did a fine job of hiding it from me.

Brown's onslaught was a rare public demonstration of his notorious intemperance. It came in the days following the Milly Dowler disclosures of July 2011. Voters had thrown him and the Labour Party out of office the previous year; both were bitter and blamed, at least in part, Rupert's newspapers. The new leader of the Opposition, Ed Miliband, was happy to follow the lead of his former boss. There were old scores to be settled, and the hacking crisis provided an ideal opportunity for revenge.

Even better, David Cameron had given Labour a perfect gift in the shape of Andy Coulson. He had installed a 'criminal' in Number 10 Downing Street.

In its eagerness for revenge, Labour ignored its own hypocrisy. The party attacked Cameron for his friendship with News International and Rebekah Brooks, overlooking its own conduct and constant inveigling. Only weeks before, a troupe of Labour leaders had turned up for Liz Murdoch and Matthew Freud's epic housewarming. Self-declared arch-enemy, Tom Watson, forgot the many drinks he'd consumed at the expense of News Corp; I remember the sight of him in a jolly mood wearing a bright blue News Corp jacket, extra large, at our party to wave off a company-sponsored yacht on a transatlantic race; he seemed at home among the yachting set. And Brown was in a different frame of mind when his wife Sarah hosted a late 2007 sleepover and pyjama party at Chequers, attended by Rebekah Brooks and Wendi Murdoch. (Kath had declined her invitation. 'It's all too cosy for comfort,' she'd said. 'And besides, I'd have to buy a pair of pyjamas.')

Brooks was the most avid networker in Fleet Street and, as editor of the *News of the World* and then *The Sun*, the eagerness to be her friend crossed party lines. She could be dazzled by these supposed admirers and made a mistake in not keeping her distance from politicians. Sure enough, these counterfeit friends fled when Brooks became radioactive and dangerous to know.

As the scandal grew, fallout spread across Britain's press; every popular newspaper was under suspicion of phone-hacking and other illegal activity.

News Corp's problems increased in the United States after a source-free *Daily Mirror* report that the voicemails of the families of 9/11 victims had been hacked — nothing ever came of it. The *Mirror* itself was later drawn into the scandal, but its pain was less pronounced without the manufactured outrage of other media and self-serving Labour politicians.

After the allegations of payments to police in Britain, the FBI and the US Justice Department began an investigation under the US Foreign Corrupt Practices Act. This was drastic action, probably incited by Rupert's American enemies, and criticised even in *The New York Times*. Bill Keller, soon after leaving as the newspaper's most senior editor, wrote: 'That seems an ominously expansive use of a statute that was created to eliminate bribery as a means to obtain business or favorable regulations from foreign governments.'

All this pressure drove the Metropolitan Police and News International into a desperate cycle of over-compensation. Afraid of further charges of a cover-up, News gave the police access to information that contained even the smallest hint of a misstep. And the Met — fighting accusations of a corrupt closeness to the company it was investigating — felt obligated to pursue every News International lead. If the company had provided evidence of a reporter double-parking on an assignment, I think the police would have staged a dawn raid.

There were plenty of dawn raids.

At first, these searches were directed at *News of the World* journalists suspected of phone-hacking. But on the morning of Saturday 28 January 2012, there was an alarming escalation in the investigation. Four of *The Sun*'s most senior journalists were arrested. Teams of officers searched their homes, detained them for questioning, then bailed them on suspicion of making illegal payments to police officers.

The Sunday Telegraph's account was typical of next morning's newspapers: 'Senior executives at *The Sun* newspaper who were closely associated with Rebekah Brooks ... have been arrested on suspicion of making illegal payments to police officers. They were detained in a series of dawn raids after information was handed to Scotland Yard by News Corporation, the tabloid's parent company. Sources within Rupert Murdoch's publishing group described the process as "draining the swamp".'

Draining the swamp? I was furious. I had worked with these people for years. Fergus Shanahan, who had been Brooks' deputy on *The Sun*, was a friend; Graham Dudman, the paper's managing editor, was a quiet, affable man; Chris Pharo was a demanding and effective news editor; and Mike Sullivan was one of Fleet Street's most respected crime reporters.

Sixteen days later there were other dawn raids. Five more senior journalists from *The Sun* were arrested: Geoff Webster, the deputy editor; John Sturgis, deputy news editor; Nick Parker, chief foreign correspondent; John Kay, chief reporter; and John Edwards, the picture editor. Kay was one of Fleet Street's most garlanded journalists and a friend since we were reporters in the 1970s. Edwards I had known since he was a child; he was the son of *The Sun*'s famed royal photographer, Arthur Edwards. These newspapermen were at the heart of making *The Sun* Britain's biggest-selling and most influential newspaper. Their arrests were based on information provided by News International, their employer. I had no idea what they were alleged to have done, but I felt a bitter anger towards the callous fool who branded them swamp dwellers — as if their arrests were part of a plan by lawyers, PRs, and others to sanitise the newspaper and company for which they had worked so long and so hard.

More arrests followed, week after week, and stories spread of the early-morning ordeals of journalists' families; crying teenagers, woken at 5am, whose rooms and possessions were searched; silent children watching as a parent was taken away. We heard stories of the mental pressures — the anti-anxiety medication, the breakdowns, heavy drinking, and two suicide attempts. Careers and normal lives would be suspended while journalists waited for months and years to learn whether or not they would be charged.

The entire upper echelon of *The Sun* was gutted. Morale was crushed; it was a miracle the newspaper was coming out at all. The anger spilled beyond the boundaries of *The Sun*. Trevor Kavanagh, *The Sun*'s associate editor and political columnist, went public in an angry column attacking politicians and the police for treating journalists 'like members of an organised crime gang'. He took an unveiled shot at his own management, writing: '*The Sun* is not a "swamp" that needs to be drained.' He went on BBC radio to attack 'certain parts of the company — not News International I hasten to add, not the newspaper side of the operation — (that are) actually boasting that they are sending information to police that has put people ... into police cells.' Kavanagh became *The Sun*'s public champion at a time when almost no one in the company was brave enough to do so. Fortunately for him, Rupert might have secretly approved of what he did. Rupert thought highly of Trevor and he remained a regular guest at his dinners and private parties.

Among some at the top of News Corp, there was shock and remorse, as if a government had seen its air force bomb the wrong target. In March 2013, disregarding the advice of lawyers, Rupert met *The Sun* journalists who had been arrested. He told them the company was being 'picked on'. He pointed the finger at 'the old right-wing establishment ... or worse, the left-wing get-even crowd of Gordon Brown'. He criticised the 'incompetent' police investigation and promised: 'I will do everything in my power to give you total support, even if you're convicted and get six months or whatever ...' His words were secretly recorded — not everyone present felt warmly towards him by this stage — and were leaked around the world, bringing accusations from his ever-hopeful enemies that he was aiding and abetting criminal activity.

In the summer of 2011, at the height of the hacking outcry, David Cameron had ordered a public inquiry into the practices of Britain's newspapers. The inquiry was to be led by Sir Brian Leveson, a 62-year-old judge from Liverpool.

Although the inquiry lasted 16 months, and cost taxpayers more than £5 million, it was not long enough for Leveson to grasp how modern media was changing. His pronouncements and judgment on the internet astounded the industry. While digital was demolishing the business models of old print, Leveson blindly ruled it did not deserve his attention: 'People will not assume that what they read on the internet is trustworthy or that it carries any particular assurance or accuracy,' he said.

Other findings were tough, but not without some merit. 'There have been too many times when, chasing the story, parts of the press have acted as if its own code, which it wrote, simply did not exist.' And politicians, he said, had become close to the press, 'in a way which has not been in the public interest'.

After 20 years in America, I was fascinated by the British impulse to control newspapers. In the US it is never an issue, given the First Amendment guarantees of free speech. British newspapers must obey the nation's laws like every other institution: phone-hacking is a crime and journalists accused of it should rightly go to trial and face imprisonment; libel laws are more stringent than America's and newspapers have navigated them for years; like every business, media is subject to anti-monopoly rules protecting new entrants, and regulators have powers to assure a plurality of opinion.

But among many in Britain there has long been an appetite for special powers to constrain the British press. It's a truism that free media is a vital ventilator that every healthy society needs. It's also true that this freedom comes with occasions of excess, error, vulgarity, vindictiveness, prejudice, and every other epithet aimed at Britain's wild and free newspaper industry. The belief that a centralised body of arbiters blessed by the state can guarantee the good behaviour of the British press, as well as being insane and sinister, ignores the true threat to a healthy information environment that comes from the developing technologies driving modern communications. The digital age has made market entry more affordable and opinion more abundant, yet at the same time British homes and workplaces are being flooded with lies, libels, violence, and pornography from sources far beyond our borders, where no courts or law enforcement can reach. But, while the internet runs amok, Britain must listen to the anachronistic ranting of politicians fighting old wars, and tolerate the sublimely ignorant deliberations of judges such as Brian Leveson.

But Leveson went ahead with his little ideas and proposed a new watchdog for newspapers operating with 'state underpinning'. He recommended that newspapers refusing to accept the authority of this state-approved regulator be subject to punitive costs in court cases. The industry's reaction was unsurprising. Editors protested that they were being blackmailed into compliance and overwhelmingly rejected the Leveson plan.

These dramas were the backdrop to my own continuing encounters with the Metropolitan Police, News Corp lawyers, the US Justice Department, and a committee of politicians dominated by Gordon Brown's personal axe man, Tom Watson.

In a conference room on Third Avenue, New York, five lawyers representing News Corp confronted me. Over three hours they questioned me, producing long-ago expense accounts they considered suspicious, even though they showed only the occasional lunch or dinner with Brooks, Coulson, and Colin Myler. They presented me with old letters and emails; none was in the least incriminating, and I already knew, thanks to the warnings of friendly company insiders, that many of them had been sent to the police and Parliament.

I spent a day at an innocuous looking house in south London, being interviewed 'under caution', as the Metropolitan Police considered whether the company should face charges of corporate liability. After I refused to meet at a central police station — I was wise enough by this stage to know my attendance would be leaked to *The Guardian* — the police suggested an anonymous building usually reserved to examine and interview young victims of sexual abuse. A doctor's examination suite was next to the room where I was questioned. It was a haunting place, made worse by the coloured cushions and other attempts at cheerfulness. Three police officers were present, as well as someone in another room who aimed a video camera at me. I arrived from New York with Chip Loewenson and another Manhattan attorney from Morrison Foerster; in London, another of the firm's attorneys, Kevin Roberts, joined us. A police sergeant asked most of the questions. Her boss, an inspector, occasionally interrupted using a more aggressive tone. I think they were employing a good-cop bad-cop routine. If there were a theme to the questions, it was an effort to have me express criticism of the conduct of others. They were also seeking to understand the complex structure of Rupert's UK companies. I made several attempts to help them, but was not convinced I succeeded. This ordeal stretched over nine hours. The sergeant was a committed smoker, mercifully increasing the frequency of breaks.

After the interview, I took Chip and his team to my favourite local pub in Marylebone. Kath, who had spent the day at home worrying, was pleased to drink a few beers with us. She was less pleased that one lawyer was sympathetically bringing me a large whisky with each pint. The next day, I slept in for hours.

Later, in downtown Manhattan, I spent three hours at the Justice Department facing a fierce battery of four government attorneys and five FBI agents. They were deciding whether to recommend corporate charges in the United States. By this time, I felt almost calm in the face of the same questions and fabricated fierceness. I had already faced my most persistent tormentors in the members of the House of Commons Culture, Media and Sport select committee. The Culture committee summoned me on three occasions to answer questions about phone-hacking. I had appeared before parliamentary committees previously and found MPs, with few exceptions, friendly but lamentably ill informed. These experiences made me far too relaxed.

My first appearance to discuss phone-hacking was in March 2007, soon after Clive Goodman and Glenn Mulcaire had been sentenced. It was uneventful, except for my answer to one question. The chairman, the Conservative MP John Whittingdale, asked: 'You carried out a full, rigorous internal inquiry and you are absolutely convinced that Clive Goodman was the only person who knew what was going on?'

I answered honestly: 'Yes, we have, and I believe he was the only person, but that investigation, under the new editor, continues.'

My response would haunt me years later when the committee persuaded themselves it constituted a lie.

My next session was in September 2009, three months after *The Guardian* story that News International had secretly paid off hacking victims. This was not a friendly meeting; the committee members were irritable and suspicious. I soon realised I had made a mistake agreeing to appear. I had left Britain two years earlier and no current senior News International executive testified — neither Rebekah Brooks, then chief executive, nor James Murdoch, who had personally authorised the payment of £700,000 to Gordon Taylor of the Professional Footballers' Association.

Kath, familiar with the ways of Labour politicians in particular, kept telling me not to testify — especially as Brooks and Murdoch weren't going to — but I didn't think there was any reason to worry. It was foolish of me. I didn't even take legal advice.

It was a nasty and bad-tempered session. I had no idea what questions the committee would ask, and knew few of the answers. Many centred on events that took place after I had moved to New York; the rest dated back to 2006 and 2007, and I either didn't know the answers, or couldn't remember.

The committee regarded my every lapse of memory and moment of ignorance as deliberate deceit. I was drained at the end — and furious with myself for agreeing to do it.

When the committee reported early in 2010, it accused me and other witnesses, mostly *News of the World* staff, of 'collective amnesia': 'Evidence we have seen makes it inconceivable that no one else at the *News of the World*, bar Clive Goodman, knew about the phone-hacking.'

By the time of my final appearance, the hacking drama was a super-storm. It was October 2011, three months after my resignation from Dow Jones. Rebekah Brooks had been arrested; James Murdoch was poised to quit and leave London for good; the *News of the World* no longer existed; and News Corp had been forced to abandon its bid to acquire the 61 per cent of British Sky Broadcasting it did not own. It was a bitter setback; Rupert's high-risk creation of Sky 20 years before almost cost him the company, and News Corp's total ownership was a long-held wish.

This time, I spent hours preparing under the legal tuition of my lawyer, Chip Loewenson and his team at Morrison Foerster. I knew that members of the committee were intent on finding me guilty of lying to them previously, and of being in contempt of Parliament — an offence some MPs wrongly believed could lead to a prison sentence. I appeared by video link from a hotel meeting room on Fifth Avenue, New York, hoarse with stress, but furious at the purpose of their summons.

MPs at select committee hearings are protected against libel charges by parliamentary privilege. This means they can basically say anything they want. They might not be conscientious in preparing for meetings, but they can harangue and insult witnesses without fear of repercussion.

I batted back all their predictable accusations and insults. *The Guardian* coverage, which had not always been flattering, said: 'Geoffrey Boycott would have been proud.' This comment might, or might not, have been meant as a compliment, but it pleased me. I thwarted Tom Watson in his efforts to pressure me into pointing a blaming finger at the Murdochs; and I even helped out one confused Labour MP, the former corporate financier Paul Farrelly, when he misunderstood a piece of evidence.

As the session ended, a still-open microphone picked up the committee clerk's view: 'He seems quite credible,' she said. Whittingdale appeared to agree: 'Interesting, but no bombshell there.' Informally, I was led to expect a rap on the knuckles, and wasn't sure why I deserved even that.

I knew I had dealt persuasively with every effort to prove I was untruthful, but I also knew Whittingdale carried little weight with Labour members. He was a decent enough man, but a docile politician, and no match for Watson's bruising style. I particularly distrusted Watson. He had built a recent reputation through his attacks on Rupert and News International, and I knew he wouldn't want the select committee report to be a damp squib. Before the committee even delivered its report, Watson published a book — titled, dispassionately, *Dial M for Murdoch* — saying I was guilty of misleading Parliament. I knew then it was a stitch-up.

On 1 May 2012, as I expected, the report accused me, and others, of lying in our testimony, and therefore of being in contempt of Parliament. I found out the day before the report's release on *The Guardian* website — some members of the committee had been leaking to *The Guardian* for months.

The report was debated for two hours in the House of Commons. Labour MPs, including Chris Bryant, called dramatically for prison sentences, while others more moderately demanded public admonishment in front of the entire House of Commons.

I knew Bryant was either ignorant of parliamentary rules, or guilty of wishful thinking, and that Parliament had no power to imprison citizens, but I was still enraged at being publicly attacked without any opportunity to defend myself. I was determined to fight the committee's 'verdict' and had already sent a detailed protest to both Whittingdale and the speaker of the house, John Bercow.

Select committee reports are typically nodded through Parliament; the House accepts their findings and the world moves on. My objections — and the accusations by my lawyers that the Culture committee was in breach of the European Convention on Human Rights — stopped the report in its tracks. Instead, Parliament referred it 'for review' to the Committee of Privileges, the House of Commons ethics watchdog.

For four years, Kath and I, working closely with my lawyers, argued with the Privileges committee. Thousands of words, some bad tempered, were exchanged as the committee repeatedly delayed its work, citing the risk of prejudicing ongoing investigations and court cases. These excuses may have been valid, but we were also sure that the committee would prefer the whole thing to just go away. Its members were MPs, too, with the usual allegiances and enmities: there was no doubt that its members did not enjoy challenging the findings of their colleagues.

In September 2016, Parliament finally conceded it had made a mistake. In a long analysis of the allegations against me, it acknowledged the Culture committee had been wrong and that the evidence did not support the finding that I had lied.

My former colleagues at *The Wall Street Journal,* in a prominent and satisfying editorial headlined 'Les Hinton's Vindication' wrote:

> Les Hinton must be wondering to which office he should go
> to get his reputation back. The question was first asked by
> former Secretary of Labor Ray Donovan after he was acquitted
> of trumped-up fraud charges ... [Hinton's] parliamentary
> vindication is, as he says, 'too little and too late,' but it should
> be a warning of the damage that political frenzies can do to the
> lives and careers of honorable men.

It had been a long wait, but the door had finally closed for me on the most difficult period of my working life.

By then, for me at least, the worst was over. The US Justice Department, whose lawyers interrogated me in Manhattan, decided against prosecuting the company. The Crown Prosecution Service reached the same conclusion; three years after my police interview, Detective Sergeant May Robinson of the Metropolitan Police sent me a letter: 'I am now in a position to inform you that the Crown Prosecution Service has decided to take no further action in relation to the Company, and by extension yourself.' She thanked me for my cooperation.

There were no more arrests. More than 100 journalists had been questioned under caution, arrested, or sent to trial. Overwhelmingly, these journalists were from the *News of the World* and *The Sun*. Five *Mirror* journalists were arrested, and 15 interviewed under caution. During one civil action, the barrister David Sherborne said hacking at Mirror Group titles made the *News of the World*'s exploits look like a 'small cottage industry'. But even as the courts continued to make large cash awards to Mirror Group victims, the Crown Prosecution Service announced there would be no *Mirror* prosecutions. There was, apparently, 'insufficient evidence'.

The *Mirror* allegations caused no hysteria; the Labour Party had no interest in destroying the *Mirror* newspapers, or their owners. The Mirror Group was the only newspaper group that always supported Labour. Despite proof of phone-hacking, John Prescott, once deputy prime minister and a ferocious critic of misconduct at the *News of the World,* continued writing a weekly column for the *Sunday Mirror.*

Of the 21 *The Sun* journalists caught in the investigation into police payments, all who went to court were acquitted at trial, or on appeal. Of the 29 *News of the World* journalists arrested for hacking, eight pleaded guilty and one, Andy Coulson, was found guilty at trial.

News Corp went a long way to make good on Rupert's promise to *The Sun* journalists. Several returned to *The Sun,* others chose to negotiate settlements. The brilliant award-winning John Kay was shattered by the experience, and the company's decision to reveal his sources, and never returned to journalism. Fergus Shanahan, one of *The Sun*'s most talented, was left in a state of exhausted despair. After his three-and-a-half-year ordeal with the police and courts, he decided he needed a rest from Fleet Street, bought a dog, and set off with his wife to renovate a house in France. 'I'm going to read newspapers for a while instead of sweating for them,' he said.

Public officials paid by journalists were not so lucky. Thirty police officers, prison officers, and government officials were convicted or pleaded guilty, and many went to prison. This was the other pain for the journalists — seeing sources that had trusted them fall. Bettina Jordan-Barber, a 42-year-old civil servant at the Ministry of Defence, was sentenced to 12 months. Over eight years, *The Sun* paid her £100,000 for dozens of stories she provided to John Kay. Jordan-Barber may have violated the terms of her employment, but the stories were undeniably in the public interest: a shortage of flak jackets and combat helicopters, military suicides, Army bullying, an inquiry into attempted murder at Sandhurst. In the frenzy, others were convicted on thin evidence. April Casburn, a 53-year-old detective chief inspector in the Met's anti-terrorist unit, was sentenced to 15 months in prison after calling the *News of the World* to protest that detectives were being transferred to the hacking investigation and away from terrorist and murder inquiries. The principal evidence against Casburn was that the journalist she spoke to made a note that she wanted to sell her story, which Casburn denied. No money changed hands and no story ever appeared.

Newspapers boycotted the Leveson watchdog that was 'underpinned' by the state, favouring their own self-regulatory body.

After the resignation of David Cameron, the new prime minister, Theresa May, said her government would not adopt the proposal that 'rebel' publications should face punitive financial penalties. This was a fragile victory; a future Labour government might well use a new outrage against the press to reverse May's decision

But the hacking scandal shifted into history. Politicians found other fires to feed, and the police more serious matters to pursue. Rupert's companies thrived, and his son James returned to his position as chairman of Sky and continued his rise in the United States.

But below them, in the foothills, were casualties: the victims of phone-hacking, of course, but also the innocent journalists and their wives and husbands and children, and others with shattered lives and lost careers, so many of them the collateral victims of other people's wars. It's possible to be angry with the idiotic law-breaking that happened as well as the unscrupulous exploitation of politicians and their careless destruction of reputations, and the strong-arm conduct of a panic-stricken police force, and, for me most painful of all, the carelessness of some at News Corp, and those working on its behalf, with the welfare of employees and their families.

As a reader, I had my own problems with the *News of the World*. It had become too often mean-spirited, even pitiless, although these traits did not make it unique in the changing style of Fleet Street popular newspapers. But it didn't deserve to die. The newspaper and all who worked there were sacrificed, put to the torch in the manner firefighters set strategic blazes to halt the spread of wildfires. But it died in vain; nothing could check the hungry flames and hostile winds. *The Sun* endured, and, even with its spirit crushed and much of its leadership gone, it began to recover. But the survivors, and those lost in the inferno, will never forget what happened. 'Draining the swamp' is a phrase that lives in infamy among them. No one ever confessed to using it.

Epilogue

I had been here a thousand times, but everything had changed. I didn't recognise the chrome furniture or the subtle lighting, or the artistic black-and-white photographs on the walls. The gleaming paintwork and thick carpet were as unfamiliar as the cheerful face of Melissa, sales executive and guardian of what was once the grim, brick-lined office of the editor of *The Sunday Times*.

This used to be Fortress Wapping, the ugly and intermittently embattled home of News International. Now, it was a demolition site, and the room I stood in a real estate showroom, filled with plans and models of glories to come.

I stood at the wide table in the middle of the room, looking down at the glass-encased toy town of tall buildings, landscaped squares, and tree-lined boulevards — an architect's vision of a new world, with everything that had gone before eliminated by London's forgetful rush. Outside, I could hear the clatter of machinery and the shouts of workmen.

In another decade, the former home of the *News of the World*, *The Sun* and *The Times* newspapers — the place I spent the longest period of my working life — would be a panorama of apartment blocks, shops, restaurants, and a 'magnificent choreographed central water feature'; a dancing fountain to banish the sounds of an impatient city.

I had said I was interested in buying a flat, although it wasn't true. The old Wapping plant had been sold to developers in 2012 and I couldn't resist a visit. Starting price for an apartment was £869,950. If I were considering a penthouse, it would cost me £4 million. In the 1970s, Rupert Murdoch paid £300,000 an acre.

When I came clean and introduced myself to Melissa, and told her the dramatic story of Wapping, she looked at me as if I had landed in her glossy office through a wrinkle in time in an old-fashioned police call box.

Everything was different, but I knew where I was. I could tell by the immutable grey spire of Hawksmoor's great church, St George-in-the-East, consecrated in 1729. It sat on the other side of the teeming Highway, waiting for the towering shadows of its new neighbours.

In the distance was the silvery arrow-point of The Shard; the Baby Shard next door was the new home of Rupert Murdoch's British publishing group, now called News UK; its name was changed to shake off the stigma of News International.

I'm always revisiting the places where I've lived and worked. I stand outside old homes all the time — peering through the hedge at Brentwood Park; down the overgrown driveway in Minchinbury Terrace; beneath palm trees in Singapore. I go to Westchester County, Boston, Santa Monica, Finchley, and to Bootle, even though my old neighbourhood was bulldozed long ago.

I drive past the Fox lot in Los Angeles, through streets where the *Boston Herald* once stood, and stroll often along Fleet Street. I haven't been to Tripoli yet; I carved my name deep into a seafront wall when I was nine and imagined it being there forever.

Kath is indulgent of my constant need to return to places, although I know she thinks it's weird and obsessive. She's probably right, but I can't stop. I've travelled so much, it's somehow reassuring to see the physical evidence of my life, and I enjoy putting together the memories. Perhaps, somewhere deep down, I'm looking for a coherent pattern to my untidy life, but logically I understand that's a waste of time. With a childhood broken randomly into disconnected pieces, life was so ephemeral that I think permanence came to seem unnatural — dangerous and stagnating.

Wapping was more than another lost place; it was also a symbol of how Rupert's company had evolved beyond the print business I joined in 1959. Wapping had been a powerhouse of cash that fuelled the company's American expansion, but by 2017, with profits depleted, it was struggling to reinvent itself. The magnates of television and newspapers, who once dominated the world of information and communication, were yielding to engineers and computer scientists with empires of a size and reach once unimaginable. Their new world was demolishing many businesses I grew up with, but it was also creating an inestimably better informed planet. As a teenager in Adelaide, there were two daily newspapers, a couple of television stations each providing a total of, maybe, an hour of news, and local radio doing the same. Half a century later, in the same city — any city — technology supplied an amount of information and variety of opinion that was virtually unquantifiable. The business of print might have been in doubt, and the new economics of journalism still to be settled, but it seemed sure to me that good journalism would flourish because there would always be demand. In the decimated print industry, while nothing promised the riches of old, green shoots were peeping through the tundra on the frontier of digital reinvention in places such at *The Times* in London, *The Wall Street Journal*, *The New York Times*, and *The*

Washington Post. The *Daily Mail* had stolen *The Sun*'s clothing with the introduction of a lurid tabloid website that claimed to have the world's biggest English-language audience.

By 2018, the Murdoch empire was changing. First, it had grown two heads, with the giant of profit and promise, 21st Century Fox, divorcing its weakening print partner. Then Rupert made a deal to sell to the Walt Disney Company his 20th Century Fox film and television studio, and other TV assets, including Sky TV. James, at least, seemed about to escape the powerful gravity of his 87-year-old father by joining Disney, or going his own way. Now middle aged, James and Lachlan, the princes who had flourished under their father's sponsorship, would soon make their own history or become footnotes in their father's story.

No one was sure what the next chapter of Rupert's story might be, but his had been the biggest and best media company ever created — or the heart of darkness, depending on your point of view. On the hard facts, no other old newspaper baron established big newspaper operations in so many places — not Hearst, or Beaverbrook, the Sulzbergers, or Northcliffe and the Rothermeres. More than six decades from the beginning, Rupert's newspapers still had a powerful presence on three continents. And no other television operation was ahead of his in its global spread — from Australia, to Britain, the United States, and elsewhere. Sky TV and Vodafone were arguably the two great new post-war British businesses, introducing new forms of communication and creating thousands of jobs where none existed.

His success had not met with universal admiration. Rupert could be hell to work for, and 60 years of success and tough tactics yielded for him a bitter harvest of enemies. To the bitterest, he was a scabrous, plundering capitalist debasing cultures across the world. Few books written about him were flattering. The titles said it all: *Dial M for Murdoch*; *Murdoch's Politics: How one Man's Thirst for*

Wealth and Power Shapes our World; *Breaking News: Sex, Lies and the Murdoch Succession*; *Murdoch's Pirates*. Books by wishful thinkers have been a staple: *Murdoch: the Decline of an Empire*; *The Fall of the House of Murdoch*; *The Rise and Fall of the Murdoch Empire*.

But the Rupert Murdoch they hated was a hallucination, a virtual devil, a crowd-sourced apparition created to be the object of all their rage and grief about big business, great power, global inequity, and everything else they saw wrong with the world.

No doubt, he's a driven businessman with heavy boots who bruised a lot of people. At times, he has deserved a kicking. As a boss, he could be hands-off or autocratic, charming or irascible, forgiving or fierce, and sometimes just a comprehensive pain; but he also imbued his companies with a fantastic sense of possibility and got big results. His ambition to grow seemed unending, as if he were working on an unfinishable opus. The ancient Macedonian conqueror, Alexander the Great, wept when he had no more worlds to conquer. Over the years, many were known to search hopefully for that tear in Rupert's eye. Working for him could be very tough and the attrition was high. At each of our regular management conferences, a booklet listed the attending executives; as the years passed, reading one was like looking at a war memorial. It was said of Lord Beaverbrook — a press lord from a previous generation — that never working for him was like serving in a world war without hearing a shot fired. I understand.

It took a while to acclimatise to life without the trappings and hectic hours of a Murdoch executive. But my suits don't wear out so quickly, and I've stopped, after 40 years, setting the alarm clock for 5.30am. For a while after leaving, I did nothing except tackle the hacking fallout in London. I didn't kick the travel bug. We travel so often between New York and London that it's only now and then we fail to recognise the cabin crews on British Airways. It's novel going on long trips without the company or the Army making the rules. Kath loved America so much she became a US citizen in 2014, but few moments make her happier than when we arrive back in London.

Writing your life story is self-indulgent, but it also illuminates the people who have made everything worthwhile: Lilian and Frank, my English parents; Marilyn and Duncan, my Australian siblings; Martin, Thomas, William, James, and Jane, my American children; and their mother, Mary, my first wife, who travelled the world with me and who died of cancer in December 2016. She is buried in a churchyard in Lusk, County Dublin, a walk from the thatched house she cherished and near the meadows of the family farm where she played as a child. And there are Samantha, Dylan, Lily, and Leo, my grandchildren; their mothers, Stephanie, Eliana, and Kel. And my wife Kath, dearest Kath, who has helped me with this book, and in uncountable other ways.

I can't explain what has entitled me to my life's success: the love, the family, or the career. My mother had a fierce determination and Bootle toughness she never seemed sure how to deploy. I think I took her determination and made better use of it, and I know that made her proud. My childhood travel seemed an unstable footing, but built in me a flexibility that prepared me for a successful working life. Arriving so often in so many new places, having to make the right impression with another group of strangers, made me good at slipping into new jobs and getting along with people. And yet, because the mobility came naturally, I imposed it on the family, just as it had been imposed on me, and was too self-absorbed to recognise until later how hard it could be for them.

My life and career has been wilder, happier, weirder, richer, and sometimes more disconcerting than I could ever have expected. I'm grateful for it all. I was always the new boy at the school gate. The early journeys were a unique education, and, for all the occasional anguish, my travels with Rupert were priceless. When it was tough I got through by staying optimistic; expect the future to be perfect — you can't be wrong all the time.

But there really is no place like home for me — none. It's too late. There is no everlasting destination. No cocoon. No hearth. No dust-shafted aspidistra parlour, or dependable smells, or reassuring staircase creaks. Home travels with me. It is with the pre-dawn blackbirds and the blinking Belisha at the London window; in the breezy sunsets of the Hudson Valley hills; in the sparrows of a Manhattan courtyard; and everywhere in the hot, strange smells of unknown cities. It's a baby's breath; the weight of a small child against my chest; the book-buried head of Kath; my own reflection in a grown-up child, older and wearier with the world, with all the same hopes and apprehensions.

Home is where it needs to be.

And that's good enough for me.

Acknowledgements

As a reporter, writing was mostly a hasty activity in noisy newsrooms, or on the road scribbling into notebooks, or dictating raw to copy-takers in old-fashioned phone rooms who had heard every story before; there was nothing more cheering — or rare — than a word of appreciation from one of them. Writing a book is different, and lonely. Without the imperative of an immediate deadline, with months to go before delivery, and no fierce editor hovering, an inner discipline is required; it was a struggle to find mine. You also need help to write a book, lots of it, and, without the help given to me, these pages would have been impossible.

James, the fourth of my five children, urged me to write this book at an ideal moment; I had turned 70 and was feeling reminiscent and boring him, yet again, with old stories. I started making notes and, soon after, while shopping for Cumberland sausages at Myers of Keswick, a splendid British food store in downtown Manhattan, a man from BBC radio, on one of those off-beat BBC assignments, asked me to answer his questions about the superior quality of English chocolate. It was a serendipitous moment: Emma Parry, a literary agent with Janklow & Nesbit, overheard the interview, asked if I were interested in writing a book, and then guided me through the glacial labyrinth of the book world.

All my family helped. James got me started, and William, the book editor in the family, made important contributions to the penultimate draft. Martin and Thomas, the two eldest; Jane, the youngest; and Mary, my first wife, helped me remember. Duncan, my brother, the family archivist, quarried through generations of records to help me piece together our family history. Marilyn, my big sister, had a better memory of the early years. My Merseyside cousins — Judith Brindley and Heather Harrison — filled in Bootle detail.

Dozens of others contributed, either knowingly or unwittingly, as I mined their memories over long walks, lunches, and evenings. Rex Jory of Adelaide, my oldest friend, filled in the gaps of our shared youth, and dug out newspaper clippings to verify or correct our recollections. Mark Jackson fitted this manuscript into his voracious reading schedule, offering sharp-eyed observations. Arthur Edwards applied his prodigious memory to the details of our years together on the road as reporter and photographer. Marianne Krafinski, my assistant, had diligently filed my personal papers for a quarter of a century. There were many others, including: Col Allan, Chris Buckland, Ken Chandler, Stanley Chang, Vic Chapple, Paul Dacre, Alison Clark, Mark Day, Alistair Duncan, Bill Hagerty, Sheila Hardcastle, Stuart Higgins, Trevor Kavanagh, Deborah Keegan, Todd Larsen, Chip Loewenson, Murdoch MacLennan, James MacManus, Bill O'Neill, Paul Potts, Pat Purcell, Ian Rae, Marty Singerman, Joe Stevens, Peter Stothard, Ian Weston, and John Witherow. The Liverpool Central Library was my microfiche portal back to wartime Liverpool.

Philip Gwyn Jones of Scribe Publications coaxed me out of the deep-seated habits of journalese — too many short paragraphs and too much economy in my description of events and feelings. It was not often a newspaper editor told me to 'expand and elaborate a little, say a bit more'. Molly Slight's forensic copy-editing rescued me from numerous mishaps — grammatical, stylistic, and factual.

But my greatest debt is to my wife, Kath, my first reader and frankest critic, unflinchingly honest in matters both of style and substance, exorcising solecisms and warning against the more fatuous and clunky passages in my early drafts. I didn't follow her advice every time, so any remaining fatuous, clunky, or otherwise flawed passages are my fault, as are any other failings in this work; I couldn't have done it without help, but the mistakes are mine.